FREE MEN *and* DREAMERS

VOLUME FIVE

In God Is Our Trust

FREE MEN *and* DREAMERS

VOLUME FIVE

IN GOD IS OUR TRUST

L.C. LEWIS

WALNUT SPRINGS PRESS

To my beautiful grandchildren—
Tommy, Keira, Christian, Brady, Avery, and Desmond—
and to the two tiny spirits I'm anxiously waiting to meet this year.
And to all the children of the world,
members of another choice generation.

Walnut Springs Press, LLC
110 South 800 West
Brigham City, Utah 84302
http://walnutspringspress.blogspot.com

Text copyright © 2011 by L.C. Lewis
Interior design copyright © 2011 by Walnut Springs Press
Cover design copyright © 2011 by Walnut Springs Press

ISBN: 978-1-59992-802-9

FREE MEN and DREAMERS

Dark Sky at Dawn
Twilight's Last Gleaming
Dawn's Early Light
Oh, Say Can You See?
In God Is Our Trust

FICTIONAL CHARACTERS

THE AMERICANS

Residing at the Willows Plantation along the Patuxent River in Maryland

JED PEARSON: the owner of the Willows Plantation; a former British prisoner of war; candidate for the Maryland State Senate

HANNAH STANSBURY PEARSON: Jed's wife; sister to Beatrice Snowden and Myrna Baumgardner

JOHNNY, JAMES, ABIGAIL: Jed and Hannah's children

FRANNIE PEARSON: Jed's sister; an entrepreneur; a musical entertainer

PHILLIP ST. CLAIR: a Philadelphia politician pursuing Frannie

SARAH AND CHARLES: orphans

MARKUS O'MALLEY: the Irish foreman of the Willows

JENNY TYLER O'MALLEY: Markus's wife; previously performed with Frannie

BITTY: the former slave who raised Jed and Frannie

JACK: a former slave; Bitty's brother and Jed's best friend

ABEL: a former slave set free by Jed; Bitty's husband

CALEB, ELI, GRANDY, AND HELEN: Abel's children and Bitty's stepchildren

LYDIA: widow of an escaped slave, Titus, who died at Fort McHenry

MIRIAM AND MOSES: Lydia's children

PRISCILLA: Abel and Bitty's daughter

ROYAL AND MERCY: a married couple; former slaves

SOOKIE: a former slave

NED GREELEY: farm manager who replaced Markus after his departure from the Willows

REESE SYMONDS: a farmhand at the Willows

Residing at White Oak Plantation, the neighboring farm

STEWART STRINGHAM (DECEASED): the original owner of White Oak; father of Frederick

FREDERICK STRINGHAM: the current owner of White Oak; Stewart's crippled son; former beau of Frannie

PENELOPE STRINGHAM: Frederick's wife

HUMPHREY: son of Frederick and Penelope

URIAH: a slave

Others

MYRNA STANSBURY BAUMGARDNER: Hannah's stuffy, Baltimore-based sister

DR. SAMUEL RENFRO: friend of Jed, Hannah, and Timothy; a surgeon

SENATOR TIMOTHY SHEPARD: college chum of Jed

LUCINDA SHEPARD: Timothy's wife

BEATRICE STANSBURY SNOWDEN: Hannah's sister and wife of Dudley; resides in Palmyra, New York

DUDLEY SNOWDEN: husband of Beatrice Stansbury; former prisoner of war

EMERSON HILDEBRAND: wealthy, pro-slavery nemesis; Abel's former military colleague whose prank led to the death of a private named Skully, entering Hildebrand into a secret pact with Abel and Dr. Foster

DR. RANDOLPH FOSTER: physician/militia captain during the War of 1812; protected Abel by taking responsibility for the shooting death of Private Skully

SEBASTIAN DUPREE (DECEASED): mulatto son of a Creole father and a slave; former pawn of Stephen Ramsey; as a British spy, he was promised the Willows in payment for his services; organized a band of rebels and terrorized the Willows; Arthur Ramsey and Frederick Stringham helped Jed Pearson and the Willows' men repel the attack, during which Dupree was murdered by freedmen members of his rebel band; Dupree's group scattered after his death and became an embarrassment to the Crown.

THE BRITISH

The household of the Earl of Whittington

LORD WHITTINGTON (EVERETT SPENCER): the Earl of Whittington; member of the House of Lords; British noble; widower

DANIEL SPENCER: the Viscount of Whittington; son of Lord Whittington

RUTH: Daniel's Jewish wife

The Ramseys of London, England

STEPHEN RAMSEY: (deceased) a wealthy entrepreneur

ARTHUR RAMSEY: Stephen's son; a former divinity student who enlisted in the British Army; Frannie's former beau

Others

RICHARD "JERVIS" PORTER: a British sailor who joined Duprée's band; an enemy of Arthur Ramsey

MARY MCGOWAN: widow of a murderer; engaged to Stephen Ramsey before he was murdered

MICHAEL AND HANK MCGOWAN: Mary's sons

LORD NORTHRUP: member of the House of Lords; cousin to Lord Whittington

LAWRENCE "BLED" BLEDSOE: Liverpool street hoodlum

Historical Figures

PRESIDENT JOHN ADAMS: second president of the United States

PRESIDENT JOHN QUINCY ADAMS: eldest son of President John Adams and his wife, Abigail; sixth president of the United States

MAJOR GEORGE ARMISTEAD: commander of Fort McHenry in Baltimore

PRESIDENT ANDREW JACKSON: war hero of the Battle of New Orleans, seventh president of the United States

THOMAS JEFFERSON: third president of the United States

FRANCIS SCOTT KEY: an American lawyer; the district attorney for the District of Columbia; writer who is best known for his poem "In Defence of Fort McHenry" (put to music as "The Star-Spangled Banner"), written during his shipboard detention during the attack on Baltimore

JOSEPH KNIGHT: friend and defender of Joseph Smith

LIGHT HORSE HARRY LEE: father of Robert E. Lee; a Revolutionary War hero and friend of George Washington; tortured in the Baltimore riot of 1812

CAPTAIN STEPHEN MACK: brother of Lucy Mack Smith and founder of Pontiac, Michigan; served in Fort Detroit during Hull's surrender in 1812

PRESIDENT JAMES MADISON: fourth president of the United States

PRESIDENT JAMES MONROE: fifth president of the States

JOSEPH SMITH JR.: Prophet and founder of The Church of Jesus Christ of Latter-day Saints

EMMA HALE SMITH: wife of Joseph Smith Jr.

JOSEPH SMITH SR. AND LUCY MACK SMITH: parents of Joseph Smith Jr.

Acknowledgments

After eight years of research, and five years of endless five-finger typing, this era of FREE MEN and DREAMERS concludes. This project has been life altering, increasing my appreciation and passion for America and past generations, and my gratitude for God's hand in its foundation and preservation. The Pearsons, and so many of the other characters, have become like family, living vividly in the creative portion of my brain, and though they won't monopolize my time any longer, they will always be with me.

I have so many people to thank for supporting me and allowing me to see this dream through. My husband, Tom, has been my cheerleader, financier, promotional expert, and biggest fan. No words could ever adequately express how much his support and patience have meant to me during this project. I love you, honey.

I'm so grateful to my children, by birth and by marriage—Josh, Adam and Brittany, Amanda and Nick, Tom and Krista—and my grandchildren—Tommy, Keira, Christian, Brady, Avery, and Desmond—for faithfully loving a busy, often-preoccupied mother/grandma. Every moment together with my family is a glimpse of heaven.

My enthusiasm far exceeds my skills, and I am in debt to many dear friends for their help and support. Kay Edwards, Lynette Johnson, Valerie Sanfrey, and Kelly Schuman—my beta-readers—proofed the manuscript. Ladies, your feedback greatly improved this story. Thank you so much. Michelle Mebius and Ernest and Kathleen Runge went above and beyond all possible expectations. Michelle went through the manuscript three times, keeping the details straight. The Runges fact-checked historical details and added critical cultural insights. Your help was invaluable, and I can't thank each of you enough.

Many thanks also go to Dr. Wayne Allgaier and his wife, Vicki. These friends were the first to lay eyes on a very rough manuscript, and Wayne's medical expertise kept the story honest and accurate. Thank you for seeing this project through to the end.

Writing and marketing a book is an emotional undertaking, slingshotting an author between elation and angst, with periodic pit stops at self-doubt and insanity. I'm grateful for my LDStorymakers peers and my ANWA sisters, who understand the particular concerns of other LDS authors, and whose advice and counsel has helped me grow. I'm especially grateful for Liz Adair, Braden Bell, Anne Bradshaw, and Kathi Oram Peterson, who have actively supported the series. You guys are great. Thank you!

Continued thanks go to Angela Eschler, who fanned my sometimes-waning enthusiasm to keep the series alive over the long haul, and to Garry Mitchell and the superwomen of Walnut Springs Press for taking a chance on FREE MEN and DREAMERS. Linda Mulleneaux provided another expert edit that greatly improved the book, as well as ready hand-holding and cheerleading. Amy Orton endured my handwringing, delivering another magnificent cover, layout, and marketing plan. Thank you all so much.

My gratitude is unbounded for my readers. Your letters and notes spurred me on. Thank you for taking this journey with me. You are why I write.

Lastly, I'm so grateful to know we have a Heavenly Father and a Savior. I don't know how people face this world without the hope They bring. Yes, there is much to be hopeful about.

I'm grateful for the Founding Fathers—heavenly inspired men who established a nation that could become a cradle for the Restoration. I'm so very grateful to the Prophet Joseph Smith. As a boy, he did not falter, and as a man, he did not faint. I'm grateful for a generation who listened to the Spirit and opened their hearts and minds to the Restoration and the new day it heralded.

Prophets have long seen our day, and under divine guidance, the Founding Fathers prepared for it. This is our moment. What will we make of it? I hope FREE MEN and DREAMERS has inspired you in some small way. Thank you for inspiring me.

CHAPTER 1

May 15, 1816
London, England

"Revenge goes down sweet, but it leaves the belly empty," mused Richard "Jervis" Porter as he foraged in alleyway rubbish barrels for other people's half-eaten leftovers. Sleeping on the ground in Hyde Park and foraging for food were new depredations for the British mercenary.

A greasy bundle wrapped in newsprint caught his eye. Peeling back the paper revealed the remnants of some wealthy locals' dinner—a few parsnips and carrots, a crust of bread, half a boiled potato, and a meaty, gravy-smeared beef bone. Jervis plopped the potato in his mouth, rewrapped the rest, and stuck it in his pocket for later.

The darkness and evening rain left his forty-four-year-old bones chilled. He tightened the filthy, threadbare coat around him as he returned to his favorite bench in Hyde Park, situated directly across from Arthur Ramsey's town home. A lump of humanity lay under a tree, so Jervis kicked it, but there was no movement. "Dead," he muttered, knowing he was barely better off than the corpse. His only purpose in life was denying Arthur Ramsey his peace—and he had been good at it. But revenge had cost Jervis greatly over the past year.

A pigeon landed beside him. "You're late," he groused as he retrieved the bread crust from his pocket and set it on the bench for the bird. He pointed to Arthur's house. "The sun'll be up soon. Today's an important anniversary. The Admiralty made 'im a hero whilst he denied me and mine our treasure there in America. Left us dead, or fugitives like me. Called us renegades, but what did ole Jervis find out one year ago, eh?" He cackled. "That he was a renegade, too."

A lamp's pale glow suddenly burned brightly in Ramsey's window. "You can't sleep, can you? You know I'm still here, like I 'ave been, every day and night since I saw you kiss that American woman, Miss Pearson. It weren't a kiss between two friends when you put her and her brother, Jed Pearson, on a ship bound for Maryland. Did you figure it out, that it was me who sent that letter, announcin' that you were a traitor? I've watched you suffer for a year, attemptin' to defend your reputation, and now you're leavin' London. So who's the fugitive now?"

Yes, revenge was sweet, but Jervis was still hungry and alone. He had a new plan, or at least some ideas of what to do next, gleaned from watching the families that came to the park each day. He'd never given much thought to the benefit of family, but he knew he needed an ally or two. He had always planned to throw in with other petty criminals, maybe find some young orphans and train them up as partners. There were plenty to be found, but sons? Yes, sons. And he knew just where he could find some.

Jonathan Edward Pearson was on the last leg of his journey, after weeks of meetings with British business leaders to re-establish trade after the signing of the Treaty of Ghent. Soon he would sail for home. Nervous excitement surged through him at the thought, and with it, a strange melancholy. Nothing was as it once was. Not even home.

Called Jed by his friends, Pearson was on his final errand, a visit to Arthur Ramsey, but as his carriage rounded the corner, he looked down the street and saw a ruckus in front of Arthur's London home.

Fear struck Jed. Had a relapse overwhelmed his ailing friend? He was prepared to bolt from the carriage, but his confusion mounted when he arrived and found Arthur directing the transfer of goods from his home to a wagon bound for a docked ship in the Liverpool harbor.

"What on earth are you doing, Arthur? Leaving England?"

He offered a chagrined smile. "I'm sorry, Jed. I was going to leave you a note."

"What could happen in three weeks that would warrant this level of upheaval?"

Arthur waved Jed inside the nearly emptied house to his spartanly furnished office and encouraged him to sit in one of two remaining chairs. Jed studied his friend, noting that the hollow echo of the closing door matched the emptiness reflected in his countenance. Despite being impeccably dressed, Arthur's overall appearance spoke of fatigue. His cheeks appeared more gaunt than they had just a few weeks earlier, and the glint of life was all but gone from his tired eyes. Jed laid his hand on his friend's forearm and gently asked, "Why did you make no mention of such plans even three weeks ago when I was here last?"

The Englishman's narrow chin dropped to his vest in submission. "It's for the best, Jed. I've wrestled over this during these past three weeks. Please trust my judgment."

Jed sighed in defeat and choked out the words, "If that is what you want, but at least tell me where you're going so I can inform Frannie."

Arthur pulled a letter from his pocket and handed it to Jed. "I've explained everything in this. See that she gets it, and be there when she reads it. She'll need your support."

Jed jumped up and paced to clear his head. "Are you . . . are you ill again?"

Arthur's hand clamped Jed's arm with comforting strength. "Only heartsick."

"Am I truly to have no explanation? For heaven's sake, Arthur, we're like brothers."

"I can't reveal the cause to you before Frannie hears it, Jed. It wouldn't be right. Though everything I've done testifies to the contrary, I do love your sister very much."

Jed paced away as a snippet of conversation from three weeks ago popped into his head. "Has Lord Whittington caused this? You said Daniel had written to you, petitioning you to speak to his father on his behalf, since the earl had failed to reply to his letters."

A sarcastic huff punctuated Arthur's reply. "That was another plan that went awry. What is it with fathers and sons? I'd give all I possess to be a father, but since that joy is denied me I want to shake men so blessed and tell them to ask nothing more from their children than to love them. I pray you never know the pain the earl and Daniel have put one another through." Arthur's hands flew in the air. "Daniel is now a thirteen-year-old fugitive, Jed! The earl has sent authorities searching for him from Ireland to Greece, with a warrant for his arrest. The boy had used the money he stole from his father to slip away. I'm the only one who knows he's managed to settle in Greece with a friend's family."

"The Jewish friend he met while traveling with his tutor?"

"Yes. The earl harangued me for months for information I did not have, and then Daniel began to write to me. When I tried to tell him Daniel is willing to speak to him, the earl refused to listen. He assumes correctly that Daniel is staying with this girl, Ruth, and her family. His fascination with her religion set his father off the night Daniel stole the money and ran away.

"If only the earl had listened to the boy, I feel he would have seen that he was not so much running toward Judaism as running away from the life planned for him from birth. Now the earl says he no longer has a son, nor a friend named Arthur Ramsey."

"Then this *is* the reason you're leaving England."

Arthur sat heavily in a chair and gazed out the window into the city he loved. "It is but a part of an overwhelming whole, I suppose. I'm a failure, Jed. My efforts to direct lives have all failed. Frannie, Daniel, Mary McGowan and her boys . . . I've failed in every relationship. Doing good in the world and serving mankind are the only joys left me, but I must offer that help from a distance, and I must render my service somewhere other than here."

Jed walked to Arthur's chair and leaned on the arms, bringing his face close to Arthur's. "These are all excuses, Arthur. If you want to do good in the world, make the woman who loves you happy. You love Frannie and she loves you. It's pride that keeps you apart." Jed pushed away and moved to the window. "I understood why you sent her away, but I no longer agree. Thirteen long months have passed, and you are both still alone. Come to America with me."

"I wish it were that simple." Arthur strode to the door and grasped the knob, his back to Jed. "I don't expect you to understand or accept my answer, but I've prayed to God to know what I should do, and this is the answer I received. Please help Frannie to understand."

CHAPTER 2

Afternoon, June 17, 1816
Along the marshlands on White Oak Farm, Maryland

Uriah burrowed into the thick marsh grass along the shore. He hadn't figured on the weather becoming cantankerous, raining and freezing as if it were January. The women slaves at White Oak said it was a bad omen—that God was angry and that's why the spring plantings had been frostbit. At thirty years of age, Uriah hungered for freedom, and now a white man offered him a way to be free. What would he have to do for it? *Maybe I'm the one making God angry,* Uriah thought.

He beat his arms against his legs to warm them up, and then he saw him—the man with yellow hair and a red handkerchief. He had seen him many times before they first spoke, hidden in the tree line as Uriah came and went between White Oak and the Willows. He worried whether the man might actually be an overseer instead of a businessman, and for a second the young slave thought about running as far and fast as he could. But Uriah was a bright young man, or so Miss Bitty always told him, and he figured if getting him hung had been the man's intention, he could have done that way back when they first discussed the plan.

The man stopped every few steps to listen and look, apparently making sure no one was following him. Uriah could see that rich as he clearly was, the man had just as much to lose as he if they got caught, and that caused Uriah's fear to subside.

"Do you have it?" the man demanded.

"Yessuh, but if you don't mind, suh, I'd like to see that deed first. I ain't never seen my name on any important paper, let alone on a land deed."

The young slave noticed the fine cut of the man's brown cashmere coat as he pulled a document from his breast pocket. The coat was finer than any his master had ever worn, though Master Stringham fancied himself to be a dandy.

The man unfolded the paper and held it up for Uriah to examine. There they were, the only five letters he had ever learned—U-r-i-a-h —and though he couldn't read any more words, he recognized the army insignia in the corner. This was an enlistment deed rewarded to a soldier, similar to the one Miss Bitty showed him—the one Abel got when he enlisted. Uriah reached to touch the document, but the man shot him a look of disgust and quickly snatched it back, shaking it as if it were soiled, then folded it and placed it back in his breast pocket. In return, Uriah pulled a piece of paper from the pocket of his overalls and handed it over. The man studied it carefully, his dark eyes darting over each drawing as he tapped the document.

"And this is complete and current?"

"Yessuh! Every buildin' on the Willows is there, drawn to show who or what lives in 'em. I even included the manor house on the back."

The man flipped the intricate map over and studied the floor plan of the house as pleased sighs issued from his mouth.

"I been paintin' every room at the Willows to work off Master Stringham's debt at the Willows mill, jus' like I was doin' the day you and me met up on the road."

The man tried to hide his excitement, but Uriah knew how pleased he was over his map.

"This is satisfactory, but I'll need two more favors from you. I'll be gone for about a month, but I'll return on the *Miss Elaine* on July twenty-third. I need you to return to the Willows near that date. Use any excuse necessary—tell them you missed a spot that needs painting, anything—but get in that house and follow my last two instructions before six o'clock that evening. Can you do that?"

Uriah cocked his head to the side and eyed the man. "What more d'ya need me ta do?"

"I need to know if you agree before I tell you more."

Uriah shoved his hands in his pockets and backed a step away. "I don't know 'bout this. I'll have to weave a tale to get in the house again now that my work there is done."

The man curled his lips and asked, "What is too hard when freedom is the reward?"

The question made Uriah uneasy, but freedom for himself and his wife, and twenty acres of land in the Michigan Territory, awaited him if he succeeded. Freedom was a very elusive thing, worth any price, causing the reason the man wanted his drawings to matter less. "You'll give me my deed after I do this thing?"

The man's lips smiled but his eyes sneered at Uriah. "Do as I ask and I'll meet up with you later that evening and give you the reward you've earned. Here are my final instructions—"

Uriah's mind raced and his hands began to shake as he listened. "I can't do this, suh! I'll get whipped or worse if I get caught!" But there was no way out—a white man knew he had considered escaping. And then he thought again of what he had to gain. He could not turn back, and yet he had to know. "Suh, why you doin' this thing?"

"You wouldn't understand. Too many whites don't even understand. And that's why I must proceed."

CHAPTER 3

Early afternoon, July 23, 1816
On a skiff at the mouth of the Patuxent River

The war had been an able teacher. Jed now understood what only soldiers could—that a warrior is just a man who knows what can be taken from him, who puts himself between what he loves and anyone who tries to take it. He looked around at the ragged sampling of passengers on the sloop, unable to lay his defenses aside and relax without seeing threats in every corner—ne'er-do-wells scavenging from broken farms, slavers hunting runaways, pulpit pounders harrowing up men's tired souls. And now nature was America's foe as winter crowded into summer, returning with an icy reach that stretched from New England as far south as Maryland.

The change in the air was sudden this day along Maryland's frost-damaged Patuxent. A clouded canopy of fog rolled in, dropping the temperatures and sending unprotected passengers scrambling for warmth. A mother and child huddled in the stern amid other wary passengers, including a skittish seminary student of barely twenty years, and a well-dressed man in a brown cashmere coat, whose icy eyes remained transfixed on something, or someone, near the bow.

The *Miss Elaine*'s thick-chested captain looked heavenward and groaned. "I've never seen nothing like this. Feel that air? Thick as chowder. We're in for a rough trip."

Though the captain's voice remained low, his worried countenance spoke loudly, stilling the voices of the passengers around him until dread silence swept the entire deck except for the lamenting voice of the seminarian repeating the rosary prayers in Latin. One shaking hand methodically moved across his breast, making the sign of the cross, while his other nervously worked the beads. The scene set the passengers on edge, prompting Jed to rise from his seat near the Negro family he was accompanying, to speak to the captain.

After months away, Jed was anxious to get home to his wife and son. Even strangers recognized him readily since his campaign for the Maryland State Senate had begun. He knew it was his controversial platform that caused some of these passengers to smile approvingly at him, while others scowled—or worse. He was already aware of the disparaging looks being shot his way because of his choice in traveling companions. But Jed looked older than his twenty-six years, and his tall, muscled stature and authoritative demeanor had a way of stilling contentions. He used these assets to his full advantage as he moved through the crowded deck. His canvas raincoat rustled above brightly polished boots, drawing whispers as he made his way to Captain William "Bully" Broome.

"The young priest is frightening the passengers," Jed explained.

The captain scowled and called his first mate. "Seaman Stoddard, ask the priest if he could petition the Almighty for our safety without frightening the passengers to death."

Stoddard quaked at the request, then left as the captain shook his head. "Things have been bad since you've been away, Jed. Real bad. Crops failed. Some fields have been replanted two, three times. First the war and now this? Some folks are wondering if God really is cursing the land like some of them preachers say."

Jed groaned and frowned. "The cause is geologic, not religious. Scientists in England believe a huge volcanic eruption in Indonesia is to blame for the change in the weather. Clouds of soot and ash are blocking the sun and changing the climates of many countries."

"That doesn't cancel God out of the equation. He's the God of heaven *and* earth."

"Those pulpit pounders you've been ferrying north to tent meetings have gotten to you."

Bully nodded to the passengers. "I doubt the cause matters much to them. Food is in short supply, and prices are high again. People are panicked, what with the toll the war took, and now this. Some are piling into the churches, but some are just pulling up stakes and moving west."

Stoddard returned as the sound of weak hymn-singing began. "Thank you, Stoddard."

"Wasn't me, Captain. The blond fellow in the cashmere coat threatened to throttle the young priest if he didn't stop, so the young mother back there began singing with the children."

A small break in the fog revealed a dangerous outcrop of land directly ahead. Bully spun the helm, and the ship responded with a sudden lurch. "I can't see what's ahead. Stoddard, set a man on the bowsprit with a horn to signal trouble, and have the men break out the blankets and furl the mainsail. We may have to anchor at St. Leonard's for the night."

Jed pushed down his disappointment. "How can I help, Bully?"

"Help the women out of the bow and back to the stern where it's drier. Then you can spread those blankets as far as they'll go, women and children first."

Jed crooked his arm to the Negro woman who had been sitting beside him near the bow, the dampest and coldest part of the ship. She must have noticed the disapproval on other passengers' faces, for she attempted to defer, but Jed persisted until his smile encouraged her to accept. When she stood, two children followed behind her—a small, dark boy of about seven years, and a young Negro girl who appeared to be about twelve. Jed attempted to relocate the family to a bench in the center of the ship, but the passengers there were reluctant to accommodate them. Controlling his irritation, he maintained a protective grasp on the nervous woman's arm as he scanned the group for sympathetic eyes. He found them on the mother and son sitting in the stern.

Extending his hand to the boy, he asked, "What's your name, Son?"

"Thomas, sir, Thomas Biddinger. My momma says you're a war hero and that you're going to be our next Maryland State Senator after the election this fall."

Jed smiled at the folktales springing up about him. He tousled the boy's hair. "Well, thank you, Thomas. I was a prisoner, hardly a hero, but I'd be honored to serve the good people of this state. I know about a real hero. Please allow me to introduce Miss Lydia, Thomas. And these are her children, Moses and Miriam. Lydia's husband, Titus, was killed at Fort McHenry the night the British bombarded the fort. You've read Mr. Key's poem, haven't you? Or sung it in school? You've surely heard about the rockets and bombs that fell that night."

The boy's eyes widened as he nodded that he had.

Jed knelt eye to eye with the lad while taking a reassuring hold of Lydia's hand. "Well, Titus stood by his cannon that night, even as those rockets rained fire from the sky. When other men took cover behind the fort's walls, Titus held his position. When the rains fell and the winds blew, and the great garrison flag had to be lowered to prevent the pole from snapping, Titus's squad held their positions and fired their guns, just so the British would know the fort still stood.

"Hours passed as the bombardment continued, but Titus stood on bastion two all through the day and into the evening, until a British ball exploded above him and cut him down. And when the storm calmed and the great flag was raised once again, it fluttered over four coffins, one of which held the body of a former slave who had only known a few months of freedom. He didn't have to enlist in the militia, but he risked his life so his family, and my family, and yours, could know the sweetness of liberty. To me, that makes him a real hero. Wouldn't you agree?"

The other passengers seemed as spellbound as Thomas. Before the lad could respond, the people slid left and right to make room for Moses, Miriam, and Lydia, whom Jed guided to a gentle sit. Then he released Lydia's hand with a squeeze before moving on to calm the throng.

The man in the brown cashmere coat turned to Thomas's mother. "Who is that?"

"You must not be from around here, sir. Everyone along the river knows that's our local candidate for the Maryland Senate, Mr. Jed Pearson."

"Jed Pearson," he snarled. "Of the Willows Plantation?" He didn't even wait for a reply. With a snigger that almost resembled a snort, he stood and disappeared into the crowd a moment before a bump rocked the ship. A loud blast from the signaler's horn split the air, and people scrambled to steady themselves while the captain shouted for a report on the view ahead.

"Visibility's poor and there are tree limbs in the water, Captain!"

In obvious frustration, the captain pounded on the helm. "Then we're docking at St. Leonard's for the night. Stoddard, pass the word to the passengers and prepare to disembark, and see what accommodations we can get for these folks."

As soon as the vessel was moored, Stoddard prepared to go ashore. The blond man in the cashmere coat came up behind him. Knowing him to be difficult, Stoddard placated the man. "Passengers' names will need to be checked against the manifest before disembarking, sir."

The man acknowledged the information with a nod before discreetly delivering a single blow to the back of Stoddard's knees, crumpling the seaman, who toppled into the water with a loud splash. Chaos ensued as a voice cried out, "Man overboard!" and the blond man slipped over the gangway to shore.

The vessel lurched to the right as too many people rushed to the scene, then port as the captain ordered them the other way. Eventually, the hands pulled a soaked and freezing Seaman Stoddard from the water. When he was able to speak, Bully and Jed questioned him.

"I want the name of that man before we disembark!" Bully soon ordered.

The men checked the passengers against the manifest. Every registered soul was accounted for, but Jed knew who was missing—the blond man in the cashmere coat.

Jed spoke to the woman who had been sitting beside him. The report was disturbing. Bully rubbed the knuckles of his bear-like hands. "Are you saying a stowaway got on my ship in Baltimore, assaulted my crew, and escaped just as anonymously?"

Jed leaned close. "He's also the man who threatened the young priest. The woman who sat beside him claimed his only other words during the trip were questions regarding me."

"Have you ever seen this man before?"

"I've asked myself that same question a hundred times this hour. I don't believe I have."

Bully drew in a long breath. "You'd best have your men keep an eye out for this fellow."

Jed winced at Bully. "My men? You mean me and Markus and four freed slaves?

"Then you'd better get some more help, Jed. What cause would such an ornery man have to ask about you and then jump ship? It can't be good. You know it can't be good."

The man regretted wearing his precious cashmere coat this day. Tree limbs and ragged brush tore at it as he plowed through forests and fields. He had won the coveted apparel playing dice in a bar in Richmond on a cotton-buying trip—took it right off a plantation owner's back. People treated him differently when he wore it, with the respect he no longer enjoyed in Baltimore. It had served him well.

The timing of the plan had been critical, but the ship's delay now threatened everything. He had to reach Uriah, so he raced on beyond fatigue until his legs felt rubbery, his lungs burned, and sweat poured down his back despite the unseasonable cold.

Perhaps the basic plan could still be salvaged. It would be months before he could return without raising questions. He knew now he had been right to raise his sights. The problem would only continue to escalate unless he struck powerfully at its root, and thanks to Uriah, he not only had the will, he now had the means. He thought about his shortsighted brothers. They didn't see the danger. Their parents' misdirected altruism had blinded them. Such men would be the undoing of America. Fortunately, he and others like him realized that.

His heart thundered so fiercely that his lungs couldn't draw in enough breath. Fear gripped him as he peered through the dusk and fog. He couldn't be lost! He couldn't be that stupid! Then he heard a rustle in a thicket and dropped to the ground and hid.

A figure came his way with a large limb raised over his head, prepared to strike. The man's arms flew over his yellow-haired head. "Don't hurt me!" he cried out. "I've got money!"

"You?" the voice growled. "You are the devil!"

"Uriah?" He scrambled to his knees, now furious that this slave had witnessed him cowering.

With the limb still poised above his head, Uriah growled, "I changed my mind."

The man slowly rose to his feet, his hands extended to calm the slave. "You didn't follow my instructions?"

The limb dropped behind Uriah's back, but he continued to glower. "I followed your instructions, but the dogs didn't just fall asleep. I saw them suffer, and then they died. I want no part of what you got planned for them folks. Keep your deed. Just let me go."

The yellow-haired man had heard all he needed, and his confidence returned in full. "There's no running away from what you've done. I have the map, and the guard dogs are dead. You did that, Uriah. You betrayed the very people who were kind to you—betrayed your friends for a measly piece of land."

Uriah's shoulders rounded in utter defeat. "God forgive me. I just wanted to be free so I could free my family. Just let me go, suh. And please don't kill them folks."

"Ah, ah, ah!" the man warned. "A wise man knows how best to play his hand, Uriah."

The slave's chin dropped to his chest, and the man reached slowly into his coat pocket, from which he withdrew two objects—a gun and vial of powder.

"Do you want your master to find you in the middle of an escape? He'll tie a rope around your scrawny neck and force your family to watch as you dangle to your death."

Uriah looked up with terror-filled eyes and shook his head. "Massuh Stringham ain't like that. He'll beat me, but he never strung no one up."

"Are you so sure? He once watched his father whip an entire family to death for simply overhearing a conversation." He brandished the vial. "You know what you must do."

Uriah's horror revealed that he recognized the substance. "That's the powder you had me sprinkle on the dogs' meat. Please don't make me swallow that. I'd rather you shoot me dead."

The man knew that would raise additional questions. "No, this way is better." He tossed the vial at Uriah's feet. "After a few unpleasant moments, you'll simply fall asleep." Uriah's eyes darted frantically, and the man knew he was contemplating escape. Aiming the gun at Uriah's knee, he said, "If I must shoot you, I'll take your wounded body to Stringham and tell him all you've done. And what will you say? That you helped me plan an attack on the Pearsons? Ha! I'll leave you to your master's whip, and it won't be just you they'll beat mercilessly. They'll see how deep the betrayal goes. They'll beat your wife, your parents, your brothers and sisters. So choose quickly before I withdraw my offer of mercy."

The slave's hands pressed over his ears as if he could block out the horrid sounds. Then he slowly crumpled to his knees. Staring at the man, he picked up the vial, then tossed his head back and downed the powder. Mere seconds passed before his face began to twist in pain. Soon he doubled over, wrapping his arms around his abdomen, until he could no longer kneel and fell to the ground in a writhing heap.

The man stayed a moment longer, smiling as he considered the outcome of the day. His plans had begun to unravel, but things had worked out well. "What I wouldn't give to watch these two farmers try and sort this out." He chuckled. Then he turned and walked away.

CHAPTER 4

Early morning, July 24, 1816
The Willows Plantation along the Patuxent River

Jack shivered as his feet hit the cold wooden floor. After wrapping his blanket around himself, he shuffled to the wood stove to stoke the fire back to life. It made no sense that in July he should have to worry about fires and cutting wood, but little of what happened these days made much sense to him.

After dipping his washrag in a basin of frigid water, he laid it on the stove to warm before washing and dressing his lean, brown body for the workday. He scowled at the need for a coat in the middle of what should be one of the hottest months of the year. A second later he remembered what day it was. His high hopes had been dashed yesterday with the delay of Jed's ship, but perhaps today would hold great prospects for him. The last thing he wanted was to face Titus's widow looking like a fretful, old man, so he shook off his complaints. And thinking it wise to be prepared, he slung his best Sunday shirt over the crook of his arm.

Jack paused by his freedom papers, which hung in a frame near the door. Placing his hand over the glass, he bowed his head to offer his morning prayer. After the "amen" left his lips, he added a soft "thank you," then reached for his hat and headed out.

A ragged line was already forming by the mill, as it had each day since the first killer frost hit. The war with Britain was over and trade had resumed, but once the initial euphoria of peace passed, the nation recognized the grievous toll the conflict had taken on her scorched farms and lands. Farmers tilled and planted the battle-scarred fields, harvesting a decent crop in the peace of 1815, but 1816's seeds struggled to sprout in the unseasonable cold, only to be destroyed completely by a late frost that left the landscape ice-burned and bleak. Maryland's harvests had previously been measured in bushels and tons, but not in 1816. People were poor and hungry, and frightened once more.

The walk to the Willows mill was short, but Jack was cold through and through by the time he reached it. The dim glow of Markus's lantern cheered him. He only hoped his Irish friend had also lit a fire to warm the place while they worked.

The echo of water against the new dock also cheered Jack's spirits. Ships came and went from the Willows freely once again, like the vessel he looked forward to today. He nodded at the line of men, noting the printing on the bags of wheat they carried. Things were worse than he thought. Now men were bringing their seed wheat to be ground into flour, and some brought nothing but empty sacks, hoping to draw some meal from the Willows' own stores.

Jack opened the door and climbed the steps to the mill room, where the upper millstone, or runner stone, was turning. He looked to the back of the room and caught sight of Markus's red curls peeking out from below his hat as the Irishman fed the fire. "Another cold one," Jack said.

Markus glanced back at him and nodded. His face was too drawn and worried for a man not yet thirty. "A man can't provide for 'is own from frozen earth." It was the thickness of his brogue, increasingly apparent in times of stress or concern, that revealed the depth of his angst.

"How are Jenny and the baby?" Jack hoped the topic of Markus's new family would bring a smile to his friend's face.

Markus brightened momentarily. "You'd think Jenny'd wear her lips off from grinnin' at the wee bairn." He chuckled, and then his expression returned to worry." He began bagging flour for the men waiting outside. Jack huffed in resignation and joined him.

"Forgive me, Jack, I don't mean ta grouse. I'm the luckiest man on the earth—got a lovin' wife and a beautiful baby son. I wish these joys for you, my friend. It's just that twixt the war and this weather, a man finds it hard to do right by his family."

"Bitty heard from Abel. The army's got him traipsin' around the mountains of western Maryland, scoutin' out a new route for the Chesapeake and Ohio Canal."

"Maybe it's another honor bein' paid 'im. Local folks are worried that if that Erie Canal gets built in New York it'll siphon business away from Baltimore, and us."

"Maybe. Or maybe they need him because he's the size of an oak and as strong as an ox."

Markus wiped at the sweat forming on his brow. "Aye." He laughed. "There is that."

After two hours of bagging flour and cracking wheat, Markus paused to study the rapidly emptying grain bin, whispering calculations to himself as the crease in his brow deepened.

Jack wiped a hand across his brow. "Seems the same worry is crossing both our minds."

The Irishman swung his head around, his expression grim. "We can't feed everyone."

Leaning heavily on his shovel, Jack replied, "Jed'll be home today."

As if in reply to the mention of Jed's name, the bell on the *Miss Elaine* began to peal her approach. Jack quickly remembered his Sunday shirt. After setting his shovel aside, he began to change, but his middle-aged fingers fumbled as they worked the buttons.

"Doin' all that for Jed, are ya? Or could all this fuss be for Titus's widow?"

The Irish lilt of Markus's jest went unanswered until Jack's last button finally cooperated. "It may be my last chance for a family, Markus. There's not much opportunity for a freedman and a free woman to meet in these parts, let alone to marry, and who knows if she'll want me? I'm not much to look at, but I'm hoping she'll see other gifts I can offer her and her children."

Markus straightened his friend's collar. "They'd be powerful lucky ta 'ave ya."

The seven men still waiting for their flour joined Jack and Markus on the dock as their excitement over the ship's arrival temporarily distracted them from their errand. The thunder of hooves now added to the confusion as Royal, another of the Willows' freedmen, raced to the dock on horseback. Annoyed by this distraction, Jack kept his attention focused downriver, but he followed Markus as they moved to catch the snorting horse's bridle.

"Sookie and me found that new bay mare in the eastern pasture with her throat slit."

Markus's brows knit into one angry line. "Wind Dancer? Someone slit her throat?"

"I'm so sorry. Me and Sookie took off last night before dusk with two of the hounds so we could get an early start hunting this morning. She was fine when we passed that pasture."

Jack laid a hand on the Irishman's back. "Royal, is there any chance an animal did it?"

Royal shook his head as he dismounted. "That ain't the worst part. They cut her too deep to mend, but small enough to bleed her out slow. They wanted that poor animal to suffer."

Fury flushed Markus's face as he wrenched the reins from Royal's hands and climbed onto the horse. "If I can't 'elp 'er I'll put 'er down, and then I'm going to track down whoever did this."

"Just wait. The ship's about to dock. Let me greet Lydia, then I'll go with you."

"I'm the farm manager! It's my responsibility to watch over this farm when Jed's away!" As Markus jerked the reins, urging the horse into a turn, Jack grabbed the bridle.

"I thought freedom made us all equals, or were those just words?"

Markus relaxed his tight jaw, though his fists remained clenched around the reins. "They're not just words, Jack, but freedom papers or not, we know the law allows me ta protect this farm in ways it'd never allow you. We learned that all too well two summers ago—with Abel."

As unfair as it was, they both knew it was true. Jack felt his manhood seep away.

"It gives me no pleasure ta say it. Jed and Hannah've been apart for weeks. Let's not spoil his homecoming with this. Just let me handle it, agreed?"

Jack brushed his large, brown hand over his face and nodded in resignation as Markus disappeared over the ridge, then a thump behind him returned his attentions to the docking ship.

He saw Jed immediately, his face aglow with boyish joy. Then Jack saw her—Miss Lydia. He wouldn't have recognized her had she not had her hand firmly tucked in the crook of Jed's steadying arm. She had been a quaking wisp with a dirty sack-dress and natty hair when he first saw her two years ago. But everything was different now. Determination now replaced her once-fearful eyes. She stood proud and tall, dressed like a proper lady in a green plaid gown with ruffled crinolines. Her black hair was drawn into a tidy bun and covered by a red felt hat. She wrapped her free arm around her two fatherless children.

Jack had felt worthy of this widow earlier in the morning—perhaps even a little elevated because of his share of prime Willows land, his savings, and the small produce business he had begun—but after seeing her, and especially after hearing Markus's reminder about the limits of his freedom, he felt small and inadequate once more.

CHAPTER 5

Noon, July 24, 1816
The Willows Plantation

Jed led Lydia and the children carefully down the gangplank. Leaning his head close to Lydia's, he said, "You're now on Willows soil. Welcome to your new home."

Royal hurried to get the mill's wagon so he could see to the bags. The two dogs he took hunting broke into a prolonged howl, racing toward the house and nearly knocking Lydia over. Jack rushed up to steady her, and Jed noted the awe in his brown brother's eyes. Releasing his own hold on Lydia, he drew Jack to him. "I missed you. It's good to be home."

A long, relieved breath escaped Jack. "It's real good to have you home."

The men with flour sacks in their expectant arms caught Jed's eye. "How bad is it here?"

Jack rolled his eyes. "Pretty bad. We've been dolin' out grain to people every day. We need to talk, but you go see Hannah and little Johnny first. I'll settle everyone in." With a brief glance Lydia's way, Jack dipped his head and said, "So sorry to hear about your loss, ma'am. Titus was a good man, a brave man. Abel speaks highly of him."

Lydia tightened her arm around her children. "Thank you for your kindness once again."

"Lydia, do you remember Jack?" Jed asked.

A bright smile lit her face. "I surely should, Mr. Pearson, since you've spent the better part of our trip from Philadelphia tellin' me how he and his sister Bitty practically raised you."

Jack seemed to rise two inches taller at the praise.

Lydia's eyes moistened. "But even if you hadn't spoken a word about him, I'd remember Mr. Jack for the great kindness he showed me and my family the night we ran away from White Oak and took shelter here. Such kindness is reason enough to remember any man."

"Indeed it is," Jed agreed as he gestured for Jack to take her arm. "You're in good hands, Lydia. Jack will get you settled. I'll check in on you all a little later on."

A shot rang out from the fields beyond the house, startling Jed. Silently, he looked to Jack for an explanation.

"We'll tell you about it later. Head on home now, Jed. It'll keep."

Jed began strolling up the lawn toward the manor house. Brown-faced children abandoned their teacher, the cherub-faced, blond lay pastor named Reverend Myers, and raced to loyally follow Jed, squealing all the way. Unable to resist their petitions, he joined in a few rounds of tag, darting about wildly to avoid the agile hands trying furiously to snatch hold of his coat. All the while, the dogs barked and howled and chased everyone. Jed's own pleasure was undeniable. The children's parents—slaves he had once owned and subsequently freed—left their work to enjoy the ruckus. Worry clouded the smiles of those leaving the Willows' damaged fields, but on first sight of him, their faces lit up with joy.

"Mr. Jed is home," he heard a lad say to his mother. "Things'll be all right now."

The weight of their hopes and expectations wrapped around him like a welcome blanket, and for the moment, all that mattered was that he was home, and that mere yards away, in the grand white house, his wife and their young son were waiting for him. He broke into a run.

After weeks on ships it felt good to run hard and fast, to feel his legs fly freely on the Willows' soil he had loved since childhood. He still had nightmares from time to time of being chained in the hold of the prison ship with his hands and feet fettered. He picked up the pace and ran even faster, shaking loose of those haunting images.

The front door opened and Bitty appeared, carrying her three-year-old daughter, Priscilla. Large-boned like her father Abel, Prissy was already more than half as tall as her petite mother, who struggled down the front steps with the girl on her hip. Jed's eyes suddenly locked on the gray tuft of hair peeking out from beneath Bitty's bandana and on the lines etching her tired eyes.

"Give her to me, Bitty. She's too heavy for you to cart around."

Relief swept over the little woman as Jed lifted the child from her arms. Tightening her shawl around her, Bitty said, "I get the same advice from Jack, and from Abel in his letters." She positioned her soft, brown cheek to receive the kiss Jed offered, and then she laid a loving hand against his face. "I hauled you around just like this when you were her age."

"But you were younger then, Bitty. You're nearly forty now."

She jutted one shoulder forward in a visible harrumph. "I only know one way to love, Jed Pearson. I can't give her less just because she was last. 'Sides, there isn't a better way to go than to wear out from lovin' a child." She patted Jed's cheek again. "But when I get to heaven I will ask God why all these children had to be so large, like their father."

The pair laughed as Jed's hungry eyes set upon the house. Bitty chuckled sadly. "She's been missin' you, too. Guess it's only right, seein' as how you've barely had but a few weeks together here and there. Hannah sat up till well after dark last night, expectin' you to walk in any minute. I just left her in the kitchen. Set Prissy on down and go find her."

The hounds began howling again from beyond the brown thicket that separated the manor house from Markus and Jenny's cabin, and then their barking ceased.

"They must have seen a rabbit. Game's become scarce."

Jed nodded absently as he headed along the side of the house and around the corner to the kitchen door. He peered through the glass, watching Hannah check the clock before grabbing a shawl from the coat tree and heading for the front door. Once inside, he watched her search the property. Then she moved to the pillar by the steps and leaned her lean body into it as she peered downriver. With her head resting against the cold wood and her long, dark hair moving softly in the cold breeze, she seemed childlike and lost, and Jed knew he was the cause.

He slipped into the parlor and grabbed the velvet throw he had brought home from England when he returned from the war. Moving quietly, he came up behind Hannah and wrapped it snugly over her shoulders. Though she was clearly startled at first, Jed knew she quickly recognized the body enfolding hers, for she relaxed and settled into him, allowing her hands to slide along his arms until they were tangled in one another's embrace. Jed tightened his hold, and she melted into him even further.

"I've missed those arms."

The depth of her want stung him. He tenderly lifted the hair from her neck and brushed his lips there, eliciting a soft sigh. "I've missed you, darling, so much. And Johnny—I can't wait to see how he's grown. Where is he?"

"Napping. I kept him up late last night waiting for you, and I was late laying him down this afternoon as well. He needs his rest. And—" Hannah turned to face Jed "—perhaps it will sound selfish of me, but I'd like some time alone with you first."

Cupping her chin in his fingers, Jed tipped her head back, noticing changes the past three months had wrought—the unmistakable fatigue, the circles under her eyes. He kissed her softly. "Have you been well? You look so tired." He felt her noticeably slump. "Is everything all right?"

Glossing over the question, she smiled. "I'm fine, now that you're here."

She snuggled into his chest, and his arms instinctively tightened around her. He surveyed the barren land with more realistic eyes, reminding himself that he had left his young wife yet again, for three months this trip, during hard times. She had agreed, knowing it would strengthen his bid for the state senate, and even though he wasn't seeking office for personal gain, he had, nevertheless, left her again.

There had been so little time together since their marriage in May 1813—weeks here and there, under the excruciating stress of war. Other militiamen had made similar sacrifices during the War of 1812, but Jed's capture had left him a prisoner on a ship bound for England during Hannah's last months of pregnancy. Providence had intervened, landing him in Arthur Ramsey's compassionate supervision, where he received news of his son's arduous birth. He had nearly lost Hannah and the baby, and were it not for the miraculous intervention of his friend and surgeon, Dr. Samuel Renfro, he most certainly would have.

Jed knew so little of the grisly day. Hannah had withheld most of the details to spare him, and when he asked the others for information, they too were reluctant to revisit the perilous circumstances that forced Samuel to cut the child from Hannah's womb. Johnny had been born, healthy and strong, but his mother had lingered near the veil of death for days before Samuel felt confident she would live. *Bless Samuel,* Jed thought. *And bless Jenny.* He knew he had Markus's new wife and her keen nursing skills to thank as well.

After he had returned home from his detainment, Jed had noted how Hannah began and ended every day on her knees, giving thanks to God, and even though his religiosity paled when compared to hers, he sometimes joined her. Yes, he was grateful to God, but it was easier for him to focus his immeasurable gratitude on beings he could see and touch, to people rather than to an amorphous entity. Yes, as he saw it, had it not been for Samuel and Jenny, he would have returned to a cold, empty house. The thought caused him to shiver.

Jed tilted Hannah's head so she met his eyes. "Have you fully recovered from Johnny's birth? I know it's been more than a year and a half since the surgery, but you look so pale."

"It's not because of the delivery, Jed. It's the fatigue of day-to-day mothering. Bitty says I'm a good mother—I devote every waking minute to Johnny, and I adore him—but he runs me ragged until I actually look forward to his nap times. He's so sweet and cheerful, but he still won't sleep through the night. And he's so . . . busy. He climbs on everything and jumps to his peril at least a dozen times a day. You'd think I neglect the poor thing for all his bumps and bruises. I've been so worried, wondering if something was wrong with our baby."

Brushing Hannah's hair back from her face, Jed asked, "What does Bitty think?"

The question was met with a playful scowl as Hannah poked her finger into her husband's chest. "She says he is you in every way."

Jed smiled proudly. "Having had only sisters, you know only of girls. We'll manage fine if our son's only problem is that he's a precocious little boy."

"He is a precocious little boy who needs his father."

Jed felt the urgency in the statement. "I'm sorry I've been away so much. You're exhausted, but I'm home now. I'll watch over Johnny so you can rest. And I promise you—"

Hannah put her hand up to halt the conversation. "Don't. Please don't. Do not promise me things you cannot fulfill. I want no expectations to be crushed, no hopes to be shattered when the next crisis presents itself and calls you away. I have come to expect only the here and now. I'm twenty-four years old, and I've already learned to accept that this is my lot, and I do accept it, but you must accept it too, and not promise me more."

Her eyes were resolute, and Jed knew he could offer no reasonable rebuttal. He simply nodded, then tightened his arm around his wife's shoulder and led her into the house.

"Bitty and I prepared a roast with all the trimmings. I'm sure you must be hungry."

"Only for you and your company."

The words lit Hannah's face. "Then could we sit a while and just talk? I want to hear about your trip, and news of Arthur and Frannie. I'm starved for any news that doesn't have to do with the bleak weather and economic hardship."

"All right, but it's as cold as an icehouse in here, Hannah."

Her brow wrinkled. "I hadn't noticed the cold before."

"I may have left the back door open when I arrived. If you'll check, I'll stoke the fire."

Returning a few moments later to a roaring fire, Hannah carried two cups of tea, which she set on the side table. Jed led her to the parlor divan, sat in the corner, and drew her back against him. "I have something to show you."

He reached into his pocket and withdrew his leather billfold. From it he pulled a hand-sized square of red woolen cloth, which he held out to Hannah. "Guess what that is."

Hannah took the piece of cloth and turned it over and over. Seeing nothing unique about it, she shrugged. "Is it more than what it appears?"

"A great deal more. You are holding a piece of history in your hand. It's the corner of a stripe from Baltimore's famed star-spangled banner. Major Armistead and his missus cut sections from the flag and mailed them to friends across the country to rally the spirit of patriotism. I had heard that the major—now Lieutenant Colonel—Armistead was ailing, and I called on him. He gave me a square as a keepsake."

Hannah seemed appalled. "He cut up the banner? How could he?"

"He felt it was a national treasure that served a greater good by being shared, since it was no longer being flown above the fort. Most of it is still intact, in the Armisteads' care."

"I certainly hope Mr. Key doesn't hear about this."

Jed chuckled out loud. "I've missed your rapier wit."

Hannah snuggled back against him. "Now that I've entertained you, tell me of your trip."

"Very well. My biggest news is that I was able to secure a trade agreement between five major British exporters and our state. They're anxious to resume shipments of our tobacco and produce. I also caught up with Juan Corvas, who was visiting Arthur in London. He's established a merchant route that carries him to every major port—London, Italy, Spain, Persia, Africa, and the Far East, then back to the islands and America. He was going to sail into New York, but I convinced him to make Baltimore his American stop. He thinks he can make three trips a year, which will open our markets considerably, and bring wonderful goods here at reasonable prices. If only this weather would cooperate . . . I—I'm sorry. I promised to speak of happier things."

"It's all right. Having you here takes my fear away."

He drew her head back and placed a lingering kiss on her lips. "I hope you know how much I need you, Hannah. Even when we are apart, you are my strength and purpose."

She leaned against him, all but ignoring the comment. "We had some excitement here as well. Remember how you told me you saw lights lit with gas in London? Well, Rembrandt Peale has now used gas to light his museum, and he's begun a company to bring gaslights to all of Baltimore. Perhaps there's a way to bring gaslights here as well."

"Frannie was at Peale's gala. She's a wise investor, that one. She bought stock in a Philadelphia gas company at the start of the war, and now she also holds shares in Peale's."

"She's a marvel. Now tell me more of your trip."

"I rode on the maiden voyage of a steamboat called the *Eagle* from Baltimore to the mouth of the river."

Hannah turned to Jed excitedly. "You did? I can't wait to take a ride in one!"

He played with her hair as he continued. "She'll be handling runs up and down the Patuxent next month. It will bring commerce we so sorely need in this region, especially with this devilish weather ruining crops. I've seen the suffering it's causing in Europe, and sailors say the effect on New England is worse yet. Measurable snow killed crops in Vermont last month. I'm worried about your sister Beatrice and Dudley."

"They've left Tunbridge, Jed. Beatrice and Dudley are expecting a child, and they've moved to New York State to open a shop. Beatrice's last letter explained how Dudley's imprisonment during the war left him too weak for the rigors of farming. His militia friend, Stephen Mack, returned to Michigan to reestablish his trading posts and open new settlements, and he's encouraged Dudley to open a store along the route of the proposed Erie Canal."

"Really? That could prove very lucrative. Has he chosen a site?"

"Yes, a town called Palmyra, in the western part of New York. I suggested they might want to add Willows tobacco and grain to their inventory."

"Did you now? I'm blessed with a wife who's both beautiful and a shrewd businesswoman."

"Are you surprised? Didn't Frannie and I do a good job managing things while you and Markus were off to war?"

"Absolutely. You're a very smart woman, Hannah." It came out sounding more like a confession than a compliment.

"All I want is peace, Jed—for us, for our friends, for America. Securing that trade agreement should give you the push you need to get elected, and once you're in office, you can pass legislation outlawing slavery. Then you'll come home to me, and to Johnny, for good."

Jed marveled at how simple it was to her—not simplicity born of naiveté, but of urgency. He had asked too much of her in their short marriage, been with her too briefly, and offered her too little. And in her own way, she had compartmentalized the great hurdles before them into bearable tasks. He pulled her to him. "That's my dream also—having picnics together down by the river and teaching Johnny to swim. I want to spur the horses and gallop through the meadows." He leaned close and whispered in her ear, "I want to feel you near me every night."

He attempted to nurse the moment into something more, but Hannah settled back against him, tightening her hold on his arm. "You've described all my dreams—dreams poor Frannie and Arthur will never know."

At the mention of his sister's hopeless situation, Jed was silent for a moment. Then he said, "I stopped at Frannie's house in Baltimore yesterday to deliver Arthur's letter to her. Sadly, I have nothing encouraging to report. I'm sure Frannie will be by to tell you the sad news, but suffice it to say the old enemies are still bent on ruining Arthur. He wrote to Frannie telling her he was leaving England for his father's plantation in Barbados. I believe the news crushed her." Hannah offered no response. "Did you hear me?"

"I was just picturing how happy the two of them once were, and wondering what they'll do now. The war doomed their chance at happiness, yet I think she still loves him desperately."

"She does, despite his injuries, and she would have married him had he asked," Jed said, "but Arthur sent her away hoping she would find someone who could offer her what he could not—a complete marriage and the hope of a child. It was his ultimate gift."

"Maybe so, maybe not. It's an onerous thing to have a man's devotion while being denied his affections, worse yet to have no choice in the matter. What comfort is Arthur's pledge of one letter a year for ten years, before he will see her again? Perhaps she will find someone else in that time, but what right does one person have to set the terms for both?"

Something in her comment stung Jed enough to compel him to pursue it. "You're speaking from personal knowledge, aren't you? You feel I've done the same to you."

Hannah straightened stiffly. "Our circumstances are very different. Even when you are away, I have Johnny for comfort, and the promise of what we'll share when you return."

Her answer held too little conviction. "But has that thought crossed your mind, Hannah?"

"In truth? Perhaps, from time to time. You are a driven man, Jed Pearson, a man with grand dreams and lofty goals, and we each pay a price to see those dreams and goals fulfilled. But I knew who you were when I fell in love with you, and I accept that I must forfeit some things I want to allow you to become who you were meant to be."

He felt a lump form in his throat. "Do you ever regret marrying me?"

She stretched until her face hovered mere inches from his. "Never."

Her eyes were as convincing as her words, and Jed's gratitude overflowed into a kiss. "I'm sorry a moment ever passes that you do not feel fully loved."

"After Johnny was born I asked myself, what if his birth had left me less than whole? Would you love me less?"

Jed felt his throat grow thick. "How could you even wonder?"

Hannah's mouth trembled over the question. "Then neither should you."

Jed met her mouth in a hungry kiss that set his heart racing, but the sounds of carriage wheels and barking dogs signaled the arrival of company, subduing the moment.

She smiled at his annoyance over the intrusion. "It's Frannie."

He grabbed Hannah's hand and pulled her to his lap with a laugh. "Let's bar the doors and pretend we're asleep."

She laughed and aimed a promissory peck at Jed's cheek, which kiss he swiftly negotiated into a final satisfying moment. "If Johnny weren't about to awaken, I would draw the curtains myself," Hannah said with a smile, then turned to look at the clock as curiosity clouded her face. Jed saw her strain to listen for sounds upstairs, where the baby slept. "It's noon. We should have heard from him by now."

Frannie burst through the door like a blur of blue wool, shaking a letter as she rushed over to Hannah. "Some swine contacted the British Admiralty accusing Arthur of two counts of treason—for helping to defend us against the mercenaries, and for fraternizing with the enemy!"

"No!" Hannah gasped.

"Didn't Jed tell you?" Frannie asked, swinging her attention to him.

"I just arrived half an hour ago, Frannie. Our ship was forced to dock at St. Leonard's because of last night's weather."

Her hands flew to her mouth. "Oh! I've interrupted your homecoming!"

"It's fine, Frannie," Jed said. "Come and sit."

She sat in a huff. "It's just that the more I read this letter, the more I have a mind to sail to England and shoot this Jervis character."

"Jervis?" Hannah said.

"Yes, it's such a mess, Hannah. He's one of Dupree's mercenaries. Arthur believes Jervis paid to have Arthur's father murdered so he could marry the grieving fiancée and get his hands on her inheritance. Arthur exposed him, and now Jervis is bent on ruining him in return."

"Are the British acting on the charges?"

Frannie stood and paced, working her hands nervously as she spoke. "Hopefully not. Several officers have written letters of support attesting that Arthur acted in the interest of the Crown when he stopped the mercenaries from murdering Americans—us. Fortunately, Arthur's military record is stellar, and his courage and honor have been noted by every officer who knew him."

Frannie slumped into a chair. "But this other charge—the claim that he fell in love with an American, during the war—has perhaps caused his ruin. An informal hearing was held, and Arthur admitted that he had fallen in love with me while he was on leave, but he testified that he returned to his duty as soon as he was certain Dupree's men were gone from here. His courage at Bladensburg and Washington is well documented, proving his loyalty to Britain."

"Then why is he leaving England? Jed told me Arthur is moving to Barbados."

"There's no peace for him in England anymore. Besides running his father's shipping business, Arthur dedicated himself to several charities. His war record drew wealthy supporters who made generous contributions. But Jervis has disparaged Arthur's reputation, and the charities say he is now a liability. So he's removing himself and taking refuge at his father's plantation in Barbados. Everything he loves is being stripped from him, and there's nothing I can do."

"You still love him very much," Hannah remarked.

"Yes, but what good is loving someone when they want you to love someone else? Which brings me to the other reason I'm here. I want to do what is best for you two and Johnny. I'm turning my shops over to my managers and returning to Philadelphia. Henri is reopening Le Jardin, and he wants me to be his principal singer."

"Philadelphia." Hannah sighed. "And how is that best for us? I'll miss you terribly, and you'll miss watching Johnny grow."

"It's because of the election, isn't it?" Jed asked.

Frannie raised an eyebrow and shrugged in confirmation.

"It's not like you to allow anyone to chase you away," Jed commented. "Besides, you were the toast of Washington's elite during President Madison's Inauguration."

"No one's chasing me from anywhere, Brother," she stated emphatically. "I'm simply leaving to pursue other opportunities." All humor aside, she added more soberly, "We both know that despite whatever fame and fortune I ever achieve, Maryland's polite circles will never see me as anything but a shameless entertainer. Why saddle yourself with the need to defend my character in every interview or debate? No, I've given this great thought. It's better for both of us this way. At twenty-four, I'm too young to sit here on the farm for the rest of my life, and Philadelphia will provide far more acceptable social opportunities than Baltimore. My businesses and holdings are in good hands, and Henri has secured a lovely home for me near Le Jardin."

"Very well, but do what is best for *you,* sister. I'll be fine." Jed stood and kissed Hannah's head. "I'm going to leave your good company, ladies, to check on my son."

Hannah smiled and returned her attentions to Frannie. "You deserve to be happy."

"Neither has your lot in life been easy, Hannah, but I think I'm finally done merely hoping and wishing for happiness. I'm going to do what Arthur wants. I don't need a man. I've got three little businesses going, and a home of my own in Baltimore if Philadelphia proves unsatisfying, but if there is a chance for happiness out there, I'd like to explore it."

Jed appeared on the landing. "Hannah, where did you lay Johnny down?"

"Where I always lay him—in his crib in the nursery."

Worry lined Jed's face. "He's not there, Hannah."

The women leapt to their feet. "What do you mean he's not there?" Hannah bolted up the stairs with Frannie close behind.

"Did one of the older girls come to play with him?" Jed asked.

"No. No one but Bitty and little Priscilla have been here all day!"

"Has he learned to climb out of his crib by himself?" Frannie asked.

Panic seized Hannah as the three of them began a frantic check of every nook and cranny on the second floor, and then a cry of horror caught in the back of Hannah's throat, turning Jed's knees weak as he found her pointing to an open window in Johnny's room. "What if he—"

Jed grasped the crib and shut his eyes as he leaned against the glass, preparing himself for the horror he expected to see below. From behind, he could hear the women's shuddered breathing, and he covered his own mouth to stifle his reaction if his fears were realized. Then he looked down.

Five successive shudders racked his frame before he could speak. "He's not out there!"

Hannah nearly collapsed against Frannie in relief, but the agonizing worry over where the child actually was sent Jed into action.

"Someone must have come in through that window and taken him!"

Jed raced down the steps to ring the alarm bell on the porch. Soon the Willows' Negro residents arrived from every direction, followed quickly by Markus and Jenny, who clutched her own baby tightly against her chest.

Ashen faced, Jed explained, "Johnny's been taken! Get the dogs! Search the entire farm!"

Within seconds, people were searching the farm on horseback and on foot. Jack called for the dogs. None came, but two made skittish appearances from the doorway of the barn, venturing a few steps with their tails tucked under their bodies, then returning inside, refusing to heel.

"Something's not right," Jack said.

The three men looked at one another and silently dashed to the barn. Far in a rear corner stall, they heard the whimpering of the dogs, who were poised protectively over something lying in the straw. Markus placed a hand on Jed's shoulder. "Stay here. Let me go in," but Jed shook his head and pushed past his friends.

The corner of a blanket peeked out from beneath one of the animals, drawing a gasp from Jed. "It's Johnny's crib blanket." Panic seized him. Swinging his arms wildly, he cleared the animals from the stall and then knelt to scoop the bundle into his arms. With one trembling hand, he pulled back the cloth to reveal Johnny's peaceful, sleeping face, but his little body seemed cold.

"Johnny? Johnny?" he cried as he shook the toddler's body. Startled eyes blinked rapidly, and the child screamed in shock and fear. Jed pressed his son against him as he checked for signs of injury. "He's fine!" Jed groaned, pressing the thrashing infant to his chest again. "He's fine!" He laughed in relief. "Someone run and tell Hannah!"

Johnny fought against the man holding him. He saw Markus and reached wildly for those familiar arms. "Johnny, it's me—it's Papa," Jed cooed, but the child would not be consoled.

"It's just that he can't see your face in this light. He'll warm up to you," Markus said.

Jed knew it was more than that. "Shh, Johnny. Papa's here, Papa's here." But the child arched his back and continued to beg for Markus. Heartbroken, Jed handed the child to his friend and slumped into a heap against the gate, allowing his earlier fear to now take its toll. In a sobbing, stumbling run, Hannah rushed in, with Frannie on her heels. She scooped the crying child into her arms before dropping into the straw beside Jed.

Markus looked at the thermometer on the wall. "It's only thirty-six degrees. We have those dogs to thank for protecting Johnny from the cold."

Hannah stared blankly at the back of the stall. "How did he get here? Do you think he did climb out of his crib and wandered here? How did I not see him?"

"It's not your fault. Johnny was brought here," Markus said as he strode to the wall of the stall, where a note hung from a nail. Jed leapt to his feet and took it from his hands.

"What does it say?" Frannie asked.

Jed read the note and angrily crumpled it into a ball, which he hurled across the barn.

"What did it say, Jed?" Hannah asked timidly.

Jed kicked at the gate, causing it to slam against its post. Several tense moments passed, and she asked again in a timorous voice, "Please, what did it say, Jed? It has to be better than what I'm imagining right now."

"It said, 'Choose sides, nigger lovers.'"

Hannah's entire frame shrank upon hearing the message. She pressed her son to her chest like a second skin and stared at the ground.

Jack returned. "I know how he did it. There are boot scuffs up the sidewall near Johnny's room, which lies directly under the chimney. I never gave that any thought before, but once a rope is tossed 'round the chimney, a man could easily climb right into the little fella's room."

"But how could an intruder get past the dogs without them alerting us?" Frannie wondered.

"Maybe they tried. Right after the boat docked, the dogs howled wildly and took off across the yard. Bitty and I figured they had caught a rabbit."

Jack produced a bloodstained muslin sack. "It was filled with poisoned meat. The other five dogs are in the thicket. They've been dead a while. Whoever took Johnny prepared days in advance, but they didn't count on Royal and Sookie taking the other two dogs away."

"The dogs must have chased him off before he had time to steal a horse and get away." Jed twisted the bloody sack in his hands. "Hannah, I want you to take Johnny and go with Frannie to Philadelphia until after the election."

She offered no argument, but Markus jumped in. "You're still plannin' to run?"

Jed was shocked by the question. "Yes. Since I know Hannah and Johnny are safe, I'm not going to let this menace distract my plans."

A deep furrow creased Markus's brow. "By all means, keep your family safe, but what about my family? And what about the other families and their children?"

"You're in no danger. This was intended to derail my senatorial campaign and stop my push for an end to slavery. We'll go away for a while, and things will die down."

"I don't agree. I can click off a number o' things goin' on 'round here that might've provoked that note. You know folks are still fumin' over you freein' the slaves and makin' 'em landowners, but then Abel and Jack got cornered in Calverton after Washington burned, and Abel accidentally let on that he's educated."

Jed's cheeks burned red over the disclosure. "I didn't know that."

"There's a lot ya don't know."

Frustration thickened Markus's brogue, and Hannah's eyes began to dart nervously between the two tense friends.

"I've been home from England for months," Jed said. "You should have told me."

"You're in and out so danged often, I can't remember what ya know and what ya don't."

"You knew where I was for the nine months after Washington burned—being marched off to the hold of a filthy prison ship and then incarcerated. You knew I wanted to be here."

"Yes, but how much have you been here in the year since? You're a good military man. You know ya can't fight a war on so many fronts with limited resources. We're spread too thin, and we're worn weary from bein' on edge for four years defendin' everyone from one threat or another. Besides, Johnny's takin' wasn't the only warnin' today. Someone slit a mare's throat and left her bleedin' out in the eastern pasture. The poor dear ran wild in fright, leavin' a bloody trail until she finally collapsed. I had ta put 'er down. Now the rest of the stock is crazed with fear. There's too much blood to even follow a trail. It looks like Bladensburg back there."

Jed swallowed hard, noticing the blood on Markus's knees for the first time. "The kidnapper could have done that, too, to create a diversion."

Hannah glanced nervously at Markus as she quickly stood and grabbed Jed's arm. "Can you men finish this later? Jed, let's take Johnny back up to the house."

Softening his voice only slightly, he answered, "Go on ahead. I'll follow along shortly."

When she didn't move, he drew his arm around her waist and returned his attention to Markus. Jed's words were cool and measured. "Then what do you suggest we do?"

"We need ta hire and arm more men."

The air echoed with Jed's derisive snort. "We can't do that! If word got out that we hired our own militia, we'd have even bigger problems on our hands!"

Markus jutted his chin forward. "Don't ya think it's a mite late to be worryin' about what the neighbors'll think?"

"That's enough, boys!" Frannie said as she stepped between the men.

But Jed pushed past her and squared off again. "No! He has something on his chest, and I want to hear it." Jed moved to within an arm's distance of Markus. "I thought we were building something here, that we believed in the same things. What happened to you?"

The women sucked in audible gasps. Jack's sorrowful gaze shifted back and forth between his two best friends, and then, hanging his head, he silently turned and left the barn.

Markus's eyes followed the former slave until he disappeared, and then, visibly seething, he turned back on Jed and glared at him through glistening eyes. "How dare you challenge my loyalty ta Jack and the rest o' the freedmen? You manumitted 'em, but who's been here, week in and week out, defendin' them against those that still see only their color?"

"That's why I'm running for the senate. To change things!"

"Then don't also go stirrin' things up, Jed. Lydia described the scene on the ship today—how you went on about Titus when people wouldn't grant her a place to sit. I heard some fella jumped ship after nosing around about you. You may have sent a new enemy here."

Jed clamped down so hard on his jaw it began to ache. "Don't presume to know my business, Markus. Have you got something solid to bring to me? When you do, come to me."

Markus cast knowing glances at Frannie and Hannah, who returned his silent petition with almost imperceptible shakes of their heads. Jed caught the exchange but held his tongue. He returned his arm to Hannah's waist and said, "Let's go home."

After they left, Markus glared at Frannie. "It's time, Francis. He needs to know."

"Hannah will bear the brunt of the fallout, Markus. She has to agree first."

He worked his jaw and rumpled his hat as his eyes searched the ground. Tense moments passed before he spoke. "I'll go see to that mare." Then he stormed from the barn.

CHAPTER 6

September 22, 1816
The Ramsey country estate on the outskirts of London, England

Decades of warring had taken a hefty toll on Britain, but the cost was most apparent in the children. Poverty abounded, particularly in homes of men the war left too broken to work—or those who never made it home. Too many children would never know their fathers at all, and some had no mothers, either. An abundance of these waifs roamed the streets, their cause overwhelming the system in place to protect them.

Mary McGowan and her husband Trevor had been products of London's streets. It led Trevor to a dismal life of crime and suicide, leaving Mary at thirty widowed and alone with two small boys. Her family's fate changed when wealthy Stephen Ramsey fell in love with her. A marriage was planned, and then, as if the fates were attempting to pound her back into her rightful place, Stephen was murdered. This final blow had finally shattered Mary's spirit, making her easy prey to a passing fever, from which she never recovered. She cursed her weakness, knowing she was too far spent to rescue her boys. She had to save them from a childhood on the streets. Time was short, prompting her desperation this day.

She wiped the tears from her eyes and surveyed the cluttered state of her once-lovely cottage and furnishings, gifted to her by Stephen's son, Arthur Ramsey, in recognition of the widow's importance in his father's life. They had a housekeeper who came in a few days a week to do the cooking, shopping, and laundry, but the small chores fell to the boys, who at six and four bore responsibilities too grievous for their tender ages. Mary knew what must be done.

"Michael, Hank," she called out weakly. The two boys appeared from the dark confines of the back room where they slept. Michael was the oldest, a wary, dark-haired child with his father's piercing eyes. He was already far too acquainted with the hard truths of life. Hank was already as tall as his older brother, with Mary's fair complexion and stocky build. He rarely spoke. He was a child content to play for hours with a few sticks and stones, but when he wanted something, he took it forcefully with no regard for consequences, be it food or a toy or baby bird. Mary saw such incongruity in the pair. One understood far too much for his age. The other, far too little.

Michael stoked the ashes and added some kindling and wood. Mary forced a smile, saying, "Thank you, m'little man." She patted the bed, and the boys climbed up and hugged her close. "There, there, my loveys."

"Can you cook us porridge today, Mama?" Michael asked, his chestnut eyes hopeful.

Mary's eyes began to sting as she drew her weak arms around them. Hank laid his head on her breast and smiled up at her as her hands brushed along her sons' brows. "You, my brave boys, must quickly dress and ride the pony ta town an' deliver this letter'n' money ta Mrs. Hewitt. She'll feed my two little men and accomp'ny ya 'ome with a few days groceries. She'll tidy up a bit, and most importantly, she'll 'elp Mama contact Mr. Ramsey."

"Will 'e 'elp us, Mama?" Michael asked.

Mary pursed her lips together tightly and forced a smile. "Don't ya worry, my loveys," she finally replied. "Of course 'e will. 'E's 'elped us already, hasn't 'e? And 'e loves God, and hasn't Mama told you that them what loves God 'elps those in need? We may not go ta church ev'ry Sunday, but didn't Mama teach her loveys to grow up

57

good like Mr. Ramsey did, and ta use your inheritance ta do good ta others as Mr. Ramsey's done ta us?"

"Is there money enough to get you well, Mama?" Michael asked, his eyes shining.

A cock crowed in the yard, and Mary tightened her arms around her boys. "Listen ta that, will ya? It's half past mornin' already. You boys hurry and dress and get on yer way to town." Hank slipped to the floor and ran off, but Michael hung back at his mother's side. "Get along with you, Michael. 'Twill be all right. Mama needs yer 'elp."

He trudged away, glancing back at her. Mary maintained her feigned smile until he slipped out of sight, and then she turned to the side table where her unfinished letter lay. She had been nearly illiterate when she began working as Stephen's housekeeper. Estranged from his own son, Arthur, Stephen took an interest in her boys, patiently teaching Michael to read and write, unlocking the boy's bright, inquisitive mind. Hank's simplemindedness touched a different but sympathetic chord in Stephen's heart, and he came to love them both. When he discovered Mary was also illiterate, he began teaching her to read and write, encouraging her to speak as a lady, and during their nightly lessons, the pair had fallen in love.

She caught her reflection in the silver hand mirror Stephen had given to her. Her once-plump face was ashen and lean, sagging at the jaw. Dark rings framed dull eyes, and her hair was nearly gray now. The deterioration on the outside now matched the state of her heart.

She wrote a few final lines and folded the paper. By the time she slipped back beneath the quilt, her limited reserves were spent. Another weak smile was pasted across her lips as she handed the letter and money to the boys and sent them on their way. She had no family to call on, and her benefactor had moved far away. She uttered a prayer that God would wing this letter on to him, and help her fulfill her dying wish to save her boys.

Michael helped Hank onto the pony and then stood on the block and hefted himself onto her back. A fortyish man came around the corner, his smile revealing a few missing teeth.

"Hello, lads. Where are you off to on this fine morning?" Michael backed away from the man. "Don't be shy, lad. The name's Richard Porter. I'm an old friend of your ma's."

Michael gave the pony a kick, but Mr. Porter took the reins and stopped the beast before the animal moved a foot. "Don't be rude, boy! First tell me, Michael, how is your ma?"

Michael's eyes began to tear at the question.

"That bad, eh?" Porter clicked his tongue rapidly. "That breaks my heart, it does. There was a time when I was very near to bein' your pa. Do you remember that?"

Michael scrutinized the man's face. "You lied ta Mama. You made 'er cry."

"Boys cannot understand the doin's of grown-ups. It weren't me what got your mama upset. It was that Mr. Ramsey. He sullied my good name and confused her. If not for him we'd be a family right now, we would. And there'd be someone to tend to you and your brother."

"Mr. Ramsey'll 'elp us. Mama's sendin' for 'im." Michael shook the letter at the man.

"Is that so? Let ole Mr. Porter read that note, eh, boy?" Porter snatched the letter from Michael's reluctant hands, and a smile curled on his lips as he read it. When he finished, he folded it up and stuffed it into his pocket, then laid his hands on the boys' shoulders. "Mr. Porter will 'ave a talk with your mama. Now you get on to Mrs. Hewitt's cottage for a bite, eh? When you get back, things'll be just fine. You'll see."

His smile was so sincere, his way so commanding that Michael dared to hope it could be so. Mr. Porter slapped the pony's haunches, and she took off at a canter. When Michael looked back, the man was opening the cottage door.

★ ★ ★ ★ ★

Mary heard the squeak of the outside door and noticed the glow of sunlight filtering into her bedroom. She opened her eyes, expecting to see Michael standing there, but to her horror she saw the charlatan Richard Porter. His concern had been so convincing after Stephen's death. Were it not for Arthur Ramsey, she very nearly could have married him.

"What are you doin' here? Murderer!" She gasped, clutching the bedcovers to her.

"Shh, Mary. Ya'll only do yourself more 'arm by gettin' riled. I know you're sick. I've kept my ears tuned to news of you. And now I've come to help you and the boys."

"I want nothin' from you. I know you killed my Stephen. Get out!" she ordered.

He held his hands up innocently. "These hands committed no crime."

"They may not've held the knife, but they paid the hands that did. I know all about you, Jervis. That's the name you go by, isn't it, Mr. Porter?"

"Call me what you wish, but I'm your only 'ope now." He pulled the letter she had written from his pocket and tossed it into the fire. "Arthur Ramsey will not be comin' to save you. Ha! I had no idea my haranguin' him would cause 'im to leave the country entirely. However, I am here, and I will make you an offer that should bring you some measure of peace."

"Where are my boys?"

"I sent them on to Mrs. Hewitt's so we could talk privately." Mary curled into a ball and began to cry. "What kind of man would I be if I left you alone in your hour of need? No, no, no. I know you're dyin'. Mrs. Hewitt told me everythin'. For a few shillings, that housekeeper would sell her own young. She was kind enough to tell me how Ramsey released the total inheritance to you. Wasn't that lovely of 'im? But I'm not here to hasten your death or to cause you further pain. I'm offerin' to be a father to your boys, as we originally planned."

"All you ever wanted was their trust money. Get out!"

"True, I want that money, but I'm not without a heart. I'm tired of bein' alone. I promise I'll care for your boys."

"Like you cared for Stephen? Never!"

"What options do you have, Mary? Arthur Ramsey isn't comin' to rescue them. They'll be tossed into an orphanage, or worse yet, into the streets. Surely I'm a better option than either of those. I'll fetch a parson. Agree to wed and give the boys to me. I've got adoption papers here, namin' me the boys' guardian. If you refuse, I'll make the constable aware of your situation, and your last view of your boys will be of them kickin' and screamin' as they're separated and dragged away."

"No, no!" Mary closed her eyes against the horror, but she could see no other way.

"Use what little time you have left to 'elp ease the transition, Mary. Give the arrangement your blessin' and help the boys accept me. Time is short. What will you do?"

CHAPTER 7

November 15, 1816
Annapolis, Maryland

The past seven days had been a fairy-tale week for Hannah. It began with a cryptic note from Jed summoning her to pack, followed by his arrival by private carriage at Frannie's Philadelphia home. Bundled up under down-filled quilts, the couple set off on a leisurely, three-day trip home, curled in each others' arms with Johnny tucked between. As the miles passed, Jed fed Hannah from the wondrous basket of exotic treats he had purchased at Philadelphia's markets, while sharing the details of his senatorial win and the news about Jack and Lydia's engagement. Each afternoon they stopped at some elegant inn with lovely views of the Susquehanna River, and well-appointed rooms that caused Hannah to marvel over the fuss Jed was making. Had he missed her as much as she had longed for him? When he pulled her into his arms and made her feel like a new bride once more, her doubts and questions dissolved.

She knew the route well enough to know they had bypassed the main road to the Willows on the third day, but her questions were met with a smile that brought a twinkle to Jed's eye. It was late afternoon when they arrived at a splendid, two-story brick home situated across the circle from the Maryland State House in Annapolis. The driver leapt to the ground and opened the carriage door. Jed took Johnny and helped Hannah out, grinning as he took her arm.

"Can you feel it? The history? The opportunity? We can make a difference here."

"We?"

"Yes. We—together. Come with me," he said with the excitement of a boy. He led her to the elegant Maryland State House, which sat on a knoll before them. "This is where the legislature convenes three months every year. Isn't it beautiful?"

"Yes, very beautiful. So this is where you'll be while you're away from me."

He tapped her playfully on her nose as he extended his arm to her. "Allow me to give you a tour, madame. Annapolis and this state house actually served as the nation's capital for almost nine months beginning in November of 1783. Imagine it, Hannah—the Continental Congress met here! George Washington stood before them in that very building when he resigned his commission as the commander-in-chief of the Continental Army. And when the Treaty of Paris was brought to America to be ratified, ending the Revolution, this is where the votes were cast. President Monroe resists change, but a new era is dawning. It's a time for new beginnings."

Jed tightened his hold on her as he swung his other arm to the left, pointing to a narrow brick building. "That's the Maryland Inn, which welcomed some of the greatest diplomats of the Revolution. Isn't it exciting to imagine Benjamin Franklin, John Jay, and John Adams there?"

Jed turned to his wife, a hint of melancholy in his eyes. "We can accomplish a great deal of good here, Hannah." Their eyes locked for several seconds as he traced his thumb along her jaw. "I know I've put you through a great deal in the past, but just strive with me a while longer. I want our future to be sweet, and I don't want this new political adventure to hoist new burdens upon you, either, so I've made a few decisions. I hope you'll approve."

She looked askance at him. "This all sounds a little ominous. What have you done?"

He led her back to the brick house where the carriage was parked, withdrew a key from his pocket, and unlocked the exquisite home's front door. "Until these new threats against the Willows are settled, I don't feel safe having you there." After handing Johnny to the driver, Jed lifted Hannah into his arms and carried her across the threshold.

"Whose home is this, Jed?" she questioned as she surveyed the papered walls and Oriental carpeting. She noticed a few familiar furnishings. "Isn't that our clock and credenza?" Her brow wrinkled in wonder. "Why are our things here?"

He set her down and took Johnny from the driver's arms. "Because this is our home now, Hannah, at least whenever the General Assembly is in session. I rented it furnished from a family who moved abroad for a few years, and I moved a few of our things in to make it feel like home. I couldn't bear the thought of us living apart while I serve in the senate." Her mouth hung agape, so as she surveyed her surroundings he rushed on.

"And we're moving the wedding here—a quiet affair we'll host before my senatorial party, which the restaurant adjacent to the Maryland Inn will cater. We'll use a portion of that food for Jack and Lydia's reception. You need only set the menu. And beside the inn sits a fine rooming house. I've purchased a night's stay there for Jack and Lydia."

Hannah eyed him skeptically. "A honeymoon in Annapolis? Will they be welcome?"

"I've become friends with Maryland's new governor, Charles Ridgely, who is quite awed by the equality we enjoy on the Willows. Though he still runs his grand Hampton estate on slave labor, he is known as a gentle master who admits the institution is wrong. He frees his slaves at age forty-five, and plans to free all his slaves upon his death. In a token of good faith, he convinced the proprietor to accept Lydia and Jack for a night—for a sizeable fee, of course. Afterwards, I've arranged a week's stay in Washington, where they'll be more welcome."

Jed looked at Hannah cautiously. "I know I've overwhelmed you, but would you mind if we live here for a time?"

"Oh, Jed!" she cried. "This is the greatest gift you could have given me!"

He seemed amazed by the intensity of her reaction. "You're really happy about it?"

"Of course I am. All I want is to be with you."

His surprise changed to tenderness. "We'll be happy here, Hannah. You'll see."

The next three days sped along as Hannah organized the home and met the staff. On the fourth day Frannie, Bitty, Jenny, Lydia, and the children arrived to prepare for the wedding and the party to celebrate Jed's election. The men were to follow the next morning with Reverend Myers, when Abel arrived on leave.

By mid-afternoon of the following day, with the preparations completed, the women set about to dress. Feeling lightheaded, Hannah sat down beside Bitty in the upstairs parlor, gathering the rustling yards of her violet gown around her. "I detest corsets," she confessed as she leaned her head back on the chair. She gazed at Frannie's fuller but definitely more comfortable form. "You always look gorgeous, but don't you feel scandalous for not wearing at least a cincher?"

"Better that than wheeze and walk around as pale as a sheet." Frannie raced to her sister-in-law's aid. "Let me loosen these ties before you asphyxiate!"

"Only a little," Hannah replied weakly. "Unlike you, I bow to convention." Jenny laughed as Frannie's disdain increased with the release of each tie.

The front door shut loudly, and the women all jumped. Frannie moved to the landing at the top of the stairs, where there was a large window. Her report to the ladies was brief. "Jed's upset."

"What time is it now?" asked Bitty as the clock began to strike four. Her smile faded into a grim line. "Where are the men? Something's terrible wrong. Jack wouldn't be late today unless—" Her bottom lip quivered. "I'd best check on Lydia. She'll be worried sick."

Frannie's gaze followed Bitty down the hall. "She's right. They'd be here if they could."

Hannah groaned and cupped her face. "I've been watching that clock all day, Frannie."

"Then it wasn't the corset. You were worried sick about the men. We've made a big mistake in keeping Jed in the dark, Hannah, and the men may have paid the price."

"Not *we*. *I* did it." Hannah returned to the chair and doubled over.

Frannie took her hand. "You wanted to protect Jed while he was imprisoned. That's understandable. The fire, the gunshot that killed the attacker, and then nearly losing you and the baby—we could scarcely bear it. We agreed with your decision to hide the news from him until his return, but he's been home for eighteen months now, and he needs to know."

Hannah turned to Jenny. "I know how difficult I've made things for Markus. He's been trying to protect the farm from an enemy Jed doesn't even know exists."

"Secrets get more snarled the tighter we hold on to them, Hannah," Jenny said kindly. "I know that well enough from my own mistakes."

"You're right. We've all been forced to live a lie to protect Abel, and my keeping it from Jed has compounded the deception, but he's so nervous and easily riled since coming home."

Frannie bit her lip as she glanced at Hannah. "Perhaps we've given him cause. Our original secretiveness would have wounded him, but he would have understood if we had explained everything to him when he first returned after the war. But now? He'll see it as a grave breach of trust."

Hearing her own fear expressed so openly caused Hannah to pale. "I convinced you all to let me tell him in my own way—in my own time—but in truth? I dared hope we'd never have to tell him. I only pray my delay hasn't caused the men harm today."

Frannie stood and began to pace. "We clearly have enemies."

The remaining color drained from Hannah's taut face. "I just pray we don't have to get into it all today. Perhaps the men are delayed by wagon trouble. For now, just help me calm Jed, and if circumstances require an explanation, help me, all right?"

Frannie took her sister-in-law's hand. "All right."

The two women descended the staircase into a flurry of hired staff adjusting their preparations to accommodate the delay. Jed leaned against the window, staring out into the busy brick circle surrounding Maryland's picturesque state house, clearly lost in his own thoughts. Hannah went to him, startling him with her touch. His hand instinctively reached for hers and drew it to his lips.

Seeking some words of comfort, Hannah looked to Frannie, and Frannie obliged.

"Maybe Abel couldn't get leave from the army, and Jack and Markus waited for him."

"Abel or no Abel, Jack would have come. Wild horses couldn't have kept him away."

The creak of an upstairs door drew their attention to the landing, where Lydia appeared, clothed in her handmade wedding dress. "Has there been any word from Jack?"

Pain filled every angular curve of Jed's face. After a hard swallow, he replied, "Not yet." Then, as if he needed to be alone, he turned away from everyone, rubbing his pounding temples. "Perhaps I should have listened to Markus. Perhaps I've been so blinded by my ambition to end slavery that I've ignored a real and present danger."

Coldness settled into Hannah's bones, causing her to shiver. She knew Frannie felt the same chill when she wrapped her arms around her midsection as she characteristically did when trying to settle her nerves.

"If he'd given me something concrete to work with," Jed continued, "but he's been almost secretive. Rather than tell me our troubles straight out, it's as if he's laying a trail of breadcrumbs for me, hoping I'll discover the answer on my own."

Jed returned to his vigil at the window, and his sister moved to his side. "Perhaps he thinks he's protecting you. You've taken on a huge load for a man of only twenty-six."

Jed spun on her with his eyes narrowed. "Protect me? Has he said that?"

Her hands came up as she stepped back a pace. "No. I was just . . . just thinking out loud."

"Do you think me incapable of handling my own affairs, Francis?" Before she had the chance to answer, he turned on his wife. "Do you?"

Shocked by his reaction, Hannah froze, and she noticed Frannie stiffen as well. Immediately, Jed moved to soothe them. "I'm sorry. I'm so sorry for overreacting." Obviously embarrassed, he slumped against the window frame and appeared to resume his search of the street. "I can handle my political responsibilities, and the work the farm requires, but there is something weighing on me—a discomfort I feel on the Willows, as if I'm a guest on my own farm. The closeness Markus and I once shared hasn't been the same since I returned home after the war—" he turned to stare at Hannah "—though you two have become very close."

Hannah's hand rose to brush at the prickles rising on her arm, but then Frannie's blessed voice broke in. "I think I see them!"

Pressing his face near the glass to peer down the street, Jed confirmed their arrival. In a moment he was out the door and in the brick street, waiting for the carriage.

Hannah was grateful to have him out of the room.

"I've never seen him like this," Frannie said anxiously.

"What am I to do?"

Frannie's eyes grew wider as she began to slowly shake her head. "I don't know, Hannah. Jed suspects something. I'm afraid the time to handle this comfortably has passed."

A clamor erupted on the upstairs landing as Bitty and the other women appeared. "They're here! Moses saw them through the window!" She clapped her hands and pushed Lydia back into the room. "We're gonna have this weddin' after all."

Frannie placed a hand on Hannah's shoulder. "Go help Lydia. I'll see what's caused the men's delay."

Hannah was grateful for the diversion. Moses stood at the upstairs window, shouting down to the men. She caught a glimpse of their faces—relief, worry, fatigue were all apparent. Mighty Abel, still dressed in his uniform, leapt to the ground to help Jack down. Noticing what looked like a patch of blood on Jack's shoulder, Hannah glued her attention to the window, where she listened in on the conversation.

"What happened to Jack? He's been shot," Jed said. Markus glanced at Jack, who spoke up with exaggerated cheer. "Had a little trouble's all. Probably nothin' compared to what Lydia'll do to me for arrivin' late at my own weddin'!"

The reply didn't seem to relax Jed as Markus and Abel unloaded their few satchels.

Frannie intervened by refocusing the conversation. "Good to see you, Reverend, Abel," she said with a well-feigned smile. She caught Jed's arm in her right hand and Jack's in her left. "We're an hour late. We've got to hurry and get on with this wedding before the governor and senators arrive for Jed's Inaugural party.

Jed looked back as if to resume his interrogation of Markus, but Frannie jerked his arm and asked, "Is that what they call the celebration for a new senator, Jed, an Inaugural?"

Her brother muttered something and allowed her to lead him into the house, but as soon as they crossed the threshold he turned to face Markus and Abel.

Markus brushed past Jed, offering a cursory explanation. "We had some trouble today, Jed, but what happened can't be settled in a few minutes, so let's set this aside until later, and celebrate all the good things first."

A brief standoff occurred before Jed said, "All right. But I want to know everything this time, Markus." He raised an eyebrow for emphasis. "Everything."

Markus rubbed his tongue along the inside of his lower lip and nodded before following Frannie and the other men upstairs to change. As he passed Hannah a worried look was exchanged, and when her glance shifted to Jed, she caught his narrowed eyes on her.

The wedding was lovely, and the turmoil circling the Willows did not mar Jack's happiness, though the tension within the group became increasingly apparent during the abbreviated reception. Jack and Lydia didn't wait around for Jed's senatorial party to begin. They greeted the few early arrivers they recognized—Timothy Shepard, Jed's former college roommate and former rival for Frannie's hand, who arrived with his Washington socialite wife, Lucinda; and Dr. Samuel Renfro, who had saved Hannah and little Johnny during his birth. Then the newlyweds took Jed's generous gift and headed across the street to the rooming house to begin their marriage. Bitty tucked the children in an upstairs bedroom and enjoyed a few hours at the high-society affair.

She fit neatly under Abel's handsomely uniformed arm. The medals hanging from his muscled chest shielded him from the scrutinizing glances of Annapolis's gentry, reminding the guests that he was a hero of Fort McHenry. Bitty had never been prouder, and when the pair danced, she seemed far younger than her forty years.

"You're beautiful, Bitty," Abel said softly.

She reached a hand up to caress his cheek. "Thank you. I might never take this pretty dress off again."

Tightening his grip on her small, work-worn hand, he pulled her from the line of dancers and into a corner. Then he moved her hand to his mouth, his eyes never leaving hers, and placed a kiss in her palm. "The dress is pretty too, but you, Bitty, are beautiful."

A shy smile broke across her lips as her other hand covered the warming of her cheek. "I feel like a princess, dressed all pretty and in the company of a fine and handsome soldier like you. I don't want this night to ever end."

Abel danced her around until they moved to the veranda, stepping out into the crisp evening air. "I ride back to Fort McHenry day after tomorrow, Bitty. There are a few things we need to attend to while we're together."

"I'm listenin'."

"The deed arrived to the land I received as a signing bonus with the army. I'm having the land deeded in your name—as Bitty Miller."

Her brow bunched up in confusion. "I know you was legally addin' Miller to all our names in honor of the profession your father gave you, but why are you puttin' the land in my name?" Her slim frame trembled within his hands. "You and Markus are telling Jed everything tonight, aren't you?"

Abel's eyes bored into hers before he nodded. "I want you and the children to be secure in case things don't go well. There's a storm brewing in Jed, and I can't be sure how he'll react."

The previous happiness was erased from Bitty's face. "I don't know the cause of it, but he's been different since he returned from England. Dr. Renfro said it happens to some folks after a trauma like war. Some fold up like Hannah's sister Myrna. Some see threats that aren't there. Some can't bear the demons in their head and they . . ." She buried her face in her hands.

"He's been pressing for answers, but Hannah begged Markus for more time. Something happened today, Bitty, and we can't delay any longer. Markus plans to tell Hannah that tonight."

Hannah was never more than a few feet from Jed throughout the evening as he guided her from one group of politicians to another, making introductions. Markus tried in vain to catch her alone, to warn her of the coming discussion, but no proper moment arose, so he tried to relax and enjoy the festivities. The food was divine—the best he could ever remember eating—but a few bites were all he could force down, and even they rose in his throat each time the events of the day replayed in his mind. Worse yet was the moment Jack and Lydia made their exit. As thrilled as Markus was for Jack's happiness, he hated to see his friend leave the party. There was strength in numbers, and tonight they would need all the strength they could muster.

Jed announced the evening's musical performance, and for a few brief moments, Markus relaxed and marveled over his beautiful wife as Jenny and Frannie performed six duets, ending with Key's "Star-Spangled Banner." When Jenny returned to his side, he took her hand and pressed it to his cheek. "Thank ya, darlin'."

"For what, Markus?"

"For givin' up the stage for the life of a farmer's wife." Broad and muscled, Markus was barely an inch taller than Jenny. She tipped her head and brushed her cheek against his, eliciting a contented sigh from her husband. "I hope you can hear that thunderin' applause hammerin' in my heart for you, Jenny."

"I can. And that means more to me than a standing ovation in any Philadelphia hall."

He took Jenny for a few turns around the dance floor until a maid waved to her from the upstairs landing. With a wry smile, she shrugged, "Our son is calling for me."

They held hands as she moved away from him until the distance caused them to break their grasp. Markus shoved his hands in the pockets of the trousers he wore at his own wedding. His stomach lurched as he felt the piece of brass he'd found earlier in the day. He'd brought it along to speak to Jed about it. He quickly withdrew his hand and found Abel watching him from across the room, silently asking if he had attended to the needed task. Markus shook his head and again sought a chance to catch Hannah alone.

Frannie must have seen the tense exchange between the men, for she moved close to Markus and asked quietly, "You're telling Jed tonight?"

"Aye. I want to at least warn Hannah, but she's been glued to Jed's side."

"Let me tell her. She needs to know."

Markus watched Frannie slip her arm in Hannah's and lead her away with nothing more than a smile to Jed for an explanation. Moments later they reappeared, with Hannah visibly paler and shaking. She sought Markus, and when their gazes met, the fear in her eyes sent chills through him.

The last of the guests were two state delegates. After they said their goodbyes to Hannah, she excused herself and slipped away. She found Markus in the alcove near the kitchen. "I need to speak to you. I'm worried." She bit her lip. "Perhaps—"

"No, Hannah. I'll not stall Jed anymore. Too much is on the line—for all of us."

"Then let me tell him, please. The truth will hurt him terribly. I never intended that."

"Then what *did* you intend?" The voice was Jed's. He appeared from around the corner, his eyes narrow and glowering. "I stumble upon my best friend and my wife in a dark alcove, whispering secrets. Shall I call Jenny down to hear this tale, too?"

The kitchen staff quickly vacated the room. As the two men squared off, Hannah stepped between, the pain in her eyes as cutting as any knife. "How dare you! Has your mind so degraded that you could believe such filth about your best friend and your wife? I was actually worried about you. I wanted to spare you pain, and yet you stand here, inflicting it upon those whose only thought was to protect you?"

"Protect me? From whom? Those I relied on? Those I trusted?" Jed's breaths came in long, heaving gulps. Then he thrust his arm forward, sword-like, at Markus. "Imagine how it appears—my best friend, a man I regard as a brother, standing in the dark, stealing glances and whispering secrets with you. And not just tonight. It's been happening since I've returned from England, like a private joke behind my back."

"I needed to speak with Markus before he told you today's news. Regardless of how it appears, search your heart, Jed. Do you believe either of us is capable of such betrayal?"

His mouth still hung agape. "I'd rather die than believe such a thing."

"Then don't," she begged. Her hands were tentative as she placed them on his pounding chest, but he remained unmoved. "Your fears are completely unfounded. The secrets we've kept were about attacks on the Willows. Markus wanted to tell you. I begged him not to."

The rumble of voices drew the rest of the Willows group near in a nervous cluster. They kept their distance, but Jed saw Hannah's worry in their faces also. "There were other attacks?"

"Yes. We've got trouble, Jed. We found a drowned slave floating offshore today. His hands, feet, and mouth were bound." Markus reached into his pocket and withdrew a four-inch brass teardrop with a "P" engraved on it. "This was tied to his gag. Do you recognize it? It's the clapper from the dinner bell at the hunting cabin."

Jed's eyes fixed on the clapper. "He was seeking asylum at the cabin." He staggered to the kitchen and dropped into a chair, with Markus and Hannah close behind. "You said there were other threats against the Willows. I didn't listen."

"Don't blame yourself."

"Oh—" his voice dripped with acrimony "—I don't, at least not entirely." He bolted to a stand and again pointed at Markus. "You should have told me everything so I could make informed decisions."

Markus nodded silently before saying, "Yes, I should have."

"It's not his fault, Jed. I'm the one who—"

"Stop!" Jed raised his hand, but he knew it was the pain on his face that silenced Hannah. "Please just stop. I need to write a letter, resigning from my seat in the senate now."

"What?" she cried in disbelief. "Why?"

"Someone knows I'm aiding runaways. They know I'm breaking the law. Besides, what will the senate lose by the resignation of a man who can't even manage his own household?"

As he exited the room he passed Abel, who called out, "You don't need to resign, Jed. We believe we know who did it, and if we're right, he won't ever tell another soul. But there's more, Jed, a terrible part." The large man drew a deep breath. "It's bad . . . real bad. Jed, I killed a white man."

Jed stopped as he felt the last drop of blood drain from his face. He looked at Hannah, suddenly feeling detached from the closest person in the world to him. "Is this the secret you've kept from me?"

Her gaze dropped. "Tell him, Abel. Tell him everything."

Giant Abel closed his eyes as if in prayer and began. "There were hard feelings between me and two white soldiers, both privates, after the battle of Baltimore. On November twelfth, Captain Foster, Caleb, and I were returning home on leave, but Caleb was acting very strange. I soon found out why. Those men had whipped him in the night, Jed . . . just dragged him from his bed and beat him until his back bled. Then they told him they'd kill us if he told me before we crossed the Calvert County line. I thought freedom would keep my son from ever knowing the feel of the lash, but he now bears scars on his young back, too."

Jed's fists clenched into tight knots. "Who dared do that?"

"Their names were Skully and Hildebrand. Caleb told us they were waiting for me at the Willows. I feared what they'd do at the farm, so I left Caleb with Captain Foster and sped home. They had the women and children barricaded in the church with the reverend, all except my mother and baby Priscilla. Skully kept a gun on them, while Hildebrand set fires around the building."

Abel's voice caught as his eyes welled with emotion. "All I could hear were the screams of the women and children, Jed. Hildebrand said if I tried to stop the fires, Skully'd shoot my mother and baby. The only way I could save everyone was to surrender, and I would have, Jed—I swear I would have given myself up—but there was no way to be sure they'd let them go.

"So I created a diversion, and I fired my rifle. I killed Skully as Captain Foster arrived. It was then that Hildebrand told me it was all a joke. They knew the church wouldn't burn because it was newly built of green timbers. They set it all up to get a noose around my neck. I don't know what they'd have done to me, but hanging would have been better than what happened afterwards."

The sight of the mighty man slumped against the wall tore at Jed, but something Abel had said earlier left a knot in Jed's stomach. "Wait . . ." His attention shifted back to Hannah. "November twelfth was the day before Johnny was born—"

She clasped Jed's hand, which remained closed and hard. "I was in the church too, along with Beatrice, Myrna, Bitty, and the children. I went into labor thinking I would die in that fire."

"You—you never felt a need to tell me this?"

"I cried out for you that day, but I knew this time you couldn't come to my rescue or our baby's. How could I tell you about that day, knowing it would cause you hurt?"

"How could you not? I'm your husband."

He turned to leave but Markus caught hold of him. "Jed, Hannah did what she thought was best, and we went along with it, but we were wrong, and so will you be if you walk away now. You want ta lead the Willows? Then you need ta know the rest."

A silent standoff occurred, and then Jed stormed to the parlor with Markus and Hannah on his heels. His hard-set eyes met Hannah's again. Her pain was real, he knew that, and he set aside his own long enough to hear Markus out. "Tell me all of it."

Markus glanced at Abel and picked up the tale. "Hildebrand threatened to have Abel hung for killin' Skully, but Captain Foster knew Hildebrand could be charged for the attempted murder of three white women, so he struck a deal to save Abel. He took responsibility for killing Skully, and in return, he let Hildebrand walk, locking all three men into a pact. Either they would all agree to stick to the plan and remain free, or all three would go to prison."

"What you mean is Foster purchased Abel's freedom with a lie," Jed said. "We all became imprisoned that moment. Captain Foster must realize it, too. I noticed he wasn't here tonight."

A conspicuous silence hung in the air like smoke until Frannie spoke up. "Surely you lay no fault at Abel."

Jed walked to the window, where the only noticeable light shone from a street lantern on a pole. "For the shooting? Of course not. Unjust laws caused that situation." He pressed his forehead to the glass and shivered, suddenly feeling cold. "It was all so clear to me as I sat in that ship. Stripped of my dignity and ripped from my home, I suddenly understood the savagery of slavery on a personal level, and I vowed I'd find a way to end it. And now, when I have a platform from which to affect that very change, I must resign the power to do it."

Frannie hurried to her brother and grabbed his arm. "But no one needs to know, Jed. Hildebrand can't risk drawing attention to himself. He could end up in prison for life."

Jed turned to Abel. "Where is this menace now?"

"I don't know. We served together for another seven months, then his enlistment ended and he left. I was asked to deliver some final papers to him at his family's home in Baltimore, but they hadn't seen him in months."

"Then how do we know for certain it even was Hildebrand?"

Markus cleared his throat. "He left his callin' card. Someone shot at Jack . . . and now Foster's dead." The news hit the room like a bombshell. Markus continued in a raspy voice. "His son told us they found 'im swingin' in the barn this mornin'. It was all rigged up ta look like a suicide, with a note pinned to Foster's shirt that said 'Tell Abel.' We don't believe Foster took 'is own life or left that note. It was surely a message from Hildebrand, clear and simple. He's settlin' the score in 'is own way, and he wanted Abel to know he's comin'."

Jed moved to a chair in the most remote corner of the room and dropped into it. His body bent forward until his face filled his large hands. Soon his fingers began digging into his brow and up into his scalp as if harrowing his head would render any sense from the news. No one moved. No one spoke.

Finally, the reverend broke the silence. "Randolph Foster was a martyr for freedom. Surely God will reserve a place in heaven for such a man."

Jed's head shot up, his anger flaring. "How much better would it have been to both serve freedom and live? Two men are dead this day because you all kept secrets from me."

"What would you 'ave done?" Markus snapped. "Murdered Hildebrand? Filed charges against 'im and risked settin' the law on Abel and Foster? There're no good choices 'ere, Jed. You don't know if you could 'ave stopped this."

Jed flew from his chair and jutted his finger at Markus. "That's exactly the point! We don't know, and we never will, because I was denied the opportunity!" The heavy rise and fall of Jed's chest punctuated every angry breath. "It wasn't your call to make," he repeated sadly. His eyes swept those of every person in the room and returned to Markus. "Each of you betrayed me with your silence, but you, Markus, you undermined me. I can't trust you anymore."

The words propelled Hannah from her spot. "You don't mean that, Jed! It wasn't Markus's fault, it was mine! Blame me, not him."

Jed showed no reaction to Hannah's plea as the two men locked eyes. Jenny appeared on the landing, and Markus's attention shifted to her. "If that's how you see it, Jed, my family and I will take our leave."

"No!" Hannah cried. She moved from person to person, seeking someone to end the madness. "Jed, stop this! Do something, Frannie. Say something to him."

"There's no sense in makin' this any worse, Hannah," Markus said softly. "I'll forward an address where you two can send a bank draft for my share of the land and horses."

Jed turned his back to him. "No need to disturb the baby. You can leave in the morning."

Without another word, Markus ascended the stairs to Jenny. The two entered the room and closed the door. Soon the sounds of their trunks scraping the floor resonated above.

Hannah pressed her hands over her ears to block the sound. "Stop this, Jed!" she pled again. "I accept my part in this, but you're destroying everything.

Pain twisted Jed's bearing, from the slump of his shoulders to the hollow emptiness of his downcast eyes. "Please leave us," he muttered to the others in the room. Empty, like so many ghosts, they silently scattered, leaving Jed and Hannah alone.

"Please sit," he urged quietly as his hand pointed to the divan. Hannah sat stiffly on one side, and Jed sat on the other, leaving a painful gap between them. They appeared like two wooden carvings of the hopeful people they had been that very morning. Each clasped their hands in their laps and hung their heads, their eyes searching the floor. Jed took three haggard breaths, struggling to settle his emotions, and then asked, "What has become of us that we could wreak such havoc?"

"Everything I did was out of love."

"Love requires trust. Do you see me so damaged that you need to coddle me? Am I less of a man since I came home from the war?"

He felt the divan shift as if Hannah's body shook at the question. "How could you ask that?" she said.

"You yourself said you were trying to protect me."

"From yourself, Jed, not from our enemies. I admit that I first withheld the truth from you to spare you additional worry while your own freedom was at risk, but when you came home, I simply wanted *you*. I knew as soon as you heard about Hildebrand you would race after him and leave Johnny and me again. Things were quiet. I hoped they would remain so, but I should have known better." Her voice took on an angry edge. "I should have simply told you the truth. In the end, you still found other reasons to leave us. Other priorities."

"They were once our shared dreams."

"We have a child now, Jed. He also deserves to be the focus of our dreams."

The comment caused Jed to finally look at her. "Everything I've ever done was intended to leave a better world for our children. Now two men are dead, in part because of our follies. I can't carry on as if it never happened. Some atonement is required."

"Then speak to the reverend."

"No." Jed shook his head. "I need to find my own answers—alone."

"Then I'll leave with the others in the morning." Hannah stood, causing him to rise in abject courtesy. He didn't offer her any argument as she headed for the stairs. As her foot hit the first step, she called back over her shoulder through a broken voice, "When will you follow?"

He coughed to steady his voice. "I need time to decide whether or not to resign my seat. If I remain in the senate, my duties will require me to remain here for a time. I'll speak with Jack in the morning and ask him to manage the farm until I can hire a new manager."

She tightened her hand around the banister and ascended the steps without another word.

After a restless night spent on the divan, Jed awoke to the sound of steps on the stairs. A small parade of his sober-faced loved ones carried bags and babies to the waiting wagons. Jed called out to Markus, and the departers held their collective breath.

"Thank you for seeing Hannah and Johnny home safely. Would you mind staying on at the farm until Jack arrives? I'll feel better knowing you're there, with Abel returning to the fort."

A sarcastic chuckle escaped from Markus. "Don't worry about Hannah and little Johnny. *I'll* not abandon 'em." He turned for the door but then spun back around. "I know you believe in God, Jed, but I've often wondered why you kick against the idea of Him bein' an all-knowin' God that intervenes in the affairs of men, and then it dawned on me. You think that's *your* job."

Jed's face flushed crimson as he watched Markus exit the door. Hannah, with Johnny in tow, was the last to descend the steps. She wore a blue traveling suit and a hat that obscured the pain in her eyes. Jed moved to her to carry the baby for her, but Hannah wrenched her arm back, placing her torso between father and son. "I can manage," she said. And then she was gone.

CHAPTER 8

April 1817
The Willows

The fragrance of spring along the Patuxent coaxed Hannah from her malaise. Along the river road, she had seen glimpses of yellow and white blossoms in the ground cover and caught the scent of the coral honeysuckle before she saw the first sight of their reddish blooms peeking through the thickets. The terrain and climate, and therefore the plants growing here, varied significantly from those she remembered from her childhood in Baltimore County. Many of these plants constituted Bitty's medicinal inventory from which she prepared her teas and poultices. Last year's three-season winter took a toll on her supplies, but now, with spring bursting so gloriously, the little woman would be in her heaven once more.

As the road rounded the last curve where the Willows property line began, Hannah's hand instinctively moved to her emerald wedding ring, wondering whom and what to expect on this return. The heaviness returned as she recalled Markus and Jenny's departure from the Willows.

Hannah had begged them to stay on for the winter, but Markus's pride would not allow it. She had received two letters from the O'Malleys, posted in Virginia, which reported that they were settled and content. Markus had returned to the trade he knew best—buying tobacco and captaining a tobacco barge—but he was also learning to be a cotton buyer. And with a ship big enough to accommodate Jenny and baby Sean, the family traveled together most of the year.

Together. Hannah recalled the day she had learned about the Annapolis town home Jed had rented. She had only seen her husband once since their parting five months ago. He had arrived at the Willows unexpectedly on the evening of December 23 with bundles of gifts for everyone, and special treats to add to the holiday meal. He cajoled Jack into playing cards until after she retired to bed, and the men had already left to hunt by first light.

That evening, after Reverend Myers's Christmas Eve program, Jed had handed out his gifts to all the residents. Bitty and Lydia used the opportunity to pull Jack aside and deliver some stern advice. Twenty minutes later, Jack announced he was suddenly unavailable for cards.

When everyone filed away to their cabins, Jed followed them into the night. Hannah's heart broke as she heard the latch on the door click shut. Needing comfort, she scooped up her son and buried her loneliness in the softness of Johnny's brown curls. She began to carry him upstairs for bed when the door burst open and Jed reappeared, his arms filled with two packages wrapped in red satin and secured with white ribbons.

He set them on the floor, laying the smaller of the two, a flat package, to the side before inviting Johnny to open the largest one. The boy huddled against his mother, requiring considerable cajoling before he would pull the tail on the giant bow, releasing the fabric encasing his gift—a beautiful red barn. Jed reached inside and withdrew eleven small items, each wrapped in paper. He unwrapped the first, a cow, and handed it to his son. "I meant to make an even dozen, but I ran out of time."

Hannah examined one of the animals—a horse, carved with such detail she could almost count the hairs of its mane. It was a talent she had not been aware Jed possessed. "You made this?"

He nodded, seeming embarrassed by her attention. "I've been working on them in the evenings, after the assembly ends its day."

Knowing his evenings had been filled with thoughts of Johnny renewed Hannah's waning hope. "They're wondrous." She unwrapped the other animals, and Johnny swooned over each gift, dropping one to focus on the next. In a moment that caught Jed completely off guard, the toddler plopped down in his father's lap to play, bringing Jed unabashed joy. He moved delicately as he reached for the other package, as if fearing to break the love spell he and Johnny were sharing. Then he handed the gift to Hannah, whispering, "I hope you like it."

She unwrapped a beautiful, hand-carved picture frame. Intricately detailed daffodils, her favorite flower, adorned each corner and trailed down the side. She traced the outline of one of the daffodils with her finger, wondering what images would eventually fill this frame. "It's beautiful, Jed. Thank you."

"There's a motive behind my gift, Hannah. I've arranged a portrait sitting for you with a wonderful artist named Anna Peale, in Philadelphia."

Her head tilted sideways as she eyed him suspiciously. "You're sending us away?"

"I'm boarding the hunting cabin up to close down our runaway shelter, but some could still arrive. It's still too dangerous here. I'm working on getting more help, but until then I'd—"

"Fine." She hadn't wanted to debate their past mistakes, and so she packed and left with Johnny the next day. That had been three months ago.

She dipped her head and closed her eyes, relying on prayer to settle her nerves. Today, she tried to focus on the blessings of spring. Tiny golden marigolds dotted the fern-covered banks that hugged the Patuxent River's lazy flow. Small, white blossoms fluttered through the carriage window, and then the view suddenly became obscured by a white storm. Hannah asked the driver to stop, and after she lifted her two-and-a-half-year-old to the ground, mother and son stood beneath the canopy of willow trees that lined the Willows Plantation's portion of the river road.

The heavy blossoms were dropping in a blizzard of white willow petals fluttering to the ground in the April breeze. Hannah urged the driver on ahead so she and Johnny could play. She twirled around and watched as the hem of her blue skirt sent the blossoms swirling. Johnny looked skyward with his hands extended, giggling as the petals landed on his face. Hannah took his hands and twirled with him as the blossoms fell on his dark curls and shoulders like snow. The boy squealed with delight, marching through the swirling beauty, but then he stopped suddenly.

Hannah peered through the lacelike sky to a white stripe created by the last vestiges of real snow, protected from the sun by the heavy boughs of the evergreens behind the mill. Three mounted riders were nestled in the tree line. She didn't know how long they had been there, but the view was too obscured by the falling blossoms to recognize their faces.

One rider began to advance. Hannah grabbed Johnny and moved him behind her as she searched the bank for some cover in which to hide. The rider called out, "Hannah, it's me. It's Jed."

For an instant, she thought she saw him smile at her, but as soon as their eyes met his countenance sobered. Was it sadness she saw there? She couldn't tell, but the curiosity of the scene was not lost on her. As she stood in the birth of spring, he stood in the last moments of winter. It seemed sadly poetic.

Jed dismounted and slowly approached his wife and son, looking more like a trapper than a senator. His face was covered by several days' growth of beard that caught strands of his dark, wavy hair. A heavy flannel shirt collar peeked from under his coat. It was Hannah's favorite, and it complimented the calm reflected in his face. She rubbed the rising hairs on her arms as she noticed how young he looked. Seeing him this way wore down her preplanned defenses.

He stopped in front of her and removed his hat, lifting the other hand to brush a few stubborn blossoms from her dark hair. His hand lingered there, and as he withdrew, her hair slid through his fingers. "I didn't mean to frighten you. It's so good to have you home."

"How long will we be welcome to stay this trip?" she asked with forced coolness.

Jed's mouth pressed into a thin line, reflecting his receipt of her barb. "Forever, I hope. I've hired new men on. The Willows is safe now." His eyes fixed on Johnny. Slowly lowering to his knees, he extended his hand to the boy. "Hello, Son."

Johnny reached back to grab a handful of his mother's skirt, demonstrating the increased rift the separation had caused between father and son. Hannah bent low and whispered to her boy, "Johnny, say hello to your papa."

He buried his face deeper into the blue folds of fabric, but when Jed again extended a nervous hand to the lad, Johnny offered his own.

The child's simple gesture brought a mixed reaction to his father, whose smile reflected an equal measure of sorrow. "Are you glad to be home?" he asked the energetic toddler. The answer was obvious as the boy turned and ran up the lane.

Jed fiddled with his hat before finally placing it on his head again. "Jack and I are riding the fence lines with Mr. Greeley, the new farm manager. I'll come up to the house later, after you've had time to settle in."

Hannah nodded and the couple went their separate ways, as they did so often these days. She wondered what the evening would hold. Maryland's congressional session was over, and Jed was home once more. How would things be between them? She didn't know.

Looking up the Willows lane, Hannah could see that Bitty and Abel's youngest children, eight-year-old Helen and four-year-old Priscilla, had already swept Johnny away to play. Hannah was grateful for a moment's solitude to adjust to the changes on the farm. Her eyes shifted to the cabin where Markus and Jenny had lived. As happy as she was for her friends, she still grieved for them, and the Willows fell a little short of feeling like home anymore.

Hannah noted the conspicuous presence of the new men Jed had hired on to replace Markus. They were white, middle-aged, and armed at all times, and Hannah wondered if the three were as familiar with a hoe as they were with a musket. She dreaded meeting the new manager, Mr. Greeley, who according to Bitty's letters was a most disagreeable man. In her brief correspondence to Jed, his response had been simply that the man had come highly recommended.

Waves and shouts came from every direction as the residents welcomed Hannah home. Some were in the fields, working for wages; others were putting in hours to pay for extra land Jed was allowing them to purchase. Plows were harrowing soil in fields to the north and south, where crops would be rotated to restore richness to the soil. Jed believed this practice was the reason the Willows produced larger harvests of sweeter tobacco.

New birth was evident everywhere as spring foals, calves, lambs, and chicks skittered about the land. Thick patches of marigolds spread across the foundation of the house like a welcome banner, and the windows were open wide. She assumed Bitty was airing the house out for her. Hannah could not deny that she loved it here, and with each step her anxiety lessened. The only question that remained was how she and Jed could close the abyss between them, and whether it was even possible at all.

Bitty appeared on the porch, her arms reaching out to Hannah. "Come here and let me get a look at you." She hurried up the stone steps and into Bitty's arms. The little woman stood on tiptoes, and Hannah bent to close the gap in their height.

"Welcome home, darlin'. Welcome home." Bitty took her by the hand and led her through the house and into the kitchen. "You must be starvin'. Little Johnny already ate two biscuits and jam. My, my how that little fella has grown!

"I'm not very hun—"

"Sit down," Bitty directed, then hauled bread, meat, cheese, and bottles of fruit from the shelves. She scanned Hannah's lean frame and harrumphed. "I'll bet you've lost ten pounds. I know Frannie doesn't cook, and I bet she doesn't have a cook worth her salt, either."

Hannah bit into a slice of cheese and sighed. Food just tasted better here. She felt her muscles relax and caught Bitty smiling as the change began.

"I won two blue ribbons last month at the Calverton Winter Fair."

"That's wonderful!"

"Penny Stringham's teachin' me how to cook French cwee-zeen. I figure it'll help if Jed decides to do some fancy entertainin' here from time to time."

The familiar ache returned at the mention of his name, but Hannah pushed it aside as she considered her sweet, oppressed neighbor, Penny Stringham. "Penny told me she trained at a French culinary school before she married Frederick. How did you arrange cooking lessons?"

Bitty's face sobered. "She lost a baby early in the year, Hannah. Frederick Stringham was so worried about her that he sent for me. I tended her a few days, and in return she offered to teach me to cook fancy." Bitty dumped two bowls of dough on the table, indicating for Hannah to begin kneading one of them.

Hannah washed her hands and set to work. "Poor Penny. You say Frederick Stringham actually showed some regard for her?"

Bitty rolled the dough out and dotted it with softened butter before folding it over on itself and repeating the process. "I can't say whether it was for her or for the baby, but he was as worried as I've ever seen him. Surprisin', isn't it?"

"Very." Hannah watched as Bitty repeated the buttering, folding and rolling again.

"He's made more mistakes than a man ought—been cold and hurtful to his wife. It seems he's sorry and wants to change. How could a woman trust a man who's done what he's done?"

Hannah pondered the question. "As hard as it is to believe, I know she loves him. I suppose if he's really changed . . ."

"Really?" Bitty emphasized her doubt with three more pushes on the roller. "Could you forgive him after all he's done?"

Hannah again pondered the situation. Suddenly, her kneading stopped as understanding hit her. "We're not talking about Frederick and Penny anymore are we, Bitty?"

Bitty shrugged, dodging the question. "How's that dough coming along?"

"What kind of dough is it? It's getting tougher the more I work it."

"Uh-huh. That's my blue-ribbon pie crust recipe, but it's probably ruined now. The more you work pie dough, the tougher it gets. But see my pastry dough here? It gets flakier and flakier as you work it, but you got to butter it up a lot and work it real long and gentle."

"Is that so?" Hannah said. "If this is one of your fable lessons aimed at helping Jed and me, you're speaking to the wrong person. Jed accused me of—of horrible things. He pushed me away. His pride caused this."

Bitty's hands came up to calm Hannah. "I know he made some awful mistakes, but try to look at this through his eyes. He came home after sufferin' wounds we can't imagine, but you were his hope. All he wanted was to get home to you and Johnny. You know that, don't you?"

"Yes, but things changed once he was here."

"Yes, yes, they did, but imagine how it must've felt to come home and see that life went on pretty well without you for nine months, and to hear whispers of secrets behind your back. What if your wife not only managed just fine, but expanded your holdin's while you were away? And what if your best friends handled all your work like you weren't even missed, and your own son loved them more than you? Might you feel a little unnecessary? Maybe even look for something else to make you feel needed?"

The image Bitty painted was one Hannah had never considered.

"You said you could forgive Frederick. Can't you forgive Jed?"

"He hasn't asked for my forgiveness. And how can you forget what he did to Markus?"

Bitty shook her head and leaned into her dough. "You can't get nowhere pushing Jed hard, Hannah. He's like this pie dough—the more you push him the tougher he gets. Markus knew that, but by the time he tried to tell Jed the truth, Jed was overwrought. You can mend things, Hannah. Talk to him. Work him soft and gentle."

"He barely even speaks to me."

"He talks in his own way—gestures, looks, gifts. Can't you see it?"

Hannah heard the creak of the door and the unmistakable sounds of Jed's footsteps. Bitty tried to abruptly change the conversation, but Hannah saw an opportunity to speak her peace.

"Jed's gestures aren't enough anymore. I can't be the peacemaker and pretend everything is all right. His accusations cut too deep. I can't forget them, or how he made me feel."

The footsteps stalled outside the door, close enough that Hannah knew Jed had heard every word. Seconds passed before he entered the room. He set his pained eyes on Hannah, holding her in his gaze, neither one moving or speaking.

The standoff left Bitty silent until she finally glared at Jed and then Hannah. "Look at the pair of you, both of you parched, standin' before a well but neither willin' to drink."

The moment became unbearable, and Hannah dropped her eyes to the floor as she slumped into a chair, turning away from Jed.

Jed took a tentative step forward. "I had hoped . . ." When Hannah didn't respond, he retreated again. "It seems the hurts are still too deep. I'll gather my things and move into Mark—into the cottage with the reverend and Greeley until I return to Annapolis."

CHAPTER 9

Late May 1817
The Willows

Though the usual spring work filled the busy weeks, the Willows was a different farm this year, and everyone felt the change. Tobacco had always been a petulant crop that required constant vigilance against rot and pests, but gone was the friendly banter and teasing that made the labor pleasant. Jed was wound as tightly as anyone had ever seen, and Hannah retreated into the library with Johnny whenever her work was completed.

For the most part, the new men were capable hands, and though Greeley proved to be as knowledgeable a farm manager as Jed had been told, it was no secret that his knowledge was equaled only by his open arrogance in his dealings with Jed, and by his disrespect for the freedmen. Everyone could see how sorely Markus's absence was felt. He alone knew enough about business, and about Jed, to provide the necessary sounding board Jed needed, and everyone knew that without it Jed would break under the strain.

Though silent on the matter, Hannah saw it too. She had spent the last five weeks torturing herself over Bitty's words: *Imagine how it must have felt to come home and see that life went on pretty well without you for nine months, and to hear whispers of secrets behind your back. What if your wife not only managed the family business but expanded your holdings while you were away? And what if your best friends handled all your work like you weren't even missed, and your own son loved them more than you? Might you feel a little unnecessary? Maybe even look for something else to make you feel needed?* Hannah knew it was true . . . all true.

Jed had come home from his detainment in Britain still shaken in many respects. She had gladly soaked up his love and effusive attention, returning it word for word, and touch for touch, but love alone was not enough to erase the dark memories that haunted his sleep months after his return.

She now knew she had ignored his fundamental nature. He was a worker with a need to protect those he loved, and she had left him nothing to do. She had used the last of her inheritance to make everything perfect before his homecoming. The men freshened up the manor house, mended fences, and painted the barn. The older children took over the smaller chores like milking the cows and weeding the garden, and the few odd tasks Jed found to do were completed by well-meaning friends before he had time to strap on his boots. He tried to turn his time and attentions to winning Johnny's heart, but the toddler fussed in his father's strange arms while laughing and cooing for those familiar to him, and clearly Jed saw no reason to upset the child.

With little to fill his day, his mind fixated on his nine-month absence, noting how others had capably filled his shoes. It had been Abel, not Jed, who had saved Hannah from Hildebrand and Skully. Samuel had replaced Jed at Hannah's bedside when she delivered Johnny, and at the church when she buried her parents. It was Markus who had protected the farm and its people during Jed's confinement. On and on the list grew as the evidence mounted in Hannah's mind, proving Bitty right.

Hannah recalled the melancholy underscoring Jed's praise for her decision to use her inheritance to purchase a buffer of land to protect the Willows from pro-slavery buyers, and Frannie's courage in crossing an ocean to succor her brother and Arthur in their hour of need.

Hannah could see it all so clearly now. Their efforts to ease Jed's burdens had actually left him feeling replaced and unnecessary. It was no wonder he ran for office, fighting for issues where his support was needed and appreciated.

His flannel shirt lay over the arm of a chair. She picked it up and pressed it to her nose, drawing in the familiar scents of fresh-cut wood and traces of citrus in Jed's European eau de cologne. The beloved fragrance made tears spring to her eyes. What had she done?

Gratefully, there had been some progress. Abel's release from the military had brought a host of changes. Fifteen-year-old Caleb had grown a foot in each direction, and with Abel's return, Bitty's family simply didn't fit in their old cabin anymore. Jed and the men built a new cabin for Greeley and the hands, making Markus's home available to Bitty, Abel, and their children. Jed moved into the downstairs guest room, but despite living under the same roof, he and Hannah rarely crossed paths during the day.

Abel's return prompted another change as Bitty declared that "meals will be eaten sitting down like a family instead of people grazin' 'round the table like a herd of cattle." So, as requested, the dinner meals were now shared, using Bitty's and Jack's families as buffers between Jed and Hannah.

And Jed made time for Johnny every day. The first few visits were painful, as Johnny clung to his mother's skirt, refusing every awkward offer Jed made, but consistency and commitment finally paid off. The day finally arrived when Johnny actually went to the window to watch for his father's arrival. Eventually their adventures became the highlight of the little boy's day, when they would take walks, collect eggs, go fishing, or simply throw rocks into the river.

Hannah moved to the window and pushed the curtain aside to peer out at her husband, who was cajoling Johnny to join him by the row of shrubs. Once the lad arrived, Jed knelt and began digging in the dirt. Fishing worms, she assumed. Sure enough, six fat, wriggling beauties soon dangled from Jed's fingers. Johnny squealed as one was plopped into his chubby palm. Hannah found herself laughing, as a hunger to share the moment nearly propelled her out the door.

She marveled at Jed's patience. He encouraged his son to deposit the worm in the bucket, but Johnny would not comply. In the end, Jed gave up, laughing as he picked up the rods and encouraged Johnny to follow.

She watched them pass a cherry tree, heavy with blossoms. Jed pulled out his knife and cut several small shoots until he had a small bouquet, which he handed to Johnny. Minutes later, Hannah heard her son running down the hall, calling her name so he could present his gift.

She knelt down in surprise. "Are these for me?" He nodded proudly. "Thank you very much. Did you cut these all by yourself?"

His eyes wide as saucers, Johnny shook his head as if he were revealing a great secret. "Papa did it," he whispered, "but he said they're for me to give to you."

The boy darted out the door to deliver his report, while Hannah returned to the window. She soon scolded herself for her childishness and headed for the back door to thank Jed herself.

By the time she reached the door, she heard elevated voices out back. Johnny and eight-year-old Moses hurried inside, looking frightened.

"Moses, who's fighting?" Hannah asked. The boy cowered, so she tipped his chin and said, "It's all right, Moses. You can tell me."

"Mr. Greeley and Uncle Abel. Mr. Greeley slapped Priscilla on the back of her legs with a willow switch, and Uncle Abel is mighty angry."

Anger flushed through Hannah as well. "How dare that man hurt Priscilla!"

"He said it was 'cause Priscilla didn't fetch him a glass of water when he told her to."

Hannah moved to the kitchen and placed an arm around Bitty, who was shaking like a leaf and saying, "Don't do it, Abel—don't lose your temper."

After a final squeeze, Hannah left Bitty and moved to the back stoop. Priscilla sat in Abel's arms, burying her face in her father's shoulder, while Abel, towering a full half foot above Greeley, glowered down at the white man, whose lips curled in fury. Other men of both colors began gathering at the scene, but Hannah's eyes were glued on Jed, who had just rounded the corner with Jack close behind.

Abel tore a new willow switch from a tree and shook it at Greeley. "Don't you ever touch any of these children again."

"Touch me—touch any white man—and you'll soon see what a joke your freedom is!"

"What's going on here?" Jed asked as he moved between the two men.

"Just instilling a little discipline," Greeley sneered. "Even the children here are uppity."

Abel's eyes never left Greeley's face as he addressed Jed. "Your farm manager whipped Priscilla with a willow switch. I won't have it, Jed. I won't have it!"

Jed placed a hand on Priscilla's leg, where an angry red welt bulged. He spun on Greeley and grabbed him by the shirt. "You have one hour to get off this property. Do you hear me?" he growled, releasing the man with a shove.

Greeley looked at his three crewmen and laughed as he passed Jed. "Come on, boys. Let's get out of here. This poor little rich boy can't manage a handful of slaves. No wonder he isn't man enough to keep that pretty little wife happy."

In one move, Jed spun the man around and planted a fist in his right cheek. Greeley reeled and went down hard. Then Jed pointed to the other three. "Choose your side. You know what we're about here. You're either with us or you're not. If you're not, get him and get out!"

Hannah breathed a sigh of relief when the three men stepped away from Greeley and toward Jack, showing their loyalty. Then Greeley reached inside his boot, and Hannah saw a glint of steel. "Jed!" she screamed. "He has a knife!"

Jed pushed Abel and his daughter to the side and dove headlong into Greeley. The blade sliced through the air as Jed slammed the man's arm to the ground. In a flash, Jack was there, kicking at the fist that clenched the blade, while Abel set Prissy down and pinned the man.

Once the blade was secure, Hannah noticed the red stain spreading across Jed's upper arm. She flew to his side and pressed her apron to the wound. The care and concern flowed so naturally from her that for a moment she didn't understand the surprise on the men's faces, including Jed's.

When Jack stepped in to assist in Jed's care, she waved him off. Instead, she rested her husband's wounded arm across her shoulder and wrapped her free arm around his waist to help him inside. And in a final effort to align her loyalties, she eyed the three hands and asked, "Would you three drag Mr. Greeley to his feet and see that he and his things are escorted off our property?"

Bitty held the door open wide for the couple. After placing a kiss on Hannah's cheek, she looked heavenward and whispered, "Thank you, God!"

Within fifteen minutes, Greeley's gear was crammed into satchels and tied to his horse by his three former friends. "You're really not coming with me?" he said as he climbed onto the animal.

The three men looked at one another and mutually answered, "No."

"Do you really want to work beside a bunch of niggers?"

The hand named Reese slouched at the comment and then replied, "So long as I get a fair wage and good treatment, I don't mind who I work beside."

Greeley spit on the ground near the man's feet. "Not me. I'm glad to be gettin'." He mounted and the three others followed suit. "You don't need to follow me out," he snarled. "I won't even bother lookin' back on this place."

Greeley heard the three men's horses behind him, but at the halfway point along the lane they peeled off and headed for the fields. It was then that he noticed Pearson's son Johnny playing with Moses, and Greeley saw a chance to get some retribution.

"You still lookin' for worms?" It didn't surprise him that the boys cowered from him. He knew he needed to up the ante to make his plan work. He called out again. "I know a spot that's got lots of good fishin' worms, and some buried treasure, too."

He saw the boy's eyes light up, and he knew he had them. He pointed to the spot along the fencerow where a forsythia bush grew. He had found the nest just the other day but hadn't taken the opportunity to warn the others. He laughed as he watched the boys head to the barn for a shovel. "Now, you take your shovel and dig down real deep, ya hear? Your pa is never gonna forget the day he fired Ned Greeley."

CHAPTER 10

Late May 1817
The Willows

Hannah led Jed to the table in the kitchen and sat him down. She turned to bring a towel and some water, but he pulled her back to him. She looked at the floor, purposely avoiding his eyes. He lifted her chin until their eyes met. "The arm can wait. Tell me what's happening here."

She tried again to avoid his gaze, but he shifted his head in tandem with hers until she surrendered and looked at him again. "I want to clean that wound to see if you need to be stitched," she said softly.

"That's not what I meant, and you know it. In six months we've barely spoken, barely shared a civil word. I need to know if this is real, or if this was just for Greeley's benefit."

Her brow fell softly against the warmth of Jed's lips, but he drew upon every reserve to withhold his kiss. Instead, he brushed her hair back to frame her face. "Talk to me, Hannah. Just being this near you hurts."

She closed her eyes, and her lips moved silently until the words finally came. "This isn't about Greeley. I've been trying to find the words and the right moment for days now."

"The right moment for what?"

"To tell you I love you—that I've never stopped loving you. I'm so ashamed of myself. I was just so . . . so angry because of the things you said—"

Jed stopped her and hung his head. "If only you knew how desperately I wish I could take those words back. I don't know what happened to me. I just felt so threatened, and I lashed out like a child."

Hannah fell against him. "It wasn't just you. I meant well, but I left you no purpose here. I'm the one who drove you away, and then I made you feel guilty for going." She pulled away, her eyes heavy and filled with love. He took her hands and pressed them together, placed a kiss there, and then covered them with his own.

"A few honest words from me could have set things straight, but I was too proud to admit any weakness. Instead, I saw enemies in every quarter. I still do at times." The light returned to his eyes once more, and he began to chuckle. "As juvenile as it sounds, I think tangling with Greeley was quite therapeutic." The pair laughed together, and then Jed became somber once more as he reached around Hannah's waist and pulled her close. "Today was the first I've felt truly like myself. It was good to feel needed here, but it's wrong to want that, or to need that. The residents are free, and they need to feel free, not dependent on me."

Hannah slid her arms around his muscled frame. Her attempt to speak came out almost as quietly as a breath. *"I* need you, Jed. And so does Johnny."

He clutched her to him. Carefully assessing her reaction, he slowly brought his mouth to hers. When she received his kiss willingly, every repressed memory of being with her returned, and instinct took over. His lips moved to each tender point—to the side of her neck, causing her to shiver, and to her wrist, making her shoulders limp. She moaned softly, and his kisses moved to the hollow of her throat, erasing all thoughts of his wounded arm. In response, Hannah laid her weakening arms around his, but she recoiled as the moistness of his wound penetrated her sleeve.

She pushed away. "Your arm, Jed!" He tried to pull her back but she resisted. "You're still bleeding."

He cast a dismissive glance at the wound, mounting one more attempt to pull her into his embrace. His efforts failed as she broke free and fetched the rag and water. "No, no, no! I'll not get you back just to have you bleed to death on the same day."

His hand never left her waist as she cleaned his arm. When she finished she said, "I'm going for Bitty. This needs to be stitched." Before Hannah could leave the room she stopped cold, her ears tuned to a sound nearly indiscernible to Jed. She shot a look of panic at him and exclaimed, "Johnny's hurt!" before racing out the door.

Implicitly trusting her fifth sense, Jed followed after her. The two flew from the room and down the lane in the direction of the cries. Moses was running about, flailing wildly at the air, but Johnny was thrashing on the ground screaming.

"Bees!" yelled Moses as Bitty, Abel, Jack, and Lydia now raced to the scene.

"Dear Lord, help us!" Bitty prayed as she tore her apron from around her neck to cover one of the boys. Hannah did likewise and Jed raced past, ripped his shirt off, and rushed to Johnny's side. He quickly swatted at the invaders surrounding his boy. Then he covered Johnny, scooped him up, and shot back toward the house, with Jack carrying Moses right beside him. The women had already begun the return trip to the house when the men caught up.

Bitty began barking orders to the gathering crowd of residents. "Get me some river clay, and fetch some ice from the icehouse! Gather some stinging nettle plants!" To Abel she ordered, "Fetch me my bag!" In an instant, help was coming from every quarter.

Once they got inside, the men laid the boys on the kitchen tables. Johnny's groans were animal-like and panicked, while Moses continued to reach for Lydia, screaming, "It burns! Help me, Momma! It burns!"

Multiple welts were already appearing on the boys' bodies, and Bitty knew time was critical. She looked to Jed, Jack, and Hannah for help. "Get their clothes off!"

She grabbed Lydia by the shoulders. "Get me two clean, white sheets, and hurry!"

Moments later, Abel arrived with Bitty's bag, and she rifled through her supplies. Then she pulled Abel aside, her eyes drilling the urgency of her message into him. "Ride to Calverton and fetch the doctor!"

Bitty had enough evidence to assure her she was dealing with yellow-jacket venom. She had a few specimens of the wasps, and she had seen a shovel lying in the grass. These boys had evidently come upon a large wasps' nest and made the residents very angry with their digging.

She checked the clock and estimated that three minutes had passed since the attack. *Hurry, hurry. What's the fastest treatment?* She pulled the sodium bicarbonate from the shelf and dumped it into a bowl. From her bag she pulled a bottle of glycerin and stirred it in, forming a white paste. Lydia arrived with the sheets, and Bitty had new directions for her. "Tear one into wide strips," she ordered as she pulled two mixing bowls from the shelves. Into one she poured white vinegar and soaked the torn cloth. Into the other she placed ice and water to soak the whole sheet. She then began slathering the gooey ointment over the sting sites. Moses flailed as she began, and then he quickly calmed, but Johnny barely uttered a sound. Hannah gasped at his stillness, but Bitty watched the rise and fall of his chest and smiled. "He's just worn out."

She laid the vinegar-soaked cloths over Moses' limbs, and the boy again expressed relief—and some wonder—as the ointment made a sizzling sound under the cloth. "Don't worry none," his aunt said. "It'll take the fire out." Confident that Moses was safe, she turned her full attention to Johnny. The mud arrived, and Bitty fetched a wool blanket off the sofa, calling out, "Jed, lift Johnny up." Once she had spread the blanket over the table, she had Jed lay the boy back down upon it, and she added, "Now go brew up some willow-bark tea. It'll ease his pain."

Next she laid the ice-cold sheet on top. The shock of the cold drew a reaction from the boy. Bitty smiled at the child. "Don't you worry, sweet boy. We're gonna fix you up." She then emptied the buckets of clay over him, and Hannah and Jed spread it in a thick layer. Bitty drew the extra sheet fabric up over the child's body like a shroud, then drizzled the ice cold water over the top, eliciting a weak cry of protest from Johnny's shivering lips.

"Jed, your father once threw a rock at a hornet's nest. My mama helped tend him. He was a bit older and bigger than Johnny, but he must have looked just as bad, or so she described it. Your grandfather was a good friend of the Piscataway Indians, as you know. He learned a bit of their medicine, which he taught my mama. Those teachin's are the basis of all I know, so in a way, your grandfather is helpin' us today, and probably watchin' over his little namesake, too."

Bitty looked up and saw some lessening of the panic etched along Jed's face. Pleased, she moved on to the final step, which was to draw the woolen blanket up and around the whole of the treatment. When finished, she stepped back. "You can carry him upstairs to bed now, Jed."

He looked at his helpless son. "And then what do we do?" he choked out.

"I'll grind some stinging nettle and bring it up when it's ready. "That's the only other thing I know to do." Bitty's eyes were shining as she laid a loving hand on each parent's arm.

"The rest is up to God, Jed," Hannah uttered. "We must pray very hard together."

After settling Johnny in, Hannah took Jed's hand and led him to his knees. The normally awkward exercise came naturally to him on this occasion as he knelt by his wife to petition the God she believed in so fully, asking Him to save their son. Hannah provided the voice, but Jed's trembling lips repeated every word, and his heart pled with God in earnest.

The doctor arrived in record time when he heard Senator Pearson's son was in danger. His examination was punctuated with approving snorts and nods and raises of his brows. "Have you administered anything internally?" he asked Bitty, who looked to Jed for a translation.

"She had me give him willow-bark tea," Jed replied.

The doctor nodded approvingly as he snapped his bag shut. "Senator, I'd say this woman has done all that could be done for your boy, but I'd like to stitch up that arm of yours before I go. Let's go to the kitchen where the light is better."

When the last stitch was sewn, Jed asked, "Doctor, Johnny will be all right, won't he?"

"It's in God's hands now. If the boy survives you'll need to be very cautious about future stings. Such a vicious episode can leave a person highly sensitive, especially a young child." Jed stood to escort the doctor out. "No need, sir. I'll return in a few days to check on your son. Call for me if the child takes a turn for the worse."

Moses was up the next day. Bitty kept applying the ointment, and Moses carried around a chunk of ice to rub over the more painful stings. Johnny's situation was more worrisome. Having fallen on the ground, he had sustained more stings on his small body.

Hannah lay in the bed with him, holding him in the damp bundle, while Jed sat in a chair pulled near so he could rest his head beside his boy's.

Bitty checked on the family near dusk and found them all asleep in the same bed. Johnny stirred as she checked on him.

"Shh." She laid a finger to her lips. "You gave us quite a scare." She brushed his hair with her hand, and with a final wink, she backed away toward the door. The boy's restless squirming now caused Hannah and Jed to awaken, and when they saw their son's agitation at being bound up, they looked at one another and teared up with relief.

Jed caught a glimpse of Bitty as she made her exit. "The worst is over, isn't it?" he asked.

She stuck her head back in the room. Johnny's arms had wriggled free, and he strained to rid himself of the rest of his wrappings. "Now that is a happy sight." The thing that made Bitty happiest was seeing Jed's free hand stretched across Johnny's body, secured in Hannah's. The little woman pressed her brown hands together in prayer position and pulled them to her lips. "Yes, the worst is over." Her bright eyes glanced heavenward. "For all of us. Things are right as rain again."

She closed the door, not knowing that for Jed, one great hurdle still remained.

The issue came to a head during the following weeks as Hannah kept Johnny under a loving incarceration. The doctor's warnings about the dire consequences of future stings caused her terror of bees to now rival her dread of mountain lions, poisonous snakes, and Red Coats. Johnny stood at the window day after day, crying and begging to go outside and play with the other children. When Jed would exit to attend to the farm, Johnny would cling to his leg and cry until both parents' nerves were spent.

Soon, Hannah designed a "bee suit" for Johnny to wear. The one-piece outfit, made of heavy broadcloth, resembled long johns and went over the boy's socks and to his wrists, meeting the cuff of mittens that protected his hands, and it had a hood for his head. The child was so grateful for the chance to play that he tolerated the ensemble at first, but once he became hot and realized how limited his movements were, he fell on the ground and cried.

Jed picked his despondent son off the ground and carried him to the house. Burying her face in Jed's shirt, Hannah cried, "It's for his own good."

At dusk, Jed took her by the hand and encouraged her to walk outside with him. "Let's count the bees we see," he suggested, hoping she would come to a certain conclusion on her own, which she did.

"Almost none are out during the evening. I never noticed that before."

Jed knew the new trust developing between them was fragile, and he was unwilling to impose his opinions on her, so he asked tentatively, "Would you feel safe allowing Johnny to play outdoors at dusk?"

"Without his bee suit?"

Jed retreated again. "Whatever you think is best." Eventually, he risked another comment. "Hannah, I trust your instincts more than anyone else's on spiritual things. God talks to you. Listen to Him. What does He tell you now?"

Her smooth brow rumpled as she pondered. "I know God can do more to protect Johnny than we can. But my faith falters when fear jumbles my thinking."

She fell against Jed and wrapped her arms around him. For that moment, nothing mattered more than being united again. He kissed her head and laid his on top. Soon he felt Hannah lift hers to look at him. "That's how you felt, isn't it? So filled with fear that you couldn't trust the things you've always relied on?"

The movement of his lips was slight as he smiled his affirmation of her assessment.

"I fear to make the wrong decision, Jed. I feel so paralyzed, yet I notice you defer to me on everything now. You're still feeling that way, aren't you?"

Another taut smile confirmed the point. "I fear I'll fail you again."

"We can't live this way. I don't want to live this way. In some ways, we were happier during the war. At least we were united against a common enemy. Now we see enemies everywhere, and though we stand together, we each still feel alone."

Jed cupped his hands behind her head and searched her face. "You have no cause to fear what I will say. I'll never blame you for any judgment you make. I trust you completely."

Could she say the same? He would never ask, but it was the question he had tried to lead her to, and now he felt stripped bare as he waited for her response. A cloud of confusion passed over her face, giving way to compassion.

"I never said that to you, did I? You think . . . you think I don't trust you anymore, but I do! I'm so sorry. That's what I've missed. Your strength, your fire, the way you see things. You're all passion, and I'm all temperance. You'd help Johnny reach for the stars while I'd restrain him in a bee suit." She chuckled with embarrassment. "We're a good team, Jed. Better together than separate, remember?" She entwined her fingers with his, the symbol of their bond. "So speak your piece to me. Tell me exactly what you think. Don't be half of what you are. I married the whole of you—the dreamer, the snarler, the man who barrels into situations swinging when he thinks his family is in jeopardy. Bring *him* back to me."

"Better together. I know it's true for me." He softly kissed their joined hands.

Hannah's shoulders slumped ever so noticeably. "All right. We'll let him play unencumbered in the evening." In the next breath she added, "But will you support me in making him wear the suit during the day, for now at least, until my nerves settle?"

The McGowan cottage on the outskirts of London, England

Michael McGowan struggled to carry his end of the small trunk that contained what his mama had called her "important papers." When they reached the wagon, Hank laughed at his older brother and lifted the small leather and wood box onto the bed himself.

"I believe that's it, boys," said Jervis, who now was referred to only as Richard Porter.

"I hope my family and I will be as happy here as you and yours have been," said the cottage's new owner. "And never you mind about your missus' grave. We'll keep it weeded real nice, and the girls will put flowers on it every Sunday in the spring and summer."

Porter removed his hat and placed it across his heart. "Thank you. It's 'ard to leave the place, but I know it'll be easier on them to make a fresh start elsewhere. Do you mind if the boys and I pause by their mother's grave one last time before we take our leave?"

"Not at all. We'll be busy moving our things in. See yourselves off when you're done."

Michael felt Porter's hand fall on his shoulder as he led the boys to Mary McGowan's grave. "Say your goodbyes to your mother, boys. Then we'll be off."

Michael planted his feet firmly. "I don't want to go. I want to stay here, near Mama."

Porter closed his eyes. Michael was curious about the man. Clearly, he didn't love the boys as Mama had, and yet it seemed important to him that *they* like *him*. Why?

"We talked about this months ago, after your mama died. It's what she wanted."

Michael had anticipated that phrase. Porter frequently used it when the boys were reluctant to follow. Porter kneeled close to Hank. "The city is filled with shops where a boy could have his fill of whatever he fancied. You'd like that, wouldn't you, Son?"

A broad grin stretched across Hank's face, and he quickly climbed into the wagon.

Michael knew Hank could be easily won. Now it was up to him. He knew if Porter took him from this place, he would somehow lose his mama—and himself.

The man who now called himself "Father" turned his full attention on Michael. "And you, my wise scholar—I have big plans for you. Wouldn't you like to be enrolled in a real school with a fine teacher and more books than you could ever read?"

Michael's innards knotted at the way the man looked at him, as if he were a prize horse rather than a boy. He wiped a dirty sleeve across his nose as Porter rose to his full stature, his eyes locking onto Michael's as if connected by a wire, while his expression shifted from annoyance to something that bordered on disappointment. Michael couldn't read this man. Mama was always easy to read. Love was always behind every expression. But Richard Porter?

"No answer, eh? I'm deeply pained. I promised to take care of you 'cause you 'ad no one else. I sacrificed my quiet life so you boys could stay together and be a family, and this is the thanks I get? I must say, after all the grand things your mama said about you, I expected better."

Michael's eye grew moist and he began to blink rapidly as his mother's name was invoked once more, but he would not allow a tear to fall.

"Would you really like me to go, Michael? Would you like to be left here . . . alone?"

Would you leave me? The chill of fear set in Michael's heart at the thought.

"Hank and I are leavin', but I won't force you. You're a smart boy. Do as you choose."

Michael watched Porter begin walking away from him. Each slow but deliberate step seemed to divide them by acres of lonely, terrifying terrain. Ever so slightly, Michael's chin began to drop to his chest. "Wait," he muttered.

Porter stopped with his back to the lad. "What did you say?"

He hated the need to verbalize his concession. "I'll come."

With his back still turned to Michael, Porter said, "I only want you ta come if it's what *you* want. Is this what *you* want, Michael?"

The boy could feel his face flush red hot. "Yes."

Porter turned to face him. "Then say it, boy. What do you want?"

Michael had seen a man break a horse once by denying it water. He watched its muscles quiver as it yearned to bolt but remained because the master held out a bucket of water. He felt like that horse on this day. His mouth was dry as he said, "I want to come with you."

A half smile curled the corners of Porter's mouth. "Then you must come as my son, and accept me as your father. Are you sayin' you accept me as your father?"

Michael cast his eyes toward his mother's grave. He never knew his real father, and his mother's face was already fading from his memory.

"I'm waitin', Michael."

"Yes."

"Yes what?"

"Yes, Father." Porter's hand reached out to him, and Michael took it. Together they walked to the wagon, and Porter lifted him in. Seven-year-old Michael looked over at his mother's grave one final time. "I'm sorry, Mama," he whispered as the wagon lumbered away. Somehow, he felt his name had just been scrawled on her stone as well.

CHAPTER 11

Summer 1817
The Willows

Johnny was a robust, tireless little boy again, and Jed and Hannah were as happy as they had ever been. Life for the rest of the Willows' family had likewise been good and sweet, yet the Willows would never be the same.

The onward march of change that began the summer of 1817 escalated over the ensuing years. The question regarding the hiring of another farm manager was quickly tabled. The three workers who remained behind when Greeley left—Reese Symonds, Hank Acker, and Robinson Guyton—proved their loyalty and their worth over time. Hannah convinced Jed that with their help, and with Abel's return, they could run the farm when Jed was away filling his state duties.

Hannah proved, once again, to be an able business partner to Jed, and with Abel running the mill, and Jack's knowledge of farming, things proceeded smoothly, allowing Hannah and Johnny to join Jed in Annapolis during his three months of service in the Maryland General Assembly, and on long weekends when the lure of the city's attractions wooed them away. The period proved blissful, and for the first time in their marriage, Jed was able to push the world back and focus solely on Hannah and their son.

The only nagging worry marring their happiness was Jed's failure to reach Markus. He missed his friend more than he could have imagined, and each letter that was returned undelivered, and each one that never produced a reply, tore his heart anew.

More change occurred early in the summer of 1818, with the announcement that Penelope Stringham had delivered a long-awaited child, a son named Humphrey, on the neighboring, slave-owning White Oak Farm. Frederick Stringham planned a July party, using the occasion to unveil not only his heir, but also his extravagant new manor house.

Hannah insisted Jed attend the baby's christening party, though he groused as he dressed for the event. "I cannot abide that bombastic traitor, nor his grandiloquent speeches."

She raised an eyebrow as she continued tying Jed's cravat. "And yet I know you'll hold your tongue and be a perfect gentleman regardless."

He huffed. "I cannot guarantee that if he boasts about having saved the Willows again, leaving out all the less flattering details, like how his own wife fled here for protection from the mercenaries he and his father were harboring."

"We know the truth, Jed, and so does he. All Frederick has left are his stories, and his troubles. What have we to fear from either? Besides, there are rumors he's in financial trouble again. White Oak's slaves have passed gossip over the fences to Bitty. They say he's been in a snit for weeks, ranting about money and returning purchases left and right."

"That explains the party. He's attempting to head off the rumors."

"So you'll be sociable, for Penny's sake?"

Jed rolled his eyes. Hannah wrapped her arms so tightly around him that her crisp blue gown rustled between them. Raising an eyebrow, he teasingly pulled on the pins holding her piled black curls in place. In retaliation, she hovered her wriggling hands over Jed's head, assuring him she was ready to inflict an equal assault on his own dark waves.

"I stand down," Jed announced, giving his wife a kiss as a token of surrender. "Let's get this over with and return home so I can pull those pins out without arousing your anger."

"You're incorrigible, Mr. Pearson."

"Guilty as charged, Mrs. Pearson!"

Soon, they loaded in the carriage and rolled up White Oak's lane. The sprawling, three-story manor house far exceeded Frederick's parents' original home. The fire that destroyed it and took the owners' lives had miraculously spared a stand of arborvitae that concealed the lot upon approach, and when the home finally came into view, it was a spectacle.

The home was brick- and stucco-built, with two breezeways connecting a summer kitchen on one end and an extravagant glass enclosure, called an orangery, on the other. Jed knew there were few homes in the region, let alone the state, that could rival it other than Governor Ridgely's Hampton Estate, and the palatial estates that lay on the tract of prime Georgetown land called The Rock of Dumbarton— the Dumbarton House, Dumbarton Oaks, Tudor Place, and a few other architectural gems. But those homes were owned by wealthy merchants and land speculators who capitalized on the movement of the nation's capital to Washington, or men of high government station. Most of the original owners were American blue-bloods descended from such families as the Washingtons, the Lees, and signers of the Declaration of Independence—men who could afford to hire architectural geniuses like Dr. William Thornton, the first architect of the Capitol.

It likewise was no secret that many of these homes enjoyed the dubious reputation of having broken the financial backs of their owners. Though Jed could not deny a spark of envy at having such a magnificent mansion barely a stone's throw from his own more modest home, he had no doubt such a dwelling was likewise breaking Frederick's back as well.

Relief washed over Frederick's pale, thin face as soon as Jed and Hannah entered. After making a few hasty introductions, Penny drew Hannah off in one direction, while Frederick pulled Jed off to a barren, oak-paneled library that echoed with the closing of the door. Frederick swept a bony hand through his thinning hair and quickly set about to discuss business.

"I have a proposition for you, Jed." His mood was nearly manic. "I'm offering it to you first because of our long history, and because we once were dear friends and very nearly family."

"Two relationships *you* ruined. And I am well aware of how you coerced Hannah into accepting your last *friendly* opportunity. Your threats to sell land to pro-slavery buyers who might harass the Willows will not impress me. Cash is hard to come by right now, but acreage is plentiful. Farms are folding all along the river."

"Fine!" Frederick's arms flew in the air as he stomped his foot like a whiny child. "I've been less than forthright, but is it impossible to expect some benevolence from the beloved, charmed Jed Pearson? Can a man so blessed understand why a failed man might want the trappings of success in the hope of giving his son a modicum of standing in the community?"

"Such ambitions corrupted your father. Neither did they bless you, Frederick."

The man turned a woeful, nearly gaunt face to Jed. "I have no grand ambitions of power, Jed. I simply want to enjoy a comfortable life and improve life for my staff."

"You mean your slaves."

Frederick cringed but went on. "I mean you no pain, but I know your plans have shifted away from horse breeding since Markus left your employ. Jed, I would like to fill that void. This is one area in which I excel. You cannot deny that I am an excellent horseman with an eye for good breeding. Raising horses will require fewer acres and much less labor than cotton or tobacco. I may be able to reduce the number of slaves I own, or free them altogether. Can't you see, Jed? This is my chance at redemption. I want to build something worthy to leave to my son."

The idea had surprising merit. "And how will you support this grand lifestyle while you get established?"

"My stallion, Marquis, is arguably the finest stud in three states. The sale of the land will provide the money I need to buy a few additional brood mares. I haven't told Penny yet, but her father is so pleased over Humphrey's birth that he has provided a sizeable trust for the boy. As executor, I can draw upon that money. Aside from the three main rooms, the rest of the house is as empty as my bank account, but I'm prepared to live a spartan life to allow things to grow."

Another thought crossed Jed's mind. "Have you ever had any trouble with poachers or hunters on your property? Has anyone harmed any of your animals at any time?"

The question appeared to cause a momentary panic in Frederick. "Good heavens, no! My animals are fine, but I did find one of my slaves dead a while back. Why do you ask? Are you having problems?"

Jed debated whether or not to confide in Frederick. "No need to be concerned."

The feel of a child in her arms again made Hannah hunger for another baby of her own. She could barely take her eyes off the squirming bundle, with his auburn curls and rosebud lips. "He's wondrous, Penny. Just perfect."

Though still dressed in maternity clothes to fit her bulky frame, the mother beamed with a joyful beauty Hannah had never before seen in her. "I've never been so happy," she replied. "I have everything I've ever dreamed of."

"Are things better between you and Frederick since Humphrey's birth?"

Penny placed her finger in her son's tiny fist and smiled as she gazed at him. "In some ways. Need may drive him to my chambers someday again, and if it does, I will receive him, but if it does not, I have all I need—someone to love, and someone to love me. Frederick and I may not have the typical marriage, but I think we shall be good parents together. I've seen him stand by Humphrey's cradle with such a look of awe on his face, touching the baby and humming to him. I can't help that despite the coldness he's shown me in the past, this gift of motherhood, and seeing him with our son, makes me love him more than before."

The conversation made Hannah want to cry for her love-starved friend, making Jed's arrival especially welcome. He marveled over the size of the tiny babe. With a gentle touch to Penny's arm he said, "He's beautiful, Mrs. Stringham. Clearly he favors his lovely mother."

Penny blushed and dipped her head shyly. "Thank you, Mr. Pearson. You are most kind. I should take Humphrey around to meet the rest of our guests. If you'll excuse me, please."

Jed took Hannah by the arm and led her to a corner as his eyes followed Penny's retreat from his simple compliment. "Bless that dear woman. She can't even bear a kind word anymore. What a blessing this child will be to her."

The comment gave Hannah the opening she had hoped for. "Wouldn't it be wonderful to have another child, one you could enjoy from his birth?"

"After your harrowing delivery of Johnny? I'd say it sounds frightening."

"This time things would be different. We'll be more prepared. At least say you'll hear Samuel's opinion on the matter."

His eyes were wide with worry as he replied, "All right. And you were right about Frederick's finances. He wants to sell another thousand acres off and turn his attentions away from agriculture and toward horse breeding."

"Does he even know anything about horses?"

"Frederick is probably the finest rider I've ever seen, and he can read a horse's conformation like a book. Their love and pleasure of horses was one of the interests that drew him and Frannie to one another. Once upon a time, he could coax greatness from a nag. If only he were equally adept as seeing greatness in people." His gaze fell on Penny Stringham again.

"How much is he asking for the tract?"

"More than we have in ready cash. He needs brood mares. I've invited him to come by and see if he'd like any of our stock in partial trade, but we'll need to raise additional capital."

Hannah grew wistful. "Those mares are the last we have from Markus's stock."

"The same sad thought crossed my mind, reminding me that the money I transferred into Markus's bank account in payment for his share of the mares has never been drawn against. Like the deed for his acreage, everything sits in the bank as if forgotten. I need to find him, but first we need to decide if we even want this land, and if so, how we'll pay for it."

Frederick agreed to take the Willows' five best mares against the purchase, leaving a balance that required the liquidation of one of Jed's finer Baltimore properties. He struggled over the decision for days, but he signed the deal in August, completely blind to how that single purchase would change the course of Willows history forever.

One winter night, Jed held a meeting to discuss the best use of the land, and British-born Reese Symonds spoke up. "Would you consider farming it to halves?"

Jed leaned back in his chair and tapped his ciphering pencil against his lips. "Sharecropping," he drew out thoughtfully.

"Have you thought about it?" Reese asked. "I've got dozens of relatives in tenements in the city who'd give their eye-teeth for a chance to move their families to the country."

Abel perked up as well. "Soldiers from Fort McHenry used to dream about little farms. Some took their enlistment grants and moved west, but I know plenty who'd like to stay local."

Jed worked for days, sketching maps, drawing up documents, and juggling crop projections. He'd call Hannah, Bitty, Jack, and Abel to weigh in on the developing plans, and then he'd return to his study to make the suggested changes. In March, when he felt he had all the details set, he and Hannah called everyone together for a meeting. "What do you think?"

Wonder lit Bitty's eyes as she traced the map with her fingers. She began at the river where Jack's produce stand and the mill sat. Between the two, a road curved from the river road and straight back along the old property line, where a separate lane veered right toward the meadows in which the current cabins sat. The road then wound deeper and to the left, where the new thousand-acre parcel was divided into fifteen rectangles, each bearing the numeral 30. "There are fifteen 30-acre farms here? And roads? You've designed an entire village, Jed!"

He turned the map and pointed to various marks. "It seemed wise to lay out a plan we could grow into. See this area?" He pointed to a rectangle not far from the dock and the mill. "This will be an open-air market. If we end up with fifteen more families living here, we'll have enough produce and fruit to draw vendors here."

"I could sell pies to the people on the ships!"

"You could, Bitty." Jed beamed. "And your children can have their own farms, and businesses too someday. All of you will get first choice of the new plots if you'd like to trade your current land for acreage in the new section. Workers who want to stay on working at the Willows for wages will take over the older cabins. Then we'll slowly welcome new families who want to sharecrop, and see how they fit in. If things go well, we'll offer them a long-term, renewable lease so we're building a stable community of people we can trust."

The room buzzed with excited chatter. When the hour grew late and everyone finally left, Hannah stood behind Jed and wrapped her arms around his waist. "Your plan is wonderful, Jed. But I can't help thinking there's more to this than you're saying."

"I'm just looking forward, planning playmates for that houseful of children you want."

"We will revisit the topic of another baby, dear husband, but first tell me what's really behind this community you're building."

"I wouldn't worry, Hannah. You know how obsessed I am with seeing traitors in every shadow, but there is reason to be concerned about the future of free people of color, and those sympathetic to their cause. A group of wealthy politicians and businessmen believe the best future for Negroes lies in relocating them to separate colonies."

"Like Britain's Sierra Leone. I've read about the plan to create a colony in Africa to repatriate freedmen who want to return."

"Not just those that *want* to return. Some of these pro-colonizers, men like Francis Scott Key, truly think this option will shield freedmen from the prejudice they suffer from whites. But many of the group's founders simply don't want to share their society or rights with freedmen. President Monroe was one of the founders. I'm still unsure about where he stands personally on the matter. There are already laws in some states regulating freed slaves' liberties if they remain in America, and their numbers are increasing. For the last four years they've been gaining support. Maryland now has her own colonization group. To better understand their intentions, I've been asked to travel to New York this summer to investigate a cluster of colonizers preparing to buy land on the western coast of Africa after the New Year."

"So this sharecropping plan is really about security."

Jed pulled Hannah close. "I want neighbors I know and trust, and I want eyes on every corner of this property, especially if I'm away. I heard some anti-freedmen rhetoric at the Stringhams' party. If it escalates, men like Hildebrand and Greeley could return to cause us trouble again."

By late summer, as Jed prepared for his trip north, he drew comfort in knowing new cabins were rising on seven of the new sites. All were occupied by families tied to other trusted Willows families. Hank Acker and Robinson Guyton resigned as day laborers to take up sharecropping, and while Reese Symonds remained on as a hand, grateful immigrant relatives of his filled three more tracts, with freedmen friends of Abel's filling two others.

A stiff, dry wind blew across the land on the late August day Jed left home. As Hannah and Johnny walked him to the dock, he couldn't shake the sense of foreboding settling into his heart. Life was right again, but despite all the hard work he and Hannah had invested to shore up their marriage and home, Jed knew more change was coming.

He tried to identify the source of his unease. The house was well stocked and supplied. Hannah and the women had seen to that, though the toll of long hours drying, salting, bottling, and pickling summer produce had left her looking tired and pale. He left the *Eagle* twice and returned to the dock to receive another of Hannah's embraces and to kiss his son once more, but even as he did he couldn't shake the feeling. Was it the stranger the children had seen lurking by the mill? The sudden drop in the price of tobacco? The new people walking across his land every day? He couldn't say.

"I'll write to you daily. I should be home by the first of November," he pledged each time, then, chiding himself for his foolish worry, he gave a final set of hugs and boarded the steamboat. As it moved down the Patuxent, he watched his wife and son shrink away until they disappeared into the horizon. When he could no longer see them, he set his sights on a clipper ship docked in Baltimore's harbor, and his mission to protect the rights of freedmen.

CHAPTER 12

August 27, 1819
The Willows

A knock on the door pulled Hannah from her work. She found Reverend Myers there, a study in contrition from his face to the hands that clenched his black, brimmed hat.

"May I have a word with you, Mrs. Pearson?"

"Of course." She unconsciously brushed her dark hair back into place before stepping onto the porch, where she pointed to one of two wooden rockers.

The reverend bowed and waved her off. "If you don't mind, I'd prefer to stand."

"This sounds serious. Do you mind if I sit? I'm more tired than I realized." She sighed as she took one of the seats. "What's troubling you, Reverend?"

"Ma'am, you do recall that I'm not a real reverend, don't you? I was just an apprentice military chaplain when I came here. I've no license or diploma, no credentials of any legitimacy. I just stayed on to fill in the void left by Jerome's death."

Hannah remembered the great blessing the reverend had been, arriving in the company of a militia group soon after the murder of Abel's father, who had served as the spiritual leader on the farm. "We're so grateful you chose to stay with us. You've been a patient counselor to everyone, and a fine teacher for the children."

"Thank you, ma'am. I've loved my time here, but as my father has stated in his most recent letter, I am five years older with no prospects, and no more qualifications to earn a living or support a family than I had at twenty-one. He insists I come home and either enter fully into a religious vocation by returning to college, or take my place in his store as he always planned."

Hannah heard the disappointment in the reverend's voice. "I see. And which path have you chosen?"

He huffed and leaned back against the porch post, his frustration now evident. "I don't know for certain. I know I love God's word, and that I've been happier these five years than ever before in my life, but like many of my peers, I still wrestle over the same doctrinal issues that caused men of conscience to break with the Church of England a hundred years ago. I've listened to pastors quote the same scriptures and pull entirely different doctrines from them. How can I lead a congregation when I don't know what God intended in His word?"

It pained Hannah that someone who had answered her spiritual questions was now in need of the same from her. She didn't want to misspeak, or oversimplify a concern that weighed so heavily on his mind. Finally a question of her own presented itself. "You've said you believe the Holy Ghost can enlighten individuals. What is it telling you?"

Peace softened the young man's face. "It tells me to go north, back to New York to attend the religious conferences held there. Perhaps I'll hear something that will unravel my confusion."

The news hit Hannah hard. "Then you must go there and find your answers."

Reverend Myers's relief was palpable. "I've made preparations. Caleb has become a fine teacher. He's ready to take over the school. And I won't leave for another month or so."

"Thank you for staying on until others were ready to fill your shoes."

"Empty shoes, I fear. My father also points out that I may have spiritually handicapped all of you. I've satisfied your spiritual hunger without having the authority to provide soul-saving ordinances God will recognize."

Hannah's head tipped at the confession. "I thought you questioned whether a diploma from a divinity school, by and of itself, opened the conduit to heaven."

The reverend dropped his eyes to the ground. "I see my father is right. Rather than strengthening your faith, I've successfully passed my questions on to you."

"That's not entirely so. You strengthened my faith. I've loved our discussions."

"Thank you. Sookie has become quite a proficient reader of the Bible in the past year. He's also become an eloquent preacher, and as qualified as I to lead the congregation's scripture study, but I must ask you to promise me you'll seek out a real church and a true pastor who can baptize Johnny and the freedmen. I may not have answers to all my questions, but God's word is clear on the necessity of baptism, and I have caused everyone to procrastinate on this matter."

"All right, Reverend. I will. You'll be missed, but I wish you well in New York."

Jack came loping up the lane on horseback, wearing a mile-wide smile. The reverend turned and grinned at his friend. "Jack may be the most amiable person I've ever met in my life."

Hannah smiled broadly as she rose to greet their friend. "Hello, Jack. We need some good news. The reverend just announced he's leaving us soon."

"So, you're goin' home after all, eh, Reverend?" Jack chuckled as he removed his worn field hat. He pointed it at the reverend before sweeping his shirtsleeve across his sweaty brow. "He's been arguin' with himself over that decision for nigh on to five years now."

"Well, I for one am glad it took him so long to decide," Hannah said. "We'll miss him."

Jack's smile faded into contentment. "Indeed we will. You're a good man, Reverend—helped a lot of people. Look what you did for Jenny when she was all knotted up inside. Now she has a good life with Markus and little Sean, and a new baby girl named Emily . . ."

Hannah's ears perked up. "A new baby girl? Where did you hear that?"

Jack's smile began to creep bigger and bigger across his face again despite his efforts to remain nonchalant. "From the ferry driver a minute ago. He said he was in Calverton talking to a tobacco barge captain from Virginia who told him Markus is back in Hampton. He was away in Kentucky for the past two years, but he and the family returned to Virginia."

"That's why he never replied to Jed's letters! Oh, Jack, I need to get there and patch up the rift between him and Jed! Wouldn't it be wonderful to have them all come home?"

"It would indeed. Lydia and I'll take you if you can wait past the tobacco harvest."

"I can't wait, Jack. Johnny and I'll go right away. I can't afford to risk that they'll move along again before I get there."

"I'll escort you, Mrs. Pearson," the reverend chimed in. "We can take Caleb along to keep things proper. It'll give me a chance to lay out lesson plans with him before I leave for home."

"Could you?" she asked, and without allowing him to answer she added, "I'll pack Johnny's and my things today. Could we leave tomorrow? Does that suit you?"

The young cleric laughed. "Yes, that suits me just fine."

The trip to Virginia proved less of a delight than Hannah had imagined. In her excitement, she had skipped supper the last night home, but the next morning ate two pieces of leftover fried chicken that sat in the bowl on the table. An hour later, she felt sick, and the jarring of the carriage only added to her discomfort. By noon she had to ask the reverend to stop the team so she could vomit in the weeds. After a rest, she felt well enough to continue.

The illness lingered as the familiar Maryland flora broke into stands of Virginia's green magnolias, scrub firs, and wisteria. They followed the James River to Hampton Creek, where the sign for Hampton sat at the edge of town.

A few inquiries by the reverend revealed the location of the Ryan O'Malley home, where Markus and his family were currently residing. Hannah recognized the name of Markus's beloved uncle from her friend's retelling of Ryan's blarney-filled pirate tales. Suddenly other stories came to Hannah—painful memories Markus had shared about his ship, the *Irish Lass,* and about his beautiful, red-haired wife Lyra, and the cottage he had built for her in Hampton. Hannah recalled the dull agony in his eyes when his thoughts would return to Hampton, and she ached for Jenny, who faced the challenge of building a life where those powerful ghosts lingered.

The reverend led the team to a gray clapboard house in a large clearing. A woven basket cradle sat on the porch, surrounded by wooden toys. Before the reverend was able to help Hannah down, Jenny's gentle, welcoming voice drifted to their ears. "Please tell me you are not a dream!" She bounded around the corner with clothespins in both hands, smiling as if it were Christmas morning. "I prayed you here. Did you know that?" She pumped the reverend's hand and then wrapped her arms around Hannah. "I've missed you all so, and I've prayed day and night that one of you would come by and call on us."

Hannah pulled back. "Didn't you get any of Jed's letters? He's written so many, begging Markus's forgiveness and asking you to return to the Willows."

Jenny stared at Hannah and placed a hand on her friend's brow. "Are you all right? You're positively green!"

"It's nothing. I ate something that disagreed with me a few days ago, and I haven't been myself since. Besides, I came here to talk about you, not me, and to see if I can convince you to come home."

"Where's Markus?" the reverend asked.

"He's away on his ship, the *Irish Lass.* He claims he's checking the tobacco markets, but I know the truth. He needed time away . . . to think."

Jenny led everyone inside the snug frame house. Sean was asleep on a rug, snuggled close to a yellow Labrador. The closing of the door awoke the boy to a house filled with playmates. Jenny made the introductions, and within a few minutes, Sean, Johnny, Caleb, and the reverend were off to the yard with the dog and a stick.

A cradle tucked into the corner of the room nestled a chubby bundle with a tuft of red hair. Jenny pulled back the coverlet, revealing a rosy-cheeked baby girl. "This is Emily," she said proudly, "the apple of her papa's eye."

"She's perfectly beautiful!" gushed Hannah. "Oh, Jenny, I'm so hungry for another baby, though I've been so tired and prone to stomach ailments lately I scarcely know how I'd manage."

"Is that so?" Jenny suppressed a giggle. "I believe you're managing just fine."

Hannah tipped her head. "What's so funny?"

Jenny cupped her hands on either side of Hannah's face. "I'd wager anything that you're already pregnant! You speak of nausea and fatigue? Can't you feel the changes in your body? I'd bet anything that beneath that green is the glow of motherhood, my friend."

Hannah was taken aback. "No . . . do you think?" Now she began to giggle at the thought of such a blessing. "So much has been going on that I hadn't even thought about such a possibility. Oh, Jenny, I miss you! Please return to the Willows. And Jed misses Markus terribly. He's dreadfully sorry for the things he thought and said, but it wasn't entirely his fault. I made his return uncomfortable for him, and he lashed out."

Jenny covered Hannah's hand with her own. "Markus saw the storm brewing, but he didn't want to cross you. He read the few letters he received. I think they gave him much comfort."

"Then won't you come home with me, or has Hampton become your home now?"

A sad laugh preceded a long, deep sigh. "The water was once Markus's home. He should be happy here. He tried working a tobacco barge when we first arrived, but that made him miss working the soil. So we moved to Kentucky and bought a little farm there, but farming brought him no joy anymore. He couldn't understand why, but I knew. He misses Jed and the Willows, but he won't admit it. So we sold our place and moved back here, and he's still a lost soul."

"There are so many difficult memories for him here," Hannah said gently. "And for you as well, I'd wager."

Jenny's eyes fixed on a box on a shelf. She walked to it, opened it, and withdrew an object—a watch fob made of braided red hair. She passed it to Hannah as she sat. "Lyra made this for Markus so he'd always have a piece of her with him. He asked me if I minded if he kept it once we were married. I told him I didn't, and it was true at the time. I knew she was his one true love, but she was gone, and he had chosen me, and I felt I had nothing to fear from her. It was so in Maryland, but it's not so here, Hannah. She's everywhere—in every building, along the harbor, in the church. I can't begin to fill the void, and it grows larger every day we're here."

"Then come back to the Willows, Jenny," Hannah pleaded. "You were happy there, until I mussed things up. When will Markus be home? Let me speak to him in Jed's behalf. Let me at least ask him if he'd like to come back to the Willows."

"Oh, I know he'd like to, but he's stubborn. You do remember my husband, don't you? Irish, red haired, part mule? As dear as you are to him, nothing short of a face-to-face apology from Jed will get him to return."

Hannah felt they were finally getting somewhere. "All right. Jed will gladly do that! We've been searching for you for ages. Jack caught some news of you from a barge captain last week, and I came right away. Jed would be here himself were he not on a trip, but when he gets back, I'll send him straight here to speak to Markus."

Hope returned to Jenny's eyes. "I think that would do it! When will Jed be back?"

"I'm not certain, but sometime around the first of November."

A little squeal erupted from Jenny, which set off an echoing squeal from the baby. Jenny clapped her hands together like a happy child. "We could be home by Christmas!"

CHAPTER 13

September 2, 1819
London, England

Lord Everett Spencer, the earl of Whittington, cursed the morning cold and drew his blanket more tightly around him. Each year, it seemed he was less able to tolerate the chill. In truth, he was less able to tolerate many things, and the chill he felt was not only a product of the weather.

Daniel would be eighteen in a few months. The earl hadn't seen the boy in nearly five years, since the night of the holiday party when they quarreled. He looked down at his hands, recalling the sting as they rendered the first blow ever issued to the boy. He clenched them tight and closed his eyes, hoping to conjure a happier image of Daniel, but the face he remembered was fading, and he had no idea what the young man looked like today.

"One hundred pounds . . ." he muttered. It was the amount Daniel had stolen from him to fund the escape that eventually landed him somewhere in Greece, where his Jewish friends lived. And there was now turmoil brewing in Greece.

How the earl hungered to bring his boy home and have him stand by his side, training to fill his responsibilities in Parliament as they had always planned. But he needed Daniel to return on his own, not out of compulsion or coercion. Anything less was against the earl's principles, and it seemed all he had left were his principles.

His loyal, elderly butler, Ridley, entered the room carrying a tray with a letter on top. "This just arrived for you, my lord."

"Thank you, Ridley." The servant turned and left as the earl broke the seal, immediately recognizing the penmanship and the casual reference "Whit." It was from his cousin—Lord Marshall Northrup:

Whit,

Everything you heard was true. The Filiki Eteria or Society of Friends of Greece is moving to a new phase. There is no timetable for the onset of battle, but those closest to the leadership of the organization believe they will most assuredly revolt against their Ottoman oppressors, and Salonika will be in the eye of the storm. I urge you in the strongest means possible to go there and bring Daniel home. Forgive him, Whit.

Forgive him and accept him back under any possible terms. Let him be a doctor, or a Jew, or whatever he chooses. He is all you have. Hurry and save your boy.

Yours,
Marshall

The note further angered the earl, reopening the wound rather than assuaging the hurt. *Doctor! Jew!* Every clear choice Daniel had made struck at the heart of his father by directly opposing everything he was and stood for. He balled the note and tossed it across the room, then swept his bed table clear of its lantern and contents. He found some relief in the shattering crash of metal and glass. It exactly expressed what he felt inside—feelings for which he had no dignified release.

For all he knew, his rebellious son was one of the rebels inciting the revolt! It was his nature. Daniel loved America and longed to go there and bask in his perception of her liberty. He wanted to be a physician. Why could he not find the same pride and liberty in Britain's proud traditions? Was she not the liberator of many oppressed peoples? Had she not been in the forefront of the fight against the slave trade? Could he not come home and serve the needs of his own people instead of dreaming about the greener grass of another land, another citizenry?

The earl leapt from his bed and moved to the window to look across into Hyde Park, where good Britons gathered as neighbors, exchanging news and cheering one another's days. Beyond the signs of affluence lay dark streets littered with the city's poor and underprivileged. He knew such dismal circumstances could be found in regions throughout Britain. These were all his people—his concern. He had pledged his life to improving their lot. Why couldn't Daniel understand how similar they were in thought and passion?

Perhaps it was time for a shift in position.

Salonika, Greece

Daniel Spencer had just crested the last rise on the rutted road for home when he caught a glimpse of Ruth standing on a rocky knoll, her hands raised to shield her eyes from the afternoon glare as she tended her father's flock of sheep. He thought how like the great, chiseled works of the masters she looked, with her long, dark hair flowing in the Aegean breeze, and her empire dress flowing lightly across her figure. She was as beautiful as a goddess, and when she waved a hearty welcome to him he immediately forgot his fatigue.

Adjusting his woolen cap and pushing his brown curls beneath it, he urged his ox team to pick up the pace. So anxious was he to share the day's good news that he abandoned the team on the side of the road and broke into a run, scattering the bleating sheep left and right. Ruth rebuked his childish behavior, but her scolding was mingled with laughter, and when he caught up to her and swung her around he understood her dismay. She was no longer the girl he met more than five years earlier, but a woman with many suitors in her tightly knit Sephardic Jewish community.

He held her suspended in the air for a moment, taking advantage of his large stature and hoping she saw him as a man equal to those her father hoped she would encourage. For a moment he saw it—the tender shift from friendship to ardor. As he gently lowered her to the ground she obscured her face from him, and when she finally returned his gaze she had composed herself and was once again merely his dear friend.

"Your day was good?" she asked with a warm, bright smile that cheered his heart.

He flopped to the ground and stuck a blade of grass between his teeth. "Very good. So good, in fact, that I now have enough money to pay my father *and* for my schooling!"

Ruth's dark eyes widened, and she clapped her hands together. Joining him on the ground, she mentally calculated the day's tally. "But how? You had but one wagon."

His hands became as animated as Ruth's did when she spoke. "That Spanish ship was in port today. I drove my cart straight onto her deck and convinced the captain to buy everything!" He leaned back, relishing in his success. "He paid me twice what some of the items were worth!"

"Twice? Why would he do such a thing? What did you take to market today?"

"The same items I always take—produce, wine, olive oil, and some tapestries. I was the only merchant he bought anything from. I satisfied his every need!"

Ruth's eyes shot heavenward. "Praise be to God! Your debt will be paid. Now you'll have peace."

The sweetness of relief sent Daniel to his back, and he looked up at the azure sky that blended into the blue of the sea. "Now I'll be able to begin my formal medical training."

"And where will you go for your schooling?"

With his hands intertwined behind his neck, he lifted his head and studied Ruth's face, which reflected the same concern he heard in her voice. He crossed his legs and sat up. "That all depends on how my father responds when I return the money to him."

"So you will return to England."

"For a time. I'd prefer to handle the transaction through a bank, but your father said a man handles his problems face to face, and since earning Bezalel Abrabanel's respect is crucial to me, I must see my father in person."

"My father's respect? He already treats you like a son. What more could you want?" Ruth asked coyly.

Daniel searched her face, wondering if she really didn't know. He took her hands in his and tenderly explained, "I'm honored to be viewed as his son so long as I'm not also viewed as your brother." Ruth's head dipped shyly, and he drew his face near hers. "I'm not blind. I see the suitors your father brings home. We both know he's determined to arrange a marriage for you—and very soon. I love you, Ruth. I think you love me too or you would have selected one of your many admirers by now. Am I right?"

She shivered but did not meet his eyes. "What good does it do to speak so? My father will never allow me to marry a Gentile, and you say you are not ready to convert."

His sigh was filled with lamentation. "A friend once advised me to strengthen my understanding of my own faith before converting to another. I've tried to do that, and what I've discovered is that I have believed in the Lord Jesus Christ all my life. I would be a liar if I denied that. I can't believe your father would prefer a liar over a Gentile."

Ruth swallowed hard. "You are wise, Daniel. When will you leave for England?"

"Soon. I want to talk to the schoolmaster here and see if there is a place for me in the next class. If there is, I may return quickly. If not, I may have to begin my schooling there. I detest the thought of being separated, but I'd write, and I'd come to you whenever I could."

Two tears fell onto Ruth's lap. Daniel lifted her chin and smiled, hoping to help her see possibilities in their difficult circumstances. "Don't cry. It would just be for a few years, and then I can stand before your father and ask for your hand knowing I'm able to care for you in a manner that would please him."

Her head remained bowed. "It is a wise plan."

Daniel did not know what more to say, and they sat in silence. He traced her jawline with his finger, attempting to coax a smile from her. He barely realized he was drifting forward until their mouths were mere inches apart. Anticipating their first kiss, he closed his eyes. Nervous and tentative, he felt his heart begin to race, and then an angry voice rang out.

"Go home, Ruth!"

Daniel felt ice flush through his veins at the disappointment in Bezalel Abrabanel's voice.

"Do as I say. Go home before your spectacle becomes fodder for the gossips' tongues." Ruth didn't argue or look back as she rose to her feet and ran in the direction of her home.

"I can explain," Daniel said, but Bezalel Abrabanel was already tearing the fabric of his own shirt, his face so twisted by obvious disappointment that Daniel's words caught in his throat.

"I treated you as a son! I fed you, sheltered you, taught you as have others in our community, even though you rejected our ways. Now take what we have shared with you and return to your own people." Bezalel turned his back to Daniel and began gathering his sheep.

"But I love her," Daniel cried out to him.

"What good can come from such love? You don't believe in the same God, you don't share the same traditions. She will marry a man who can protect her life *and* her faith."

"Isn't love more important than religion?"

Bezalel turned with his hand raised, his finger punctuating each word. "We can trace our lineage back nearly six millennia, yet we are a scattered people, driven from one adopted land to another." He looked down at his curled hands. "We were forced from Iberia. We left our lands, our goods, everything we had built over generations, and we found refuge here. We started over, carving out a life with our bare hands. Again, we became a mighty people—a productive, respected, affluent people—and now there is a growing concern that we are too many, too affluent. People whisper that the Jews must go once more. And if this comes to pass, do you know what will help us survive? It will be our faith, and history, and those traditions you so easily discard. The discussion is over. You will leave tomorrow for England."

"No! I love her, and she loves me! If I go she will go with me!"

Bezalel Abrabanel's expression darkened. "How could the elders have been so right and I have been so wrong? I suppose I didn't believe you could betray me in this way, turning my daughter against her God. No matter. You might as well know. The arrangements are made for Ruth's betrothal. She will be gone when you reach my home, and tomorrow her future husband will carry her away to another land, where her marriage will take place."

Before the last word fell from Bezalel Abrabanel's lips, Daniel abandoned his cart and began the race to find Ruth, but as her father had said, she was nowhere to be found in the village, and no amount of pleading could pry her whereabouts from the townspeople. Daniel felt tainted and banished, completely unwelcome in the place that had opened wide its arms to receive him years earlier.

With his small bundle of belongings, he sat in the village center by the common well and called her name. When he became too hoarse to say the words, he groaned her name until people began throwing stones and closing their windows to shut out his wailing. Bezalel found him there in the morning. Daniel looked into the man's stony face and begged once more. "Please—she is all I have."

Bezalel offered no words of comfort as he lifted Daniel to his feet, then escorted him to the port where a ship docked in the Aegean Sea awaited his arrival.

He fought the men who assisted Bezalel's efforts to drag him on board. When the ship left the port, he considered tossing himself into the sea. If he made it safely ashore, he would begin his search again, and if he drowned, his death would at least deny them their peace. As he steeled his nerve to make the leap, he saw Ruth standing on a hilltop as still and stiff as marble, while a man stood beside her, his finger pointing to Daniel then sweeping across the horizon as if sweeping Daniel's memory away from Greece. Daniel held Ruth locked in his sight, but she never moved as he watched her silhouette grow smaller and smaller until it finally disappeared from view.

Three weeks later, Daniel's ship reached the Liverpool port. Two days after that, he stood on the stoop of his father's London home. Gone were the comfortable linens he wore in Greece; he had abandoned them along the way. Instead, he bristled under layers of stiff fabric—a blue tailcoat and brown fall-front trousers, a white waistcoat, shirt, and cravat. He removed the beastly top hat as he banged on the door with the lion's-head knocker.

The stalwart Ridley gushed over him, herding him inside and to the imposing doors of his father's study. "Allow me a moment to prepare your father, Viscount Whittington."

"Just Daniel, Ridley. Please simply call me Daniel."

The gentleman nodded worriedly before slipping through the door. A moment later he swung the door open and gestured for Daniel to enter.

His father was standing in the center of the room, though the change in his appearance left Daniel unsure it was even him. Daniel now stood a few inches taller than his father, who seemed to have aged more than a decade in the five years they'd been estranged. His thin frame no longer looked robust. In short, the mask of invincibility was gone, leaving a mere mortal behind. The change left Daniel shaken, and it was reflected in his voice.

"Hello, Father. I've come to repay the money I took the night I ran away, and to fulfill whatever penance the law requires of me. I know there's a warrant pending."

"Have you only come home to pay your debt? Will you not sit for a moment before we deal with the legalities?

The earl's desk served as a barrier between the two men as they sat. Moments passed as the earl studied his son. Unable to bear the scrutiny, Daniel burst to his feet and set the bundle of money on the desk. "I was wrong to take it. I make no excuses for my behavior. I'd like to know where we go from here."

Sorrow creased the earl's eyes. "You've become a man. I've missed so much, Daniel."

Upended by the softness of his father's voice, Daniel dropped the stoicism and returned to his chair. "We're two very stubborn men."

"How was Greece?"

Daniel flinched at the reminder of what he had been forced to leave behind. "The time there was good for me."

"For me as well. I've missed you, and I'm willing to admit the many mistakes I myself have made. I'd like you to come home. I'd like us to make another attempt at being a family."

"I must tell you first that my plans have not changed, Father. I still have every intention of becoming a physician."

The earl winced and then acknowledged the report with a deep sigh. "Very well. You're a few weeks late into the term, but I'm sure we can get you seated."

His father's retreat from his former adamancy took Daniel aback. "Are you saying you will support me in this?"

"Will you agree to begin with two years of study? In return, at the conclusion of those two years, will you revisit my desire for you to someday fill my seat in Parliament?"

Daniel felt the hairs rise on the back of his neck. Had his father really changed, or was his generosity merely a tactic to lure him back in? He wasn't sure, but he knew he was no longer a timid, dependent boy. Perhaps they could enjoy a respectful relationship, and if they could not he would be two years further along in his studies with some resources of his own with which to continue. "I'll agree to that."

The earl stood with his hand outstretched. As he stepped toward his son, the distance between the two men seemed insurmountable. Fumbling in their efforts to bridge the gap, they shook hands first, and when that gesture seemed completed, neither man could initiate the release. They stood arms' distance apart, staring at one another like two rams on a hillside deciding who would yield. Surprisingly, it was the earl who melted into loving submission. He took a step, and then another, at which point Daniel closed the gap, filling his father's waiting arms.

"I've missed you, Son. This is an answer to a thousand prayers."

With its mahogany panels, dark drapes, and carpeting, the room seemed stifling to Daniel. He missed the bright beams of sunlight, and the smells of the Aegean Sea. He longed for the light airiness he knew in Greece, where muslin and silk fluttered in the Mediterranean breezes. He hungered for the soft lowing of animals in the rugged hillsides. He physically ached for Ruth.

Moisture filled his eyes as the memories flooded him. His father must have noticed and interpreted the tears as a reflection of Daniel's happiness at being back in England, for he said, "It's all right, Son. You're home now. It's all right."

Daniel hadn't the heart to tell him where he truly longed to be.

The wind howled around the harbor like the lone wolf Stephen Ramsey had smuggled onto his estate. The animals had been hunted to extinction in Britain, so when Stephen had found a cub in Spain he brought it home. Michael thought about him often these days—how that wild, hunted creature had been rescued from its predators, while he and Hank were at Richard Porter's mercy. The man had changed their surnames legally—to Porter. *You don't want people tyin' you to that murderin' father of yours,"* he told the boys. The name McGowan never drew Michael's thoughts to his father—only to his sweet, heartbroken mother, for whom he still grieved. Michael never let a day pass that he didn't remind himself and his less-sentimental brother who they really were.

He wrapped his tattered, threadbare work coat around him and kicked at a stone in the street. *Another day, another change . . .* In the two and a half years since Mary McGowan's death, Porter had moved the boys five times, shifting them from school to school, town to town. Long gone was the promised, comfortable, country cottage on the outskirts of Liverpool. Home was now a third-floor flat in the dirty city whose only view was of other sooty rooftops where residents gathered to escape the heat and discuss their desolate lives.

Things had been tolerable at first. Porter had risen in station when he married Mary McGowan, adopting the boys and their inheritance. For a time, he assumed the role of a respectable country gentleman— enrolling the boys in a good school, and dabbling at gardening, but that was short lived. The burden of respectability grew too onerous, and eventually, like mice and other vermin, Porter sought and attracted his own kind—moochers and thieves with a penchant for gambling and liquor. His temper flared, and his language grew coarse and slurred. The money, though sufficient for a prudent family to live well, was inadequate to support both Porter's vices and the rent, and eventually he and the boys would be forced to move again.

At nine years old, Michael was a good student and could easily catch up or, as with his current school and teacher, dazzle his way to more challenging studies, but seven-year-old Hank was slow and uninterested in book learning, and eventually he was no longer expected to attend. Michael worried over this for many reasons, beginning with the sorrow it would have caused their mother. But more importantly, it meant that Hank was now Porter's shadow and a daily sidekick to him and his nefarious friends. Hank had all but abandoned all discussions of his mother and what she wanted for her boys; he had become as attached to Porter as a son is to his father. This left Michael on a lonely and precarious precipice.

As pitiable a man as Porter was, Michael recognized that his adopted father longed to be—and have—something better, but he was unable to get a firm hold on it. Porter believed character was like a coat he could simply slip into, rather than wool he needed to weave into something meaningful. Michael knew Porter was a pile of uncombed, unwashed wool, and he would likely ever be so. Still, as detestable as he was in many ways, and completely unaware of the critical needs of children, he occasionally surprised the boys with treats and treasures. They barely had enough coal for the stove, but they each had a pocket watch—filched from a shop by one of Porter's friends, no doubt. And though meat and dairy were luxuries, they generally had day-old cakes and biscuits, and each had a modern boar-bristle toothbrush.

Most importantly, Porter had never laid an angry hand on them, though Michael felt certain that day would come. And perhaps the thing that kept him from taking his younger brother by the hand and running away altogether was this—Porter was all they had now.

For days, Porter had hinted at a new change to their already undisciplined routine. Wearing a dirty shirt and smelling of ale, he sidled up to Michael. "I'm goin' ta teach ya a new game—one that'll also bring a little extra income into the house."

Michael knew they were about to cross the line he had been dreading.

"We'll play to your natural talents. Me and Hank have already been practicin', Michael. We just need to lead ya along."

Michael watched the glint in Hank's eyes as he smiled up at Porter's gap-toothed grin.

"Let's see some actin' here, Michael. Can ya give me that hungry look . . . the one ya give me when there's no milk in the pitcher?"

Michael felt his brows knit together.

"Don't give me that haughty look, lad! If ya can't play along, me and Hank will go it alone, but them what works gets the rewards, and that reward just might include a steamin' meat pie for supper."

Just the mention of hot, nourishing food etched the look of want on Michael's face.

"Yes! Now that's right close to perfect! Now all ya have ta do is walk up to folks, make that face and say, 'Do you have a shillin' for a poor hungry boy?'"

Michael's head shot back in disgust. "You want me to beg?" The comment caused an equally vitriolic physical response from Porter.

With his hands on his hips, he leaned down close to Michael's face and sneered. "You came from a long line of beggars and worse, boy! Your papa's people were all thieves and miscreants. He was pulled from a Barbados prison by Stephen Ramsey 'cause he needed a lackey to do his dirty work, like kidnappin' the earl's son and killin' his governess. And it weren't just him. Your mama begged near every day to keep food in your belly. And were it not for Stephen Ramsey's guilt over your father's suicide, she'd've still been on the streets beggin', or liftin' her skirts like a tart ta keep you fed!"

"Liar!" Michael threw himself at Porter. "Don't say that about my mother!"

"So, you do have some fight in ya!" Porter laughed as he easily subdued the boy.

"I don't care what my real father was. My mother was good and kind, and Stephen Ramsey was to be our father. He loved our mother and us, not like you."

"Now, there's all kinds of love, lad. I got the survivin' kind of love for you boys. Ain't we done all right so far?"

"We'd have money enough if you didn't drink it up or gamble it away," Michael said.

Porter straightened and frowned. "Now that hurts me, Son. I've got some problems, I'm not denyin' that, but I was doin' just fine before I took you in. And don't I go out every day and make an extra bob the best way I can? Only I can't keep workin' forever. It's time you boys pitch in, and till you're old enough and smart enough ta get a real job, well, we got ta make use of the talents the Lord already gave ya."

So that was it. The line Michael vowed never to cross was clearly drawn, and now he had to choose. Moments passed, and then without another word, Porter turned and walked up the street. He had barely taken ten steps when, after a single look of disappointment at his older brother, Hank sped to catch up to Porter, then clasped his hand and walked double time to keep up. Michael clearly saw how it would be.

"I'm smart! I'll get my education!" he called after Porter, but neither Porter nor Hank acknowledged him. "And someday I'll get a good job—a fine job!"

The distance between them increased.

"I'll make my own money and do something ta make my mother proud."

Richard Porter stopped. Silence filled the space between them. Porter finally dropped Hank's hand and turned to face Michael. "Let that dream fill ya with fire, boy. Let it make ya work hard for that future, but until then, ya gotta do what ya can."

Michael felt his jaw tighten in resolution. "Only till then."

"Fine. I'd expect nothin' less of ya. Trust me, I believe in ya, Michael. I've got big plans for you. Now come along and learn your part."

He dropped his eyes to the stone streets and counted each one as he made his way to Porter's outstretched hand. Fifty-seven stones separated him from the values his mother instilled in him and the life he was about to enter. Fifty-seven stones . . .

CHAPTER 14

September 16, 1819
The Willows

The sunrises seemed more effulgent, the rivers glittered more vibrantly, and the sky was more dazzling each night as the little party traveled home to the Willows from Virginia. Hannah had finally come to accept that she was expecting a new child. Adding to that joy was the very real hope that Jenny and Markus would accept Jed's apology and return to the Willows. But the crowning joy was the decreasing number of days until Jed would be home to hear the news.

Hannah ignored the still-present bouts of morning sickness, amplified by the jostling of the carriage. Instead, she used the days to play little games with Johnny, realizing that her time alone with him was drawing to a close. They observed the fall change of colors and made a game of counting animals—one point for a bird, two for a squirrel, five for a deer. Johnny sat on the carriage floor and looked up, harvesting dozens of points with each passing flock, though his view was obscured by his mother's position. Over and over, he advised her to sit on the floor as well, so she too could count the birds. She declined, assuring him that he was simply far superior in his skills. The pair read books, played cards, and practiced Johnny's letters. He was an exceptionally bright boy, in part due to the excessive amount of time he spent playing indoors during the summer, since he had now developed a deathly fear of bees and insects.

Hannah knew she had imparted her own fears to her son. Jed was concerned about the development, but he hadn't forced the issue. She could see, however, that she must begin whittling away at the child's fears. For now, she was content to have him all to herself, to have her arm around her four-and-a-half-year-old boy and to see his sleepy head resting on her lap. She fingered his curls that were so like his father's, and watched him smile contentedly as his snores fluttered out with each breath. She tried to imagine him holding the hand of a baby sister or brother, and her heart warmed at the thought of her growing family.

She could hear snippets of conversation between the reverend and Caleb as the clergyman grilled the boy on aspects of history and with quotes from the great literary masters. She tried to play along and found herself somewhat alarmed by how many of the answers eluded her now. She would need to increase her personal studies to prepare to tutor Johnny.

As the carriage neared the Willows in the late afternoon of September sixteenth, Hannah noticed how the two men had grown conspicuously quiet. She paid more attention to the surroundings, and disturbing signs began appearing along the river road. The sheriff was speaking to some locals at the end of a neighbor's farm lane, and two of Reese Symonds' relatives were standing at the Willows lane with muskets in their arms.

"Has there been trouble?" the reverend asked them.

"A considerable number of oddities," replied one man in a thick British brogue.

"Too many ta just be a coincidence," the other man added. "Jack and Abel are at the main house. They'll fill you and Mrs. Pearson in."

The reverend urged the team on to the house. Jack and Abel met them out front.

"Did you see Markus?" Jack asked Hannah.

"No. He was away, but I had a very positive chat with Jenny. She thinks Markus will listen if Jed apologizes to him personally and asks him to come back."

"We could use him," Abel said. He helped Hannah down from the carriage and set the boy down as well.

"The Symonds men mentioned trouble while we were away," she said anxiously.

"Nothing you need to worry over," Jack said with a wink in Johnny's direction.

Hannah caught the hint and leaned close to her son. "Darling, why don't you run off and find Moses? Tell him about Sean and the big yellow dogs."

Johnny's brows knitted together and he frowned. "I'm scared, Mama. I want Daddy to come home."

"He will come home in a few weeks, but until then we're home, safe and sound, so go and play. All will be fine. You'll see."

Johnny was reluctant to leave his mother's side, but Caleb led him away so the adults could speak freely. Again Hannah inquired about the trouble, and Abel began.

"Some building supplies are missing from the homesteads, and there's been damage done to the water wheel. We've made most of the repairs and it's running again. I'm more worried about the carcasses of two steers we found in the back pasture."

Hannah shivered and began rubbing her arms.

"Could animals have killed them?" the reverend asked.

"Yeah," Jack said, "but it don't add up when you figure in the rest."

"I suppose it doesn't," Hannah agreed reluctantly. "We saw the sheriff on the road."

Abel nodded. "The Symonds wrote out a report for their lost supplies. He's been checking the other farms, but so far, we're the only place with anything to report."

Hannah bit her lower lip. "Jed was worried our enemies might return. He thought having more families here would keep us safer. I suppose they're not any more afraid of a few sharecropping families than they were of freedmen and a few women."

"If it's Hildebrand or his kind, the arrival of these new families might just be what drew them here," said Abel. "Half of the new families are freedmen too, and whoever is harassing us probably doesn't like the idea of colored people becoming landowners and businessmen."

Hannah crossed her arms and looked down the long lane. "So what should we do?"

"We're going to herd all the stock into the closest pastures and tie all the dogs out tonight. If anyone comes on this property, somebody will hear them."

She nodded her agreement, though her nerves were still on edge. "That sounds wise."

Jack laid his hand on her arm. "These fellas haven't bothered us in over three years, Hannah. It's likely they just wanted us to know they're still around. I bet they won't come by for another three years, either."

She offered a half smile. "Let's hope you're right, Jack."

No new evidence of raids or trouble turned up the rest of the week, allowing the reverend to feel comfortable taking his leave of the Willows for New York State. A late Indian summer had swept across Maryland, and like a gift from God, the brief extension of warmth lifted the spirits of those hard hit by the good man's departure. The autumn colors were vibrant and rich, while the temperatures lured people from their homes to play and picnic under nature's kaleidoscopic umbrella. Everyone found excuses to be out of doors, and whether they were busy with chores or play, children dotted the landscape.

All except Johnny. He had been thrilled with the cooler autumn temperatures that finally set him free, but the hot air and sunshine left him fearful to be out of doors again.

On September twentieth, Hannah dragged the rugs out for a final beating before the cold locked everyone in for the winter. She turned her face skyward until her cheeks grew hot. At twenty-seven, she possessed a childlike longing to lie under the open sky and allow the sun to bake her skin brown. She looked for Johnny, hoping to use her son as an excuse for an hour's folly, but a glance at the house revealed his sober face at a window. She motioned to him to come outside, but he shook his head. Again she coaxed him, yet he refused to leave the house.

"What's the matter with Johnny?" asked ten-year-old Moses.

Hannah bent down as if sharing a secret mission with the boy. "Let's see if we can't convince him to play, all right?"

Forty minutes of cajoling, a plate of Johnny's favorite molasses cookies, and innumerable promises that the world was safe from bees and bad men, finally lured him to the porch, and from there to the yard.

"Let's go build a soldier fort like Fort McHenry," Moses said.

"Yeah!" Johnny cheered.

It pained Hannah to renege on the promises that the world was perfectly safe when her own nerves were still a bit raw regarding the intruders. "Let's stay close to the house, boys, all right? Perhaps you can make a fort in the barn. The stalls would make a perfect fort."

The boys caught her vision and raced away to the barn as she returned to her rugs. She had finished beating the lot of them and turned her attentions to dragging them from the line when she heard a scream. She threw the rug beater to the ground, then raised her skirts and bolted for the barn. Reese Symonds was tending the yearlings in the corral with Royal, who ran for Bitty, while Reese sped toward the barn and the scream.

Johnny lay at the base of the ladder, his body twisted and his leg misaligned. Trickles of blood flowed from the back of his head and out of his ear. He called for his mother and tried to reach for her as a hoarse moan escaped his lips. Hannah began to scoop him to her, but Reese stopped her, warning, "Best not move him until we check him over."

It took every particle of restraint to wait patiently as Reese ran a rudimentary check of her boy. When she saw his eyes roll around in his head and then drift closed, she gasped aloud. Moses stood a distance away, tears streaming down his chubby brown cheeks.

"Moses, what were you two doing up there?" Hannah shrieked.

"Th–th–the loft was our lookout tower. Johnny saw a moth and thought it was a bee. He swatted at it and walked right off the edge."

Her fears, passed on to her child, were the cause of his injuries. That realization was too much to bear, and once again she begged God to save her son. Bitty arrived and knelt by the boy, with Jack, Royal, and Abel close on her heels. Johnny was relocated to his own room, his leg was splinted, and his wounds addressed, but he could not be awakened.

The local doctor who attended to Johnny after the bee stings returned again and advised Hannah to rush the boy to a hospital for a surgical consultation. Within the hour, plans were made to move Johnny to Baltimore by steamboat where the family's friend, surgeon Samuel Renfro, lived and worked. As preparations were being made, Moses came to see his friend. Tears pooled in his eyes as he arrived with an offering in his hands—five molasses cookies. "They're for Johnny, for when he wakes up." Hannah thanked the boy numbly, then returned to the last of the preparations.

Word of the senator's son's injuries spread wide and fast along the river and beyond. Bitty dashed off notes to Jed at his Annapolis office, as well as to Frannie, and to Hannah's sister Beatrice. Jack rushed the letters to Calverton, where postal carriers would begin the journey to deliver them to those far-flung destinations. Abel and Bitty prepared to accompany Hannah and Johnny, while Reese Symonds raced ahead on horseback with two more of Bitty's notes— to Hannah's Baltimore-based sister, Myrna, and to warn Dr. Renfro of Johnny's impending arrival. With every possible preparation in place, Hannah and her party set their hopes on the hospital attached to the Maryland School of Medicine, and the skilled surgeon who had miraculously delivered Johnny nearly five years ago.

Reese was waiting at the Baltimore harbor with Myrna and her rig when the ship arrived. A new symptom had begun during the trip as Johnny's breathing became a labored snore, leaving Hannah frantic to race to the hospital through Baltimore's newly gas-lit streets.

Soon, the little group burst through the hospital doors like a hurricane. Though Dr. Renfro's girth was nearly equal to his height, he rushed to greet them quicker than Hannah had ever seen him move. The arms of his compassion wrapped around her from the moment their eyes met.

"My sweet girl, you and Johnny are two patients I wished to never tend again," he said.

Hannah guided him to the unresponsive child. "He fell from the barn loft, Samuel. He won't awaken." Try as she did to remain brave, her words came out in a forced staccato. "His breathing is now labored. You can help him, can't you?"

"Bring a candle here," Samuel instructed a medical student. One at a time, Samuel lifted Johnny's eyelids and held the candle near enough that Hannah could see the flame reflected in her son's dull eyes. After giving the candle to the student, Samuel carefully ran his large hands along Johnny's skull, settling on several spots along the back. Hannah saw the crease of the surgeon's brow deepen as he examined the boy more intently. He instructed two medical students to carry Johnny into an examination room. "I need to examine him more thoroughly, Hannah. Wait in the family conference room. I'll come to you when I've finished."

The normally cantankerous Myrna was the essence of solicitousness in her younger sister's hour of need, remaining by her side and offering constant words of comfort and support. Hannah soaked it in like parched ground as the tortuous minutes ticked by. Samuel reappeared in the company of two other white-coated colleagues. Hannah studied his face and found his expression so unnerving that she couldn't find the strength to rise from her seat until Bitty took one of her hands and Myrna took the other, supporting her effort.

"This is Dr. Llewellyn," Samuel said as he nodded to the older of his two colleagues, "and this is Dr. Pense. I asked them to consult on Johnny's condition. Tell me again how his accident occurred. Where did you find him? Was he near the ladder?"

"I wasn't there when he fell. I found him at the base of the ladder."

Samuel nodded somberly. "Hannah, we are all agreed that Johnny experienced at least two dangerous blows to the head. He probably hit the ladder and then the barn floor. In any case, it seems blood is effused under his skull in two areas, compressing sections of his brain."

Bitty's and Myrna's hands tightened around Hannah's. "What can be done?" she asked.

"Your workman told me Jed is out of state. When is he expected?"

"Not for a few more weeks, Samuel, but I am here now. Tell me what can be done."

"Hannah, you should not have to make this decision on your own." He placed his hands on her shoulders and looked into her eyes. "We must perform a series of operations called trephinings, wherein we remove circular pieces of bone from Johnny's skull to release the blood and thereby decrease the pressure."

"Bore into his skull?" Hannah's lips began to quiver uncontrollably but she did not falter, fearing if she did they would not allow her to sanction the treatment. "Is that our only option?"

Samuel glanced at his two colleagues, who nodded their affirmation. "We believe it is. I must be blunt with you, Hannah. This is a grave procedure. I've only assisted in five. Most of those were on soldiers during the war. There is no guarantee the procedure will work at all because the damage to the brain may already be permanent. And there is the obvious risk of harm from the procedure itself, or infection that could result."

Hannah's hands moved to cradle her overburdened head. "What will happen if we do nothing? Can we not wait to see if he recovers on his own?"

"His breathing is very labored. His response to stimuli is poor on one side. We must proceed soon to give us the best chance of success."

Her eyes fell to the polished wooden floor as if divine guidance could be found there. She clasped her hands together and closed her eyes. "Oh, dear God, please help me," she prayed softly. A rush of warmth, like sunshine, began in her chest and radiated outward. She raised her eyes to Samuel and said, "Let me hold him in my arms for a few moments."

Samuel took her hand and guided her into the examination room, where on first appearance Johnny seemed to be merely sleeping. But as she drew nearer, Hannah noticed the deepening of the bruises, the swelling that altered his appearance. She cupped his cheeks in her hands and pressed her lips to his brow, spreading kisses from corner to corner. The last kiss lingered over his right temple, and she began to sing a song from a book called *Rhymes for the Nursery,* which Jed had brought home for Johnny after the war.

"Twinkle, twinkle little star . . ." she began in a broken voice. "How I wonder who you are. Up a—" She coughed to clear the growing lump from her throat and began again. "Up a—"

She felt Samuel's hands on her shoulders, and she spun into his arms. "He didn't want to play outside, Samuel. I made him terrified of bees but I didn't want him to be afraid, so I coaxed him out. I did this. Oh, Samuel! What have I done to my boy?"

"Shh . . . There now. You did no such thing other than love your boy with all your heart. If love were enough to keep him safe, our little Johnny would live for a thousand years. I know that. Jed knows that too. Now let me see what's causing this angel to sleep."

He led her back to the family conference room and signaled to the women to come for her. As he began to leave her side, Hannah reached her hand out and took his again, drawing his eyes back to hers.

"Samuel, please . . . please . . ."

The surgeon's eyes were now glassy. "You needn't remind me how precious this child is to you, Hannah. We will do our very best. Pray that God will grant us wisdom beyond our own."

Hannah stifled a cry as Johnny headed for surgery on a litter borne by the two medical students. She barely sat during the long operation. The hollow echo of her boots on the wooden floor became unnerving as she repeatedly paced the path from the window to the surgical room, with Myrna and Bitty matching her step for step. At last the door opened and Dr. Renfro appeared. His long-faced demeanor froze Hannah in her place.

"He made it through the procedures. I can't say more than that, I'm afraid."

She crumpled over in relief. "May I see him?"

"Shortly." His chin lowered when he took her hand as he had so often that difficult day. "There were complications, Hannah. The dura mater—oh, how can I explain this?"

His eyes darted about the room as he searched for the words. As each second passed, Hannah felt her hope, and her son, slipping away.

"The outermost covering of the brain is a membrane called the dura mater. After we used the trephine to remove a section of the skull, this covering began to swell until it protruded through the opening. We applied a dressing and a pewter plate to cover the site until the swelling reduces sufficiently to replace the segments of skull. He's been through quite an ordeal. Now all we can do is wait."

Myrna attempted to persuade Hannah to come home with her, but she refused.

"Take Bitty and Abel home with you," she said. "I'm not leaving this room."

"You're well beyond exhausted. You'll do your son no good if you collapse."

"Then I'll collapse here, by his bedside." Hannah issued her sister a look that ended any further argument.

Nine days passed, and Johnny showed no sign of improvement. Abel spent his time visiting the fort, while Bitty and Myrna took turns running errands and sitting with Hannah at Johnny's bedside. She sang and read and prayed until she was hoarse, and when she could not utter another word, Bitty and Myrna took their turns doing the same.

On the tenth day, Dr. Renfro pulled Bitty aside. "Is there any word from Jed at all?"

Bitty wrung her hands. "No, and none from Frannie, either."

CHAPTER 15

October 1, 1819
Philadelphia, Pennsylvania

Frannie Pearson had no sooner stepped off the ship in the Philadelphia harbor when she heard her name being called by a man dressed in a dapper striped suit, holding a bouquet in one hand and a sign obscuring his face in the other. She moved toward him and read the sign with anticipation. "'Shall we dine?' Well, I suppose that depends on who is behind that placard and under that top hat." The sign was lowered, revealing a man in his forties with a well-trimmed beard and a jaunty glint in his eye. "Mr. St. Clair, you are indeed a man of your word."

"Of course. I told you I'd be waiting at the docks in ten days when you returned from your trip to New York." Phillip St. Clair crooked his arm and waited for Frannie to take it.

"Excuse me for a moment, won't you? I need to arrange for the transport of my things."

He offered to handle that detail, but Frannie refused with a flick of her wrist and a flash of a smile. Moments later she returned to find him sulking and quiet. "Whatever is the matter?"

"Really, Francis. Sometimes you make a man feel . . ." Apparently unable to find a suitable term, he simply groaned.

Frannie took his arm and looked up at him. "I warned you I'd wear down your last nerve. You should escape before I cost you the price of supper and a subsequent headache powder."

He began to laugh and soon settled into a casual pace as they made their way to his carriage. "I secured the endorsement of the mayor. With his support my seat on the City Council is assured, and he asked me to consider a run for his office when he retires."

"That's wonderful. I'm very happy for you."

"I lack only one thing to make this a perfect day, Frannie."

She withdrew her arm and stopped dead in her tracks. "Don't do this, Phillip."

He framed her face in his hands and forced her to meet his eyes. "We make a good team, Frannie. Why can't you abandon this attachment to a man who offers you nothing?"

She stormed off, and Phillip shouted across the walkway to her. "I love you, you know. I'm here, and I'm not going anywhere."

Frannie noticed the attention being paid to them. Her face flushed hot and she looked for a place to run away, but she was penned in on every side. Cornered, she turned to face him and spat out, "Stop it. You're embarrassing yourself."

He hurried back to her side. "You mean I'm embarrassing you. You say you don't care what other people think, but that's not true at all. You actually care very much. That's a side of you I didn't expect, Frannie. You pretend to be impervious, but you're actually more vulnerable than people know. You needn't fear me. I won't leave you. I'll wait out the last five years of your emotional imprisonment to Arthur Ramsey if that's what it takes for you to believe that."

She walked away again and began hailing cabbies on the street.

"Don't run away. Show me how brave you can truly be. Come with me to dinner and celebrate with me. Please?"

A cabbie pulled his carriage up close. "Need a ride, miss?"

Frannie hesitated for a moment before finally lowering her hand and placing it in Phillip's. "No, thank you. I believe I'll accept the gentleman's offer."

Frannie had not felt this vulnerable in years, and the feeling was both uncomfortable and exhilarating. Dinner was a lazy, drawn-out, two-hour affair, and the carriage ride home was filled with banter—

and with Phillip occasionally reaching to squeeze her hand. When they reached her Philadelphia home, he took her hand firmly in his and simply said, "I won't ask you to marry me again, Frannie, because my previous proposal stands until you accept, or send me away."

Overwhelmed by the implication, she remained still as he moved toward her, his eyes searching hers as if seeking any sign she would reject his kiss. She did not. Five years had passed since her last kiss, the emotional test Arthur had placed on her lips, and though she had not sought Phillip's overture, she welcomed it at the first touch. Suddenly she realized how starved she had been to feel loved, to feel anything that even resembled love. The moment so engulfed her with warmth and safety that she began to reconsider Phillip's proposal. She pulled back and studied his face, curious to see what emotion she'd find reflected there now after their kiss. She saw passion and a hunger surpassing her own, but she also saw what she sought—concern and love, and she yearned for more.

"Phillip, I—I—"

The door burst open and Frannie's housekeeper, Mrs. Standish, came bursting out. "Thank heavens it's you! I saw the carriage pull up and wondered who was lurking about—"

"That'll be all, Mrs. Standish!"

The woman huffed at the rebuff. "A letter arrived by special courier nearly a week ago, and as I've always said, nothing good ever comes by special courier." She spun on her heels and reentered the house.

"I should go," Frannie said.

"Very well." Phillip slipped to the ground and came around to help her down. "Can I see you tomorrow? Let's say brunch at that little café along the Schuylkill?"

She actually hated to see the evening end. "All right."

Phillip brought her hand gently to his lips. "Till tomorrow then."

When she slipped inside, Mrs. Standish was standing in the foyer, flapping a letter in the air. It occurred to Frannie that the housekeeper's manner bore a striking resemblance to another busybody—Myrna Stansbury—and she wondered how she hadn't noticed that before.

She rolled her eyes at Mrs. Standish as she broke the seal. The handwriting was immediately comforting—Bitty's hand—a feeling that turned to instant panic as Frannie read the first line of the message. Tossing the letter on the foyer side table, she raced up the stairs as she called out instructions to Mrs. Standish. "Fill a canteen and throw a day's provisions in a bag!"

She stood at the top of the stairs, trying to decide how to proceed. Should she send for Phillip? No, too awkward. A carriage? Too slow. She would ride to Baltimore on horseback!

She yelled down from the landing as Mrs. Standish raced up the stairs. "I'll do the packing. Please tell Mr. Bowers to saddle my horse! And hurry!"

She ransacked her drawers until she found the men's pants and shirt she tucked away for emergencies, knowing she'd be safer traveling alone if she were dressed as a man. From her nightstand she pulled a pistol. In seconds it was loaded and tucked into her saddle bag, along with some cash. Next, she hastily threw some additional clothing into a satchel, then grabbed both bags and raced downstairs to find Mrs. Standish off in a corner, reading Bitty's letter. The woman jabbered some inane excuse that Frannie abruptly cut off, adding a stern final instruction.

"Since you now know the full nature of my business, please see that Mr. St. Clair and my business associate, Mr. Dunlevy, are equally informed about my departure and destination."

Frannie was out the door and mounted in five minutes with her bags secured and her pistol at the ready. At her firm kick, the horse bolted down Baltimore Road, and Frannie began a sleepless race to reach the ones she loved.

Someone or something was creating a stir in the hospital's foyer. Bitty and Myrna stuck their heads out of the room and gaped at the scene.

"What is it?" Hannah asked.

"Some filthy, unkempt man is creating a disturbance," said Myrna.

Bitty covered her mouth in surprise. "That isn't a filthy man. It's Frannie!"

When Frannie crossed the threshold, her hair was a nest of auburn tangles that poked haphazardly from beneath the brim of a worn leather hat. Dust and mud covered her face, turning her eyes into two white circles. Her clothes, men's and two sizes too big, were ridiculous by any standard.

After offering a brief hug to Hannah, she moved directly to Johnny. She took the lad's hand and pressed it to her cheek, her tears flowing in two dirty streaks. But the moment became an emotional contradiction, for while Hannah's eyes welled in shared sorrow, she couldn't help the chuckle that escaped her mouth.

Frannie looked at her sister-in-law in complete confusion until Bitty brought a mirror over. Frannie laughed and cried as she clutched Hannah to her. "I'm so sorry. I was away. I jumped on my horse and came as soon as I heard."

"You rode from Philadelphia? On horseback?"

Frannie wiped the back of her hand across her eyes, nodding. "I left around eight and rode all night, switching mounts in Delaware and Havre de Grace."

"Oh, Frannie! Thank you!"

Samuel entered and was clearly pleased to see Frannie there. He exited just as quietly, calling Bitty into the hall with him. "Has there also been word from Jed?"

Bitty pressed her lips tightly together and shook her head.

Samuel's face was grim with worry. "Tell Frannie there's a rooming house across the avenue where she can bathe and rest."

Six hours later, Hannah stood at the window, staring at the starry sky, holding Johnny's hand as she and Frannie sang every verse of "Twinkle, Twinkle" to him. Myrna spent the days working on the knitting she had brought from her home, while Bitty busied herself rolling bandages for the hospital.

Two days later, Phillip St. Clair showed up unexpectedly. Flustered, Frannie made hasty introductions and quickly led him from the room. "I told Mrs. Standish to tell you where I was so you wouldn't worry. I never intended for you to come."

"Of course I would come. I love you. I want to help."

Frannie's hands flew up like a barricade. "I can't entertain you. Hannah and Johnny need me. You should return to Philadelphia."

He took her by the shoulders and spoke in soft, loving tones. "I made arrangements to be away for as long as necessary. Forget I'm even here, but if and when you need me, call for me. I may be of some service, particularly until your brother returns. All right?" He handed her a piece of paper with the number of his room at the Lord Baltimore Hotel.

Phillip did prove to be a valuable asset, freeing Abel to return home to tend to the farm. Samuel attempted to insert a tube with a funnel at the end in Johnny's throat, to allow him to be fed broth, but that caused new complications, and Hannah came to a decision. When Samuel arrived on rounds, she said, "I want to take him home."

No one seemed surprised by the decision. Samuel simply asked, "Are you certain?"

"Very certain. You say you've done what you can, and if it is now a matter of waiting for him to awaken, I'd rather he do it at home, in his own bed, surrounded by his own things." She drew a deep, shuddering breath and paused to steady herself. "And if he never wakes up, I would still want my last days with him spent in our home. When do you think we can leave?"

"I'd like him to remain here another week at least, until the risk of infection is past."

"Very well. A full month then."

Samuel gestured for Bitty to follow him into the hall. "I think you should contact Timothy and Markus. If the outcome isn't positive, Hannah and Jed will need more support."

Bitty quietly moved to Samuel's office and dashed off two more notes, bound for Washington and Hampton, while praying that God would still perform a miracle.

CHAPTER 16

October 12, 1819
Palmyra, New York

An explosion rocked the air, and Jed jerked so abruptly that his horse nearly threw him. When the horse settled down, Dudley Snowden placed a gentle hand on Jed's and smiled. "They're blasting rock out of the path of the canal some eight miles away." At Jed's sigh, Dudley added, "It took months for me to bear the noise without scrambling under the table."

"I'm not sure I could bear that noise for the next few years."

"We do what we must. The war certainly taught us each that lesson, didn't it?" Dudley's pensive tone revealed that he neither required nor expected a reply. "I simply tell myself that each blast means increased security for Beatrice and the children."

Jed cast a sideways glance at his frail brother-in-law as he rode along beside him. He remembered his first impressions of Dudley from their introduction in 1810. Back then he was a sturdily built, thirtyish artillery officer with a firm and ready handshake. Two years in British Melville Island Prison had transformed the genial man into a frail, thin shadow of his former self, though his smile and spirit actually seemed to have increased in vitality since his ordeal.

"I must thank you and Beatrice for your hospitality. I'm sorry I haven't visited sooner. I'm afraid I've allowed—"

Dudley raised a hand to stop Jed. "No apologies a
know the good work you've been involved in since re
And no doubt your adjustment was not without its com,
I know mine was. Dear Beatrice nearly drove me to drink with no.
effusive efforts to nurse me. I wondered if things would ever feel
normal again, and they could not, of course, because neither of us
were the same people we were prior to the war. But we love who we
each have become even more than we loved one another before. And
so we moved on."

Jed heard an involuntary groan and was surprised to realize it
had come from him. "I've no right to complain. Your suffering was
far worse and far longer than mine."

Again, Dudley stopped him. "Suffering is suffering, Jed. When
we're in the crucible, it matters not how hot the fire grows. We all
are changed by it."

"You used your adversity to grow even wiser, my friend."

Dudley shrugged off the compliment. "I simply came home with
different questions."

"I returned with the old ones intensified." Jed swatted absently at
a low-hanging branch before him. "Perhaps that's why I had trouble
settling into my old life when I returned home. What you said makes
perfect sense. We came home changed, to wives who were also
changed—more independent and capable than those we left behind.
It wasn't an easy adjustment, but like you, Hannah and I made it
through the difficulties, and things are sweet again. I miss home, and
I'm delighted that's my next destination."

Dudley smiled. "On the next visit the canal will be able to bring
you more than halfway. The construction of the middle section, from
Utica to Seneca, is complete now, and navigation is set to commence
in May. When the canal is completed, people will be able to travel
one hundred miles in a day! These are amazing times, are they not?
I'm glad we survived to see it all."

"I knew Hannah would be vexed if she knew I was so near and failed
to stop by. I'll arrange a return trip with her and Johnny very soon."

"Myrna will give us each a tongue lashing if she is not included when the sisters meet."

They passed the sign that marked the edge of Palmyra Township on a wide street that boasted a notable abundance of shops and services. "It's a fine town," Jed remarked.

"We've almost three thousand residents now. We're no longer just a frontier village."

On the west end alone Jed noted an impressive array of stores intermingled with attractive frame houses, two blacksmiths' shops, a tavern, a stable, a saddler, and offices for a doctor, a lawyer, and two pharmacists. Dudley guided his horse off the main road to the next street on the north side of the town where a sluggish creek flowed, and then they rode three blocks further east. "This is what I wanted to show you. The canal will run parallel to Mud Creek until it crosses Main Street at the eastern end. The Jessup Basin will extend off the canal at the eastern end of town to permit barges to dock for loading and unloading. Two other basins will be located at the town center, and at the west end of town, where an elegant dry dock will also be built.

"Things will never be the same. We'll be a gateway to the west for settlers and for merchandise. But even good change has consequences. The canawlers will work hard on the canal all week, then come into town with their pockets filled with money and a hunger for entertainment. And not every newcomer passing through will be God-fearing, either. We'll have our work cut out for us to keep the peace and maintain the gentle tenor of the town."

"At least you'll have the revenue to hire more officers to enforce the law," Jed said.

Dudley chuckled thoughtfully. "We've got something better than that."

"And what is this secret weapon?"

"The Methodists' annual week-long Genesee Conference. Last July over a hundred Methodist circuit preachers from the western Hudson Valley and lower Canada convened just thirteen miles from here, in Vienna."

160

Jed huffed sarcastically. "That alone would be reason for me to move."

"Really? I attended," Dudley admitted. "I wanted to feel the power of dozens of men on fire with the word of God, all vying for men's souls. I'm not afraid to admit that I came home from the war with unanswered questions about God and heaven."

"I thought I had met God personally during my trials, but I have not been able to find Him again, in that same way, since my return. Did you find your answers at the conference?"

"Not all, but every possible denomination seems to be lit with a fire of revivalism in this area. I'm not afraid to search until I find my answers. Are you?"

The two men's eyes met, but Jed couldn't bear the soul-searching tenderness in Dudley's expression, so he changed the subject with, "Show me your store." He gave his horse a nudge and moved away, forcing Dudley to urge his own mount on.

Soon, they passed Snowden's Mercantile, where a brisk amount of traffic was passing through the doors. "How soon would you like me to begin shipping tobacco to you?" Jed asked.

"Full leaves won't serve me as well as rolled cigars." Dudley held an invisible cigar up to his lips and wriggled his fingers.

Jed groaned at Dudley's pantomime, and the tension was gone. "I'll see what I can do."

"I do hope you'll bring Hannah and Johnny here in the spring. I'd love my Rachel to meet her cousin, and by then the baby will be crawling. I'd cart my family south to Maryland, but it's getting harder and harder to hire enough help to leave the store these days, what with the canal company paying men eighty cents to a dollar a day. Who can compete with those wages? It's three times the wage most of the immigrant men earned in their homelands."

"The Erie Company's success has men reconsidering another canal near the Potomac."

"Ah, yes, the Patowmack," Dudley repeated, using the Indian name of the river that also served as the name of the first canal attempted in the Maryland–Virginia region. His voice was thoughtful and his gaze distant. "I rode a barge on the Patowmack Canal from Georgetown to Cumberland when making my way to Detroit."

"That's right. We bumped into one another in that little ivy-covered tavern. You were meeting Harry Lee for drinks. It was the last time I saw you."

"I left on a canal boat that evening. Weeks later, Detroit fell and all the regulars were marched to prison." A sense of melancholy suddenly hung in the air, but after a time Dudley chuckled, lightening the mood. "There's some irony in the fact that one canal led to my imprisonment, and another canal will lead to my financial independence."

Another silence ensued. "There's another connection," Jed finally said. "Light Horse Harry died last year."

"I didn't know . . ."

"He was recuperating at Dungeness Island off the coast of Georgia from the injuries he sustained during the Baltimore riot."

"The Baltimore Riot? I suppose that is another sad bit of history I need to catch up on. I missed so much while I was in prison. But dear old Harry! He was a good friend and a great patriot. I'm glad he lived to see the republic survive the war. I wonder what's become of Anne and the children. He was especially proud of little Robert E."

Jed didn't have the heart to burden Dudley with the sad details of the Lee family's economic misfortunes. "No prouder than you are of your family, and now with a new baby arriving any day."

"Yes. What a joy to be a father. Family is the only true treasure on earth, but good friends come close. My dear friend Stephen Mack led Beatrice and me to this town and its opportunities. He's preparing to move his family from Tunbridge to the Michigan Territory to join him. With my store and his westward trading posts, we've formed what I think will be a successful partnership. We won't see one another often, but fortunately we have the company of Stephen's sister's family—the Smiths—but I'm sure Hannah has told you about them."

"They have the boy who suffered with the typhoid infection."

"Yes, Joseph. He would have lost the leg had it not been for the good fortune of having a skilled surgeon in the area. He still has a limp, but even so, like his father and his older brothers, he's a hard worker, though a sober-minded child. I suppose like us, he's spent sufficient time in the crucible to have his own heart changed." Dudley pulled his horse up short. "Look at that. We're back home again. I jabbered on so I didn't even realize how far we'd come."

The men rode into the yard of the Snowdens' twelve-acre homestead and up to the hitching post by the porch of the red brick home. Beatrice and Dudley's three-year-old daughter, Rachel, ran out of the house to greet her father. "I've missed you, Papa, and Mama has missed you so much she is crying."

Dudley's brow furrowed. "She's crying?" Without waiting for an answer, he dismounted, tossed his mount's reins to Jed, and rushed into the house, leaving Jed in the company of Rachel. Minutes later, Dudley returned grim-faced. Beatrice followed him with a handkerchief pressed to her cheek. A piece of familiar stationery fluttered in the breeze as she extended her hand to Jed. "The postmaster rushed this out to us after you two left on your ride. It's from Bitty."

Jed dismounted, feeling the blood drain from his face and then from his limbs. "A note from Bitty?" Steadying himself against the hitching post with one hand, he took the letter with the other. The note was brief, but its few lines hit him like a rocket that threatened his world.

Dear Beatrice,

If you can, please come quick. Johnny fell from the barn loft and hurt himself bad. Jed is away and we don't know when he'll be back. We are at the hospital in Baltimore.

Bitty

★ ★ ★ ★ ★

Guilt and fear beat upon Jed along every foot of the race for home. He traded mounts when he could and bought new ones when he could not, spending twenty hours in the saddle each day during the two-hundred-mile, two-day race for Albany. He was beyond grateful when he reached the dock and found a steamboat departing for New York City within the hour. Dirty and nearly delirious from fatigue, he crawled into the luggage compartment to stretch out and rest, but the peace of sleep eluded him. Instead, he was haunted by images of Johnny, bent and broken on the barn floor, and of a grieving Hannah who was, once again, handling things without him.

He thought back to his conversation with Dudley over religion. He wanted to challenge his pious brother-in-law and ask him where God was the day Dudley and Beatrice's first child died, or the moment Johnny fell. At times Jed sensed the wisdom in teachings about faith, about God's timing, and the need for man to be long-suffering, but at other times they were unpalatable. There had to be answers, Jed concluded. There had to be more, and yet he continued to ask the same questions. Why did he? He knew. The truth was, he *did* believe in God.

During his ordeal on the *Iphigenia,* Jed had heard the voice of an angel, Jerome's unearthly voice, telling him to trust in God. Jed had followed the advice and had been delivered from his hell. And when he believed his cause was lost in the British military court, and prison was to be his lot, he had again been delivered. Yes, he had experienced the sweetness of God's intervention, but he had also seen the anguish when God's delivering hand was stayed. Why were the sick and dying men in Dartmoor Prison not delivered from their hell before death? Why had Jerome not been spared from death by a devil like Dupree? Why had it been necessary for Dudley to suffer for two years in Melville Island until the life was nearly sucked from him, before he saw relief? Jed didn't know, and still he marveled that his brother-in-law's faith seemed stronger than ever.

Jed knew if he planted corn, corn grew. But when he prayed, he couldn't be sure of the outcome. He didn't know if God would answer his prayer and spare Johnny. That singular uncertainty terrified him, and yet, after another long wrestle over these spiritual matters, he squeezed in between the barrels and crates, found a spot between two trunks, and lowered to his knees. Then he poured his heart out to God once more until he fell asleep crouched over that trunk.

A lurch, a bump, and calls for lines awakened Jed, who slowly untangled his tall frame and rose stiffly from the dirty floor. He ran a hand through his tangled hair and tidied his rumpled clothes before exiting onto the New York City pier. He quickly located a sleek clipper ship departing for Baltimore within the hour. His return had proceeded so perfectly he could almost see and feel God's merciful hand in the flawless aligning of his itinerary, and hope began easing the knots tangling him up inside.

CHAPTER 17

October 13, 1819
Washington, District of Columbia

Timothy Shepard brushed his coat sleeve, removing the dust picked up during his construction inspection of the magnificent Capitol Rotunda. He and his assistant moved through the nearly completed wings of the building, noting items that still needed repair. He examined the decorative capitals that crowned the columns of the reconstructed Senate Chambers. "Benjamin Latrobe may have been slow and expensive, but his details are exquisite."

"Are you not as pleased with Mr. Bulfinch's work since Mr. Latrobe's resignation?"

"To the contrary, I say God bless Charles Bulfinch for getting the Supreme Court, the House, and the Senate back in their chambers so quickly! And mark my words, this domed Rotunda will become the symbol of this republic. Both architects have served us well, and thanks to Mr. Bulfinch's speed, we'll see the government return to its proper home in December."

"How did the Congress ever seat everyone at Blodget's Hotel?" asked the young intern.

"Quarters were tight and none too comfortable on that first day the Congress reassembled after the Washington fires, made more so by the painful task of inquiring over the failures in the war. The brick Capitol constructed on First Street served the Congress well during the following years, but this was meant to be the home of the legislative and judicial branches of government. And it's even more magnificent than before."

"As is the President's House. All is right with the world again. And if all goes well next November, you'll no longer be the assistant to a U.S. senator, but a senator yourself."

Timothy ran his hand through his brown hair, boyishly mussing it. "I hope the Virginia State Legislature will be able to see past my shortcomings and into my heart. I love this nation. All I've ever wanted was to serve her, but I'm only an adopted son of Virginia since my marriage to Lucy five years ago, and they may pass me over on that fact alone."

"You're legally qualified."

Timothy raised a dubious eyebrow at the young man. "Family connections trump legalities, friend. My father has been a state senator in New York, which to some Virginians makes me a man of questionable heritage. Lucy's family is well connected, but I am still the dark horse." He shrugged. "But no matter. First things first. Let's get these notes to Senator Gregg so he can set Mr. Bulfinch's men on the final repairs."

Another intern raced up the steps, calling out, "Mr. Shepard! Mr. Shepard!"

The urgency in the boy's voice sent Timothy running. "Is it Lucy? Is the baby coming?"

"No, sir. Your wife sent me with this note about your friend—Mr. Pearson. I'm to tell you she's readying a bag for you, and that you should clear your schedule to travel immediately."

The seal on the note was broken, and Bitty's unfamiliar handwriting and signature took a few seconds to register with him. Now it all revealed the urgency of the event detailed.

After racing home to his wife and daughter, Timothy found a packed bag waiting by Lucy's feet. "You must hurry. The letter was sent to our old address, delaying its delivery."

"I'm not sure I should leave you now," he said as he took her in his arms.

"Of course you must. The baby isn't due for weeks, and Mother is near. Jed and Hannah have so little family—if they lose their child, they will need the strength of their dearest friends."

He gazed into her dark brown eyes, which seemed like two chestnuts against her rosy complexion. He couldn't believe his fortune at having won the hand of this good woman. He had been at a ball, earnestly courting Frannie Pearson, when this famed beauty passed by, dressed in pale yellow on the arm of her fiancé, an infantry captain. Timothy's fascination turned to love after her fiancé was killed in the war, and Frannie had cared enough for Timothy's happiness to decline his offer of marriage, advising him to seek Miss Bainbridge's hand instead.

He stooped to pick up Nellie, his daughter. "Maybe we should all go, Lucy."

"In my condition I'd be little help. I'd simply be another body to be housed and fed. And Frannie will surely be there. You haven't seen her since our wedding. You two need to speak."

He paled at the thought. "That will surely be awkward."

"It will be worse if I am there. But you might find things surprisingly cordial. She is rumored to enjoy a prestigious circle of friends, including a new romantic element in her life. Apparently, she has not one but two rivaling beaus—a possible Philadelphia mayoral candidate and a prestigious young Baltimore businessman named George Peabody. They met while he and Elisha Riggs were opening their Philadelphia office. Johns Hopkins is also her good friend."

Timothy peered curiously at his wife. "Frannie knows George Peabody, Elisha Riggs, and Johns Hopkins—three prospective titans of commerce? How do you know all this?"

Lucy began toying with her husband's tie. "No woman is more appealing than one nursing a broken heart, and I am not so confident or so naïve that I would not want to know what my husband's former love was up to. And I read the paper's society pages."

Timothy roared with laughter. "Very well then." He hugged his daughter as his mood sobered once again. "I'll go and see what service I can offer. The Pearsons' road has never been an easy one."

"Which is why you must go, even though you'll miss the first event for the candidates of next year's election."

"Perhaps a senate race is all a foolish lark. I could leave my post as Senator Gregg's aide and begin my law practice. It would be wise financially, and with the new baby—"

Lucy pressed a finger to his lips and smiled. "Don't abandon your dream. You love the government, and I love you. I'd rather wear last winter's bonnet and live with a happy, contented man than have my turn in every millinery shop in town. Now go and comfort your friends."

October 14, 1819
Holetown, Barbados

The sad news of the senator's injured son was the chatter among Baltimore's sailing community. The Willows port was a destination most local seaman knew, and Senator Pearson had personal connections to many of the ships in the harbor, having either sailed on or shipped his tobacco on most. A Baltimore ship captain who knew Senator Pearson carried the report of Johnny Pearson's injuries to his next destination—the Bahamas—where the Spanish captain Juan Cortez was docked. Juan immediately pulled up the sleek *Inez II*'s anchor and set sail for Barbados to tell Arthur Ramsey the tragic news.

The Holetown Port was familiar to Juan. Some fifteen years ago, when he was barely twenty, he had captained his deceased father's ship and its lawless crew to find the mercenary Dupree. Today he focused on the ever-changing shoreline that spread before him like a white ribbon strung along a sea of blue satin. Only patches of forest remained to testify of the island's past. European colonizers had deforested most of the land to make way for plantations of tobacco and sugar cane. Stephen Ramsey, Arthur's father, had grown rich from just such an enterprise, using a combination of free prison and slave labor.

Juan guided the ship past the public Holetown docks, where shirtless and barefooted black-skinned stevedores loaded and unloaded ships. Some were shackled; some bore whip marks across their broad backs. The legs of most were raw and bloody or scabbed. The crew of the *Inez II* silently stood along the starboard deck, observing the all-too-familiar scene.

The ship sailed a few hundred yards along Paynes Bay to the private dock of Ramsey's Ixora villa, where dozens of ratoon bundles of sugar-cane stalks were stacked and awaiting transport to a mill. Once the ship was docked, most of the crew, including Amado, the son of Juan's first mate and cousin Ferdinand, headed off to find Bridgetown and her many intrigues.

Ferdinand slapped a hand on Juan's shoulder. "Are we old now, Juan?"

Juan smiled and patted his cousin's hand. "No. Our mothers just raised us well, to be obedient and sober, to love the Lord, and to fear the Holy Father."

"It's brought us loyal wives and good children who wait for us to return from sea. Do not worry about the ship or the men. I'll be here. Go and see your friend."

"Very well. I'll be at Señor Ramsey's villa. If I leave Ixora, I'll send word.

Before Juan reached the dock, a chiseled, dark-skinned man of not more than twenty years greeted him and led him across the white sand and through the thick foliage, where nine broad fields of sugar canes rose in various stages of growth. His manner was confident and his accent clearly Jamaican, though his English was smooth and clear.

"We be harvestin' da last field a cane dis week. Mista Artur be wid da workers."

Juan suddenly felt overdressed in his black pants and coat as he walked in on a sea of scorched cane fields dotted with men and women clad in soiled white linen. He didn't recognize Arthur until he was practically upon him, since the man was dressed as a common field worker with only a broad-brimmed white hat to distinguish him from his employees, who wore bandanas on their heads. Juan was cheered by Arthur's strong gait. He had picked up weight, rounding out his previously gaunt face and bony frame, and though he carried a walking stick, he only leaned lightly upon it when he stopped to talk to a worker. When he saw Juan, he lifted the stick high and waved it in greeting.

"What brings you here, friend?" As soon as Arthur asked the question, the reason for the trip sobered the Spaniard.

"Can we go inside and speak privately?"

Arthur's previously bright smile faded to worry as he guided his friend to the white-stucco manor house glistening in the sun. A young maid dressed in a brightly colored dress quickly came out to the veranda. "Sit you down," she said as she placed a cup of tea before Arthur and a mug of rum before his guest.

"And could you bring some sandwiches, Anna?" Arthur asked.

She pinched his cheek and winked at him. "Anating for djou, Mistuh Artur."

Arthur shrugged sheepishly at Juan, who pointed a finger at his friend and laughed. "You're blushing. I thought you looked surprisingly improved. Now I understand why."

"No, no. It's not like that. They're just appreciative because I freed everyone the week I arrived four years ago. In return for kindness and respect, they treat me well."

Anna returned with a plate of fruit and saltfish. "Dis be good till da sandwiches come."

"Thank you, Anna." As she left, Arthur leaned back, studying Juan. "The news must be terrible to bring you this way. Have you seen Daniel Spencer again since locating him?"

"Weeks ago. He is growing into a fine young man—strong and confident. I overpaid him for his goods as you requested, and I'm proud to report you lost eighty pounds sterling in the transaction."

Arthur sipped at his tea and smiled. "I hope he will soon have enough money saved to pay his debt to his father and repair the rift between them."

Juan raised an eyebrow and shook his head. "I spoke with the viscount as we haggled over prices. He spoke only of a local young lady he hopes to win, and plans to attend medical school. He may not use the money in the way you envisioned."

A visible slump in Arthur's frame confirmed his distress. "Once you reported having seen Daniel at Salonika, I thought I had devised a perfect path to reconciliation. Now I see that I am no better at playing God than my dear friend Jed Pearson. Instead of hastening Daniel's return home, I am financing his escape. End it, Juan. Make no more purchases on my account."

Juan nodded as the mention of Pearson's name sobered his own countenance. "It is news of Jed Pearson's family that brings me here."

Arthur sagged into the back of his chair. "No."

"The Pearsons have suffered a painful tragedy. Their son was badly injured in a fall in late September, and from what I hear, his situation is grave."

Arthur winced and stared at the table. "My last conversation with Jed was about fathers and sons. I told him I hoped he and Johnny would never allow anything to cause them to become estranged from one another. This will break his and Hannah's hearts as nothing else could."

Juan nodded quietly and toyed with a leaf that blew onto the table. "This will pain Frannie as well, will it not?"

A new level of sorrow washed over Arthur. "Yes, they're very close. She will suffer too."

"Then she will need your support, eh? Let me carry you to Maryland on my *Inez II*. She is the fastest ship on the sea. Hurry and pack." Arthur didn't budge. "Surely you will come?" Juan implored.

Arthur's gaze drifted to an undisclosed spot in the sky, where it held for several seconds before falling back to the tabletop. "Frannie does need someone, but I am not that man. Instead of setting her free, I seem to have challenged her to a contest of self-deprecation, which she appears determined to win."

"She may turn to someone else for the comfort she seeks."

Arthur smiled sadly. "She has many beaus now, or so she said in her final letter." His index finger absently traced the water ring left on the table by his glass. "She was trying to make me jealous so I'd come to her. I almost did, several times, but now I see how this game must end. Her grief will cause her to open her heart to one of these men. It is as it should be."

"As you choose, then." Juan studied the scenery, desperate to find a new topic. "It is beautiful here, a paradise amongst so much slavery. I saw the scars on the backs and legs of the slaves at the docks today."

Moments passed before Arthur finally processed the change in the conversation. "The slavers brutally whip their workers' backs, then they send them into the cane fields without clothing to protect their arms and legs from the sharp leaves. They treat their animals better."

"I was once a part of that world. It has left a terrible stain on my soul."

Arthur blushed with embarrassment. "I didn't mean to say . . . You never chose that life, Juan. My father threatened to kill you if you refused to carry those slaves from Africa."

"Ultimately it always comes down to choice. I simply chose to save my life over protecting theirs. But you have sacrificed your life for others. You forfeit your desire for Frannie to give her something more, just as you've surrendered your life in Britain to free these people."

Arthur shrank back from the praise. "I am a shell of a man with a hollow life. I forfeited little in either case, but here I live in beauty where I can do some good for a time. But I've finished trying to control the outcome of events in people's lives, Juan. I released the McGowan family's inheritance money to them, and I've heard nothing from Mrs. McGowan since. I have no idea if my actions proved to be a blessing or the ruin of her and her family. I am finished playing God."

Arthur pushed back from the table in frustration, and turned to stare blankly at the sea. "I've made a disaster of my own life and added distress to all I've tried to help. I'm a failure in every possible way."

Juan leaned forward and grasped Arthur's hand. "Look around you. Look at these people, and then deny the good you've done."

"A random goodness here and there does not a good life make."

"Your life amounts to much more than a random series of good deeds, Arthur. You have a purpose. I believe you are being led to some thing or some work God has for you."

"You're mistaken, my friend."

"No. You are one of the finest men I have ever known. Your dreams were simple—to serve God and your country, to have a wife and family. I know you still love Francis Pearson. Because of love you gave her up. I do not believe God would close such a sacred door without opening another. Be faithful Arthur, and I believe God will yet show you your purpose."

Chapter 18

October 20, 1819
The Willows

The women took turns drizzling drops of broth into Johnny's mouth and caring for his needs, but as each day passed the child grew more gaunt and frail, until the twentieth of October when Hannah told Samuel the time had come to leave the hospital.

"I wish I could have done more, Hannah. I'm so sorry." His shoulders rounded as he looked at his empty hands. "If I had one miracle in these, you know I would give it to Johnny."

She walked to him, and his portly arms opened wide to her. "You've been wonderful, Samuel. I don't know how I would have gotten through this without you."

He patted her back gently, then rested his hand on the nape of her neck. "Despite all we know, so much rests in God's hands alone. I hope you find some comfort in knowing that it is somewhat of a miracle that Johnny is still with us. Try to see God's loving mercy in this added time He is giving you to say goodbye. I only pray Jed will arrive home in time."

Phillip made the arrangements to transport Johnny back to the Willows on the *Eagle*. The ship reached the Willows dock on the afternoon of October twenty-first. A wagon was quickly summoned, and all forty-three Willows residents arrived and lined the lane in a show of support.

After settling Johnny in, Hannah closed the door to her boy's room and crawled into bed beside him, holding him in her arms and savoring every second of his little head tucked into the crook of her neck. She hadn't thought much about the child growing within her since Johnny's fall. In fact, she hadn't told anyone she was expecting. It would wait until Jed arrived.

Frannie was leaning against the porch, observing Phillip's distress over the condition of his hands as he came up from the barn. He caught her eyeing him. "I'm not much of a farmer," he said.

"You have other talents."

"Come walk with me and let's see if one of them is brightening your smile." Reluctantly, she agreed, and they strolled down to the shore, where she instructed him in the fine art of rock skipping. He paused mid-throw and said, "I need to return to Philadelphia for a few days."

She tried to appear nonchalant about the comment. "You've been away far too long."

Phillip let his rock fall to the ground. "Must you be so indifferent? I realize you are trying to be stalwart for Hannah, but can't you admit you'll miss me a little?"

"Please do not ask me to think of romance or the future now, Phillip."

He stepped away from her and rubbed his fingers deep into his temples. "Forgive me. I won't distract you further. I'll pack my things and catch the next ship to Baltimore."

As he strode away, Frannie picked up a handful of stones and tossed them all into the water in a vent of frustration. She heard the familiar clop of a horse. When she turned she found Timothy Shepard astride a bay, studying her with disappointment in his eyes. "And how long have you been lurking in the thicket?" she asked coolly.

"Long enough to watch you spurn another suitor. And I wasn't lurking. I didn't want to disturb you."

She picked up another stone and hurled it as far as she could into the middle of the river.

"No one can question your ability to throw things away, but I beg you, don't cast another opportunity for happiness away as easily as that stone."

Her head swung slowly while she delivered a stinging glare. "It appears marriage agrees with you."

"I won't apologize for being happy. We both know you didn't love me, nor do you now. And I am happy, Frannie. I want the same for you. Everyone does—except you, it seems."

She raised her skirts a few inches and began storming away from him, but Timothy was determined to say his piece. "Lucy urged me to come here to support Jed and Hannah in this terrible time, but perhaps you're the one who most needs my help. Don't squander this chance, Frannie, please. Go after him." He slid from his horse and caught up with her. When he reached her he attempted to grasp her arm, but she jerked free of him. "Fine!" he tossed back. "Don't tell me you're still pining after Arthur Ramsey."

The mere mention of Arthur's name seemed to energize her anger. "You don't understand. You never did."

"I do understand. It's about loyalty and fidelity, and about devotion against all odds. It's about the type of allegiance others denied you in your hours of need—your parents and Frederick." Then Timothy added soberly, "And me. But you've passed the test, Francis. No one can ever question your constancy. You're in pain. What can your ghost do for you now? Was he the one who came to you? The one who offered you comfort and love? For once, admit that you miss the company and companionship he denies you, and drink up what this man is offering you."

Myrna was on the porch, simultaneously watching the interchange between Frannie and Timothy, and watching as Jack helped Phillip load his bags into the wagon. Frannie called out to her as she approached, asking, "Myrna, will you please show Mr. Shepard inside after he tends to his horse?"

As Myrna and Timothy disappeared into the house, Jack caught the message and quickly exited as well, leaving Frannie and Phillip alone and awkward. She noted the mud on the only pair of boots he had brought, testifying that he had rushed to her side in haste, and that he was leaving with equal hurry. She looked at the chipped and soiled nails on the future politician's normally manicured hands and smiled.

"You needn't have seen me off," Phillip said. "I was wrong to press you when you're rightfully torn. We'll speak when you return to Philadelphia."

Frannie took his hand. "I will miss you . . . very much." She moved to stand close to him and whispered, "You're a dear man, Phillip." And then she kissed him.

After the wagon departed, she wrote a letter to Arthur detailing the tragedy with Johnny and how desperately she had needed someone to lean on. In closing she said simply:

> *I've met someone, and I am finally going to grant the last request you made to me, at the port of Liverpool five years ago. I choose to be happy, Arthur. I wish you the same.*

After Jed reached Baltimore and discovered his family had returned to the Willows, the Lord's mercy blessed him again, with a moonlit night safe for sailing. He arrived home, bedraggled and exhausted, sometime after two in the morning. He ran from the docks, past the sentries, and into the house without a word, ignoring the barking dogs, who quieted as soon as they caught his scent. A beam of moonlight cut across the bed, displaying Hannah there holding a fragile being that looked like a marionette of their son. Bone-thin and pallid, he lay somewhat rigid in her arms, his face so gaunt Jed's shock came out as a moan that awakened his wife.

Hannah slipped from the child's bed and flew to Jed's arms without uttering a word, though her groan of relief spoke volumes to him of her suffering. They clung to each other and cried over their boy, then crawled in bed with him nestled carefully between them until sleep overtook them.

Sometime later Jed awakened, feeling his wife's finger wiping traces of moisture from his eyes. A flood of apologies ushered forth as each parent voiced responsibility for the situation. On and on, the emotional flogging went until Jed admitted the real source of his disappointment. "I prayed so hard—every mile, every moment. Where is the blessing?"

Hannah swallowed hard and sat up. "This is it. You're here with me, together, and God allowed Johnny to live long enough for you to say goodbye."

Jed rose and moved to the window in silence. Moments passed before he felt Hannah's trembling hand on his shoulder. His head bent and he rubbed his cheek over the softness of her skin. "It's not enough. I want more." His words eked out as broken as a child's.

"I know," she replied as she stepped into his arms.

"What good is faith if this is the hollow reward you get for trying to live well?"

Hannah lifted her eyes to meet Jed's. "Faith is not currency. We don't do good to collect rewards to buy what blessing we want. It gives us courage and hope to face what comes."

"Hope of what? Please help me understand."

"Of answers in heaven, I suppose. I don't know for certain. I can only tell you what I feel, and I feel a sense of assurance and love, Jed, and peace I didn't have days ago. I know they are from God, helping me to bear this. Spend time with Johnny, and pray for these things, and you'll feel them too."

She stepped away and made a soft turn in the room, scanning its interior. "Can't you feel it, Jed? There's something special, something sacred in here, as if unseen angels are present. I began to feel it in the hospital. I watched Johnny wither, day by day, and I listened to the rattle in his breathing and the moans he makes, and I was terrified, but not anymore. Now I have peace that he's not alone. And I've felt his joy, as if his spirit is already somewhere beautiful and joyous, leaving this shell behind to give us time to accept his passing. But I do have one terrible fear. Do you realize we never had Johnny baptized? Reverend Myers made me promise to have the ordinance performed, but Johnny fell before I could. I want to attend to that today." Hannah's face had a glow to it, attesting to the depth of her belief in the concepts she had espoused.

Knowing Johnny's breathing grew more shallow with every moment, Jed asked Abel to fetch a reverend to administer the rite of baptism. While a pitcher of water was brought and the clergyman was organizing himself, little Johnny slipped away, and the reverend stopped before pronouncing the sacred words.

"I'm very sorry, madam. I'll give the child last rites, but I cannot baptize a dead child."

"But you must! What of that verse in the fifteenth chapter of Corinthians? Please!"

The reverend's empathy disappeared at the mention of such a request, and he began packing up his things. "There is nothing in current liturgy for such a practice. It would be heresy."

"Please do not leave here with him unbaptized."

"It is already too late, I'm afraid." And with that, the reverend left.

Countless people visited to pay their respects on the morning of the funeral. Jed noted that the tension in Hannah's face had shifted into understandable sadness. When he asked how she was, she replied, "I keep telling myself, God knows we tried to see to Johnny's baptism."

In the afternoon, the mourners gathered at the Willows cemetery, where Jed and Hannah buried their son beside so many others they loved. The grim words spoken by the clergyman hurled Hannah back into despair. Jed cradled her protectively against him and took her upstairs to rest.

She cried herself to sleep in his arms, but restlessness drove him from the bed to the front porch, where he heard the steady approach of a team of horses. He peered through the darkness and saw a wagon rolling up the lane. Several seconds passed before he could identify the driver. A chill began in his chest as he prayed God would not bring more trouble to this sorry house this day.

The darkness obscured the travelers' faces, but Jed could see the driver jump down from the wagon, where a woman sat cradling a baby. He watched as the man removed his hat, clutching it in his hands and twisting it nervously. Another head popped out from beneath blankets in the wagon bed. Light reflected moistness in the man's eyes, and then Jed heard the man speak in a thick Irish brogue. "We came as soon as we heard, Jed. I'm sorry—I'm so awfully sorry. God bless ya."

Jed spread his arms wide, moved to Markus O'Malley, and swept him into his embrace. "Forgive me, Markus. I was a fool."

"There's nothin' to forgive. I just needed to get home ta my brother."

CHAPTER 19

Winter/Spring 1820
The Willows

The first few weeks following Johnny's death slogged by like a forced march. Myrna left first, which was actually a relief to Hannah, who frequently found herself comforting and entertaining her older sister. Frannie's departure hit Jed and Hannah much harder, but after a month's absence from her beau, her businesses, and her career, her return to Philadelphia was critical. Jed and Hannah found great comfort in Markus and Jenny's return, and in work that wearied them so they could sleep, so every seasonal task and every neglected chore was attended to.

The men busied themselves with seeding the winter wheat, digging the potatoes, hunting for rabbit and deer, and slaughtering twenty hogs from which they rendered hams, middlings, sausages, and both salted and smoked pork. When the smokehouses were full, they took an excursion to the bay to rake oysters and hunt ducks. In between all this, they raised a new house for Markus and Jenny on Markus's tract of Willows land.

Hannah and the women kept equally occupied with autumn's tasks. During the day they churned butter, made cheese, pickled oysters, rendered lard, and put up pear preserves. At night they laid out linsey and flannel and cut out the winter clothes. All the while, the women urged Hannah to share the news of the expected child with Jed, but she resisted, fearing neither of them were prepared for the upheaval of emotions the announcement would cause.

On the evening of November twenty-first, a bright light shot across the sky with unimaginable velocity, moving from east to west.

"Make a wish! It's a shooting star," Markus said.

Everyone's eyes were riveted on the sight until the ball of light fell from their view. The disappearance was followed by a shattering explosion that shook the home's porch like an earthquake. The frightened children cried out, "It's a rocket!" as they grabbed for their mothers' skirts.

"No, no," Jed assured. "It's a meteorite—a rock falling from the atmosphere. As Markus said, some see it as a sign of good fortune."

Jed brushed Hannah's long, dark hair that night, noticing how quiet the evenings had become—no lively chatter about Johnny's doings that day, no plans being made for the next. "Did you make a wish on the star tonight?" he asked.

"No, it was gone before I thought about it."

The motion of the brushing stalled as he recalled his wish. "I did, but I can't tell you what it was or the wish won't come true." He kissed her cheek and was rewarded with a coy smile.

"Good night," she said, then rose and slid into bed. Moments later she felt his body slide in beside hers. She watched the light fade as he turned down the lamp. His breathing didn't settle into the lazy cadence of sleep, and though she knew he was awake, she pretended not to be.

Something awakened Hannah in the dark of that next November morning. She rolled onto her back and looked over at Jed, who appeared to still be asleep, as she acknowledged the first flutters of life within her. She laid her hands gently over the spot in her belly, and when the subtle internal tickle repeated, inexpressible joy surged through her, rekindling the awe of motherhood that had all but been extinguished by Johnny's death. She lay there for several minutes, marveling at the gift she had all but ignored.

Jed rose up on one elbow, his hair in utter disarray, and caught her smiling. "It's as cold as the icehouse in here, yet you're grinning from ear to ear." He stood and threw his wrapper around him. "You were just lying there, waiting for me to stoke the fire, weren't you?"

She studied the toll the war and the loss of Johnny had taken on her young husband. His shoulders had regained the breadth and strength of his youth after the damage the war had wrought, but at only thirty years, his hair was already beginning to gray at the temples, and his smile was a rare occurrence. But it was the dullness in his eyes that most worried her, as if he were living life with his eyes half closed. "I believe it was your turn, Mr. Pearson."

Jed added a log, which quickly brightened the darkened room. "First one up tends the fire, Mrs. Pearson. House rules." He hurried back to bed and quickly burrowed beneath the quilt.

Another flutter caught her off guard, and her eyes widened in surprise. Again, she smiled.

Jed looked at her oddly, and she knew he realized her mood was about something more than the fire. "What?" he asked softly as he brushed her long, dark hair away from her shoulder, made bare by the slipping of her gown. Fear furrowed his brow. "Are you well?"

Hannah took his hand and moved it to her belly. "Soon you will be able to feel it too."

"Feel what?" he asked as his alarm increased.

"The quickening of life in our child."

He remained motionless except for the slight tilting of his head. "Another child? We're having another child?"

Her nod was subdued as the word "another" harrowed up images of Johnny's beautiful, absent face. "In the spring. Late March or early April."

Jed closed his eyes and pulled her so near to him she couldn't see his face to read his expression. "You must have known this for weeks. Why haven't you told me?"

"Whatever confusing feelings you're feeling right now, I've struggled with them as well, wondering if I could love this child as much as I loved Johnny, and feeling guilty for even carrying another baby so soon." She wriggled free of Jed's embrace, barely able to meet his eyes. "I found out soon after you left, but I thought I was carrying a brother or sister to grow alongside our boy, not a child to fill empty arms after Johnny was gone."

Jed cupped his hand along her cheek. "And yet I caught you smiling."

"Because I do love this baby, Jed. I already love it. Is that wrong of me?"

Cradling her against him, he assured her, "Oh, no, sweetness. Don't let fear rob you of your happiness. I've longed to see the light return to those sad green eyes. No child will ever replace Johnny, nor will we ever stop loving or missing him, but we'll make room in our hearts to love this new baby."

"Then you're happy about the news?"

His voice was raspy with emotion. "It was my secret wish last night."

They shared the news that Hannah was expecting another child, though their happiness was more restrained than it had been with Johnny. With the bulk of the Willows' winter preparations completed, Hannah and Jed packed their things and headed their carriage down the lane on the road to Annapolis before the Maryland General Assembly prepared to meet.

A heavy melancholy set in as the couple exited Willows land. Hannah felt it immediately, and she struggled to fill the silence with conversation. "I suppose we'll need to find a new house for next year's session, since the Murphys are returning to the States and will want theirs back."

"You're assuming I'll still be a senator," Jed said.

"Of course you will. Your constituents adore you."

"I haven't decided whether I want it anymore, Hannah."

She cocked her head toward him. "What? But your plans, your dreams—"

"I have new dreams as well. *Our* dreams. Smaller in some ways, but just as important." He took her hand and placed a kiss there. "Competing factions are beginning to divide the local legislature. Everyone expects President Monroe to enjoy a sweeping re-election, but the same factions splitting our state are beginning on the federal level as new parties rise and parties rally to their own agendas instead of the nation's. I'll watch and see what direction things take. Perhaps we'll find a better way to serve."

Except for a two-week return to the Willows for the holidays, Jed and Hannah spent the next three months in the bustling city of Annapolis, shopping, dining, and enjoying the entertainment it afforded. The Annapolis newspaper was fascinated with the Pearsons, who kept to themselves and seemed to never be more than an arm's distance from one another after the legislature closed each day. From dredging up the painful details of Johnny's death, to the effusive excitement about the coming child, the writers managed to spread the couple's lives across their printed pages each week until Jed was as anxious to leave the area as Hannah.

Over the course of the preceding ninety days, he had watched new political parties arise both in the state and in nearby Washington, playing tug-of-war over issues and working the citizenry into a lather. After a long discussion, he and Hannah had their decision.

The gavel fell in the State House on February nineteenth. As Jed attempted to make a hasty exit from the session, he was approached by members of various parties hoping to sway him toward their differing camps. Listening to the diverse arguments, he felt he was looking into a crystal ball and getting a glimpse of what would befall the young nation. It only strengthened his resolve when a reporter stood on the steps of the state house, pressing him for a decision regarding his political intentions.

Pencils scribbled wildly as he replied, "I cannot confirm my interest in re-election without first expressing my gravest concerns over the dissensions I see erupting within the ranks of our state and national leadership. This does not serve the interests of the citizenry. We would all be wise to re-read President Washington's Farewell Address and his counsel on the matter, that the disorders and miseries which result in party politics cause men to seek security in individuals rather than in the constitutionally derived powers of government, therefore threatening public liberty. We would be wise to discourage and restrain such party divisiveness."

Hannah watched the scene from the stoop of their Annapolis home. Jed swept her inside when he arrived, away from the public crush of those who wanted to question him further.

"I heard what you said to them. This is exactly why you need to remain. You are a voice of reason, a friend of the Constitution and the Bill of Rights. Your point of view is important."

"And you're certain you want me to do this? Now, with the baby coming?"

"Very certain. It's who you are, Jed. It's who I want our child to look up to."

He pulled her to him and rested his chin on her head for a moment. "You're a strong, good woman, Hannah. I've always known it, though never more clearly than in the past few months. But this must be our new political arrangement—we do it together, all of it. And from now on, wherever I go, we go together. Agreed?"

She smiled broadly. "I doubt the assembly will look kindly upon a baby in their session."

"All right," he said with a laugh. "You're exempted from meetings, but beside me on everything else."

The next day, Jack and Markus arrived with a wagon to carry all the Pearsons' belongings back to the Willows. Jed and Hannah spent a few weeks on the farm before they moved to their Baltimore home, a residence Jed had inherited from his parents, to be near Samuel and the hospital, should Hannah's delivery warrant such intervention.

The family butler, sixty-five-year-old Bartholomew, his wife Lily, and their adult daughter and her husband—Sarah and Elijah— lived at the residence year round. When they received word that a baby would be born in the home, the women prepared a perfect nursery, complete with hand-made quilts and embroidered gowns. These were added to the complete new layette Hannah had made for this child to avoid using Johnny's things and dredging up memories that were still too tender.

One other preparation eclipsed all others in importance—that of finding a church and a pastor to bless this new baby. The Pearsons attended a different church each week until Hannah found one with doctrine she found comfortable.

"Comfortable?" Jed scratched his head in wonder. "We're not shopping for a settee, Hannah. We're choosing a religion, a dogma within which to raise our child. Shouldn't we have some attachment to it stronger than comfort?"

"The pastor was congenial, and his preaching was my favorite of all those we attended, yet I question why they speak more about the fear of God than they do of His love. This preacher at least struck a balance."

"But he won't be our preacher when we return to the Willows."

"Then we'll begin searching again when we get home," she snapped. Momentarily contrite, she turned her lumbering body around. "I'm sorry. I just want to be sure this child is christened as soon as possible, in case—"

Jed took her into his arms and calmed her. "I'll speak with him right away."

As with Johnny, the onset of Hannah's labor began prematurely. On that snowy March night, Jed sent Elijah for Samuel while he remained by Hannah's side, holding her hand and daubing her brow with a cool sponge. When the delivery seemed imminent, Lily and Sarah urged him to leave but he refused, vowing not to go until

Samuel arrived. Hannah watched the surreal mix of wonder and terror that struck him each time the women grabbed her hands to support her through a body-knotting contraction.

Samuel fought his way through the accumulated snow and arrived in a panic, obviously fearing a repeat of Hannah's last delivery, but it was not to be so. Instead, Samuel was greeted with an air-splitting wail that reset the pace of his worried heart to normal. When he tried to examine the tiny boy, he was met with the kick and punch of a prizefighter, which sent the good doctor off in a string of raucous, relief-filled laughter, made all the more joyous when he was able to declare both mother and child to be perfect in every way. Despite his assurance that all was well, Jed pressed Samuel to repeat the blessed report three times before allowing him to leave.

Again, the gift of motherhood awed Hannah, and she was equally awed by her husband's reaction to the miracle of the tiny child's birth.

"Look at all that hair!" he marveled.

Hannah only saw how precisely the baby resembled Johnny on the day of his birth.

Jed barely left his little family's side, sharing Hannah's waking hours marveling over their son, whom they named James Edward. Frequently she would awaken to find Jed marveling just as dreamily over her.

Couriers were sent to deliver the blessed news to Frannie in Philadelphia, to Beatrice in Palmyra, to Myrna, who lived only a few blocks away, and to their loved ones at the Willows. Beatrice and Dudley were unable to attend, but everyone else gathered on the second Sunday after James's birth for his christening. They stayed for days, filling the house with laughter and love, taking turns swooning over the baby, and Frannie's engagement ring, given to her by Phillip St. Clair. Her fiancé encouraged everyone's efforts to press her to declare a wedding date, a thing she would not do. Hannah stood solidly as her defender, whispering quietly in her sister-in-law's ear that she needn't forget the past and move forward until she was ready.

The statement of support for Frannie was actually a summary of the conflict afflicting Hannah's own happiness. For the first few weeks after James's birth, her joy was full. She thought she had never felt so happy, never known such peace, but as each day passed and the company disbanded, a heaviness began suffocating those joyful feelings, leaving her drowning in a relapse of grief Jed was powerless to relieve. But she knew who could.

She was in a state of tearful melancholy when she said to him, "I need to see Beatrice, Jed. Please take me to New York."

"Travel now? With the baby?"

"Please, Jed. Besides you, Beatrice is the closest person to me. Only she knows the anguish of a mother who has lost a child. I need her. Please understand."

Jed struggled to remain calm. "I do understand, but the timing, Hannah. Be reasonable. I could do nothing to protect you when you delivered Johnny, but I can and I must do all I can to keep you and James both safe this time. I promise we'll go to New York this summer, when the baby is older and the weather more temperate."

"You know I wouldn't ask if I didn't feel such a sense of urgency. Please, Jed. It will be all right—I know it will. I can't explain it more than this."

She watched her sensible husband wrestle over her nonsensical plea, knowing the flailing he would inflict upon himself if anything went awry. But in her heart she knew it would not. As sure as her instincts had ever told her anything, she knew she needed to hurry to Beatrice.

Jed studied her face, silently pleading with her to withdraw the request. When she did not, he said simply, "I'll make some inquiries regarding the weather and route. You add a line in that letter imploring Beatrice to arrange good medical care when we arrive. I want everything in place should we require it. And you must promise to trust my final judgment on this, agreed?"

She hugged him tight. "Of course I will, but I know you'll find a way."

In mid April they set out on Jed's intricately planned itinerary, with Hannah's agreement that at any sign of bad weather or ill health they would stop in whatever city they were in and wait out the trial. They set out on a sleek Baltimore clipper ship that slipped through the water like a skater on ice, depositing them in the New York City harbor in less than six days, which Hannah called a miraculous feat of the modern world. She and James had borne the trip better than her fretful and overly protective husband, who tried to lure her into resting on dry land for a few days with tempting offers of fine cuisine and entertainment. But Hannah's heart was set on reaching Beatrice, so the Pearsons boarded the next arriving steamboat in Robert Fulton's eight-ship Hudson River fleet, for the trip to Albany. Every new sight and sound revived Hannah's mellowed spirit, and Jed began to relax and enjoy the adventure with her.

After a long winter that had lived up to the region's reputation for snow and cold, spring had finally kissed the area with more temperate weather. The Mohawk River was still too blocked with ice flow to make for safe travel, so at Albany, the Pearsons booked passage on a coach, which slogged along the muddy, rut-filled river path.

The ice had melted sufficiently to allow traffic on the water at Utica, so the Pearsons boarded a seventy-foot passengers-only packet boat that, unlike its cargo-carrying counterparts, was pulled by three draft horses that moved along the towpath on the man-made portion of the canal. This venue offered exquisite views of the dense pine forests, budding trees, and wildlife along New York's western frontier. Nature's show was magnificent, and adding to that beauty was the lulling song of the canal-boat drivers, whose sing-song commands directed traffic on the waterway. The ride was restful and smooth, with accommodations suited to a genteel clientele.

Small coal stoves heated the two main cabins, though passengers still pulled out warm, thick quilts as needed. Though the boats had hanging berths for sleeping, the Pearsons opted to disembark at lock towns each night and stay in cozy inns. All in all, the $3.50 ticket price proved to be a delightful two-day investment.

The canal ran through Rome and would soon be open for travel clear through to Seneca, but as it was not yet available, travelers were forced to debark and book passage on a jostling, springless stagecoach for the remaining 105 bumpy miles of the journey. The cost of a ticket was $3.00, and the ride was said to require only fourteen hours in good weather, but the soft, sloppy roads, which were more like paths, turned the trip into a three-day, bone-jarring endurance trial that left the passengers longing for the canal boats once more.

Hannah was beyond relieved when the stagecoach driver announced they were finally in Palmyra. Jed left his wife and baby at the station while he walked to Dudley's store to alert him of their arrival. Hannah was working the feeling back into her numbed limbs when she noticed a wagon and team rolling her way. Jed was a passenger in the driver's box, but she didn't know the driver in the white shirt, black pants, and suspenders. Then she realized to her sorrow that the wisp of a man was Dudley.

None of Jed's warnings had prepared her for the visible toll the war had taken on the once-sturdy, energetic captain. It had been eight years since she had last seen Dudley, before he had been captured at Detroit and imprisoned at the start of the war. His head was nearly bald now, and it appeared he had aged three years for every one that had passed, until at less than forty years, he looked more than fifty. Still, once her initial shock settled, Hannah couldn't deny the fatherly love shining in his eyes as he looked at her.

She began walking toward the wagon, her speed increasing as she closed the distance. For a second she remembered how she once blamed Dudley for stealing Beatrice away from her, leaving her and Myrna behind in their dismal home. In reality he had rescued them, as well, allowing his and Beatrice's home to be a respite from their crazed mother. Now, Dudley slipped to the ground and called out, "My dearest Hannah!"

Shifting James to her side, she reached her arm around her brother-in-law's thin neck and hugged him tight. "I've missed you so terribly, Dudley. I prayed for you every day."

"And we, you," he replied with a sniff. After a time, he released her and stepped back. "Let me look at you." He studied her face until his eyes became moist. "Where a pretty debutante once stood, a beautiful woman now stands. How can that be?"

Hannah didn't feel beautiful, with her pinned hair falling out from beneath her bonnet, and her boots and the hem of her green traveling suit caked with mud, but she received the compliment warmly. "I'm still your little sister—always," she said as she returned to his arms.

"Always."

A loud squeal erupted. "Dudley, I want you to meet our son—James Edward Pearson."

"Hello, James." Dudley offered a quivering smile. "He's a fine son. A very fine son. We've each known some hardship, haven't we? But the good Lord has seen us through and reunited us. I truly thank Him for that. Come, let's get you to Beatrice. We'd received word about the terrible state of the roads and wondered whether you'd make it through."

They loaded into the wagon for an equally emotional scene at the Snowden home. Beatrice rushed from the house with her hungry arms waiting to enfold her sister. Hannah marveled that her oldest sister was even more lovely at thirty-eight than she had been in her youth. Both women soon retired to the house, and when the initial crush of excitement passed, the babies were laid down to nap, while the older children were sent outside to play with their father and uncle so the women could prepare the evening meal.

"What is Myrna up to these days?" Beatrice asked. "She rarely writes anymore, and when she does the letters seem a bit, well, fabricated. One would think she was running Baltimore herself."

Hannah responded with a tight-lipped smile. "For once I am able to report that her life really is as grand as she says. She began a women's auxiliary at the hospital. Our friend, Dr. Renfro, tells us she has raised a small fortune in contributions—enough to add a new wing to the facility—but he also tells me that after working closely with her, he has no desire for a wife."

Beatrice laughed until her face grew red, but then the conversation became stilted. The two sisters were peeling potatoes when Beatrice said, "You'll feel much better once you speak of it." Hannah returned her questioning gaze, and Beatrice added, "I know you. You still chew your lip when you're worrying over something."

"I didn't realize . . ." Hannah's hand rose to her mouth and remained pressed there for a moment as she struggled over whether to raise the tender topic. "Tell me, did you have . . . difficulty loving Rachel? I mean after—"

"—losing my first baby?" Beatrice finished.

Hannah's chin dropped. "Yes. I feel like a terrible mother when I look at James and see Johnny. And then I feel guilty when I don't. Did you ever feel that way?"

Both women's hands stilled. Hannah slipped into a chair and stared at hers, whereupon Beatrice placed a loving hand on her sister's shoulder. "I did for a long time, though I'm grateful to report that the guilt eases. But you have no reason for such feelings."

"Don't I? I planted the fear in Johnny that caused him to panic and fall."

Beatrice brushed the comment away with a knowing smile. "You were trying to protect him. That's what mothers do. I lost my child by being foolhardy, and still God forgave me."

Something in her voice caught Hannah's attention and caused her to study her sister's face. "Yes, I can see it in your face. You've found your peace."

Beatrice moved past the comment, taking Hannah's hands. "Don't allow the past to cause you to miss a moment of James's life, and don't be afraid to love him as fully as you did Johnny." She stood and flushed with embarrassment. "But why am I telling you all this? You're the spiritual one in the family. What has God been telling you?"

"He told me to come to you, just as quickly as I could."

Beatrice's brows knitted together. "To come to *me*, or to come *here?*"

194

"What do you mean?"

Before Beatrice could answer, the men returned and the conversation was suspended. Later that night after the children were tucked into bed, the four adults retired to the parlor, where lovely European and unique frontier items filled the room, creating the most eclectic décor Hannah had ever seen. A crimson Brussels carpet with thick loops lay in the center of the floor before a green Chippendale sofa, while a bearskin rug hung across an entire wall, and oil lamps topped tables resting upon four vertically mounted deer legs. The overall look was a fascinating blend of American and European styles, and the Pearsons shared their enthusiastic opinions with their hosts.

"The benefits of partnering with Stephen Mack," explained Dudley as he urged Jed and Hannah to sit. "He's truly a pioneer on the frontier, but he still loves the finer things of life."

"He's been a good friend to you," Jed remarked. "I'm glad your service in the war at least brought you one good thing."

Dudley's glance shot to Beatrice. "Much more than one, wouldn't you say, my dear?" She touched his hand and he continued. "I venture the war will be recorded very differently by men of differing experiences. I will record it as the spiritual turning point in my life. And if I were given the chance to get those months in Melville Island back but lose what I learned there, I would refuse, and go through it all again to hold on to that knowledge."

Intrigued, Jed leaned forward. "And what did you learn?"

"A great deal about many things. I saw great suffering, but I also saw great majesty there. At times, when men hungered for a simple crust of bread, I saw them give it freely to satisfy another's need. And there were other acts of tremendous compassion extended by otherwise hardened men. We were all changed at Melville. Strangers became brothers, and we understood governing in a sacred context, as a means of caring for the weak while strengthening them. We thought more of the next world than of this one. God became as real to us as you are sitting there, and our faith became as accessible to us as this chair. That is what Melville taught me."

His closing words were soft and reverent, and the mood hung in the air like maple wood smoke, a sweet breathable essence that warmed the insides while slowly settling over everyone.

"Jed, I told you I came home with different questions. They concerned the question of baptism. So many of the men at Melville feared they would die having never attended to this, and sadly, many did. Upon their death beds we made a pact that those of us who survived prison would search for a way to save our fallen comrades' souls." Dudley took Beatrice's hand. "Little did I know I had a son in need of the same mercy." He looked to Hannah. "I know you understand."

Tears sprang to Hannah's eyes, though her voice was strong as she asked, "Do you have an answer? The pastors we've spoken with have crushed our hope for such a mercy."

"We've had the same response, but my heart told me there had to be another answer, particularly for innocent children. I couldn't reconcile a God who would condemn a child's soul because of a parent's error."

Hannah nearly bolted from her seat. "Neither could I! I felt peace wash over me at Johnny's graveside, easing my worry."

"Dudley, have you found a minister who confirms these feelings?" Jed asked.

Again Dudley looked to Beatrice. "No. Not yet. But our hope is stronger than ever."

"Have you read something? Have the synods released some new doctrine?"

"Nothing as concrete as that. But where others fear a punitive God, I see the God of love. Yes, He's also a God of law and justice, but isn't being *just* the essence of justice? I think we have somehow lost this aspect of His nature in our religious teachings. There must be something that reconciles the God of these two testaments, since we are taught He is the one true God."

"I have said as much to Hannah." Jed's hand shot forward, emphasizing his point. "But what is the answer if no church teaches such things?"

"Not yet, but do you believe in miracles, Jed?"

Growing suddenly quiet, Jed settled deep against the sofa.

"There's been a stir in town in the last few days," Dudley began. "One of the preachers told a member of his congregation about a local boy who has been wrestling with his indecision over churches and their various doctrines. This lad went into a grove seeking privacy to pray for an answer to his questions, and he claims to have had a vision. The preacher dismisses him as a devil-possessed dreamer, but I think they should hear him out."

Hannah watched Jed's dubious expression from the corner of her eye as she asked Dudley, "What kind of vision did he claim to have?"

Dudley also studied Jed's face before responding. "He saw the Father and the Son."

Jed huffed, and his body relaxed like an empty bellows. "I thought you were being serious."

Dudley rushed in, hands raised, as if holding back the tide of disbelief. "I'm fully serious, Jed. Hear me out. Remember the Genesee Conference—the religious gathering of Methodist preachers that occurs each summer? Beatrice and I attended to see if we would hear something that would ease our hearts. We attended four or five sermons in a single day, but one on the program caught our attention. It was given by a preacher named George Lane, whose very discourse was titled, 'What Church Shall I Join?' I saw the boy we speak of attending Lane's sermon, and I knew by his face he was as affected by the preacher's words as I."

Jed leaned back, tipping his head to the side. "And what were these miraculous words?"

"They weren't miraculous at all. In fact, it was as pragmatic and sensible a sermon as any I've heard. He referenced a verse I had read many times but which struck me powerfully on this occasion—James 1:5—which reads, 'If any of you lack wisdom, let him ask of God, that giveth to all men liberally, and upbraideth not; and it shall be given him.' He as much as extended an invitation for each listener to take their questions to God and expect a reply."

Hannah began rubbing at the prickles on her arms. She turned to her husband and said with awe, "Jed, that's exactly the essence of what Reverend Myers taught." She turned to Dudley to explain. "A young lay-chaplain stayed on at the Willows after Jerome was killed. He left us last fall to attend some religious conferences being held in New York. He believed as well that we could ask God and receive answers individually through the Holy Ghost."

"Then he may well have been amongst us that day."

Jed tightened his grasp on Hannah's hand. "Who is this boy? You heard the same counsel. I assume you've prayed since then, and yet you've had no visions. Why did this lad?"

"You'd have to know him to understand," Dudley replied. "He's a good boy, as honest as the day is long. And though he has a youthful heart, he also has a sober nature in regards to the topic of religion, taking his meager education and using it to study every aspect of God. And perhaps it has nothing at all to do with what he has done. Perhaps the time is simply right, and he is the right vessel."

"You know him, Hannah," Beatrice said. "It's Joseph—young Joseph Smith."

Hannah bolted forward in her seat. "Joseph saw God and Jesus Christ? You believe he has received some answers that will give us peace regarding our sons?" She swung her head around to Jed, her face filled with hope.

"It's late, Hannah. The baby will be up soon." Jed stood and helped her rise, ending the conversation. Turning to Beatrice, he bowed and said, "It's been a long day. Thank you for the lovely supper and your hospitality. Hannah should rest before James awakens." Addressing his brother-in-law, he added, "Thank you for the story, but we'll turn in now if you don't mind."

Dudley was clearly dismayed by the abrupt end to the discussion. "Of course. Are we still planning to go fishing in the morning?"

"I'll be ready." Jed drew his arm protectively around Hannah, and as he began leading her away she turned her head to glance back at her sister. "See you in the morning, then?"

"Yes, dearest. Sleep well."

A slight tension hung in the air the following morning as chores were shared, meals prepared and eaten, and the men departed on their fishing trip. As soon as the door closed behind them, Beatrice cornered Hannah and asked, "We upset Jed last night, didn't we?"

Hannah shrugged as she sat and toyed with the corner of James's blanket. "You have to understand what we've each been through since Johnny's death. It was weeks before I saw Jed smile. And he hasn't known what to expect from me or how to help. It's as if I've been bobbing along in the sea—one day floating along just fine, the next day crashing on the shore in a wreck. Our marriage has been sorely tested between the war and his work and travel, and also by the troubles caused by my insecurities. We were finally happy. We finally had a mutual plan and we could see our way, and then we lost Johnny. Jed's terrified the peace I've found will evaporate if I set my heart on some wild notion. And you have to admit, Beatrice, it sounds incredible."

Beatrice pulled out a chair and sat down, facing her sister. She wiped at the table absently and then spoke in a tone filled with conviction. "You know me better than anyone, Hannah. I'm not prone to wild action or reaction, yet I believe Joseph's story." She covered Hannah's free hand with hers and squeezed it. "He reminds me so very much of you—the way you saw things in the Bible that caused such a stir with the pastor growing up."

"I was a child, Beatrice."

"God has often worked through the unfettered heart of a child, has he not?"

Hannah released her hand from Beatrice's. Her gaze returned to the blanket.

Beatrice went on. "I know from previous conversations with his mother that Joseph had been involved in a serious study of the Bible before the revivals began. He had begun to see the Bible differently than most—not merely as a record of God's past involvement with man, but as an invitation for mankind to learn from the past and receive their own answers in the present."

Hannah weighed that idea for a moment. "That's what Reverend Myers said."

"Yes. I was in town the other day when I ran into Joseph's brother. He told me the entire Smith family has suffered criticism since the preacher shared Joseph's experience with others, yet despite everything, they stand beside Joseph and his story. Imagine how much easier it would be to simply tell the boy to recant his story as a tall tale rather than bear the hostility he now does. But he will not recant it, nor do they want him to."

Hannah continued to listen quietly.

"And just imagine what it would mean if his story were true! Imagine the love of God if He would speak to a mortal boy and introduce him to His very Son. Consider all He is revealing about His true nature and appearance through that visit!"

Hannah's head jerked up in surprise. "Two Beings, as Stephen described in the book of Acts in the Bible?"

"Yes."

Hannah raised her hand to halt the conversation. "Consider what you are saying, Beatrice. You are describing something— something—"

"Miraculous?"

"Even . . . even more than that," Hannah sputtered. "You're speaking of another religious reformation!"

"Or a restitution? Remember how many times we prayed for a miracle for our tortured mother? You would recite that scripture from Acts chapter 3 about the restitution of all things, asking why the miracles of the New Testament weren't available to us in our day. Maybe, Hannah, just maybe the heavens are about to open to man once more. Perhaps the promised restitution is about to begin."

"That's enough, Beatrice!" Hannah abruptly stood and stepped toward the door. "My fractured spirit is being held together by a single thread of peace, and you would now dangle me over some spiritual cliff with nothing but more questions for support? This is not what I need."

Beatrice stood and rushed to comfort her sister, but Hannah held her at bay.

"I'm sorry you're upset, but I don't apologize for what I've shared." Beatrice thumped her fist over her heart. "Something has changed inside me since hearing about Joseph's vision. I know it's true . . . in here. You said the Lord told you to come here to see me. Perhaps it wasn't me you were being sent to find. Perhaps you were meant to hear about Joseph's vision." Her voice broke, and she quickly rushed to compose herself. "I'll speak no more on the matter now, but please, ask the Lord if these things are true, and when I have something more to share, I'll write you. Agreed?"

"I need to walk." Hannah took her wrap from the coat tree and exited the house.

Her hands shook and her heart thundered within her breast as she pondered and wrestled over the ideas Beatrice had replanted in her mind—unconventional ideas she had slowly abandoned to obtain some measure of spiritual peace. It was a curiosity to her that though America was largely founded on the idea of religious freedom, by and large churches were tightly defining religious thought.

And now God may have communed with a boy?

Hannah wished her friend Emmett Schultz was still alive. She missed their religious chats and all the wisdom he had shared from his theological training, teaching her about courageous religious scholars like John Wycliffe, William Tyndale, and Johannes Gutenberg, who, despite great opposition and frequently at great risk to their persons, translated and published the Bible so it could be accessible to all people. Emmett believed God had inspired them, as well as great reformers like Martin Luther and John Calvin, who also risked life and legacy as they fought for the freedom of men and women to worship freely, and to have access to the word of God.

What would Em say about Joseph Smith?

Hannah remembered a conversation they had shared nine years ago. She and Beatrice were staying with Emmett in Hanover, New Hampshire, after Beatrice had taken sick with the typhoid. Hannah felt as helpless as she had in dealing with her mother's mental illness. She had trusted Emmett with her most intimate spiritual questions.

> *". . . This restitution of all things—I can't get anyone to agree on it. What do you think that means?"*

> *He leaned forward thoughtfully. "I believe we must be faithful to His established word, and that Christ will again reestablish His original Church in the manner and time of His choosing.*

Dead hopes began now to stir within Hannah. She remembered how she once prayed for a miracle to heal her mother's mental illness, but a rigid pastor had assured her that the power Jesus and His Apostles held no longer existed on the earth. When she had spoken with Emmett about it, how had their conversation gone?

> *"And what of Jesus' authority, Em, and the healings and the miracles He performed? Do you believe these will return also?"*

> *"I do. Perhaps not in my day, but I have asked God, and I have felt Him confirm these feelings in me. I don't believe He would whisper an untruth to one of His children who came to Him in prayer, seeking an answer."*

Neither did Hannah. But there was more. What else had Emmett said? About America? About her?

"God has great plans for this nation, but first he must prepare a generation to receive what He brings forth. Perhaps you, Hannah, are part of that generation."

How could I have forgotten that? Hannah longed to share this memory with Jed, but he had made his position on Joseph Smith quite clear, so nothing more was said about Joseph or religion during the rest of that visit, and the Pearsons and Snowdens carried on as if the previous conversations had never occurred. In parting, Beatrice hugged her sister tightly and whispered in her ear, "Pray about what we discussed."

Hannah refrained from speaking of Joseph and his vision on the trip home. Instead, she decided to wait to hear more from Beatrice before reopening the conversation with Jed. But secretly, in her heart, she already believed it was true.

Chapter 20

Summer 1820
The Paxutent River

Hannah lifted her head from Jed's shoulder and reached skyward to stretch. The action jostled little James, who lay across her shoulder, and he responded with a stretch of his own. She caught Jed beaming at the pair. She readjusted the baby, who fell back asleep almost instantly. Snuggling against her husband's dusty shoulder, she said, "I'll be so glad to get home."

"We've hardly been home in months," Jed replied as he gazed out across the river from their seat on the steamboat. His smile slowly slipped into a somber, thoughtful expression.

"You're thinking about Johnny, aren't you?"

Jed turned and kissed Hannah's head and tightened his arm around her. "It's as you said. I don't feel frightened or worried about him, but I'll never stop missing the sight of him running through the grass chasing butterflies. Sometimes" —he stopped and cleared his throat— "sometimes I still hear his voice and I turn, expecting to find him there."

He watched her free hand move to her mouth to still the quivering of her lips. "I know," she said quietly.

"Love doesn't die when a body stills. I think I've always believed that. It's what gave me courage during the war. I knew that no matter what befell me, the warmth of love would follow my soul. That's what I feel when I think of Johnny—warmth, love, peace—but I still miss him."

The pair smiled at one another as comfort slowly pushed back the grief. From the bow, the steamboat captain called out a thirty-minute stop in Calverton.

"Shall we get off and stretch our legs?" Jed asked. "We should check to see if there are any packages or letters."

"And get a bite to eat—perhaps a sandwich to hold us until we reach home?"

"Good idea, since no one at the Willows even knows to expect us."

The stroll, though brief, felt delicious to Hannah, and they quickly purchased some food and stopped at the postal office to see if any mail was waiting. The postmaster produced a few letters and a package wrapped in brown paper. News updates of local interest were scrawled on a chalkboard in the building. The day's reports included news that another new American flag design would be unveiled on the Fourth of July to commemorate Maine's statehood, bringing the total of states in the Union to twenty-three, with the admission of Indiana, Louisiana, Mississippi, Ohio, Tennessee, Illinois, Alabama, and now Maine, since the end of the war.

Maine's admission was part of the hotly debated Missouri Compromise, which was intended to limit the states where slavery would be allowed, but more importantly, it was a political concession to keep the balance of congressional power even between the rivaling pro- and anti-slavery factions. Again, Jed saw division and danger on the horizon for the nation. Even former President Jefferson had emerged from the quiet of his private life to weigh in on the matter. He too feared that the issue over slavery and the balance of party power could prove to be the unraveling of the still-fragile Union.

The whistle on the steamer blew. Jed had just begun to hurry Hannah from the building when a neighbor approached them. "Senator, are you two coming or going?" he asked.

Jed sensed concern in the man's voice. "We're headed home. Why do you ask? Is there trouble at the Willows?"

"There's a good deal of smoke in the air up that way. It could be coming from Stringham's place. Just thought you ought to know."

Jed searched the skyline where the man was pointing. He hadn't noticed it before, but now he could detect a haze in the north. Hannah's face turned anxious and white as he quickly urged her onto the boat.

The short ride seemed interminable, but when the ship docked at the Willows pier, things seemed calm and eerily quiet. Hannah and Jed left their belongings at the dock and hurried up the hill in the direction of the haze, but before they traveled far Jenny came by in their wagon, looking as if she hadn't slept in days. Her golden hair was tangled, and her face was smudged with soot and dirt. Her two children, just as ragged, were nestled in the back.

"Has there been another fire?" Jed nearly shouted.

"Yes. Either we've had a terrible rash of coincidences, or our 'friends' are back. Things were perfectly quiet the whole time you were away, until two days ago. When we woke up, all the new horses Markus bought were roaming loose because a fence was down. While the men were herding them up, the bull broke loose and gored one of the stallions. The men started a small fire to heat a rod to cauterize the wound. They were managing one problem or the other all day, but they managed to stop the bleeding and save the animal. Then, late that afternoon when things were finally settling down, Abel and Bitty's new house caught on fire. The official explanation is that the men didn't completely douse the fire they used to heat the rod, setting off an ember that fell on Abel's roof."

"But I take it you don't believe the official explanation," said Hannah.

"Let the men tell you what they think. You're just in time for supper. The women are about to set food out for the workers."

They reached Abel's house and found nearly everyone from the Willows there, engaged in framing a new cabin beside the smoldering frame of the first. Work stopped as soon as they saw Jed and Hannah.

The women piled in the wagon to take Hannah and the baby to the house, while Jed and the men talked.

"Do you agree with the sheriff, that a stray ember set this fire?" Jed asked.

Abel kicked at the ground, and Markus shook his head. "There wasn't much of a breeze, and if the wind was carryin' embers, we'd've seen some other spot fires."

Anger was evident on Abel's face as he surveyed the burned home. "I salvaged Bitty's hope chest and a few personal things, but the house and most of the furniture are a complete loss."

Jack laid a hand on his brother-in-law's shoulder. "We'll have this new cabin under roof in a few days. We'll make this right, won't we, Jed? And by the way, did you happen to check the mail? The sheriff said he'd leave us a note if any strangers were reported in the area."

Jed turned back to the wagon and pulled the mail from a pouch. "No, there's nothing from the sheriff." For the first time he noticed the word "Urgent" written across the package he had picked up in Calverton. He quickly opened it and pulled out a framed portrait and a letter signed by Samuel Renfro. At quick glance, the portrait of an anonymous family meant nothing to Jed, so he began to read the letter.

June 5, 1820

Dear Jed,

Please show this portrait to Abel. If he confirms that the man on the right in the back row is the soldier he served with at Fort McHenry, he may be the same man who attacked the Willows. Take immediate heed. I have reason to believe he will be heading your way once again. I will explain as soon as I am able to come south.

Samuel

Jed studied the portrait again, pausing over the mentioned face, which now seemed familiar. It was a younger face, clean-shaven and more peaceful than the one it resembled from Jed's recent past, but the blond hair confirmed it. Hairs rose on Jed's arms. "It's him!"

"Who?" Markus asked.

"The man who jumped ship that day I escorted Lydia and the children here."

"That was the day Johnny was kidnapped," Markus muttered under his breath.

Abel came up from behind and gazed down from over Markus's shoulder. His large, brown finger came down forcefully upon the same image. "That's Emerson Hildebrand."

"You're certain too?" Jed said more than asked. "If only we had gotten Samuel's warning sooner . . . perhaps we could have captured this devil and saved your home, Abel."

"We know he's probably our arsonist, and probably Johnny's kidnapper," Jack said, "only, tidy as this all seems, we can't do nothin' about it without implicatin' Abel, right?"

Jack's analysis smothered the men's excitement.

"We've got other problems, too," added Markus. "Frederick Stringham came to investigate the smoke. He's all riled up, worried we're involved in something that could endanger his family. We told 'im the sheriff was making a full report, but that didn't satisfy 'im much."

A cloud of dust stirred on the river road. Markus raised his hand to shield his eyes from the sun. "Rider comin' in. I don't think it's Frederick."

Jed squinted into the light at the awkward, bouncing rider and uttered, "Bless you, friend," before saying more loudly, "It's Samuel!"

The horse slowed to a trot, bumping Samuel Renfro up and down in the saddle like a kernel of popping corn. Before he reached the group he began calling out, "I saw the smoke! Is everyone all right?

I tried to get a warning to you. Did you receive my letter and the portrait?"

Jed ran over and grabbed the animal's bridle. "It's him, Samuel. It's Hildebrand."

Samuel slid from the horse. "Abel recognizes him from Fort McHenry?"

"Yes. He's also the man who jumped from my ship the day Johnny was kidnapped. Sit down and rest, Samuel, and then tell us where we can find this devil."

Samuel pulled a handkerchief from his pocket and mopped his worried brow. "I'll tell you what I know, Jed. This past week I was summoned to the estate of a man named Solomon Hildebrand, to attend to his wife, who suffers with a weak heart. I had never met the gentleman or any member of his household before, but something about the butler seemed familiar to me.

"My patient was Margaret Hildebrand. She was being tended by a lovely young Negro woman named Belle. She had a little son, about six years of age, who followed after her as she went about rubbing warm oil on the woman's feet, calling Mrs. Hildebrand 'Auntie Marg.'

"I spent several nights there tending Mrs. Hildebrand before her passing. She and I shared many conversations about her life and family. She had four sons, the youngest of who was named Emerson. My ears perked up at the mention of his name.

"Margaret was raised on a Virginia plantation by a slave named Naomi, who accompanied her north when Margaret married Solomon Hildebrand. Naomi eventually gave birth to Belle, who was born the year after Emerson. The two children grew up alongside one another.

"As the slave woman grew older, Margaret Hildebrand promised Naomi that Belle would never be sold away from the family, and having no daughters, Margaret felt a special affinity for Naomi's child, who loved her in return. When Margaret became ill, it was Belle, not Margaret's daughters-in-law, who nursed her and attended to her every need.

"One day, Emerson and Belle were found together. The young woman had been badly beaten. I know because I attended to her the summer of 1814, before the British landed. That's why the Hildebrand's butler seemed familiar. It was he who brought the battered woman to me. He used no name, presenting nothing but an envelope of money and a written request asking me to use it to treat the young woman and then to send her home when she was again well.

"Margaret revealed that this assault in 1814 produced a child—the young boy I told you about. Recognizing that their own son was the child's father, Solomon and Margaret emancipated Belle and offered her the option of remaining with the family or moving to a new home of her own. Having no one else, Belle chose to remain with the Hildebrands."

"I'm assuming Emerson didn't take the news very well."

"An understatement, Jed. He felt his parents were flaunting his indiscretion, and he went on a rampage—striking Belle again, destroying property, threatening to kill the child. He demanded that Belle and her baby be sold and sent away, but his mother refused. His father finally got him calmed down by offering him a trade of sorts. Believing some military discipline would do his youngest son some good, Solomon arranged a prestigious assignment for Emerson at Fort McHenry—and in return, Solomon promised to remove Belle and the baby from the house. That was in July of 1814, just before the British invaded Washington."

"So he entered Captain Nicholson's company right before I arrived at the fort."

"Yes, Abel, right after he and Skully joined the American Colonization Society. Between that, the situation with Belle, his parents' decision to remand him over to the military, and the upheaval after Washington, Emerson's fury against Negroes was already ripe. And then you arrived, winning Captain Nicholson's favor—bigger, stronger, smarter, willing, and *Negro.*"

Markus huffed in disgust. "—Who won a commendation for bravery and was lauded in that newspaper article. That was the match that lit Hildebrand's fuse the day he whipped Caleb, and then came here and attacked the women and children."

Samuel's face sobered at the memory. "I cross-checked that time frame against his mother's memory. Abel, I believe you mentioned that Emerson Hildebrand was supposedly escorting his friend Skully to Baltimore for medical treatment, and that it was on his return to camp that he beat Caleb and executed the attack."

"That's right."

"Mrs. Hildebrand remembered that visit clearly," Samuel continued. "Emerson and Skully came to the family home and found Belle and the baby still there. Not only that, the Hildebrands had built them a small cottage on the family estate and purchased a new rig with a matched set of bays to pull it. All of it was paid for using funds drawn from Emerson's accounts. Worst of all, Skully had discovered his secret. He tortured Emerson over his indiscretion with Belle and their child during that visit, calling him a nigger lover. That's when something snapped in Emerson. He needed a grand play to prove his position on Negroes once and for all."

Jed felt disgust roil in his gut. "So the coward vented his fury upon Abel and everyone associated with him. We've heard enough. Just tell us where we can find him."

"It's not that simple, Jed. Emerson Hildebrand and Abel have each other by their legal throats. And I didn't come here so you could kill the man. I hoped knowing him and his thinking might help you use other means to stop him, and if you listen I think you'll see an opportunity."

"Samuel's got a point, Jed. The more we know about 'im, the more predictable he seems. Like 'im murderin' Wind Dancer," Markus said. "She was a bay, and now we know why he has an angry streak where bays are concerned."

"I don't want to understand him," Jed replied. "I want to stop this beast without jeopardizing Abel."

Samuel let out a long breath. "Skully's death should have been a relief to Emerson, but now he had the American Colonization Society behind him—other like-minded men hoping to rid the country of freedmen. They gave him power and insulated him from the law. By now he also had a drinking problem.

"In another effort to salvage his son, Solomon relocated him to a family business in Alabama where he could make a fresh start, but each time Emerson came home to make a report of his enterprises, there was trouble.

"Solomon Hildebrand was afraid to even tell his son about Margaret's passing, fearing the uproar his return home would bring. As expected, Emerson again demanded Belle's removal. The exchange became so charged and ugly that legal action has been taken. While I was there, Solomon Hildebrand asked me to personally witness a change to his will that will strip Emerson of all family holdings if he becomes embroiled in any further legal incidents. In short, Emerson's financial future is tied to his efforts to reform, and all his brothers are aware of this codicil and are determined to enforce it."

"Is Emerson aware of this codicil?"

"I'm sure he is. That's why I felt you were all in possible danger. Emerson knows his livelihood is now at risk if he is involved in any further incidents, but he's just crazy enough to risk everything on a final act of revenge. At least you know more about him now."

"Thank you, Samuel, but what's stopping him from simply hiring other miscreants to do his dirty work? There will be no peace as long as he lives."

Another rider appeared on the road. Jed recognized him as Frederick Stringham, and his hands flew to his head to preemptively fend off the headache he knew was coming.

Frederick rode up to the group and scowled at the burned cabin. "More trouble?"

The men looked to Jed, who replied as coolly as he was able, "The sheriff thinks the wind carried an ember from the men's work fire to Abel and Bitty's roof."

"'The sheriff thinks'? At Humphrey's christening party you asked me if I'd had any trouble with vandals. Except for the mysterious death of one slave, I have not, though I know you've had quite a series of accidents lately—a schoolhouse fire, animal killings, and now this?" Frederick's body was as rigid as a wire, and his eyes narrowed. "Did Dupree escape? Are his mercenaries still roaming this area? I have a right to know, Jed. I also have a family to protect!"

"It's not Dupree," Jed said tightly. "I'm certain of that."

Frederick's face remained rigid. "You mean to say you've incited sufficient anger in someone else that they would go to these lengths for retribution?"

A flood of indignation flushed Jed's face, but before his anger could erupt into a response, Frederick chimed back in with, "I'll make you a proposition. You're spread too thin to properly patrol these lands, especially since you've added two tracts of my land to your spread. I'll provide two riders each night to patrol our common fence line so you can concentrate your resources elsewhere." Jed eyed him suspiciously and Frederick explained, "I have an interest in keeping this land safe, and if you can't do it, I'm willing to shoulder a portion of the load."

"Uh-huh. And what do you want in return?"

Frederick leaned his rail-thin body back in the saddle and tilted his head at a cocky angle. "I hear you've made some impressive contacts in the shipping trade. I'd like a personal introduction to these men and your help in securing some preferential shipping rates."

It was a small request, one Jed could easily, painlessly satisfy, but Frederick Stringham was as inconsistent as Maryland's ever-changing weather, and the past had proven him to be a louse at times. Still, the help was needed.

"All right. These are *my* terms," Jed began. "These men are my good friends, and I'll not have them offer you a favorable contract and then have you renege on our deal. So patrol the fences for two years, and at the end of that time I'll make the introductions."

Jed thought Frederick would balk at the terms. Instead, he offered his hand and said, "Agreed." Then he spun on Markus and grinned. "I respect your eye for horses, Mr. O'Malley. Once you get your stables up and running again, I'd enjoy sponsoring a little race . . . say, with a small wager, perhaps?"

Markus folded his arms. "I'd welcome it, Mr. Stringham."

Pleasure gleamed in Frederick's eyes. "Shall we say, in the fall then?"

Markus rolled his hand forward sarcastically as he bowed. "I'll await the date and time."

When Stringham rode off, Abel sidled up to Jed. "Those patrols will be a blessing."

"I think so too. So, what is he planning to ship that requires so much care and expense?"

"His horses," Markus said. "That's why he's all right with the delay. He's just gettin' started with his breedin' program. He won't have enough quality stock to ship for a number of years, but he saw an opportunity to offer you something in exchange for your help."

"So be it. It cost me nothing to get the help we needed. And now you have a race."

Markus snickered like a schoolboy. "Poor Frederick. His stallion, Marquis, is sterile, so he paid a hefty price for Bristol's Pride, a good stallion with a fine pedigree. And Bristol did race at Ascot last year. What Frederick doesn't know is that I finagled a deal to acquire the horse that beat 'im—Windmere—a sultry little Arabian formerly owned by a senator who has a weakness for cards and fine tobacco, two things I know quite well."

Jed stopped in his tracks. "You won that horse outright?"

"We won the horse. It also required a little stake. I put up half the cash you saved for me from selling my horses to Frederick, and I put up a hogshead of your finest tobacco. We got it all back with three queens!"

Jed roared with laughter. "And that's the horse you're planning on racing against Frederick's stallion in the fall?"

Markus shrugged sheepishly. "I know 'tis a terribly cruel thing ta do ta the man, but I can't 'elp m'self."

There were many surprises for Jed and Hannah during the coming months—all of them delightful. The shops he installed at the dock had become a bustling enterprise, selling goods of all kinds. Jack's fresh-produce stand was always stocked with something from the garden he, Lydia, and the children tended on their little farm. Lydia had also mastered the art of rolling cigars and now had a bustling business of her own selling the Willows' finest smokes to steamboat passengers. Bitty always had a shelf of baked goods, and Abel sold flour and cracked wheat, along with handcrafted furniture. Royal and Mercy's family concentrated on eggs and chickens, Sookie whittled small toys for children, and Reese's relatives had a large stall filled with handmade quilts and finely crafted embroidered goods. The shops were such a draw that the Willows dock became a regular stop on the river, soon prompting its own name—Willowsport.

Everyone worked together to produce the tobacco, corn, wheat, and hay needed to keep the farm afloat, but life became easier, and everyone on the Willows began to prosper.

For Jed and Hannah, it was a season of peace filled with busy mornings and lazy afternoons enjoying James and one another. They took long horseback rides and had regular picnics. They'd choose a new book—*Ivanhoe* and *Frankenstein,* among others, including the works of Miss Jane Austen, whom Frannie had taken a liking to during her time in England—and would take turns reading to one another as they lay under the canopy of a willow tree with their son lying in their laps.

Sometimes, Hannah and Jed would pack a picnic basket, hop a steamboat, and let it lead them to a new town or port, where they'd spend the night. The next day they'd pack up and sail back home. The economy along the river was still a struggle for communities hard-hit by the war, and the leisurely visits by the senator and his wife had the unintentional benefit of increasing Jed's popularity and influence.

The big race was set for September's fall harvest. Frederick had spent a sizeable amount of money promoting the event to debut Bristol's Pride and launch his stable's name. Soon, the race became a community affair, with other farms entering their horses, and vendors asking permission to sell goods and wares. Frederick welcomed the hoopla, assessing small fees for everything, until the original two-horse race became a regional Patuxent River Fair and large revenue-maker for White Oak Farm.

Hannah and the other Willows ladies bought lovely hats for the occasion and dressed in their finest party attire, just as the ladies do at the Ascot Races in England. When word leaked out about their plans, other ladies in the area followed suit, lending an added euphoria to the day. When Bitty and some of the other freed slaves rode in with the Pearson entourage, guards began to turn them away, but Frederick Stringham held his tongue and personally waved them in.

Eleven horses were entered in the race on the day of the fair. Frederick laughed at Windmere's size—a mere fifteen hands. Next to his massive bay stallion, Bristol's Pride, Windmere looked like a yearling, but this sleek, black bullet astounded even Markus with her speed. She was a dream to watch, racing as if she had been born to run full out over any terrain.

Markus had spent the summer training Royal and Mercy's son Jubal to ride the Arabian filly. Small, with cat-like reflexes and an immediate connection with Windmere, Jubal needed no whip to coax her to run. With a whisper in her ear she would bolt, becoming a blur in seconds.

On race day, Jubal's yellow shirt and cap matched the ribbons in Windmere's braided mane. As beautiful as she was, most of the local money was on Bristol's Pride, the dominating physical specimen. Aside from a few small bets, only the Willows people and one anonymous investor bet on Windmere, but when the gun fired, a small black nose edged to the front and remained there from start to finish. Bristol's Pride finished respectably, three lengths behind Windmere, while the rest of the festooned horses ran in a pack far behind the leaders.

After the race, Frederick strolled over, not nearly as upset as Jed and Markus would have expected. "You're a good sport, Frederick," Jed noted. "And Bristol's Pride ran well."

"Yes, yes, he did. But somehow I knew better than to bet against the Willows. I've come to expect that your Pearson luck could turn a thirty-year-old nag into a winner. You're the luckiest cuss I've ever met, Jed Pearson. You too, Markus. It appears the Pearson fortune has rubbed off on everyone associated with the farm, so I decided not to test fate today. I was the other person betting on Windmere."

Markus nearly swallowed his celebratory cigar. "You? You bet against your own horse?"

Frederick's head bobbed as if dodging the question. "Let's say I hedged my interests well. My good neighbors wagered heavily against you, and I profited nicely from a favorable bet. Between my winnings and the revenue the fair generated, I have enough to fund my stables very comfortably for the next few years. And, Jed, I still have your promise to help me secure favorable shipping rights, correct?"

Jed stopped laughing long enough to answer, "You do."

Frederick rocked on his heels as pure contentment oozed from him. "Mark this day, gentlemen. White Oak's luck is changing, too."

CHAPTER 21

February 7, 1821
Philadelphia, Pennsylvania

Phillip St. Clair arrived promptly at seven as promised, but Mrs. Standish informed him Frannie was not ready.

"The curtain rises in thirty minutes, Francis," he called up the stairs.

She came to the top in a nightgown and a white silk wrapper. "I'm not going."

His face paled and then boiled red. "What do you mean you're not going? Are you deathly ill? Because nothing short of that could excuse you abandoning me in this way."

"I'm quite well. I'm simply tired of serving as a curiosity for your friends' amusement."

Phillip turned and paced three steps before returning a cold stare. "You've pushed, and I've backed down. You've arrived late, left early, and utterly forgotten social commitments, and I've covered for your rudeness. You've shown a remarkable lack of decorum in conversation, and I've laughed it away rather than holding you accountable. In short, I've given in to you time and time again, but no more." His voice became softer and more steady. "Interestingly, things have grown worse since our engagement, perhaps because you know what I'm just realizing—you don't want to marry me. Very well. I withdraw my proposal. You are free, and so am I."

He turned for the door and was very nearly through it when Frannie finally responded. "I have tried to push you away, and I'm sorry."

Phillip sagged against the doorframe. "Timothy Shepard was right. You're incapable of loving someone—of actually loving someone."

Being charged as one incapable of loving another had been laid at her feet one time too many. *Well, no more.* Frannie lifted her head and shot back, "It's not fear that prevents me from accepting the trappings you associate with love—the lavish engagement; the large circle of wealthy, intrusive friends; and the enormous wedding. Those things mean nothing to me."

He shut the door and leaned against it. "All right. What would you have chosen?"

Frannie drew in a deep breath as she sought for the right words. "I'd want something small and intimate, to share with the people I love. Do you know how I came to be a performer?"

He began to climb the steps toward her. "At Le Jardin, here in Philadelphia."

"Yes, but did you know I ended up there because I was seeking a place to hide from a painful set of circumstances? It must sound ridiculous that I would hide on a stage, but somehow, up there, I felt bold and strong and detached from the world while I healed."

"Are you saying that's why you again returned to the stage and Philadelphia?"

She scanned the opulent décor of her downtown home, smiling sadly as she fluffed her wrapper's silk fabric. "Philadelphia is my fortress. My costumes are my armor."

Phillip met her on the top step. "I marveled at how different you were at the Willows."

She closed her eyes as if savoring the memory. "I don't like people to see me unmasked."

"So you sent me away."

Again she toyed with her robe. "I didn't know how to transition from the elegant woman you fell in love with to the farm girl from Maryland."

He stepped closer and ran a finger through the dangling curl on her shoulder. "The wild woman of the Willows?"

Her head dipped as she smiled. "A woman most comfortable when riding, and fishing, and walking the fields. A woman who generally prefers men's trousers over formal gowns."

"You needn't be one woman or the other. You can be both."

The words sounded perfect. Phillip took her hands in his, bringing them both to his mouth to place a kiss on each. "Jed and Hannah are still in Annapolis, aren't they? We could be there in two days and have a quiet ceremony, followed by a honeymoon in Virginia. How does that sound?"

Tiny shivers prickled her neck. "Are you serious? You could simply drop everything?"

His eyes drifted away for a moment, and then he looked at her and smiled. "Yes. Would you?"

A euphoric giggle escaped Frannie's lips. "I could be ready by tomorrow noon."

Phillip laid his hands along her neck, rubbing the underside of her chin with his thumbs. "Nothing would make me happier, Frannie, but I want you to be certain."

Like an old ghost, Arthur's face came to memory, casting a brief shadow on her joy, but she quickly banished his image. "Yes, I am certain. Very certain."

Phillip paid a rider a small fortune to carry the news to the Willows and on to Annapolis. When his carriage pulled up in front of Jed and Hannah's rented home, Frannie was greeted not only by them but by Bitty, Jack, Markus, and all their families.

The women swept Frannie and her hastily purchased dress away, and from that point on it was all a blissful blur of sewing and laughter and love, while Jed and the men whisked Phillip away to an Irish pub until well after Frannie had retired.

The reality of what she was about to do struck her the next morning when she awoke to find the re-tailored gown hanging on the door. She stared at it, imagining herself in it with Phillip standing by her side. It was easier than she expected. She tried to picture Arthur there, but she couldn't even bring his face clearly to mind.

She reached for her reticule and pulled the drawstring wide, revealing a small, jeweled box that contained a thin coil of linen gauze. It was nothing but a bit of trash to anyone else, but for her it was nearly sacred—the token Arthur had slipped on her finger mere days before the horrid explosion. Frannie would have gladly married him despite the limitations fate imposed upon him, but he wanted her to have more. *So be it, Arthur,* she said to herself as she dropped the linen ring into the flame of the lamp. The seconds of bright blaze faded back to the former tepid glow, leaving behind only the ashen remains of promises unfulfilled.

A knock on the door began the day's preparations. She remembered little about the ceremony other than Phillip's fear that she would bolt and run. She did not. Vows were spoken, rings were exchanged, and then came the pronouncement that they were husband and wife.

Wife. Frannie liked the sound of the word. She was Phillip's now, dear to him in a way no other woman could be, and as each day passed, she finally understood many things—about Jed and Hannah, and about Arthur's great gift of love.

They traveled to Alexandria and ran into Timothy Shepard, who instantly sensed the change in his old friend. He pulled her to him and whispered in her ear, "I'm delighted for you, Frannie. Be happy, my friend. Be ever so happy."

"I am, Timothy. I finally understand," she whispered back.

He smiled at her as if catching a child with her hand in the cookie jar. "It's interesting that you've married a politician. Was that not the very reason you spurned me?"

Flustered, Frannie scrambled for a response. "Yes, but the responsibilities of a city councilman, or even the mayor of a city, are far different than those of a senator."

"You think so? Phillip has ambitions of more. Help him stay grounded, Frannie, and see that you get your share of his time. Lucy is quick to rein me in when I get myself out on a limb. Do that for Phillip. He'll thank you for it in the end."

The week-long honeymoon stretched to two before Frannie and Phillip reached Philadelphia. Then came the business of merging two households into one, and announcing the marriage to the public.

A party was hosted in their honor. The press of people and their nosy questions reminded Frannie of the games she was forced to play to appease Baltimore's gentry matrons, and here she was, at nearly thirty years of age, playing the same games once more.

"You're doing wonderfully, darling," swooned Phillip, placing a kiss on her cheek as he dragged her off on his way to work the adoring crowd. She remembered Timothy Shepard's words and wondered if she was up to the task, but each time Phillip strode more than a few feet from her, he soon hurried back for her hand, and her concerns faded.

As she expected, he asked her to retire from the stage—an easy concession she readily agreed to. Instead, Frannie spent more time tending her business investments, including sketching designs for her successful millinery shop, and she used her position as a councilman's wife to advocate for the city's poor. She developed a special fondness for the Orphans' Asylum on the outskirts of town, founded by a benevolent committee of influential Philadelphians—the Orphans' Society of Philadelphia.

Frannie applauded the composition of the OSP's board of directors—busy mothers and homemakers who managed the asylum's large budget like a team of skilled businessmen. The religiously devout group seemed a bit guarded in their welcome of the ostentatious newcomer, but Frannie wasn't deterred by the lukewarm reception. She quickly moved to the music room and began playing show tunes and folk songs until, as with the Pied Piper, the children followed.

The asylum's resident matron wasn't as amused by the disruption to her rigid schedule. Bells rang, signaling each period and controlling every minute of the day. Times were set for wake up, washing, dressing, bed making, and morning chores such as cooking, milking, baking, and gardening. The standards of cleanliness and manners were high, and owing to the generous budget provided for the asylum, the food was nourishing and the children nicely dressed.

Lessons and more chores followed, with time for recreation, music, and art, followed by more chores that taught the basic skills of farming, animal husbandry, and homemaking the children would need to secure work and to establish homes of their own some day. When a child was proficient in reading, writing, and arithmetic, and when he or she was a capable worker, the child was indentured and left the orphanage to enter the world.

Frannie applauded the asylum and its plans until, as she was leaving one day, she heard crying echoing from a pantry closet off the kitchen. To her horror she found a small, blond girl about six years old, whose feet and hands were loosely tethered to a chair.

"Good heavens! Who did this to you?"

"I just need to use the latrine," the girl said with a sniffle. "I'll be quick."

As soon as she was released, she darted out the door to the outhouse. A few minutes later she returned, sat in the chair, and prepared to be bound once more.

Baffled, Frannie took the girl by the shoulders. "You're Sarah Pittman, aren't you?" The child sniffed and nodded. "Well, I'm not re-tying you, my sweet Sarah. You're free to go."

The child remained in the seat with her arms resting where the ties were fastened. "You must, Mrs. St. Clair. I'll be in a dreadful spot if you don't. I've already done two days. At evening I'll have finished my punishment, and the matron will let me go."

Try as she did, Frannie could not get the girl to leave, so instead she stormed off to confront the matron—a Mrs. Cassidy. "What is the meaning of tying Sarah to a chair?"

The middle-aged matron folded her arms across her ample chest and replied in a soft, unapologetic tone. "Have you run a home of one hundred youngsters, Mrs. St. Clair? The only way to maintain discipline is to incite a little fear of the consequences of misbehavior."

"Tying children up is barbaric! She couldn't even get to the outhouse!"

"One of the older girls is always in the kitchen working. She releases the punished child when it's time to eat or use the facilities." Frannie's brown eyes blazed with anger, but Mrs. Cassidy curled a finger at her and led her back to the pantry, where Sarah still sat in the chair.

Before the matron could address the child, Sarah spoke up, but shame, not fear, colored her voice.

"I'm sorry, Mrs. Cassidy. Catherine couldn't hear me, and I had to go."

"That's understandable, child," cooed Mrs. Cassidy. "Would you like to explain to Mrs. St. Clair why you're in the naughty closet?"

Sarah's chin dropped to her chest. "I climbed on a counter to fetch a biscuit for Charles, and I knocked a big glass jar on the floor."

"And what else, Sarah?" the woman asked softly.

The blue-eyed imp touched a spot by her eye. "It shattered and cut Charles right here."

Mrs. Cassidy looked at Frannie. "Charles could have very nearly been blinded."

Frannie swallowed hard at the thought. "But tying a child to a chair, Mrs. Cassidy? That's intolerable under any circumstance."

The woman leaned back against the door, a strand of gray hair falling across one tired eye. "No child ever died from being tied to a chair, Mrs. St. Clair, but plenty died because they disobeyed. Maybe my ways aren't yours, but I'd give my life for these children, and they know it." As if choreographed, Sarah leapt from her chair and wrapped her arms around the matron's legs. "And what's this?" asked the matron, seeming to fight the urge to smile. "All right. All things considered, I suppose you've paid your penance. Go and play until it's time to help with supper."

Sarah nodded and scampered away. Frannie was speechless. "Can we at least agree to discuss some alternative punishments besides tying the children down?"

Mrs. Cassidy's eyes dropped to the floor. "Yes, if you get me more help day-to-day."

Now we are accomplishing something, Frannie thought. "I'll take that up with the board. In fact, I'd like you to make a list of everything you need to have addressed, and I'll be your advocate."

As the weeks passed, Frannie spent more and more time at the Orphan Asylum, admittedly falling in love with the children, and with two in particular. Each night as she arrived home, her head was filled with ideas to bounce off Phillip before presenting them to the board.

Jed, Hannah, and James arrived in June for a visit, disrupting Frannie's schedule at the asylum. As thrilled as she was for their company, she could not get her mind off the children. Hannah noticed her preoccupation and said, "I think I have some news that will interest you."

Frannie blushed in embarrassment. "I'm sorry for being such dreadful company. I don't know where my mind is these days. Tell me your news. Did Windmere win this year's race?"

"Yes, but if you ask Jed about her he'll talk your ear off." Hannah reached into her bag and withdrew a bundle. "I sold every hat you sent down for the Patuxent River Fair! There's nearly seventy dollars there, and I could have sold more had I had more to sell."

"Was no one else selling hats for race day?"

Reaching a hand to her sister-in-law, Hannah gazed on Frannie with her pride evident. "Oh, there were other milliners, but the gentry ladies only wanted a Frannie St. Clair design."

Dubious, Frannie could not hide the curious pleasure that comment brought her. "The gentry preferred my designs?" The grin that brightened her face faded as she asked, "Did those old biddies realize that Frannie St. Clair is actually *me*—the former Francis Pearson, whom they snubbed and gossiped about until my parents felt forced to hide me away?"

The light of satisfaction burned brightly in Hannah's eyes. "I made each of them quite aware that the talented designer's whose fashions they now craved was in very deed my brilliant sister-in-law. And I charged them each twenty percent more than you advised."

Frannie roared with laughter as a tear moistened her eye. Dabbing delicately at it, she dropped her gaze to her lap. "Thank you for telling me that, Hannah. I've never quite managed to shake the hurt of their scrutiny. Baltimore always made me feel small somehow. I can't explain why anymore, but I never could feel truly at home there."

"Well, now you can. You're a star there, Frannie, and even if there are a few biddies who still choose to judge you, they are in the minority. You are a woman of great distinction now."

"A woman of distinction . . ." she repeated. "Isn't it funny? Such a vindication would have meant the world to me a few years, or even months ago, but now, having received it, it seems so inconsequential. I've learned what matters most, and the opinions of others are far down my list of priorities." She turned her attentions to James as he toddled about the parlor. All at once she scooped him up and hugged him close.

"I know that look." Hannah reached a hand across the divan and squeezed Frannie's.

"Is it obvious? I pray for children of our own, but two have already stolen my heart."

"From the Orphan Asylum?"

"Yes." Frannie felt warmth radiate through her at the thought of the children. "Charles is two. He has a head full of brown tousles and big, brown eyes that melt my heart. Sarah is a blond, blue-eyed angel. She's only six, but she looks after Charles like a little mother."

"Are you and Phillip considering adopting them?"

Her previous delight quickly vanished. "We've discussed it. I'd bring them home tonight, but Phillip asked me to wait a bit longer to be sure I've considered the impact two children of those ages will have on our lives." She leaned closer. "But I already know I want them. I can picture them here, Hannah, in our home and at our dining table. You and Jed manage to travel fine with the boys—" She wanted to retrieve the word as it slipped from her tongue. "I'm sorry."

Hannah's wince was subtle. "It's all right, Frannie. We think of Johnny all the time. And yes, we take James everywhere we go. We're off to New York on this trip. The American Colonization Society is establishing a colony called Liberia, for the re-colonization of freed slaves. Jed wants to make sure the society isn't coercing freedmen to leave the country. And then we're off to see an inventor who has built a motor he claims will revolutionize life."

Frannie set James down to play and clasped her hands together. "Even in this city of brotherly love, prejudice exists. I noticed there were no children of color at the Orphan Asylum, and no one wanted to address my questions on the matter. I discovered a few Quaker women who are forming a group to care for colored orphans, but they have little money or support."

"Jed is worried. Debates over abolition have led to men using pistols to settle their differences. People are beginning to call for tighter laws regarding slaves and freedmen, too." Hannah sighed.

"I wish I could take all the children in—every one of them."

"But you can't, Frannie. No one can. Just help where you are able, but don't let the fact that you can't save everyone prevent you from adopting the children you've come to love."

CHAPTER 22

July 1, 1821
Liverpool, England

Daniel Spencer's foot tapped a nervous staccato rhythm against the floor of the carriage as he stared out at the dismal, increasingly impoverished scenes. He refused to make eye contact with his father. It was no secret that he had only come along to satisfy the contractual obligation he agreed to in exchange for his father's support during the first two years of medical school. So much hinged on the outcome of this day's tour. It could decide the course of his entire future, or it could be the straw that would finally break the father and son's relationship forever.

They reached a section of Liverpool consisting of ragged shanties from which hollow-eyed children peered. Daniel shrank over the disparity between himself and them. Parents shoved children through the doorways to beg for alms, and they came calling out to Lord Whittington.

Daniel was impressed that the children knew his father by name, and then he recalled the days when he and his father would stand on Ludgate Hill after services at St. Paul's, greeting the poor and distributing coins and news of work and free food. Some of St. Paul's wealthy patrons thoughtlessly doled out their coins, but not the Earl of Whittington. Daniel remembered his father's gentle kindness as he instructed him on the privilege of serving all of Britain's citizens.

They had stayed until each person's needs had been addressed. Daniel was ashamed that he had forgotten.

The earl stepped from the carriage in a new woolen frock coat, allowing the children to press in on him despite their muddy clothes and their dirty hands, which reached to touch him. As he passed out silver coins, he asked questions of different children.

"How is your mother, Sarah? Is she taking the tonic the doctor ordered? And you, Harry, how is that cough? Better now? You seem much improved. Tell your father there are openings at the coal plant. I'll leave a good word there for him."

One by one, the children took the proffered coins, giving an awkward curtsy or bow as thanks for the gifts. The earl tousled one boy's hair and pinched a girl's chin while telling her what a beauty she was growing to be. There was no deceit in the earl's actions, only love and caring. Years of mistrust began peeling back, revealing the man Daniel had once adored.

When the earl returned to the carriage, he waved to the adults who called out their gratitude.

"Father, how do you know these people? They're not even in your district."

The earl called instructions to the driver before answering the query. "Parliament was discussing funding for a system of hospitals, and I was on the committee to decide where they should go. I made several trips here to speak to the people and to inquire after their health. The average life expectancy here is forty-six. For women it's forty-two, because so many were dying in childbirth, and one-third of all the children were dying before the age of ten. Much of the suffering was preventable with treatment which they were unable to receive."

Daniel took a deep breath. "Which is exactly why I want to be a physician."

His father nodded thoughtfully. "What treatment would your instructors prescribe for people who are malnourished, or who are cold because they haven't enough money to buy coal to keep their meager shelters warm in the winter?"

"There are no medicines to treat the weather or hunger," Daniel shot back.

"And yet, are these not as critical to health as a vaccine or tonic?"

Daniel quieted, and the carriage rolled on a few minutes before reaching a new brick hospital. It was small by London's standards, and overcrowded, with people lined up along the expansive front porch.

"This is the facility that was built as a result of our inquiries. It opened its doors last winter, and it's already overwhelmed by the needs of the community," the earl said. He pointed down the street to another brick building, where a long line formed. "St. Andrews Church provides hot meals for the children and the sick. I was able to get a bill through Parliament to fund them for another year."

"Only one? Then what?" asked Daniel.

The gravity of the situation was evidenced by the grim twist of his father's mouth. "Britain's finances have been greatly strained by decades of war, and now we're sending troops to support Greece's struggle for independence from the Ottomans."

Daniel felt the lurch in his stomach at his father's mention of Greece. *Why did he do that?* He was unsure if the earl was assessing his pain, or irritating an old wound. Daniel had heard reports of massacres where the casualties numbered in the tens of thousands, and for a moment he found some peace in knowing Ruth was far from Greece and in the protection of a husband. The two men's eyes met, and the earl rushed on.

"The question is always, 'What is essential?' Is medicine more important than food? Will a subsidy providing coal be of greater benefit than new sewers, or clean water, or a school?"

Daniel felt his hackles rise. He pounded his fist against the carriage seat. "Why not end the warring and pay for it all?"

Seconds passed as the anger in the space leveled. "Would Napoleon have cared for our people's needs if he had succeeded in breeching our borders?" the earl asked softly. The air stilled as a cloud of pain seemed to darken his eyes. When he continued, his voice sounded strained. "Or would he have crushed and murdered our people as he did so many others? Without security, none of the rest can be accomplished. What good is a bandage to a conquered people?"

Daniel called to the driver. "Please stop. I need to walk." Before the carriage had even halted and before the earl could respond, Daniel was out of the coach, pacing alongside.

The earl rested his head against the window frame. "I've done the same when the nation's problems overwhelmed me. I've likely walked a thousand miles beside my carriage over the years, working through the frustration, asking God to clear my view so I could see what needed to be done, and to show me how to persuade my brothers of Parliament to see it, too. Without an honorable government, the people suffer in ways no doctor can relieve."

Daniel offered no reply, nor any other indication he had heard, except for the constant raking of his hands through his dark curls. He was nineteen years old, a man three inches taller than his father and among the academically brightest in his Cambridge class, and yet in this minute, he felt childish and naïve. He began walking down the road, listening to the squeak and groan of the carriage wheels as they commenced again. He felt crowded and pressed, but when he looked over his shoulder the carriage was rods behind him, forcing him to admit it was the new questions his father raised that were the source of his burden.

Daniel raised a hand in submission. "I've seen enough." Stopping dead in his tracks, he let his shoulders slump. He thought he had found a better way to ease suffering. Now he realized he never had any choice at all. His bloodline and personality had unalterably chosen his destiny. He was a Spencer, and Spencers served Britain, whose needs were too great for any single doctor to mend. But a powerful voice in Parliament could ease a magnitude of suffering, not only in Britain but in the world.

He walked back to the carriage and opened the door. Once inside, he leaned forward, his elbows resting on his knees. His head shook back and forth as his breathing became gusts of disappointment. "There's no escaping this responsibility, is there?"

"You are a good man, Son, and this is your destiny."

Daniel shot back against the seat, wincing at the conundrum gripping his heart. "Please ask the driver to turn the carriage around. I'm ready to return home now."

The next few weeks sped by as the viscount was strutted about London society. He easily fell back into the customs and regimens he had been taught since birth, and in truth, it was not entirely unpleasant. He and his father went about doing much good together, which brought Daniel immeasurable pleasure as a new closeness and affection began to develop between father and son. The earl's hand frequently fell upon Daniel's shoulder, offering affectionate pats and squeezes, and he could not deny that the pride reflected in his father's eyes satisfied a deep hunger he had longed to fill. Soon, he began to relax and soak it all in.

And there was a parade of young beauties vying for the attentions of the mysterious young viscount with the Grecian lilt to his voice. Courtesy was the best he could offer them, as his heart was still irrevocably bound to the dark-eyed beauty he had loved since his youth.

It was decided Daniel would complete his medical training, which he and his father both felt would be an asset to the future Parliamentarian whose political agenda would focus on improving Britons' quality of life. The pair returned to Whittington Castle, spending a few final days together before Daniel left for school. He was surprised at the regret he felt at the impending separation from his father, whom he loved and felt loved by once more.

Daniel had barely been gone an hour, and already the castle seemed intolerably empty without him in it, but a deep warmth eased the chill of loneliness for the earl. His boy was back, and he was not merely his flesh and blood, but his son once more.

He heard the thump of the door knocker echo all the way to the confines of his library, and then came the spry steps of Ridley, announcing the cause of the commotion.

"There is a young woman at the door, sir. She wants to see Master Daniel. I've told her he is not here, but she insists if she cannot see him she wants to see you. Her name is Ruth."

Ruth. The name sent a panic through the earl he had not felt since the days of his son's youth, when the McGowan brothers stalked his home, laying a trap to steal Daniel away. The earl knew Ruth was here to do the same, but she would not need to lure Daniel away. One inkling that she was near and he would abandon everything—all their plans, their hopes, their dreams.

"You didn't tell her where he was, did you?" the earl asked with a shrill urgency.

Ridley recoiled. "Of course not, sir. I would never disclose personal information."

"I'm sorry, old friend. Of course you would not. Please, I need a moment first."

What to do? What to do? The earl knew he must send the young woman away, but how? She must be left with no hope of reconciliation so she would never return or seek for Daniel again. And Daniel must never know.

The earl rose from his chair, noting how stiff his nearly fifty-year-old body was becoming as he walked to the entrance hall. He paused before the heavy door to run a hand through his graying hair, collecting himself before facing the woman. She would be angry, and with good reason, but he could not flinch. He had stood before kings and international courts, defending Britain's stance on issues. Surely he could disarm the rancor of one young Jewess.

When he opened the door, he was unprepared for what awaited him. Even though her gray cloak and muslin dress were muddied eight inches up from the ground, she was a vision of exotic beauty and strong determination. Her dark hair was swept back in a simple braid that allowed soft tendrils to fall along her brow and olive cheeks. Her dark eyes were wide and clear, like two orbs that penetrated his soul. He could hardly meet them.

The earl stepped onto the porch. "As Ridley told you, my son is not here, nor is he expected anytime soon. And I can tell you with all honesty, he has no expectations of seeing you."

It is true, the earl appeased himself. Daniel thought she was lost to him forever, so he had no expectations of ever seeing her again.

"I only have one question, my lord. Did he receive my letters?"

This was the question the earl had hastily prepared for. "My dear, I can say with complete surety that he was, and is, as aware of the last as he was of the first." Agonizing as it was, he bore the inquisition of her eyes while she scrutinized him.

"You must forgive me for doubting you, sir, but I cannot believe Daniel would not at least reply to a dear friend who has been caught up in the bloodbath of Greece. The Daniel I know would have done far more than answer, and yet you say he ignored all my letters?"

Again, those dark eyes bore into his, and he became annoyed by her ability to disarm him. "Young woman, you shouldn't be here. Britain has aligned her allegiance with Greece, and you are an enemy to this nation and this house. I thank you for the kindness your family showed my son during our rift, and in gratitude for that kindness I have shown forbearance, but as an officer of the government, I must ask you to leave at once, or I shall be forced to execute my civil duty and have you arrested."

Despite the sorrow in her eyes, Ruth did not flinch or shy away. "I will go, my lord, but it was not my coming that caused the dread I see in your eyes, nor will my leaving ease it."

She turned and descended the grand porch like a queen, her skirts sweeping across the wet stone walkway and down to the tree-lined lane. The earl's gaze remained on her, and even after she was gone he remained at the window as if expecting some divine consequence for his lies. Remembering her final words, he drew the heavy drapes around him like a cocoon, feeling the demons close in around him as they had done once before.

"I had no choice!" he shouted to the shadows and corners. "He cannot marry her!"

"Are you all right, my lord?" asked Ridley as he raced into the room.

The earl hated the tone in his servant's voice. He had heard enough of it seven years earlier when he suffered his breakdown. Releasing the fabric, he stepped away and straightened his coat. "Nothing to fear, Ridley. I thought I saw a bat in the corner. I was mistaken."

Daniel sent the carriage on to Cambridge with his things while he nudged his horse on to a district on the outskirts of London to purchase a few needed items. His first errand was to a tobacco shop that carried Willows cigars, an American brand of which his father had grown especially fond. He had a box wrapped in lovely gold paper while he addressed the card and arranged the delivery instructions. Lastly he wrote a loving note.

> *Dear Father,*
>
> *Thank you for being so patient and forgiving, and for allowing me to find my way. Enjoy these. I bought one for myself. I'll save it for finals. Who knows? Perhaps I'll become enamored with them as well. Like father, like son . . .*
>
> *Your affectionate boy,*
> *Daniel*

He marveled at the pleasure it gave him to attend to this little surprise. Once the arrangements and purchase were completed, he headed to the tailors to buy a few shirts, then on to a pub for refreshment before heading on his way to Cambridge.

A stir was ensuing outside as a sheriff hauled a feisty young woman through the streets, drawing a crowd as he warned, "Settle down, you little vixen, or I'll be forced to tie you up."

"Let me go! Let me go! I've done nothing!" yelled the woman. Her voice caused Daniel's arms to prickle. He cocked his head in the woman's direction, attempting to dismiss the crazy notion. Again she cried out, and this time Daniel moved to the doorway and peered at the crowd surrounding the scene. At first he could see nothing, and then he saw the white muslin of her gown, with the unmistakable embroidery that adorned Ruth's clothes.

A small break in the crowd allowed him one brief glimpse of the woman. He saw the flash of fire in those unforgettable eyes and his heart thundered. "Ruth!" he cried out. He tore through the onlookers, scattering men left and right as he barreled forward. Upon reaching her, he gripped the sheriff's arm so tightly the man winced. "What is the meaning of this?"

Recognizing the viscount, the sheriff tried to explain. "She's a vagrant, my lord. I found her prowling around your castle. I asked your father about her, and he said I should arrest her."

"My father does not know her. She is *my* friend, my very dear friend."

He gazed upon Ruth and saw the toll the confrontation had taken on her. Not even his arrival could relieve the haunted look in her eyes, and when she looked at him it was as if he too were a stranger. Placing one hand alongside her face, he smiled at her and offered the other to slowly lift her to her feet. The sheriff flushed crimson and released his grasp on her, then began to gruffly disperse the crowd.

Daniel barely noticed anyone else on the street. Wanting desperately to pull Ruth to him, he caught himself and focused on the question tearing at his peace. *Is she married?* She still stared at him as if she didn't know him anymore. "Is it you?" he gushed. "Is it truly you?"

"How can you be so surprised at my arrival?" she spat. "I told you I was coming. I told you everything."

Immediately he was on the defensive. "Told me? How? The last time I saw you I was on a ship being evicted from Salonika, and you were betrothed, on your way to your wedding."

Daniel felt the sting of her silent inquisition. She peered more carefully into his eyes, and her own softened. "You never received my letters, did you? Then you don't know."

He watched her face transform back into that visage of light he had fallen in love with, taking him back to Greece and the happiest days of his life. "What don't I know?"

"I protested the arrangements made by the elders with such fury that my intended returned me to my father, declaring me too willful to make a good wife."

Daniel dared not even breathe. "Are you telling me you're not married?"

"I am not married, Daniel. No good man in my village would have me after that."

His captured breath released in a joyful rush as he clapped his hands together in jubilation. "Is it terrible of me to be so very happy about your misfortune?"

Ruth offered the first smile of their meeting. "Not at all. It is only as I hoped."

Without a second's further delay, Daniel wrapped his arm around Ruth and led her to a bench. Quickly falling into step with him, she nestled close to his side. "It feels good to laugh again. There has been no cause for happiness for months. Only sorrow and grief."

"I've read the reports of the war in the papers. It's horrible. And all this time I took some comfort in thinking your husband had carried you far away to safety."

Her response was filled with urgency. "Do not believe everything written in your papers, Daniel. The Europeans do not know the whole story. Jews were blamed for the murder of the patriarch of the Greek Orthodox Church, but our people didn't kill him. The Ottomans in

Constantinople executed the clergyman, then ordered a few Jews to dispose of the body. Now we are blamed for this murder, and no Jew is safe in Greece, or welcome anywhere."

"Has the war come to Salonika?"

A dull glaze swept over Ruth's face. For several seconds she stared straight ahead as her tears fell. "Father told me to hide in the caves with some of the other women and children. For two days we heard gunfire and screams of death. When all was finally silent, we returned to the village, but death and carnage filled the streets. The Greeks had come with pitchforks and sickles, killing and maiming every Jew they found—men, women, and even the children."

She buried her face in Daniel's shirt as he held and rocked her. "Your father?"

"Dead, like all my other relatives. I have only a cousin of my mother, in Russia. I was trying to make my way there when I decided to risk coming here to find you."

He brushed the hair away from her wet face and kissed her forehead. "If only I had known, I would have come for you. Instead God has brought you back to me. Marry me, Ruth."

"I—I—I didn't come here to—"

Daniel cupped her hands and kissed them. "I love you. Can you say you don't love me?"

She walked away, turning her back to him. "Your father will never accept such a union."

"He's different now. He's changed."

She turned to face Daniel, and he noted the tightness of her down-turned mouth and the unease in her eyes. "Has he? I wrote you so many letters, Daniel. Every week these two years I poured my heart out to you in writing. Did you ever receive even one?"

"I—I—I was away at Cambridge." He sought some answer that did not implicate his father, but he could find none.

"I went to the castle today to see you, but your father turned me away. As I was leaving the sheriff picked me up and returned me to your father's door, but again, there was no welcome waiting there for me. Instead, he instructed the sheriff to arrest me."

Daniel paced as he tried to reconcile the man Ruth was describing with the father he had recently reclaimed. "He's afraid I'll leave him again. I'll speak with him. When he sees how much I love you and knows I'll still fulfill my duty in Parliament, he'll welcome you."

Daniel mounted his horse, placing Ruth behind him, and they set off back to Whittington Castle. The opening of the heavy door brought Ridley rushing to the grand foyer, and when he saw Ruth in Daniel's company, the color drained from his already pasty face.

"Where is my father, Ridley?"

"He's . . . he's in his study, I believe."

Daniel transferred Ruth's hand to Ridley's arm. "Please get her something to eat."

As Ridley and Ruth headed to the kitchen, Daniel steeled himself and entered the study. His father was sitting in a chair reading, but as soon as he saw his son, curiosity then worry crossed his face. He rose and set the book aside. "You're back? Is everything all right?"

Daniel eyed his father carefully. "I stopped in Dunwoody, Father, where I found my friend Ruth in the constable's custody by your orders." He noticed the narrowing of his father's eyes. "When I was confused, with nowhere to go, Ruth and her father took me in, fed me, cared for me. How could you turn her away from your door and into the hands of the constable? What if I hadn't come upon her? She came to England seeking escape from the horror of war. Instead, she nearly found herself jailed."

The earl looked as if he would panic, but he quickly recovered and spoke with an air of authority. "I acted in haste. If she needs a place to stay for the evening, or travel funds, arrangements can be made, but I cannot harbor an enemy in a time of war."

Daniel offered a sarcastic laugh. "I doubt one war-ravaged woman will do England irreparable harm, Father. And what of her letters? Why did you withhold them from me?"

"They were written to a confused boy. I was trying to spare you further confusion."

"You had no right. If there was any confusion, it was solely on your part, Father. But let me clarify things for you. I love Ruth, and she loves me. And in the near future, if she blesses me with a 'yes,' we will marry, but that needn't frighten you. I don't need to choose to love one of you or the other. We can be a family together, but the choice is entirely yours."

"Do you actually believe there is room for that woman in the world you have embraced? A Jew? Really, Daniel? As a member of the House of Lords you will vow to uphold the holy Church of England. How can you do that while married to a woman who denies the Christ? No! She will go, and you will tell her tonight."

"If she goes, then so will I, Father. And there will be no further reconciliations."

The earl's voice turned cold and dark. "Leave again and there will be no *option* for further reconciliation. And you'll leave as you stand there—no money now or in the future. It will be the end of your education, the end of all your dreams. Is she worth that to you, Daniel?"

Apparently drawn by the commotion, Ruth raced into the doorway. Daniel extended his hand to her and she rushed to him. "You have forgotten the value of love, Father. She is worth everything."

The couple turned for the front entrance. The earl leapt to his feet and chased after them, yelling, "Daniel, if you cross that threshold it will be as if you never existed! Your name will be blotted from the family record. I will never acknowledge you or your seed!"

Daniel shook his head, saying, "I pity you, Father," just before the door slammed shut.

On the front porch, Daniel turned to Ruth and kissed her hand. Marry me today."

Worry filled every corner of her face. "How will we live? You are disowned, and I have nothing and no one."

"I still have all the money I earned in Greece. I sent it ahead to Cambridge with my things. If we hurry we can collect it before my father sends someone to confiscate it."

A glimmer of hope shone briefly in Ruth's eyes. "We are utterly alone in the world. Where can the exiled son of an earl and his Jewish wife find peace?"

"In America," Daniel replied. "I know a place where we'll be welcome in the meantime. We'll move to Liverpool. I'll get a job on the docks, and we'll save our money, and when we have enough we'll sail to America. I'll find a medical school there. You'll see."

Ruth framed his face with her hands and kissed him. "What are we, Daniel? What will our children be? Neither Jew nor Christian? There are truths from my religious training I cannot abandon—the teachings of the prophets, my belief in the miracles and power of God, the comfort of angels, God's holy temple. And what of your Jesus? What faith embodies all these things?"

He pulled her to him and held her tight. "I don't have all the answers, and maybe there are no answers for some of our questions. I only know that this is right—that *we* are right."

She nodded, and with that simple assurance they raced on to Cambridge and collected Daniel's money. He took nothing else—not a shirt or a shoe beyond what he already wore. A local vicar married them that night, and five shillings were spent on a simple meal and room at an inn, where they spent their wedding night.

Home was a Liverpool flat that Ruth adorned with curtains and linens made from embroidered flour sacks. Their needs were few, and though his father's decree of banishment echoed in Daniel's ears from time to time, he held fast to his name, hoping that in time his father might come seeking his only family.

The name Spencer drew curiosity along the wharf. Some thought they recognized Daniel and asked if he were the son of the earl. "Do I live like the son of an earl?" Daniel would always counter good-naturedly, never actually putting the question to rest. In time, people stopped asking the question; they were content to simply know the loving couple as the Spencers, a hard-working pair whose door was always open, and whose table always had room for one more.

Though Daniel came home bone-weary every night from loading and unloading ships, he had never been happier in his life. He soon discovered the limits of medical care for the poor, and his desire to complete his education burned within him. One weekend he traveled to Cambridge to see his professor and explain the circumstances behind his abrupt withdrawal from school.

The professor slipped a precious medical text into Daniel's hands, telling him not to surrender his dream. Armed with that book, he spent what little free time he had studying in the library, adding more knowledge of herbs and natural medicinals to what the healers in Ruth's community had taught him. With Ruth by his side, he went about offering assistance to the poor, despite Britain's laws against the practice of medicine by unlicensed physicians. Their services were limited at first—bandaging wounds, delivering babies, sitting by the bedsides of the sick—but as Daniel's confidence and competency increased, he became known as "Doc" along the port.

Week by week the little honey jar grew with coins from his dock work, and their pantry was never empty as their 'patients' paid them by sharing what little they had. Each day as Daniel passed the offices of the passenger ship fleet, he'd check the price of passage as he read the names of the ships sailing to America the next day. It had become a ritual for the clerk to ask him if he was ready to buy a ticket yet. He knew that day was still quite far off.

He'd frequently come home from his dock work leading a trail of "patients" to his door, only to find several more lined up outside, while others, whose concerns were within Ruth's level of medical expertise, were inside being cared for. One day on his walk home, Daniel found one of his regulars, a spry owner of a dozen alley cats, sitting on the ground, surrounded by sympathetic but unskilled people merely catching enough gossip to share by their evening fires. He quickly assessed the old codger, whose complaint was in his lower back.

"Two ornery thieves run me right down, Doc! One was a stocky brute. The smaller one toppled down hard when he hit me and tore his shoulder up pretty bad. I told the officer so they could find the devils."

Daniel gently helped the man to his feet. "Let's get you back to my house and put a poultice on that back, shall we?"

The old man's hobbled gait improved remarkably as soon as the aroma of Ruth's mutton stew reached the pair. Daniel opened the door, calling out, "Set another bowl, darling. I believe Henry will be dining with us tonight."

Ruth smiled brightly at their friend. "What is it today, Henry? Is your cough back?"

"The most odd thing, missy. Two hooligans nearly broke my back, didn't they, Doc?"

Ruth glanced at Daniel, whose eyebrows rose humorously over the comment.

"But here's the strangest part. One of them apologized and tried to help me up, though the officers were bearing down on the lad."

"Sounds as if he's more likely a decent lad who's in trouble than a hooligan."

"The other one was a mean cuss. He'll be someone to reckon with in a few years."

After two bowls of stew and some bones for the cats, Henry took his leave. Less than five minutes later a knock sounded on the Spencers' door. When Daniel opened it, he found a balding, middle-aged man with an overly gratuitous, gap-toothed smile, standing in the doorway in the company of two adolescent boys who fit the description of Henry's hooligans. The smaller of the two boys had a lean, mature face, though he made no eye contact. The larger of the boys retained the round-faced look of youth, though his eyes darted about hungrily, assessing everything within his gaze. Something about the boys seemed oddly familiar, and though Daniel couldn't recall having ever met them before, he felt wary and nervous about their visit.

Daniel nodded for Ruth to hide in the back room while he stepped outside and closed the door behind him. Straightening to his full height, he asked coolly, "May I help you?"

The man removed his soiled cap, and when he spoke, the smell of ale was thick on his breath. "I heard you're a fine doctor who caters to the distressed and the poor."

Daniel noted the gold pocket-watch chain peeking out from the man's tattered jacket, and he knew their distress was legal rather than financial. Those avoiding the law dared not visit a hospital or clinic, and as word of mouth spread, Daniel saw more and more of the waterfront's riffraff coming to his door. "I'm not a doctor, sir. Just a dockworker."

The man pushed the smaller of the two young men forward, whose blood-smeared shoulder was set at an odd angle. The man chortled. "My boy here said you'd say that, knowin' as he did that it's contrary ta the law for a man ta practice medicine without a proper license. And yet I know you do." He cackled again. "No need ta hide it. Folks up and down the waterfront talk about your kindness, and we wouldn't want that little bit of news ta leak ta the authorities, seeing as you're so kind to help out those who need ya."

Daniel clearly heard the implied threat. "I have no medicines— only herbs. And I have no instruments, save these." He held his hands up.

"'Twill do," the man replied, shoving his sons closer.

Daniel barred the doorway, nodding at the injured lad. "Only him."

"But I'm his father, and this here is his brother."

"I know how your son became injured. I treated the old man they ran over, and I believe you'd be as interested in keeping the law out of this as I. Those are my terms."

Anger flared on the man's face but then quickly dissipated. "You're a sly one, Doc."

Without a reply, Daniel pulled the boy in, then shut and barred the door. Pointing to a chair, he said, "Sit and tell me your name."

"Michael," was the reply, though the boy never raised his eyes. "I think I broke my shoulder."

"Really?" After a quick exam, Daniel exclaimed, "Yes, you've sustained quite a bad break. Did your father try to reset it? That would be a terribly painful mistake." The lad's silence assured Daniel he was right.

Michael ran the back of his hand across his nose. "He's not my father, not really. He just married my mother before she died."

"I see." Daniel tipped the boy's face upwards. "And is the boy actually your brother?"

Michael looked down and nodded.

"You two seem very different." Michael didn't reply, and Daniel let the conversation lag as he applied a figure-eight sling. "This should hold the shoulder in place while it heals. So you know a bit about medicine as well as the law? How is that? How old are you?"

"Eleven, but I like to read," he answered sheepishly. "I love the libraries."

"I do too."

"Why aren't you a real doctor? You fixed me fine."

Daniel winced slightly. "My situation is complicated. I help those in need where I can."

"How is he, sir? The old man, I mean."

"He's bruised and his back is strained," Daniel explained soberly, "but he'll be fine. I'd like to clean that wound on your shoulder. It could get infected."

"No need to bother. I'll tend to it. And I'm sorry. Will you tell the old man that?"

"I will, Michael. That shoulder will require a few months to fully heal. Come and see me again in eight weeks so I can check your progress."

The boy nodded, rose stiffly, and began to leave. Daniel followed and unlocked the door. "Michael, have we ever met before? You seem familiar to me."

"I don't believe so, sir."

"Hmm. Perhaps I've met your real father."

"I doubt that, sir. He died when I was very small. A few years later we lost our mother."

"I'm sorry. Well, I'm here if you ever need to talk to someone."

With a final glance back, Michael opened the door and exited the Spencers' home.

"All patched up?" asked Richard Porter.

Hank took a playful but powerful swing at his brother's wounded shoulder, forcing Michael to react swiftly and causing him further pain. "Baby," Hank taunted.

Michael paid him no regard and began walking away alone.

"Still mad, are ya?" Porter asked. "Pickin' pockets is a mite riskier than beggin'. The family's got t'expect we'll have some bad days until you two hone your skills."

"We're not a family! We're criminals!"

"Don't be so quick to judge us. You fancy that nice Doc Spencer, don't you? Well, he was once a criminal too—stole money from his father. You two share somethin' else ya might find interestin', Michael. He's the boy your father kidnapped the night he was caught."

Michael's eyes grew wide. "He's the viscount?"

"The same. 'Twas his nanny your father murdered."

The boy swallowed hard.

"It's said in polite circles that his father sent him far away ta keep him safe, but the lad was so distraught about the separation that he came ta hate his own father, and then he robbed him and ran away. The two don't speak anymore. So before you judge what makes a family, keep that bit o' history in mind."

Ruth came out from the back room. "Is everything all right?"

Daniel pulled her to him and held her close. "Word is spreading about our clinic amongst the criminals along the waterfront. The man tonight blackmailed me into treating his son." He brushed her hair back and stared into her eyes. "We spend half of what we make on medical supplies, and we give most of the rest away. It'll be months, maybe years before we can afford to sail to America. Until then, we need to be more careful. I don't want you seeing patients alone. In fact, I want you to promise me that from now on you'll lock the door when I'm not here."

"All right." Ruth pressed close and clung to her husband. "I could get a job at one of the mills. The extra money would help us buy passage more quickly."

"No. Those factories treat their workers like slaves. I'll take extra shifts on the dock. Don't worry. It'll all work out fine."

But sometimes at night, when Ruth was asleep, Daniel would worry about their situation. His thoughts would turn to his father, wondering what he thought on the day his gift box of cigars had arrived. Had he kept them? And if so, did they conjure thoughts of the son who had sent them? Daniel cast a glance at his sleeping wife, and his heart settled. Ruth was his only family now, and their course was clear.

CHAPTER 23

Fall 1822
Philadelphia, Pennsylvania

The world seemed to be changing at a galloping pace, and with advances in technology came the strain of government to incorporate these changes in their districts. The brief holiday break from work was not truly a break for Jed, who spent most of his waking hours poring over reports and charts detailing some of the marvels of their day.

Hannah would play with James in the crisp air until he fell asleep, at which time she'd curl up beside Jed with a good book, her feet in his lap, which he rubbed as he studied. There were a few pleasant diversions. Despite his protestations at being "fancied out" from Annapolis's vibrant social calendar, she cajoled him into attending the Stringhams' grand holiday ball. It soon became apparent that it was primarily hosted to promote White Oak's stables. Nevertheless, the occasion gave Hannah an opportunity to reconnect with the other local ladies, and Jed couldn't deny the pleasure he felt at seeing her fully happy and vibrant again.

The couple hosted a party of their own—for all the residents of Willowsport. Though the public's name for their area still sounded foreign to them, the Willows was now a full-fledged community, and the money taken in from the shops along the wharf had brought prosperity to all the residents. Jed finally acquiesced to the change, placing a "Welcome to Willowsport" sign at the landing the day his family departed back to Annapolis.

Their return to Annapolis was brief. Jed offered the assembly the results of his research on the topics of installing gas lighting in Maryland's major cities, labor concerns arising in Baltimore's burgeoning garment industry and cotton mills, and the cost effectiveness of switching to anthracite rather than softer bituminous coal. It was then decided Jed should visit cities that had already transitioned to these changes, to speak to their officials, and another multi-week, several-city, Pearson family trip was planned.

Their itinerary was set to coincide with a standing invitation to attend a Philadelphia party Frannie and Phillip were throwing to begin Phillip's mayoral campaign. A letter was sent ahead by special courier to announce Jed and Hannah's intended arrival date. Three days later, on January 22, they arrived with James in tow, as a chilling winter snow began to fall.

Frannie caught the cherry-cheeked toddler up in a loving embrace and kissed him until he giggled. "I've been worried sick about you three traveling in this frigid weather."

Jed dusted the snow from his shoulders and helped Hannah remove her heavy coat. "Fortunately, we had a heated carriage. Otherwise, we'd likely have never made it over the line."

Frannie slung James onto one hip. "I can't believe how he's grown. Children really do grow like weeds. I have so much to learn." Phillip tried to stop her announcement, but Frannie's enthusiasm bubbled over, and she blurted out, "We're adopting two children!"

"Sarah and Charles?" exclaimed Hannah with an excited clap of her hands. "I'm thrilled for you both. Congratulations!"

Jed and Hannah turned to offer Phillip equal congratulations only to find his face looking pinched. A quick glance back at Frannie showed hurt in place of her previous joy.

Patting his brother-in-law on the arm, Jed said, "Don't be nervous, Phillip. If a farmer can learn to sing lullabies and change nappies, so can a banker. You'll do just fine."

✶ ✶ ✶ ✶ ✶

While the women discussed the party plans, Phillip whisked Jed away to his study to discuss campaign strategies. "I feel doubly blessed to have you here, Jed. More than anything, I want to win this election and be a good mayor."

"'More than anything' is a very dangerous attitude with which to begin public service."

Phillip sputtered and fumbled with the drink he was pouring for Jed as he corrected himself. "What I meant to say is, I want to be elected so I can serve Philadelphians well."

Jed eyed his brother-in-law carefully as he took the drink from his hand. "My best advice for you is, don't lose yourself or your family along the way. Politics is an intoxicating arena. It's hard to tell your friends from your enemies because they often look and sound similar. You're blessed with a wife who loves you, and you'll soon have a family. Stay true to them and remember all the goals you set when you began."

Phillip nodded and rolled his hands as if moving the conversation along. "Yes, yes, I agree completely, but none of that will matter if I can't win the election. Surely Hannah made sacrifices while you established your campaign."

"Sadly, too many. I felt my constituents needed me more than my family, and that after the election I'd be able to balance it all. In the end, I nearly lost all I hold most dear."

Phillip's expression softened. "I love Frannie, Jed. I'd never knowingly do anything to jeopardize that. But I need advice on how to build a strong campaign. For example, should I support President Monroe's intolerance of European interference in this hemisphere?"

Jed rose in his seat. "You can't be serious."

"Will such a hard line interrupt Philadelphia's international commerce?"

Jed cleared his throat with a sound that resembled an annoyed grunt. "The Monroe Doctrine, as it's being called, rejects the meddling of European nations in the affairs of Western nations, and warns against any future plans for colonization here. How can that be but good for the nation and her businesses?"

"Well put! Now, I know you're touring cities to glean ideas on how to move your state forward. Perhaps I can help you, and in doing so, perhaps you can also help me."

Jed sat back and marveled over this man. "Then tell me about Philadelphia's labor laws."

"Labor laws? Constituents don't care about that. They care about revenue and jobs."

"Very well. Philadelphia has textile mills. Have you ever toured them? Do you know who fills those jobs, and how old those workers are? Did you know that on average, half of America's factory workers are under the age of ten?"

"I toured them . . . once. And I saw children there. The supervisor said they were the only ones small enough to move between the bulky machines and change the spindles."

"Is that a life you'd want for your children? Do you know how many hours the average factory worker puts in each day, and under what conditions? Fourteen, with an hour or less for breaks and meals. I know plantation owners who treat their slaves better."

"But what has this to do with politics?"

Jed glared at the man. "Everything, Phillip! How long have you been a city councilman?"

"I'm in my first term. I filled the seat of a councilman who retired early."

Folding his arms across his chest, Jed rolled his eyes and huffed. "Perhaps you should consider serving on the council longer before attempting to run the entire city. Philadelphia is more populated than some states. Governing requires you to preserve and protect the quality of life of your constituents, and to create a framework where the brilliance and ingenuity of your citizens can thrive, while protecting the rights of the individual. We live in a marvelous time. Inventions we never dreamed of a few decades ago are changing the landscape and improving lives, but without good governance to secure and maintain individuals' rights, we'd step back forty years and have tyrants and oppressors once more."

With a shrug, Phillip shoved his hands into his pockets. "You've given me much to think about if I'm blessed to be the next mayor, but for now I just need a winning campaign."

Not even two blankets and a down quilt could warm Frannie's bones on this, the coldest day she believed she had ever awakened to. Ice was thick in the window corners, and Phillip was burrowed so deeply beneath the covers that only an errant tuft of hair was visible.

Hating to awaken him from such a sound sleep, Frannie gritted her teeth and pulled her woolen wrapper around her. After shoving her feet into the slippers on the floor by the bed, she dashed to the fireplace to stoke the embers back to life. In a few seconds her bravery was rewarded as the fire warmed first her hands, and then her backside.

Rapid footsteps sounded outside the door, followed by an equally rapid knock. "I didn't expect you to be up so early today, Mrs. St. Clair. I'll get Cook to hurry breakfast along, and I'll get your bath drawn directly."

Frannie hurried to the door and cracked it open. "Thank you, Martha. We have a busy day today, so I want to get an early start. Have Mr. and Mrs. Pearson awakened yet?"

"Not a peep, nor from that darling little son of theirs. Shall I knock on their door?"

"No, you've plenty to do. I'll awaken them."

When she closed the door and turned back toward the bed, Frannie found Phillip smiling from across the room. "Good morning, beautiful."

She hurried across the floor and slipped beneath the covers he held open for her. "Good morning, darling," she said.

"Did you sleep well? Today is a very important day. If things go well at tonight's party, you could be awakening beside Philadelphia's next mayor come November."

Frannie tensed at the mention of the topic that so preoccupied her husband's every thought. "All the arrangements are in place, Phillip. Hannah and I just need to slip by the asylum to drop off additional blankets and see the children. They were nearly blue from the cold the other day, but we'll be back in time to arrange the flowers and plants when they arrive from the arboretum. In fact, why don't you come with us? You haven't seen Sarah and Charles in weeks."

"I can't, and perhaps you should cancel your visit to the children today as well."

Frannie stiffened. "Cancel? I miss them, Phillip, don't you? It's painful enough that the adoption paperwork hasn't cleared yet. I'd still like to have Charles and Sarah here tonight. They're going to be part of our family, and tonight is a perfect time to announce that."

Barely meeting her eyes, Phillip placed his hands on Frannie's arms and pulled her close, then began rubbing her neck and shoulders. "Look at how tense you are. You already have too many things pressing on these lovely shoulders."

"Honestly, Phillip!" she snapped, abruptly standing as she began pulling the day's attire from her wardrobe.

"I know you want the children to be here," Phillip said calmly. "I think that sounds lovely too, but we have a lifetime to share with them. Why add further stress to an already critical day?"

Frannie spun on him, not caring that her disappointment in him was apparent. "When did running for mayor switch from being a folly to being critical?"

Phillip threw the covers off and huffed. "Now you sound like your brother. He as much as said I wasn't ready to be mayor. Are you also of that opinion?"

"I'm not saying that. I'm only asking you to recall that there are concerns far more critical than a campaign party—things like keeping the orphans warm this winter. The farmers at the market agree this is one of the coldest on record, which worries me since the groundskeeper at the asylum thinks that the furnace mortar is badly cracked. If Mrs. Cassidy responds to the cold by stoking the boiler fire too high, the entire building could go up in flames."

"Frannie, listen to yourself. You're taking advice from groundskeepers and farmers now? Really, darling, that building is less than five years old, designed by the finest architects in the city, who contracted fine builders to construct it. You needn't fret over its safety."

"Say what you will, but I won't be able to concentrate on this party if I'm worried about the children. A word from you and someone would check the mortar on the coal furnace today. And what of the five new coal stoves you promised to deliver to keep the children warm?"

An exasperated rush of air preceded Phillip's acquiescence. "I don't need this today of all days, Francis, but very well. I'll see to it."

The asylum was barely warmer than the barn when Hannah and Frannie arrived to hand out the treats and extra blankets they had gathered. Then the pair spent an hour in a side room with Sarah and Charles, and Frannie introduced the children to the woman who would soon be their aunt Hannah.

"Is this the day Charles and I get to go home with you?" asked Sarah.

Hannah turned away from the scene as Frannie knelt by the little girl to explain how the court was delaying the adoption. "I wish it was today, my darlings, but I promise you if it's much longer, I'll march to the courthouse and arm-wrestle the judge to get those papers signed."

When the bell rang for lunch, the children scurried off. Frannie's hungry eyes followed them until they disappeared around the corner.

"In their hearts, Sarah and Charles are already yours. They clearly love you, Frannie."

Frannie patted her chest, her emotions rising. "I know, Hannah, but I'm powerless to get this paperwork finalized, and Phillip is too distracted with politics to attend to it himself. I suppose you heard our argument this morning."

Smiling contritely, Hannah took her sister-in-law's arm. "What time are the flowers being delivered from the arboretum?"

Frannie glanced at the clock on the mantel. "Soon, but I'm not leaving until I see the five coal stoves delivered."

"Phillip will be vexed."

A defiant smirk stole across Frannie's mouth. "I don't care!"

Two more hours passed. The stoves still had not arrived when the St. Clair's maid pulled up in a wagon to summon Frannie home. "Mr. St. Clair's in a sorry state, ma'am. He sent me here to fetch you home straight away."

Embarrassment flushed Frannie from her neck to her brow. "I'm not a bone to be fetched, Martha. Tell Mr. St. Clair I'm awaiting the delivery of the coal stoves for the school."

The woman nodded nervously. "Sorry, ma'am. He also told me to tell you he'd see to that errand personally—just as soon as you arrive home to handle the party details."

Frannie stood motionless for several more seconds before harrumphing so loudly even Hannah seemed taken aback. Frannie finally turned to her for support, but Hannah was clearly at a loss over what to do or say. "Hurry home, Martha," Frannie ordered the maid. "Tell Mr. St. Clair that Mrs. Pearson and I will be along directly."

Frannie looked down the hall, hoping to catch a final glimpse of the children before she left. Seeing no one, she resigned that she must leave them yet again, and she turned for the door, but Hannah remained stalled in the entrance, turning her head as if attuning to a voice.

Curious, Frannie did likewise, but she heard nothing unusual. "What is it?"

"Oh, nothing," Hannah said, though her brows were knitted close together. "I was just thinking that maybe we should just take Sarah and Charles home with us."

Frannie revisited that thought. "Oh, how I wish we could, but it's more critical that I get his support on pushing the adoption through, and as you said, he's already vexed."

Hannah nodded, though the crease in her brow remained.

Jed was still out when the women arrived at the St. Clair home. Flowers and plants stood in heaps in the foyer, and Phillip was in a snit, ordering the maids to begin arranging things despite their protests that Frannie was on her way. His greeting was icy as she and Hannah walked through the door. With a shake of his head, he donned his hat, coat, and gloves and stormed past the women, saying only, "You neglected to order brandy."

"Phillip, wait! I'm . . . I'm sorry!" Frannie gasped. "But what about the stoves?"

He stopped in his tracks, tilted his head only slightly in her direction, and said, "Don't worry. I keep *my* word." Then he closed the door against the frigid wind and was gone.

Unnerved by the tension between them, Frannie wasted the first hour berating herself for her error and double-checking everything else, while Hannah set about arranging plants and evergreen swags in the grand foyer and parlor. The two women combined talents in the dining room, setting boughs over the windows and doorframes and placing magnificent arrangements in the corners, and down the center of the buffet table. When the work was completed, Hannah dusted her hands off and surveyed the scene. "It's beautiful, if I do say so myself."

Frannie scanned the decorations. She had to admit the décor was everything she had envisioned, a setting that would impress the wealthy campaign donors and politicians Phillip had invited, and yet it left her somehow empty. "Yes, it is lovely, and it ought to be. Phillip gave me a scandalous budget which I spent completely."

"And yet I can see by your expression that something's still not right."

"No, it isn't," Frannie said absently as both hands moved to her hips with a smug little jerk. "Actually, something is very wrong, and I'm going to rectify it. I haven't heard Phillip come in yet, have you?" The scrape of the front door echoed down the hall. "That's probably him. I need to speak with him right away."

She nearly walked over Jed. "Oh, it's you," she said with obvious disappointment.

"Well done, ladies! I thought I was in the Queen's Garden in London." He placed a kiss on each woman's cheek. "Phillip couldn't ask for anything more lovely than this."

"No, he couldn't!" Frannie agreed with a touch of impudence. "And I deserve a reward."

"The children?" Hannah said. "I want to bring them here, too."

"Yes, the children," said Frannie. "Jed, will you help me?"

Jed was reading in the study when Phillip finally arrived home, sputtering under his breath as he hastily removed his coat, hat, and scarf. When he surveyed the foyer, his dismay quickly subsided into awe. "It's stunning, absolutely stunning," he muttered to himself.

Jed appeared and smiled. "The women did it all in a few hours. I'd say they outdid themselves, though we've all been worried you'd miss your own party."

He shot Jed a look of utter exasperation. "Was the brandy delivered?"

"Hours ago."

Phillip nodded his relief, and then a new worry crossed his face. "I've spent the last three hours racing about the city in a panic over coal stoves for the orphans. Frannie gave me an assignment to buy them days ago, which I fully intended to do, but I've been so busy. And today I got sidetracked at City Hall with my campaign chairman, and all but forgot about them. I suddenly remembered at four and have been scouring the city ever since, looking for these

257

contraptions, but the stores were either out or closed. Has she been asking for me?"

"Several times."

"Please don't mention my error to her."

"I stopped by the children's home this afternoon, and it was already uncomfortably cold," Jed said.

Phillip's hand covered his mouth as he paced the foyer. "I let her down, Jed. I let the children down, too. Frannie was right. I've lost track of my priorities."

"What can we still do tonight? Can we get a mason to check the safety of the furnace?"

Phillip waved his hand dismissively. "The furnace is fine, but I'll make arrangements to have the stoves delivered tomorrow. Right now I need to hurry and dress."

When he reached the bedroom and opened the door, he found Frannie dressed in a gown made of ivory silk, and for a second he held his breath. "You look absolutely radiant, and the house is . . . well, you've exceeded my wildest expectations, darling."

Frannie remained cool despite his effusive praise. "I thought you'd be pleased, and so I gave myself a gift. I hope you'll approve."

"You deserve it, whatever it is."

"Yes, yes, I do. Children!" she called out. Sarah and Charles entered from the adjacent room, dressed in the party attire she had purchased for them months earlier when she thought the adoption would already be finalized. "This is the reward I want, Phillip."

With a forced smile he complimented the children on their appearance, dismissing them back to their room in the same breath. "We discussed this, Francis. Do they even have the necessary grasp of etiquette needed for a night like tonight?"

"They're children, Phillip, not heads of state."

"One hour, Francis, and then I'll order the stableman to drive them back to the asylum." She began to protest but his expression was filled with pleading as he said, "Please, just make this one last sacrifice for me."

She felt the muscles in her jaw clench. Raising her hand, she pointed to the door behind which the children stood. "Do you still want this adoption?"

"Of course. It's just that the timing has—"

"Then give me your word you'll use your influence to push this adoption through."

"Don't be angry with me, Francis. Not on this night."

"Your word . . ."

"Fine! You have it. Do I now have your support?"

Frannie pasted on a smile and stood with Phillip and the children as he introduced Sarah and Charles to the arriving guests. Per his wishes, Jeffrey, the groomsman, swept the children back to the asylum before the clock struck nine. For the rest of the evening Phillip and Frannie circulated through the crowd, making small talk and watching how the guests gravitated to the heroic senator from Maryland and his wife. Frannie saw the envy in Phillip's eyes as Jed Pearson became the unexpected man of the hour.

When the door closed on another blast of stabbing cold as the last guest departed, Frannie turned to Phillip. "Thank you for attending to the stoves. I couldn't bear to send Sarah and Charles back there if I didn't know the home would be warm this night."

Jed quickly took Hannah by the hand and led her toward the stairs. "Frannie, Phillip. I'd say the evening was a great success. We'll say good night and see you in the morning."

Phillip jumped in. "I'm sure Frannie is far spent, as am I. I believe we'll turn in as well. Yes, we'll see you both in the morning."

Sometime after the hall clock chimed one o'clock, an unearthly clamor arose on the east end of town near Logan Square, causing Phillip to wonder if hell had released the dead souls confined there over the past two hundred years. Bells were clanging, and soon the cacophony of voices carried from all directions as horses and wagons began racing toward the Schuylkill River Bridge.

Phillip leapt from the bed and raced to the window. Off to the east he could see the eerie glow of fire. It was not an unusual sight in the coldest part of winter, when the city suffered more blazes caused by stray fireplace embers and faulty oil lamps. But this night, a sickening thud settled in his stomach as he looked again in the direction of the fire. *The asylum? No!* he prayed.

Sick with fear, he opened the window against the bitter cold, arousing Frannie. "You there!" he yelled down to a man on the street. "Where's the fire?"

"The children's home! It's all but lost!"

"The children's home?" Frannie cried. "Does he mean the asylum?"

Phillip sought some appropriate word or phrase to express the depth of his regret, but there was none. A groan was all he could manage as he quickly donned clothes to race to the scene. He watched Frannie's hands shake so violently she could scarcely gather her clothes to dress. In a moment Jed was there, pulling suspenders over his long johns while Hannah stood behind clutching James to her as if he too were in danger.

"Is it the asylum?" Jed asked, his eyes fixed on Frannie.

"Don't worry about Sarah and Charles. I'll look after them," Hannah offered.

Frannie covered her mouth to catch a shuddering breath. "Don't you know? They're not here. They were sent back to the asylum to sleep."

"Just say it," moaned Phillip as he shriveled with guilt. "I sent them back." He leaned heavily against the wall as he made his way toward the door. Unable to meet Jed's eye when he neared him, he simply said, "I'm going on ahead. Try to discourage Frannie from coming." Then, without waiting for a reply, he fled from the house, slamming doors shut behind him.

✷ ✷ ✷ ✷ ✷

Stumbling about, Frannie resisted all of Jed's and Hannah's efforts to comfort her. "They'll need more blankets," she muttered as she tore the covers from her bed.

"Frannie, let Jed go and help," Hannah pleaded. "I don't think you should be there."

With one manic, determined sweep of her hand, Frannie warned her brother and Hannah not to try to deter her, and she secured Jed's help. She was silent as he hitched the team, and then she took the reins from him, slapped the leather down hard on the poor horses' backs, and drove them at a merciless pace across the snow and ice toward the giant blaze. Only guttural sounds escaped her as they drew nearer and the extent of the devastation became clear.

The bells of several fire companies rang, but none had arrived. The only hope lay in the long line of men and buckets snaking across the frozen ground to an ice-topped pond from which they labored to draw water. Frannie prayed no one was still inside the blazing main building.

A large group was huddled near the willow tree in the asylum's front yard. Phillip and others were attending to the wounded and frightened children. Frannie leapt to the ground and raced there to check the children, seeking two faces in particular. Her husband shrank upon seeing her. "They're not here, Frannie. Dear God, they're not here."

She saw Mrs. Cassidy stumbling about in the yard, her face streaked with tears and soot, and her burned hands outstretched as she hoarsely called out the names of missing children. "Thomas! Mary! Where are you, children? Sarah? Charles?"

The sound of those two names sent a shock through Frannie. She ran to Mrs. Cassidy, nearly accosting the woman. "Where are they? Where are Sarah and Charles?"

"I don't know. Some forty children are unaccounted for. It all happened so quickly!"

The shattering of glass pierced the night, and all eyes shifted to the upper floor window, where two children were silhouetted.

Jed and a group of men dashed to the building, but the *whoosh* of a fireball drove them back. Another explosion rained glass and embers upon the ground. When the men looked up, the window was empty except for the red glow of death.

Jed fell to his knees, and Frannie was soon there, falling upon him, weeping over his back. From the corner of her eye she saw a haggard man with his mouth agape—Phillip. She felt empty, barren, devoid of empathy for his grief.

A cry sounded from a field near the pond. Seeking somewhere or someone to help, the men raced to the scene. Three children, burned and now nearly frostbitten, were huddled together against the barren branches of a hedge.

Wagons began carting the fifty-three survivors to hospitals, while brigades combed the fields for children who had escaped from a fiery danger into an equally merciless frozen landscape. As hours passed, one small body after another was retrieved. Frannie raced to each rescued soul, passing out blankets, offering words of comfort, praying . . . always praying.

Finally, two small forms, a boy and a girl, both blue-tinged and near death, were found in one another's frozen arms by a silo. Phillip arrived there first, and though his expression told Frannie it was Sarah and Charles, it also told her their condition was grave.

Jed and Phillip scooped the children up and placed them in the wagon, where Frannie soon sat holding them against her body, swathing them under blankets. The hospital was completely overwhelmed by the incident with too few doctors, beds, and supplies for such a disaster. Seeing the suffering and chaos all around her, Frannie made a rash decision. She took Jed's hand and squeezed it. "Please help me get them to Samuel, in Baltimore."

Four drivers stepped forward. After stopping at the house just long enough to get Hannah and James, the two-team party took off for Baltimore, leaving Phillip St. Clair and the city council of Philadelphia behind to attend to the funerals of the twenty-three children who perished.

CHAPTER 24

January 1822
The Willows

Frannie now requested the miracle denied Hannah, as the lives of Sarah and Charles were placed in Dr. Samuel Renfro's hands. The children's initial prognosis included pneumonia and frostbite, along with lung distress brought on from smoke inhalation. Samuel could offer no assurance other than that he would do his best, a modest promise made with a sympathetic glance at Hannah, with whom he had shared a similar but unfulfilled promise.

Jed, Hannah, James, and Frannie moved into the Pearsons' Baltimore home, which sat within walking distance of the hospital. Painful, tenuous weeks of waiting passed. Phillip arrived the fourth day of Frannie's vigil, laying the cause of his delay on the need to plan the dead children's funerals, and an investigation into the cause of the fire. He brought the completed adoption papers with him, which proved a great comfort to Frannie, except that the immediacy with which they had suddenly been obtained cast doubts on her husband's previous excuses.

The pair could barely meet one another's eyes anymore, particularly when Phillip divulged the fire's cause. "You were right, Frannie. The older boys stoked the furnace high, and the mortar cracked, igniting the wood framing. If I had only listened to you—"

Frannie merely grabbed her cloak and invited him to the hospital to see the children. Two days later, Phillip packed his bags and headed back to Philadelphia. Frannie didn't share the content of their conversations, or of Phillip's letters that arrived between visits, but Hannah noticed the lag between his visits, while the duration of each stay grew ever shorter.

Frannie maintained a faithful vigil by her children's bedsides. When Hannah could convince her sister-in-law to rest, she would place James in Lily and Bartholomew's faithful care and stay with the recovering children, reading books, singing songs, and cajoling them to eat. When exhaustion threatened to overwhelm Frannie, Hannah spent the night in a chair between their two beds or staring out the window that overlooked Baltimore's gas-lit streets. Her love and protectiveness for these children grew easily, and yet she felt an increased somberness growing in her that she could not explain or express, even to Jed.

In early February, Samuel announced that a critical corner had turned and his expectations were high that both of the children would suffer no residual harm from their ordeal. It was a moment of sweet bliss for the women, and Jed finally headed north alone, to complete his government assignment. Though Hannah had prayed earnestly for Sarah and Charles, she realized that they were also the source of her burden. Despite every effort to ignore the dark thoughts, she couldn't help but ask God, *If Thou blessed these children, then why not my Johnny?*

She hated that petty part of herself. She wouldn't—couldn't—deny God's existence. He had inspired her so personally in the past, but the God that preachers described seemed arbitrary and unfair, welcoming some of His children to heaven and banishing others, including some who never even lived long enough to sin. Either that, or bits of truth had been lost or altered over time.

Reverend Myers had told Hannah a reformation was once again occurring as this new generation saw more contradictions between the doctrines of churches and the written word of God. She thought of young Joseph Smith and his tales of having seen God the Father and His Son, a separate Savior, Jesus Christ.

Could it actually be true? Would God appear to a boy? And did Joseph really see what he said—two separate Beings, God the Father, and a God who was His Son?

It was so different than anything Hannah had ever been taught, yet it felt so simple and true!

To whom did Jesus pray in the garden? His Father?

But could it be? She wondered if the tender feelings such concepts stirred in her were a sign that the tales were true, or just a manifestation of her *wanting* them to be. Had precious, pivotal truths about the existence of both a Father and a Son been lost? And if so, what else had been lost or changed?

For a moment she dared not even give voice to her question, but then she heard herself utter, "Could the clergymen also be wrong about the fate of unbaptized souls?"

Hannah's inner debate came to a head on the day Samuel arrived at the hospital to sign the children's release papers. On his heels was the sweet older reverend who had come by frequently to pray for the children. After the joyous news was announced, the clergyman patted each of the children's heads, offering a remark intended to provide comfort. "God must love you children and your mother very much to have given you such a wonderful miracle."

The comment hit Hannah with such noticeable force that both Frannie and Samuel laid a comforting hand on her back. When the dear man left, Hannah moved to a corner to ponder the implication of the comment. Had God loved Johnny less? Or her? Or Jed?

Samuel came to her and took her hands. "Forgive him. He means well, Hannah."

"I—I—I know that. He's attended to us with the greatest tenderness these past weeks."

The moment became heavy. "You must know how—how much even I wish . . ."

She now became Samuel's comforter. "I know you did your best."

A weak smile graced his lips, and his shoulders rounded as he left the room.

"Can you ever forgive me?" Frannie asked. "I've been so preoccupied with my concerns, it never occurred to me how hard being here might be on you."

"You supported me when Johnny was hurt."

Frannie slipped an arm around Hannah's waist and laid her head on her shoulder. "You truly are my sister in every way that matters."

"I feel the same. I dread losing you to Philadelphia again. I'll miss you and the children."

Frannie walked a few steps away. "I'm not going back. You've noticed the conspicuous absence of my husband." She pulled a letter from the drawstring bag. "It seems Philadelphia is lauding their mayoral candidate as a hero for responding to the fire, but he says all of that becomes meaningless the minute I look at him. All he finds in my eyes is disappointment and judgment. He cannot bear to be around me anymore."

"I'm so sorry, Frannie."

Frannie walked to the window and stared out absently at the Baltimore harbor. "Oh, he assures me it is all being carefully orchestrated to protect us both. Articles began appearing in the *Times* the week of the fire, explaining my absence. First it was described as a humanitarian effort to rush a few orphans to Baltimore for treatment. The next week I apparently suffered a breakdown of sorts as a result of my devastation over the tragic deaths of the twenty-three children. Next week the papers will state that I cannot return to Philadelphia where the memories are so raw. In the end it will be said our marriage became the latest casualty of the fire."

"That's the most cowardly thing I've ever heard!" The impact of the situation finally hit Hannah. "Move back to the Willows. It would be a wonderful place to raise the children."

Relief showed on Frannie's face. "Thank you, Hannah. I prayed you'd ask."

★ ★ ★ ★ ★

Sarah and Charles took to the farm like calves to milk, enjoying the open space and leading their two-year-old cousin, James, along like a welcomed shadow. They joined their brown-skinned friends on trips to the Willowsport docks to be spoiled with treats and trinkets at every one of the twenty-odd shops now filling the burgeoning market.

Jed welcomed Frannie when he arrived home from reporting his findings to the assembly, though he sputtered off something about wanting to throttle her ex-husband. "I'll be more discerning the next time you bring a potential husband to meet me."

"There'll be no 'next time,' I assure you." She smiled as she caught a glimpse of the children on a tree swing Jack had rigged for them. "I have all I need now."

"Well, then it seems the perfect time to introduce an idea I've been toying with for some time. Wait just a moment." He left and returned carrying a scrolled bundle of papers, then led the women to the kitchen. He unrolled the papers across the table, revealing diagrams of a grand house. "This is the new home I want to build, employing all the wonderful inventions I've seen!"

Frannie cocked her head at Jed as if he were crazed. "A new home . . .?"

Hannah's expression was disapproving. "It looks like the President's House."

"Only generally, but smaller," he teased. "But it will have room enough for all of us, with a wing for you and your family too, Frannie." He pointed to a hill to the right. "We'll build it there, Hannah, on top of the northern slope." His mind leapt back to the drawings. "And see the conveniences! Indoor pumps in the kitchen and both bathing areas—which will be fitted with copper tubs. And a built-in icebox—a prototype from the inventor of the contraption. I tell you, I saw such wonders on this trip, Hannah! I foresee a day when every house will be gas-lit and plumbed with water pumped right in—even hot water! I saw steam engines inventors say will run on steel rails and move people more quickly than horses. And they have an electromagnetic device they say will also one day generate power. What a day we live in!"

Frannie lovingly rubbed a hand over the wood of one of the cupboards. "I'd prefer that my children and I remain here."

"It's old and in sore need of repair, Frannie."

"I know, Jed, but it's our history. Our grandfather built it with his own hands. Besides, the children and I will likely only be here in the summers and holidays. I'll still need to be in Baltimore most of the year to manage my businesses."

Jed suddenly sobered. "When I stopped in Baltimore to check on your children, Samuel delivered some disturbing news. Hildebrand was arrested for assault in North Carolina. His brothers found out, and they've stripped him of all holdings in the family companies."

Hannah's mouth dropped open. "He'll go off on another rampage."

"He and his friends are in jail awaiting trial, but his attorney is challenging the will and Samuel's medical integrity. They'll try to prove that Hildebrand's father was incompetent."

"When is this beast to be released?" asked Frannie.

"They nearly killed both victims, so I pray he's found guilty and issued a long sentence."

"Let me guess." Frannie huffed. "At least one was Negro, correct?"

Jed nodded. "A young freedman—a hotel porter who presumably scuffed Hildebrand's bags. Hildebrand and his colleagues were drunk, and their anger turned to violence. They tied the porter behind a horse and dragged him to teach him a lesson. A Quaker woman ran in front of the wagon, trying to stop it. They claim they didn't see her." Jed looked at the floor and shook his head. "Had one victim not been a white woman, the court might have released Hildebrand altogether, but even so, he may still be found innocent and set free."

As soon as the ground was warm enough to dig, work commenced on the new house, producing a melancholy excitement. Each advance on the new home drew the family one day closer to leaving behind the old. There would be no memories of Johnny in the new home, and Hannah wondered if she could ever feel welcome there.

On the day the house was completely under roof, Jed pulled Hannah from the kitchen and walked with her to the building site. From his pocket he pulled a blindfold, which he tied across her eyes, and then he led her inside the new structure, ignoring her questions about what on earth he was doing. Once they were in the shell where their bedroom would go, he removed the blindfold and pointed to the mantel. Hanging on the wall there was a portrait of Johnny, enlarged from their last family portrait.

Hannah stood spellbound, silent tears trickling down her face.

"Now this can be our family home."

CHAPTER 25

September 1822
The Willows

The announcement took up only six inches of a column in the *Baltimore Patriot*, an insignificant amount of notice for an event with such enormous consequences at the Willows. Emerson Hildebrand had not expected a jury in a North Carolina town to care about one broken man of color and a small Quaker woman, but they did, to the tune of eight years in prison.

Eight years—a season of peace. Though glad the miscreant could wage no further attacks on the farm and her families, the Willows men remained reserved in their joy. The big question now was whether the reality of a prison sentence and a lost inheritance would remove Hildebrand's fear of telling the truth about Skully's death. Would the felon's ignominy make him more hungry to have his revenge against Abel? They held their collective breath and waited.

In a note Frannie sent to Jed and Hannah in Annapolis in late November, she wrote:

> *The public's fascination with Phillip's heroism after the fire evidently waned during the campaign—he was defeated. He has laid the loss at my feet, saying the public wants a happily married mayor, and he*

has decided to proceed with a divorce. The true end of our marriage occurred months ago, and though I grieve over what might have been a satisfying union, I mourn more for the assault my character is undergoing.

A friend sent me clippings from the Philadelphia Examiner, *where I am cast as an emotional puddle! They are entirely ignoring the issues of negligence I raised. This must not go unanswered, and Hannah, when the children and I come home for Christmas, you must help me write an honest but appropriately scathing editorial reply.*

Still bristling over the thought of being painted an emotional wreck, Frannie enjoyed the time she and Hannah spent huddled over the kitchen table, drafting a pointed rebuttal. Their article became a scathing editorial not only about the deadly errors in construction that led to the tragedy, but also about the intolerable means of discipline she had witnessed at the asylum. It also ventured into the use of child labor in the mills and factories, and ended with a tender explanation of how Sarah and Charles were doing.

Her editorial spawned a flood of letters heralding her as a children's advocate. A month later, city and state women's groups took up the causes of orphans and child labor, and by the spring of 1823, four requests arrived for Frannie to speak publicly on the matter.

She and the children arrived at the Willows in a panic, well before summer, when they were expected for their annual respite. Hannah had never seen her perpetually confident sister-in-law so disarmed—pacing the floor one minute, and crumpling into a chair and biting her nails the next. "I think I'm going to faint! I can sing and dance before a thousand people, but I can't write and deliver a speech! You've got to help me, Hannah. You're so good at putting thoughts into words."

"Me? I don't know what to write. You're the one who spent time at the Orphan's Asylum. You know what you felt there . . . what you saw."

"Yes. See, Hannah? You help me sort things out. I need your help writing my speeches." Her eyes widened as a sly grin crossed her lips. "Come with me on these trips!"

Hannah jerked her head in shock. "That's the most preposterous idea I've ever heard! I don't know anything about the conditions in the orphans' homes or the factories."

Frannie backed up a step, placing her hands on her hips. "Well, maybe you should, Mrs. Pearson. After all, you're a state senator's wife. Maybe you should be aware of how Maryland treats their most vulnerable citizens."

Hannah pondered Frannie's point. "You do give me cause to think, Francis."

Frannie's eyes sparkled enticingly. "Two of the invitations are from cities in New York. We could slip over to Palmyra and see Beatrice!"

A surge of excitement shot through Hannah. "You are absolutely shameless!" But with her finger tapping against her lips, Hannah thought the proposition over. "What are the dates?"

"They're in the fall . . ." Frannie perused the letters again. "September . . . and we have the discretion to select the other two dates at our convenience."

"That's harvest time. Jed wouldn't be able to come along, and there's so much I need to do during that time to prepare for winter."

"Jed will be busy completing the new house before winter, Hannah, and as for the canning, you have a town here now. Hire some of the girls to do that while you advocate for the orphans. Besides, if we take a nanny along we could also bring our children. It would be a wonderful adventure for Sarah and Charles, and James could meet his New York cousins!"

"It does sound exciting, and perhaps we could do some good."

"Of course." Frannie clapped her hands together. "Then you'll come?"

"You'll have to help me become familiar with the issues."

Inches shorter and rounder than Hannah, Frannie straightened her back, assuming an authoritative posture. She held her hand out and shook her sister-in-law's. "Consider me your personal tutor."

The women's summer was peppered with visits to local orphan homes, factories, and mines. They heard grim tales of children under ten years old working twelve-hour shifts, six days a week, as threaders in mills, and diggers in the narrow mines, which ran day and night. There was no hope of an education for these meager-wage earners, but since most were from poor families who needed every penny, parents shuffled their offspring out the door of childhood and into an illiterate life of monotonous, hard labor for a dollar a week.

Horror stories were told of parents who couldn't afford to feed and clothe their children any longer, so they simply relinquished custody of their offspring to these facilities, which then became the new prison-like orphanages, with fences and guards preventing the children's escape. It was too horrible for Frannie and Hannah to fathom, and as their awareness increased, so did their anger and determination to improve these circumstances.

But there were signs of hope. Churches and teachers advocated for children until Connecticut led out, passing a bill requiring companies to provide schooling for employed children. And faithful, tireless clergymen ministered to these vulnerable citizens.

The reverends often waited outside factory gates, prepared to bandage the day's wounds. As they doled out food, they shared stories of God's love with the children, urging them to be saved through baptism. Again, the old ache over Johnny returned to Hannah's heart. Try as she did to put the concern to rest, it gnawed at her all summer.

The busy schedule made her time at home with James even more precious. She couldn't help comparing him to Johnny. At three and a half, James was part boy, part babe, ready to run and play one minute, needing a hug or a seat on his mother's lap the next. Where Johnny had been rambunctious from birth until the wasp incident, James was more thoughtful in his actions. Bright and inquisitive, he was less inclined to jabber than Johnny had been, but his thoughts and questions were profound for one of his tender age.

"It must be very sad to be a caterpillar, Mama."

"Why, James?"

"If your mother is already a butterfly, who tucks you into your cocoon?"

Hannah never tired of his observations. And as vain as it sounded, she had to admit he was a beautiful child, just as Johnny had been. James was perhaps an inch taller at three than Johnny, with large, dark eyes set against a rosy palette, and dark, straight hair instead of Johnny's bouncing halo of curls. James was thoughtful and considerate, and though he could run all day with the older children, he was careful, as if before birth God had explained to him the need for caution.

Jed loved that James was remarkably patient for a child, willing to sit on a riverbank and fish by Papa's side for hours with his own little pole and hook. Hannah would often pack a picnic lunch and go along, curling up under a tree with a book while they caught supper. She marveled at how comfortable they were together. Jed never tired of spending time with his boy, and adoration showed equally in James's eyes.

The days until the women would depart on their trip grew short. As excited as Hannah was to go, she couldn't deny a twinge of apprehension. It was apparent Jed felt it, too. One morning, she awoke to find him and James staring down at her with their fishing poles in hand.

"Wake up, Mama! We're going on a picnic!"

She brushed the sleep from her eyes and smiled at her son. "It's too early, James."

A glance at Jed revealed a sheepish grin that verified James's announcement. After a quick splash of water on her face, and a few moments to change, the three headed into the humid morning air for a family adventure. Three horses were saddled, included the loyal, aged Figaro, who carried James with a gentle, experienced gait.

"Are Frannie and the children coming along, too?"

"No. Today is just for us."

"Hmm," she swooned, wrapping her arms around Jed. "I do like the sound of that."

The three mounted their animals and headed off. "Where are we going?" Hannah asked when Jed reined the lead horse away from the docks and toward the slopes that led to the hunting cabin.

"The falls," he replied with a wink. "The best trout are in the pool up there."

James beamed at his mama as if he were about to bestow a great gift on her.

Hannah looked off to the right as the jagged cliffs broke toward the Patuxent and was grateful their path veered left to safer terrain. An hour passed, and as the hills became steeper, she caught the first sounds of rushing water flowing from Poplar Creek.

They crested the top where a flat, grassy meadow surrounded a broad pool of cold mountain water that flowed from western Maryland. Hannah hadn't ridden up here since Johnny died, and the beauty of the spot took her breath away.

Jed stopped untying the pack from his horse's back as he watched Hannah's reaction to the view. "You look as if you've never been here before."

"It's been a long time. I suppose I've forgotten how lovely it is."

"It's sad when we forget something so wonderful." Pensive, he returned to his work.

It was a curious statement, but Hannah didn't pursue it as she attended to setting up the picnic and getting James settled. She spread an old quilt under a wide oak tree that offered ample shade from the August heat. She read while the "men" cast their lines. Thirty minutes passed uneventfully at the pond, and with little cajoling, James was sent off to collect bugs and pretty stones, while Jed laid his gear aside and moved to the oak, and Hannah. He snuggled close, causing her to feign annoyance as she turned the next page with obvious deliberateness.

"I miss you already."

She smiled, eyeing him sarcastically. "You'll be so busy. You'll be glad for time alone."

"I will be busy with the harvest, and then there's the promise I made to arrange the shipping of Frederick's horses on Arthur's ships." He sighed. "But I'll still miss you two."

"We'll write you every day." She smiled again and turned another page.

"What are you reading?" Jed asked as he nuzzled her cheek.

She turned the cover toward him. *"Persuasion,* by Jane Austen."

"Another novel by the brooding British authoress."

Hannah smacked Jed lightly with the book and folded her arms in mock protest. As the promise of a kiss hung near, she taunted Jed. "After all the times you've ignored me to fish, now, when I'm engrossed in this chapter, you suddenly—" She noticed the shift in his expression from glib to glum. "I'm just teasing. I don't mind setting it aside today." She nestled against him. "If it's any comfort, it has a happy ending, like our story."

"We are happy, aren't we? I mean, we had a rough spot a few years ago. I was a fool, and then we lost Johnny, but we truly are happy now."

"Yes, we are, but what's really on your mind, Jed? Why did we come to this special spot, and why the comments about how we sometimes forget so easily?"

"Because I needed to talk to you alone, away from Frannie and the children's ears."

"What's really going on?"

"Frannie mentioned you're going to Palmyra. Are you going to talk to Joseph Smith?"

Hannah's head bent as she fumbled with the pages of the book. "I hope to."

"Why didn't you tell me?"

She sat back and let her mind wander until it found the truth. "I was afraid you'd ask me not to, and I didn't like either of the options that would leave me."

From his silence, she knew she was right.

"It's a bad situation up there, Hannah. We've both read Beatrice's letters. Joseph's family has had nothing but trouble and controversy these three years since he told the reverend his story."

"Since when have we shied away from something because of controversy, Mr. Pearson?"

"Beatrice said even long-standing family friends have turned away from the Smiths over this, questioning their morality as well as their sanity."

Hannah wove her fingers through Jed's, then brought his to her lips and kissed them. "Who knows better than you how a good man can have his name assailed? How did you feel when the British called you a murderer and a coward? And some of Washington City's fine citizens were willing to let the British hang you—an innocent man—rather than give up the real shooter. And if I recall the story correctly, you stood before the British Admiralty and told them you'd be willing to die—to be their scapegoat—if only they'd allow you to clear your good name. Does Joseph not deserve the same?"

Jed looked away from her, and Hannah knew these were not his true concerns. Whatever it was, it was something deeper and more frightening to him than the opinions of men.

"What compels you to go?" he asked softly. "Is this still because you worry over Johnny?"

Her body became rigid. Now she was the one who needed to hide her eyes. "Every time I hear a minister warn a small child that his soul is in danger if he fails to be baptized, I die inside. Did we consign our innocent little boy to everlasting hell, Jed? I worry over this every day. Am I crazy?"

"No, no, of course not. I feel the same."

A groan of relief escaped her, and her body relaxed. "I even feel him near me. Sometimes I even talk things over with him and I tell him how much I still love him and miss him. Jed, if death is the end, how is it that I still feel like a mother to my dead boy?"

"I don't know, but I feel it too—his nearness." Jed's eyes became moist. "I don't fear for him the way you do, or feel despair when I think of him, but neither do I feel he is utterly gone. Wherever I go, whenever I see something James would like, I start to buy two—one for James and one for—" Two tears fell from Jed's eyes as he looked up into Hannah's face. "My senses remind me Johnny is gone, but for that first little while, it's as if he knows I was thinking of him, and I feel that alone brings us each such happiness."

Hannah saw James chasing a butterfly in the field and smiled before resting against Jed, her head lying in the crook of his neck. "Markus once told me he feels the same way about Lyra. Jenny senses it, and for a while I felt so terribly for her, but I understand it now. I think I always did. Death doesn't end love, Jed. We pick up the pieces and move on, but the love is still there. And if, as the ministers say, Johnny's soul is lost forever, why would God allow us to continue to love him so much? It would be cruel. That's why I need to speak with Joseph. I don't know if God gave him any answers that will ease these questions, but surely if God visited a prayerful young boy, and if He speaks of His own Son, He is not a God who casts babies into hell because their parents failed to get them baptized at five years of age. I need to ask Joseph what he thinks."

Jed tightened his hold on her. "It frightens me more than you could ever know."

Hannah looked at him and saw true fear in his eyes. "Do not worry so, my darling. How could talking to Joseph ever upset us?"

278

"Believe me, Hannah. I've seen how religion divides people, even people who love one another. What if you believe what he tells you, and I cannot? Where will that leave us?"

She had considered that possibility, but she had never allowed herself to dwell on the potential repercussions. She raised their joined hands and looked at them. "We've passed through the fire and we're even stronger yet, like one being now—united in heart, and of one mind. If it's not right for you, it won't be right for me either, and I'll know it. Trust me. You'll see."

CHAPTER 26

September 1823
Holetown Port, Barbados

Arthur Ramsey watched as the last of his trunks were loaded on board the *Ramses,* the flagship of his father's shipping fleet. He was excited to return to England, but he couldn't deny he would miss Barbados in the interim.

The ruffles of Juan Corvas's chemise billowed in the island breeze. "This sun and these zephyrs remind me of my home in Cadiz, Spain." He smiled and leaned back into his mahogany chair, resting his booted feet on a coiled rope. "They make a man lazy."

Arthur laughed and drew down another gulp of tea. "Are you calling me lazy?"

Juan's own laugh was deep and resonant. "It makes one's *soul* lazy, my friend. Today? Tomorrow? They are less important here than in England. Are you certain you want to return to that stiff place? I can ship Jed's friend's horses. You don't need to attend to this."

Arthur sighed long and low. "Yes, I do, Juan. It's been eight years since I turned tail and fled. Barbados is where I live, but England will always be my home. And it's time—time to check on my properties, time to be more than a silent partner in my father's shipping business."

"*Your* shipping business."

"Exactly, so I'd better do more than read reports from managers. I need to learn how it operates. Jed merely gave me the incentive. As you said, I've become lazy down here."

"But healthy, eh? You look very good these days."

Arthur agreed that his time in the islands had been healing, and though human hands had attended to him, Arthur attributed it all back to God, who had brought him to Barbados.

He counted it no small miracle that the neighboring plantation had, as a part owner, one of Norway's finest surgeons. The two men became friends on the surgeon's annual vacation to his island investment home. Prior to one of his friend's visits, an infection had left Arthur fevered for days. Anna, Arthur's housekeeper and nurse, had applied every remedy she knew, but the illness would not abate, so he put his affairs in order and prepared for death.

He knew the most important details of his life had been attended to. He had turned the inheritances over to Mrs. McGowan and her children, who, he assumed, were self-sufficient. Through a bit of subterfuge, Daniel was supplied with the means to repay his father and return to England a repentant man if he chose. And Frannie, the only woman he had ever loved, was married. After making generous arrangements for all his staff, he was ready to submit to death.

But Anna saw things quite differently. She personally ran to the surgeon's home, past the guards, who caught her and beat upon her until the ruckus she stirred brought the visiting physician outside. Before she collapsed from the abuse, she reported Arthur's condition.

It was weeks before Arthur discovered the price of her loyalty. The surgeon's wife had personally attended to her and returned her to her family while her husband raced to Arthur's side. After controlling the immediate cause of the infection, the surgeon assured Arthur that more could be done to relieve his suffering. In the course of the next two years, two more surgeries had been performed, and his pain and bouts of infection had been greatly reduced.

"God blessed me with Anna's loyalty and Dr. Jorgenson's friendship. And though I still am not who I once was, I am well enough, and I need to go home."

"Then at least let me sail you there. You'll be much more comfortable on my ship."

Arthur turned his head abruptly in his friend's direction. "Are you slighting the *Ramses,* Juan? She's the finest ship in my fleet."

Juan's eyes twinkled as he raised his glass to his friend. "And yet your father bought me one even finer, did he not?"

Arthur chuckled over that irony. "Sometimes I forget how you came to own the *Inez II.*"

"I never allow myself to forget those days. I try to do good with what I have. So allow me to do some good for you. Sail to England with me, and let us share a few weeks together, eh?"

"But you're set to sail to America next."

"Ah! What good is it to own a ship if you cannot decide where she sails?"

Their time at sea proved to be among the most pleasant memories of Arthur's life, a bookmark upon a chapter of leisure he would return to and draw from in the coming years.

Arthur grieved at how much his sweet England had changed since the end of the war. The factories dotting the cities had lured masses of hopeful job-seekers into every cramped nook until shabby tenements were built to accommodate them. Unattended children ran amuck in the streets while their parents and older siblings worked, but when Arthur approached London authorities about the sorry state of the children, they offered little sympathy for the so-called innocents, stating that many of them clustered into packs, robbing and accosting the weak.

After settling into his London town home, Arthur made a trip to his father's country estate. His attorney had rented the grand manor house to a wealthy mining baron, whose monthly rent was sufficient to maintain all the grounds and little cottages that dotted the massive property.

Arthur cheered to see the McGowans' stone home in good repair. Chickens pecked in the yard, and sheep roamed in a sturdy pen. The remnants of a fine garden plot showed great industry, and several cords of firewood told him careful preparations had been made for the approaching winter. He felt in his pockets for the bundles of treats he had brought along for the boys, as well as a silver jewelry box he had picked up for their mother. His knock on the door was met by a cheerful woman, who opened the door and wiped her hands on her apron.

Arthur removed his top hat and bowed slightly. "Good day, madam. I'm Arthur Ramsey. I've come to pay my respects to Mrs. McGowan."

"Mrs. McGowan, you say? The mister and missus of the house are out for the day, but you're welcome to pay your respects to Mrs. McGowan. Do you know where her grave is?"

Arthur's heart sank. "Her . . . grave?"

"Yes, sir. Didn't you know about her passing? The stone says she died in May of 1817."

"Six years ago? I never received any word of her even being ill. What about the children?"

She shook her head sympathetically. "I'm sorry, sir. I just came on with the Martin family two years ago. I never knew the woman or her children."

A sense of panic began to set in. "Is Mr. Cavanaugh still living here?"

"The caretaker? Yes, sir. He's a fine man. Lives in the cottage by the mill."

"Yes, yes, I'm familiar with it. Thank you very much."

Arthur quickly rushed to Cavanaugh's cottage, where he found the caretaker pumping the pedal of a grindstone upon which an axe was laid for sharpening. "Mr. Cavanaugh!"

The older man turned abruptly and squinted at Arthur. "Yes, I'm Cavanaugh."

"I know that, sir. I am your employer."

The axe fell to the ground as the myopic man leapt to his feet and rushed over to Arthur. "So you are!" he extended his hand, which Arthur took as a matter of habit. "So good to see you, sir. How are you? What brings you back to England?"

Arthur retracted his hand. "I am most distraught, sir. Imagine my shock when I arrived at the McGowan cottage to find that Mrs. McGowan is dead and her boys gone."

Sincere sorrow clouded the man's face. "Yes, sir. 'Twas a very sad day."

"Why was I not informed?"

"I don't read or write, sir. I just assumed your lawyer would tell you the sad news."

Arthur had never known the man was illiterate. "A woman is dead, Mr. Cavanaugh! And her two children are missing. What do you know about *that?*"

"She was sick before you left the country. She just never improved."

Now it all came back to Arthur—the image of Mrs. McGowan wrapped in a shawl, the annoying cough she dismissed with a shy smile, and his desire to believe her dismissal because he was pressed with other concerns. He cleared the lump from his throat. "She never improved?"

"No, sir. And with no family to help her, she relied on a woman in town named Mrs. Hewitt to cook for the family at the end."

The image of the bedraggled woman tore at Arthur's peace. He had offered her money, when what she had needed was a friend. He could hardly choke the words out. "And the boys?"

"I don't know where Mr. Porter took them."

Arthur's hackles rose at the very mention of the name. "Porter? Richard Porter?"

Cavanaugh backed away in response to the vitriol in Arthur's voice. "I believe so. He and Mrs. McGowan married near the end, and then he sold the cottage. After the funeral the Martins moved in, and Porter took the boys away."

Arthur didn't even offer the man a word of farewell as he turned and stormed back to his carriage. On the trip back to London, he sorted through the feelings swirling within him until he was able to admit to whom his anger was truly directed—at himself. *Why didn't she write of her needs? Did she assume I was as inconstant as everyone else she had relied on?*

He reached his attorney's office in a stylish section of the city. After taking the steps two at a time, he was so breathless when he reached the top he could scarcely lift the knocker. The attorney, Mr. Reynolds, panicked at the sight of Arthur Ramsey doubled over on his stoop, his top hat lying on its side on the stonework, but when he attempted to assist Arthur, his prestigious client pushed his jacketed arm away, refusing his help.

"Are you aware Mrs. McGowan died six years ago?" Arthur asked between gulps of air.

"Come inside, Arthur, please."

He slowly rose to a shaky stand and asked the question again, emphasizing each word. "Did you know Mrs. McGowan passed away, or not?"

Reynolds leaned against his door as if the question had overtaxed him. "Not at first. I was shocked to hear she had sold the cottage, but since you relinquished control of her inheritance, there was nothing I could do legally. Then the bank president told me her husband had come by with a copy of her will. He closed all her family accounts and transferred the money elsewhere."

"Do you know who her *husband* was? Richard Porter! That lying scoundrel Jervis!"

"Yes, Arthur. I also made the connection too late, and there's nothing we can do. I went so far as to track down the vicar who married them. He's a drunkard who would marry a rooster to a cow if they paid him with a pint, but the marriage was legal and binding, as is the will and the transfer of guardianship of the boys, I'm afraid."

"You know he only married her to get his hands on the money!"

"Of course, but once he had the money he could have run off without taking the children, but he didn't. The question is, why?'"

Arthur paced within the confines of the stoop. "Do you know where or how they are?"

Reynolds shook his head in obvious disappointment. "After hearing the news of her death, I made inquiries about the boys throughout the city and in the surrounding areas, but the trail was cold."

"And you never told me a word of this?"

"What good would it do but upset you further?"

"I would have come home! I could have—I could have ferreted the scoundrel out."

Mr. Reynolds took Arthur by the shoulder. "You must accept it, Arthur. All that could have been done *was* done. Mary McGowan could have written to you or to me. She knew how to reach us, but she didn't. You must face the fact that she made a plan for her sons that was contrary to your wishes. You did all your father could have asked you to do. Richard Porter is now their father, and you have no further obligation to the McGowans."

CHAPTER 27

September 12, 1823
New York City, New York

Four large men unceremoniously ejected Hannah and Frannie from the property of the Rathbone Mill in full view of the ladies' society who had sponsored their visit.

"I advise you ladies not to return," said the larger of the four, a swarthy, muscled man. "And tell your friends to stay away, too, unless they want to be arrested for trespassing."

While the lack of welcome was not unexpected by the two women, their physical dismissal was, leaving both of them visibly shaken. It was an emotion to which Frannie was unwilling to surrender, leaving her more determined than ever to get inside.

"Fine! We'll just sit here until the mill's owner changes his mind and allows us to see the conditions the children are working in."

The large man shook his head in disbelief at his colleague, then looked back at Frannie. "Suit yourselves, but you'll find all you need to know about our safety record at the county offices. An inspector comes twice a year to check the place over."

"There's more at stake than the mill simply being safe. When do the children get to play and simply be children?" challenged Hannah.

The man jutted his face forward. "What do you Bible thumpers have to offer them? We do these kids a favor. They're discards, with no one else to take care of them. Some are orphans, some are just poor. Some are immigrants whose parents don't even speak English. You want to change their world? Tell President Monroe to fix those problems. Until then, yes, these kids work hard, but for most of them, it's either the mill or an orphans' home, and have you seen some of those places?"

Frannie sobered at the question.

"The boss wants them strong and alert, so they get three squares and a sturdy bed to sleep in. On Sundays a parson comes and preaches, and we've started a little class to teach them to read and write. So, yes, kids on the streets can play all the day long if they want, but where do they sleep at night, and who feeds them and keeps them warm in the winter? Will you?" He glared at Hannah and then at Frannie. "Or you?"

"This place is barely more than a kennel where you benefit from their labor."

He raised his voice until the rest of the crowd of placard-carrying women could hear. "If and when these youngsters choose to leave here, they will leave with some work experience under their belt, and for the smart ones, a trade—and a tidy sum to stake them. And none of them will have a prison record, or be found froze to death on the streets." His eyes narrowed and he stepped aside, his arm sweeping as if welcoming them into the mill. "If you or any of your prissy-gloved friends can offer them more, you're welcome to come in and take them now."

Frannie and Hannah looked back at the crowd of women, whose fire suddenly dimmed.

"Ladies?" Frannie said as she raised her skirts to begin a forward march, but no one seemed prepared to follow.

"Good grief, they have no plan," Hannah whispered. "It's just as Myrna said. She warned me to keep my expectations low because people often get fired up about something with no plan to follow through. She said it happens at the hospital all the time, and now here it is. These women brought us here, but they have no alternative plan for these children."

Frannie and Hannah begged the men for a moment as they returned to where the women were now circling and animatedly talking to one another in hushed tones. Frannie went to the league's president and asked, "This is your opportunity. Why aren't you seizing it?"

The woman looked left and right at her friends, whose wide eyes dropped as soon as the scrutiny moved in their direction. "This isn't what we intended."

"What *did* you intend?" Frannie barked.

"We wanted to make the mill owners treat the children better. *We* can't take them."

The men snickered at Frannie and Hannah as the crowd dispersed, leaving them standing alone. "This is going to be harder than I expected," Frannie said.

Hannah bit her lip as she watched the women walk away. "The problems are much bigger than just safety standards in mills and children's work hours. The families are failing. The cities are flooded with newly arriving immigrants, and the mill managers scour the streets, preying on them by offering their children a roof, a job, and food. I feel so helpless. We can't solve these problems."

Frannie's eyes brightened. "Maybe not, but we know who can— Jed!"

"Jed? How?"

"We need to convince him to consider a post in the U.S. Senate! He's well connected. Have him capitalize on his war record and get himself appointed so he can help these children."

CHAPTER 28

September 25, 1823
Palmyra, New York

The experience in New York City had sobered Frannie's and Hannah's expectations about single-handedly changing the world, but they continued on through the remaining speaking engagements while noting the industries most egregious in their exploitation of the youth.

They saw it everywhere and recorded every instance so they could raise enough indignation in Jed to persuade him to toss his hat into the pool of men seeking a post in the U.S. Senate. Even the canal boat ride to Palmyra was a lesson in child labor, as boys as young as ten were hired as "hoggees," or mule drivers, to keep the animals on the tow path as they pulled the boats along. A chilling, torrential downpour hit the boats one afternoon. Frannie and Hannah gathered the children, including Helen Miller, who was serving as their nanny, and huddled near the stoves to keep the children warm and dry. All the while, they fretted over a small boy of no more than ten years, hunched over the back of his mule with nothing but a slicker to protect him as he sang a melancholy tune.

The sun broke near the end of the lad's first six-hour shift. When he jumped down to change into dry clothes before the return trip home, a new nimble lad mounted the mule, and with a mile-wide smile he greeted the passengers and sang out in a cheerful cadence:

I was workin' in a line barn, a'eatin' beans and hay,
Boss a'kickin my stern every night and every day,
So I hired out canallin' as a horny and a toil,
Drivin' mules that kept a'bawlin' 'long the towpath's
    smelly shore.

On the towpath's smelly shore, me boys! On the towpath's
    smelly shore!
Driving mules that kept a'bawlin' on the towpath's smelly
    shore!"

The entire mood on board the boat shifted, as passengers clapped and sang along with the boy. When they departed at their stops, they rewarded the lad with a few pennies or a sweet, so when Hannah and Frannie's little party reached Palmyra, they followed suit and tipped the boy, stopping to talk with him for a moment. Hannah marveled over the boy's cheerfulness, which proved once again the complexities of child labor.

She recognized significant changes to the town since her last visit. Several basins, or small bays, had been built along this section of the Erie, and canal boats were busy loading and unloading passengers and goods along each. The once-quiet village had evolved into a bustling port, catering to the needs of the canal travelers with eateries and shops, while industry also prevailed, with ash shops, boat builders, and warehouses strung along the waterway.

The children were anxious to stretch their legs, and the women were relieved they had the foresight to bring along Bitty and Abel's daughter, Helen, to help care for the children. At sixteen, she already had the mothering instincts of a woman and the eyes of a hawk, two necessary qualities to keep the children out of mischief as they strolled Palmyra's streets.

The excitement of soon seeing Beatrice now captured Hannah's full attention. Remembering where Dudley's store was situated, she led the way there and to the fidgety, middle-aged store clerk tasked to be their greeter. "Yes, right on schedule! Reginald Cooper here." He smiled broadly at Frannie as he tapped his fingertips together. "Major Snowden sends his regrets. He's picking up supplies in Rochesterville, but he gave me instructions to make you feel quite welcome! Please gather a nice bag of treats for the children. And may I offer you ladies a jar of hand cream or a complimentary comb?"

Frannie's eyes widened at the man's gratuitousness. "No, thank you. We're quite well supplied on both items. Hannah, the children and I will select a few candies while you and Mr. Copper chat."

"Cooper," corrected the clerk as he glanced and smiled in Frannie's direction.

"My apologies." Frannie smiled and tucked herself into the candy corner.

"Mrs. Pearson, I've secured a rig for your use. It's tied up right there at the post. Here are the directions to the Snowdens' home." He handed Hannah a paper as he pointed down the street and to the right. "Just follow the main road. It's one of the finest homes in Wayne County!"

His hands returned to a clasp, and Hannah could barely suppress a laugh at his obvious delight over his welcoming efforts.

"Thank you. I'm sure I'll remember it as I get close."

Laughing voices and taunting jeers erupted in the street as a band of young men rounded the corner, circling about one beleaguered member. Mr. Cooper scowled as he went to the window and pulled the curtain aside. "Darned ruffians!"

"What's happening?"

"It's just a crowd of locals taunting one of our youngsters—a young man named Smith."

"Joseph Smith?"

The clerk's scowl deepened. "Did those boys tell you about him? I wish they wouldn't spread that embarrassing slander to people as soon as they step off the boats. They must know the major's out of town. Everyone knows he doesn't tolerate it."

"Then neither shall I!" Hannah abruptly turned for the door.

"Please, madam, don't involve yourself. Those boys would never pull these shenanigans if the major were here."

"So they know Major Snowden believes Joseph's story?"

"Of course not. He's just a fine gentleman who defends the weak and addled."

"Addled?" Hannah huffed. "I'll have you know Major Snowden has spoken to me of Joseph and his family with the highest regard!"

"And they are a fine family . . . a fine family. Who can fault them for rallying around their boy, but Joseph is either addled or evil, and no one could ever believe the latter of him."

With a final shove and an additional string of humiliating epithets, the crowd moved on, leaving Joseph alone to gather his wits and confidence about him once more.

Cooper shook his head. "I heard they tossed him into a pond last week."

Hannah tried to imagine the stresses upon the boy—to be so young and well liked one moment, and then so reviled the next. She felt a sudden desire to protect poor Joseph.

"It's painful to watch," Cooper remarked. "Life would be much easier if the boy would just recant his story."

"Then there's only one reason he would put himself through all this torment—because he told the truth."

"That God and Jesus appeared to him in a grove of trees on his father's farm?"

Hannah took a step back, drew in a deep breath, and struggled to hold her tongue. Just then, Frannie stepped between the pair, slapping a paper sack of candy loudly upon the counter.

"Six licorice whips, three suckers, and five pieces of taffy." She began nudging Hannah forward from behind, adding, "Mr. Cooper, we'll be certain to mention your kindness to the major this evening." Once they were outside, Frannie turned to Hannah. "What was that about?"

"Nothing. Let's just get to Beatrice's."

Minutes after arriving to a warm reception there, the women settled into the kitchen to prepare supper for the hungry children.

Equally famished for news from home, Beatrice fired off questions about Jed's government work, the summer races and the fabled hat contest, and news from Baltimore. But as soon as Hannah began describing the troubling scene in town involving Joseph, Beatrice said, "I'd prefer to change the subject."

The comment stung Hannah's sensibilities. "Surely you don't condone the way Joseph is being treated. It was you and Dudley who defended him to Jed."

Through tightly pressed lips, Beatrice muttered, "Things change."

Hannah saw how uncomfortable Frannie was becoming, but she needed to understand, so she pressed further. "What has changed, Beatrice?" Her sister's hands tightened around the potato she was peeling, and Hannah said, "It is you who has changed, isn't it?"

It came out as an indictment. Beatrice's head shot up and she glared at her sister.

Hannah softened her voice and tried again. "Tell me why. You were so excited before."

After setting the peeled potato in the bowl, Beatrice rested her hands on the table and leaned over it, her creased eyelids framing tired eyes that again avoided Hannah's. The face was suddenly so familiar to Hannah, not Beatrice's but their mother's—a face plagued by stress and fret, surrounded by streaks of gray. Pursed lips were marred by feathered lines that seem to spread the distress across Beatrice's tired face.

"Rachel!" Beatrice called out to her seven-year-old in a voice that caused the child to cower. Closing her eyes against welling tears, Beatrice forced a smile. "I'm sorry, darling. Mother is just tired. Could you please go to the root cellar and bring Mama three more potatoes?"

Frannie grabbed Hannah's hand, affording her no excuse as she pulled her to the door. "We'll do it, Beatrice." As soon as they were beyond the door, Frannie stormed ahead of Hannah and asked, "What has gotten into you?"

Hannah balled her fists and pressed them to her temples. "It's too hard to explain."

"Is this about that boy—Joseph Smith?"

"What do you know about Joseph? Did Jed talk to you about this?"

"Only that he's worried about your preoccupation over a boy you've never met, and about events you can't confirm."

Hannah's shoulders slumped as it was all so succinctly and clearly put into perspective. While they walked, she pondered Joseph's story and her impressions of him from the afternoon, and her conviction returned. "Did Jed tell you about Joseph's vision? He says he saw God *and* Jesus. They were glorious Beings but embodied in the forms of men—like us! Or . . . I suppose we look like Them," she rattled on excitedly. "But it makes sense, don't you think?—that if we are made in Their image as it says in the Bible, then we should look like Them? As if we are Their children?" The last line came out as a whisper, as if it were a disclosure of great secrecy.

"It makes more sense than a God who is a cloud, or an invisible force."

Frannie's matter-of-factness stunned Hannah. "Do you believe it's possible?"

"I suppose. I accept that God has spoken to you in ways I don't understand," Frannie replied. "And there are others who have had unexplainable miracles. I accept that God can do whatever He chooses."

"Just like that?"

"Jed and I were raised without much instruction, so we're pragmatists, I suppose, but that doesn't mean we don't believe in God. I accept Him as a loving influence. I suppose I don't really know what I do or don't believe, and perhaps neither does Jed or Beatrice. We all have times when we need to believe in *something,* and we grasp onto what gives us comfort."

"You mean like when I rushed to baptize James."

"For all the struggles you've had to define your beliefs, you've always been very passionate on issues of religion. In the face of the same confusion, some of us simply step away."

"But if Joseph did see what he claims," Hannah went on, "wouldn't that change the ambivalence?"

"Perhaps yes, perhaps no. It seems the thousands of years since Christ's birth have only broadened the confusion. Can one young man's experience rein in that uncertainty?"

Dudley's wagon rolled into the barnyard across the way. He didn't see Hannah, and her disappointment must have shown, for Frannie said, "Go. We've a lifetime to solve the problems of the universe. I'll take the potatoes to Beatrice and help her with supper. It will do you two some good to be apart for a bit."

Hannah observed her brother-in-law before rushing in on him. His frame had a contented roundness that bode well for his health, though his shoulders remained round and his gait was slow. She hailed him from across the yard. His arms extended to her and she hurried to him, no longer with the complete rush of youth, but that of a mother of nearly thirty years. She stood nearly an inch taller than him, owing to heels that added a full two inches to her stature. No matter. The embrace fit like a glove as the two met.

"My dear, sweet, Hannah," he said in her ear. "How well you look."

"It's so good to be here. I've missed you both so dearly."

"And are you girls having a good visit?"

Hannah forced her smile to become even brighter. "Very nice, though Beatrice will not miss my company for a short while."

A line of worry crossed Dudley's brow. "You two have quarreled?" he asked, and then his eyes creased in understanding. "Mr. Cooper told me about the scuffle involving Joseph this afternoon. Did you raise the topic with your sister? Is that what set her off?"

Hannah leaned against the barn door. "Yes. I didn't know her opinion of him had changed. What happened? Do you feel the same?"

Dudley squeezed her hands, then released her and returned to the work of unhitching his team. "Are you saying you now believe?"

"Have you any idea how abruptly my understanding of God was shaken by what you told Jed and me on our last visit? It confounded both our sensibilities—his more than mine—and so for three years I kept my feelings about that conversation to myself, pondering what little you told me and asking the Spirit of God to remove the confusion from me if Joseph's tale was untrue. But instead of leaving me, the ideas have filled me with a longing to know more—about the individuality of God and His Son, and about our relationship to Them. I have more questions and no answers, Dudley. And today I felt such a powerful affinity toward him—for a boy I've never even met face to face. Jed fears the disparity in our positions on the matter will divide us."

Dudley turned to her, sorrow etching his face as if a sculptor had transformed him in an instant. "And well it might."

A numbing chill coursed through Hannah. "That's it, isn't it? You believe, and Beatrice no longer does."

"And it's tearing our family apart." Dudley bit each word. He unbuckled the last of the harnesses and led the horse into a stall, then leaned heavily against the beast. "Never has a passage of scripture rung truer to me than this from the twelfth chapter of the gospel of Luke.

Suppose ye that I am come to give peace on earth? I tell you, Nay; but rather division:

For from henceforth there shall be five in one household divided, three against two; and two against three.

The father shall be divided against the son, and the son against the father; the mother against the daughter, and the daughter against the mother . . ."

"Even the husband against the wife?" Hannah said.

Dudley studied her face until his own became a reflection of the distress she felt. "If God and Jesus really did appear and speak to Joseph, it's the most important event to occur on the earth since the Resurrection, Hannah. Those blessed with a confirmation that it occurred should let nothing stand in their way of doing whatever God asks." He turned away and stared blankly forward. "But they will, because they fear man more than God."

Hannah followed behind Dudley mechanically as her mind raced back to her conversation with Jed on the day of their picnic. Dudley cast another worried glance at her as he picked up a brush to groom the mare. Hannah noticed the angry set to his face, hard like flint, and the edge also tinged his voice as he explained further.

"You cannot imagine the firestorm created by Joseph's vision. He's a poor, uneducated boy with a shining reputation. The ministers could have easily ignored his story, passing it off as the dream of an innocent youth, and his import would likely have faded away, but instead, people turned on him as if he posed some great threat. Men of influence piled on, threatening him and his family with spiritual ruin as they tried to crush him into recanting. It reminded me of the winepress Christ submitted to, and then I understood. Joseph does pose a great threat, because he is telling the truth."

With trembling hands, Hannah brushed over the goosebumps on her arms. Even her face became flushed, and the fine hairs there rose at Dudley's words. "How does Beatrice not see it?"

"She did, but she became afraid. Her fears run deeper than you know, Hannah. She was well aware of your mother's insanity long before anyone else spoke of it. For years she endured people's snickers and comments, even from supposed family friends— guests who came to the Stansbury's summer barbeques primarily to gather another year's worth of gossip about the 'crazed' hostess, Susannah Stansbury. Beatrice had no ally. Your father stood blindly by, pretending it wasn't so. Myrna's adoration of her mad mother was unshakeable, and you, the subject of Susannah's abuse, were too young to do anything. Beatrice still condemns herself for not doing more to support you, but she was powerless and sinking as well.

"She thought she had put that painful chapter of her life behind her. I was home again, our family was thriving, her relationships with her sisters were sweet—Myrna included.

"The questions we had about baptism for our lost baby, and for the dead soldiers, were the last obstacle, but no one could answer them in a way that brought us peace. And when we heard about Joseph's vision in response to his prayer, we felt that *our* prayers were also being answered, and that patience and faith would eventually lead us to the peace we sought.

"People—respectable people—maligned that poor boy." Dudley's hands tightened around a hank of mane until his knuckles bulged. "The very people who championed his good character and work ethic when they needed his labor, gathered in churches and in the streets to listen to the vitriol being spewed about him."

"Hypocrites! How could they do that?" Hannah said fiercely. "I hope he refused to help them."

Dudley shrugged and released the horse's mane. "It's not his way. Besides, it's a small town, and his family is poor. What could he do?"

"But Beatrice?"

"At first, we defended him publicly. You'd have been most proud of your shy sister. She walked out of homes when the conversations became attacks on Joseph, and she openly challenged people in his defense. When many turned their backs on the Smiths, we increased our association with the family. Beatrice even accompanied Mother Smith when the dear woman visited the homes of ailing neighbors, some of which were the very doors Beatrice had stormed out of. She made it clear where she stood. She was asked to resign from a few local ladies groups, an ignominy she endured rather well, but then the whispers and snickers began, except she was now the victim."

"Like Mother. Oh, Dudley, I didn't know."

"I had already spent time in a far more agonizing crucible to allow the snickers of ignorant people to bother me. Business declined, so Stephen Mack helped me turn my attentions to wholesaling goods out of town. But that meant Beatrice was home alone more and more, and in time, the pressure became too great. A local minister called on her at home, offering to welcome her into his congregation as a rescued sheep. The thought of belonging overwhelmed her with warmth, and she joined his congregation. She said she needed a church and a community, and since Joseph's experience had failed to provide an alternative to the churches already established, she wanted me to abandon my support for him as well and join her."

"And did you?"

He closed his eyes briefly. "To save my marriage, I ignored the counsel Joseph said God gave him, to join no church at this time. Yes, I allowed my name to be added to the same roster as Beatrice's."

Dudley returned to brushing the mare with such force that the poor beast whinnied her discomfort. Recognizing his error, he leaned across the mare and whispered his apology. Hannah heard the break in his husky voice and felt his uttered apologies were actually being issued to divine ears.

She sat on a stool and stared at the wooden barn floor as Jed's expression of his own fears haunted her. She knew she was in the same position as Dudley, and she too had made a promise. Her head suddenly felt heavy and troubled. She leaned forward and remained there as her elbows found support on her knees. "Are you happy?" she asked Dudley.

"We are a house of liars, Hannah. There is no happiness in that. I handed Beatrice an ultimatum of my own. I cannot remain here and watch what is about to unfold. I'm moving the family further west—to Michigan or the Ohio."

Hannah's head lifted. "Beatrice hasn't mentioned the move, but after what I saw today, I could never live here and watch people abuse that young man, whether I believed him or not."

"But you do believe him."

The downtrodden look on Dudley's face nearly caused her to cry. She thought of Jed again, wondering if she was seeing a glimpse of their painful future, and she suddenly needed to stand and move.

"But that belief leaves followers in a maelstrom." She noticed that Dudley did not attempt to correct her. "The divine simplicity of it—two Beings, a Father and a Son, who answered the prayer of a boy—illuminates how far religion has slipped from the true nature of God, so it makes sense that Joseph would be told to join no church at this time, but nothing more was offered in replacement."

"Nothing yet."

"I can't fault Beatrice for wanting something stable to cling to. I felt the same way. After James was born I couldn't risk another of my babies dying without benefit of salvation, so I raced to find a church to have him baptized in, even though I didn't agree with the doctrine."

Dudley's lips formed a thin, taut line as he began putting the brushes away.

"I have so many questions. I came here hoping God had revealed more to Joseph—that I could finally have my answers. Instead I'll go home more torn. It's exactly what Jed feared."

"Hannah . . ." Dudley twisted a rag nervously around his fist. "I—I don't know if this will ease your concern or add to it, but . . . I think Joseph has recently had another vision."

Again, Hannah's arms and face prickled. She stepped toward Dudley as if uncertain she had heard him correctly. "What?"

"He has said nothing, so I make this claim solely from my observations, but the Smiths have recently closed ranks around the boy. I'm not the only person who's noticed that where the Smith boys previously hired out from sun up to dark, they lately have begun rushing home before sunset each night. At first we all thought it was to assist with the construction of the family's new house, but even work on the frame house ceases early, and all the Smiths gather inside. Joseph's oldest brother, Alvin, is particularly protective of his younger brother, and I assure you, were it not for the older Smith boy's duties on the new house, Alvin would have accompanied Joseph into town to prevent just such a spectacle as occurred today."

"Then how can you leave now?" She clasped hold of Dudley's arm to anchor herself. "You must help Beatrice believe in Joseph's vision once more!"

"No one can make another believe anything if their mind is closed to an idea. I pray you don't find that out for yourself when you go home and speak to your husband about all this."

What could she say to Jed? Hannah strode to the barn door with her head down and her shoulders slumped as if an invisible boulder rested there. She turned back to her brother-in-law. "Do you think Beatrice would be vexed if I went to speak to Joseph?"

Dudley's gaze never broke from hers. The slightest raise of his eyebrow was his only response, and Hannah knew the answer.

"If I can't speak to Joseph, you must promise me something. If you hear anything more, will you write to me and tell me?"

"Of course I will."

Hannah nodded and slipped soberly through the doorway, tucking her questions about Joseph into her heart once again.

She spent another half hour walking the farm's fields before returning to the house. Pausing at the door, she rehearsed a calm expression and a few random questions to ease her way back in. Frannie's eyes opened in exaggerated wideness upon seeing her, with a forced smile that matched. The expression nearly made Hannah laugh. Dudley was perched in the parlor, reading the mail he had picked up in town, while the children waited anxiously by the door with a book in their hands, like a flock of baby chicks waiting to be fed.

The silence in the room increased the cold Hannah felt from her hour in the autumn chill. She moved to the fire to warm herself and said, "Your summer garden must have been huge, Beatrice, and it's still producing squash and kale. Did you do that yourself?"

It was a small effort, but it was the acknowledgement Beatrice needed from her sister. Her face brightened as she spoke about the joy working in the garden had brought her over the years. Hannah now understood how many lonely hours that toil had filled.

As she moved to the cupboard to gather the dishes to set the table, she caught a glimpse of Dudley. Their eyes met and he smiled at her—it was a smile with a wince embedded within it. She understood that as well. Yes, it was a house built of love and mortared with lies. Would it stand? She didn't know, but she determined it would not be the plan for her own home.

Shortly after she was certain Frannie and the children were asleep, Hannah slipped from her bed to her knees and poured her heart out to God. *Please tell me if there is more . . . And help me know what to say to Jed . . .*

The first request filled her with a delicious, warm peace that was marred by the anxiety she felt over the second. Still, she remained on her knees, facing the problems, determined to gather all the strength God would grant her.

CHAPTER 29

October 16, 1823
Annapolis, Maryland

Hannah found herself sadly grateful when the air turned colder and news the canal might freeze forced them to leave two days earlier than planned. In seventeen days, they arrived at the Baltimore harbor, where Frannie and her children parted company with Hannah, Helen, and James, who transferred to a steamboat that carried them to Annapolis.

Jed met them at the docks, and Hannah all but ran into his arms. "How did you know what boat we'd be on?"

"I didn't." A sheepish grin tugged at his lips. "I've come to the harbor to meet every boat for the past three days." He surveyed her face as if seeing her for the first time.

"It's me," she whispered to him, trying to dispel the many fears they both carried.

His eyes were moist as he gazed down at her. "Still my best girl?"

"Always and forever."

The meeting of their lips was ethereal, less a kiss than a promise of what would come. Jed pressed his forehead to hers, confessing, "You can't know how badly I've missed you."

"You forget how often I've been the one left at home to wait."

"Of course. What I meant to say is . . . I need you, Hannah. I need my family. I'm not cut out to be a bachelor." He hoisted James in his arms, and the exhausted boy nestled into the curve of his father's neck. Hannah held faithful Helen's hand, wrapping her other arm tightly around Jed's as they walked to the rig.

After they fed James and Helen and settled them into bed, Jed started a warm fire and presented Hannah with a tray of delicacies pulled from the kitchen.

"I thought you didn't know we'd be arriving today," she said. "Don't tell me you've—"

"—been buying little things every day, just in case."

Hannah took a bite from a peach tart and smiled approvingly.

"We ran into some delays on materials, so the house isn't finished yet," Jed continued, "but we'll be able to spend our first Christmas there. I'm anxious to show it to you."

"A perfect homecoming, a new house . . . You're spoiling me. Thank you for all this. I have so much to tell you, too."

Jed's face flinched but his smile remained. After setting the tray aside, he took Hannah's hands in his and pulled her back toward him. "How was your trip?"

"Enlightening, sometimes depressing. It was wonderful to visit the city with the children. We took in a few performances and visited the library. That part was wonderful, but we saw some disheartening things as well, Jed, and our eyes were opened. Children's issues begin with the troubles plaguing their families—families that are breaking down because of poverty and the failure to integrate new immigrants into work and school. Frannie and I both think these are problems the federal government should be concerned about."

"The federal government *is* concerned about these and other issues, but some of them are state mandated. The debate over what rights belong to the states and which are federal strains this fragile Union. Too much federal intervention, and some states will threaten secession again."

"But if we are the 'United States of America,' shouldn't children have the same protections in one state that they have in another?" Hannah asked.

"In theory, yes, but states maintain the right to define these protections based on their individual needs. And there are so many arguments already straining the fabric of the Union."

"Like slavery?"

"Which varies state to state, and fiscal concerns like taxation and trade, as well as western migration, Indian uprisings, boundary disputes, and—well, the list is endless."

Hannah wriggled around until she could face Jed. "Frannie and I think you should voice an interest in the U.S. Senate. I know I've balked in the past, but I now realize how right Timothy has always been on this matter. Washington needs men of good character and devotion—men who can see the needs of the entire nation, not merely those of their local constituency."

A smile spread across Jed's face. "Perhaps you should run."

Hannah rose up on her knees and looked down on him with pride. "If only such a day could ever be. For now I'd be grateful just to have the privilege to vote."

"I've been approached to fill the seat of a retiring Maryland senator. I cannot give you the right to vote at this time, but if selected, I can make your opinions heard in Washington."

"Like Dolley Madison?"

"She'd be very proud of you. *I'm* very proud of you."

"For now, you must represent both of us." Hannah snuggled against her husband, enjoying his fingers combing through her hair, and then he asked the question she knew would soon come.

"How was Palmyra?"

She couldn't swallow past the lump the words brought to her throat. Setting the rest of the tart aside, she turned once more and met Jed's worried eyes. "You were right about the possibility of religion causing a breach in a marriage. I saw it in Beatrice and Dudley's home, but I'm determined it will not be so with us." She felt Jed's arms stiffen, despite her efforts to allay his concerns. "For now, I am content to simply hope, and wait, and see what is to come. And all I ask is that you support me in this."

Jed brushed the hair away from her face. "What happened to Dudley and Beatrice?"

"They were ostracized for openly supporting Joseph. Beatrice eventually chose the sociality of her established church and congregation over waiting to see what God would reveal next. Then Dudley followed to keep peace in their home, and now they are both miserable."

Jed's gaze held Hannah's for several seconds, then slowly slipped to some faraway point.

"Jed, I can't change what I feel, or what I believe, but it won't happen to us. Trust me."

He rubbed her palm with his thumb. "I would never ask you to compromise what you believe."

"I know that. I—I absolutely know that."

He frowned in obvious confusion. "In the meantime we will be without any church or pastor or religious affiliation. Wasn't that the very situation you feared when James was born?"

Hannah threaded her fingers between his. "I'm placing all my faith in what I know about us—that we are so united in spirit that when the time comes that one of us feels they have found their answer on the subject of religion, it will feel right to both of us."

"But you've already made your decision. You already believe Joseph."

Her gaze broke momentarily from Jed's. "I believe he saw God and His Son, and I want to know more about what God said to him— in time. We don't have to have all the answers tonight. For now we can still read and pray as we figure it out together."

Jed held her close, becoming uncharacteristically quiet. The evening's conversation had opened the possibility of major changes for the family, and for now, Hannah figured simply holding firmly to one another was the best course they could pursue.

Once Jed voiced his interest in becoming a United States senator, the stars began to align to make it so. A U.S. senator from Maryland finally set his exit date for the fall of the coming year, and the state legislature quietly placed their hand of approval on Jed, who had already announced he would resign his state senate seat at the end of the 1823–24 session of the Maryland General Assembly.

The family moved into their new home in time for Christmas, and after all the moving they had done for the state senate, the adjustment was easier than Hannah had expected. The large foyer was serviced by two grand staircases that swept left and right, leading upstairs to four large bedroom suites and a bathroom fit with a copper tub and a dumbwaiter to bring water up. Best of all was the water closet, and a chute that dropped the dirty laundry to the washing room.

They celebrated James's fourth birthday quietly, savoring the last few weeks of peace before making another move, this time to Georgetown, to place Jed in easy proximity of the Capitol. Hannah assumed from her last conversation with Dudley that the Snowdens were also preparing to relocate in early spring. She assumed her questions were about to be answered when two separate letters arrived from Beatrice and Dudley. Beatrice's was dated January sixteenth, while Dudley's bore a mark indicating it had been posted in early February. She opened her sister's letter first.

Dearest Hannah,

Forgive me for not writing sooner. I have hardly been able to face my own reflection these past months, knowing how I have disappointed those I love most. Knowing that you believe Joseph, I hope you will forgive me for shifting my loyalties. Though I have never uttered an unkind word against him or his family, I banded with those who did, thus giving support to the Smiths' abusers and withholding it from that dear family in their hour of need.

You should know the Smiths' eldest son, Alvin, passed away in November at the tender age of twenty-five years. The remedy physicians used to treat his illness proved to be his demise. He was an angel of a man who honored his dear parents and upon whose shoulders laid the Smiths' security for a season of peace and rest. The responsibility for their parents' care now shifts to Hyrum and Joseph. Much rests upon that young man.

The family is despondent, and my fickle friendship provided no comfort in their hour of great need. It was then that I recognized the full weight of my mistake, having traded truth for error, abandoning the best people for those who use the Smiths' loss to further malign them. I am ashamed.

A move has weighed on Dudley's mind for some time, and the attitudes in the town have cemented his resolve to depart from Palmyra. His first choice was a move west to Ohio or Michigan, but in his kindness to spare me the rigors of pioneering, he has instead chosen a farm near Colesville, New York. He says he'll be pleased to pass the land down to the children, and that he feels well enough now to manage the rigors of farming. Its situation along the mighty Susquehanna River will also make it a suitable site for trade both north and south.

And so I must return to the work of packing up what may have been the happiest season of my life for a move to a place of unknown, both physically and socially. It is a consequence of my own weakness. Please do not judge me too harshly.

Hopefully, I am still considered your loving sister,
Beatrice

Alvin Smith's death touched Hannah on two tender subjects. The news of a child's passing, even an adult child, always reopened a thinly veiled wound in her heart. But news of it being *this* young man, the son of the same parents who raised the child God appeared to?

Wasn't God aware of this Smith son also? Hannah thought. *Surely He knew how deeply Joseph and his parents loved Alvin. Surely He could have spared this boy. But He didn't . . .*

She quickly backed away from that train of thought, assuming these were the same questions people were using to further wound Joseph and the parents who supported him. She was grateful Jed was already gone to Washington to look for homes and to meet with Timothy. She needed to put all this in some perspective before he asked her these same unanswerable questions, or it could mean the closure of his relatively open mind and his willingness to read the Bible with her as she searched for verses that supported Joseph's miracle.

Hannah was alone in the house except for James, who was playing quietly on the floor with the farm set Jed had carved for Johnny. With reluctant fingers she picked up Dudley's letter as she debated whether to add his account of Alvin's passing to her already-troubled mind. Biting her lip, she broke the seal and began.

Hannah,

I hope this letter finds you well, and that Jed has opened his mind and heart to the truths you already accept. We will soon leave Palmyra for Colesville to begin anew, but I am happy to say that recent developments have softened Beatrice's heart, and I hope we will someday be united again in expressing our support of Joseph Smith.

As I explained during your visit, Beatrice and I are no longer part of that intimate circle of trusted friends with whom the Smiths' confidences are shared, and so I ask you to forgive my silence on the matter of Joseph and his most recent visitations as I share with you what fragmental knowledge I have recently heard.

And yes, I said "visitations," Hannah, for it is rumored that an angel returned to Joseph multiple times, repeating his divine communications and sharing the most exquisite news, that God has a work for Joseph to do, and that there is a book written upon golden plates which contains the fulness of God's everlasting gospel. Imagine it, Hannah! Another book from God! The hour is nigh at hand when the spiritual confusion will be cleared. And though I do not know the specifics of the teachings delivered by this heavenly Being, one counsel has more than come to pass—that Joseph's name shall be spoken for good and evil. This I can most assuredly attest is already true.

I know nothing more at this time, for it is the matter of the gold more than the angel's words that is whispered here, but as I know Beatrice has revealed the sad news of Alvin Smith's passing, let me add that the local clergy have used this young man's passing to pound the pulpit on a matter dear to all our hearts. Alvin Smith died without baptism, and the pastors tell the family that his soul is forever lost. Knowing how beloved Alvin was to his family, I believe this topic will be one Joseph either has or will raise when next the angel visits him. And therein lies my hope that someday our greatest questions will meet with a loving resolution.

Be of good courage, Hannah, and share with Jed your sister's and my assurance that what is about to proceed is worth the price of scrutiny. Bear it well.

Your friend and brother,
Dudley

Hannah anxiously awaited the first sight of Jed's steamboat. When it arrived, she grasped Dudley's letter firmly in one hand and James's hand in the other, running to the docks to meet the boat.

Jed dashed breathlessly from the boat and scooped James up. "Is everything all right?"

"I need to show you something wonderful!" Hannah's eyes never left his face as she presented the letter. "Read it—it's from Dudley!"

Jed set James down and began to read. Hannah scrutinized his every expression as she waited for his response. He seemed to stall near the bottom, rereading the final paragraphs, the last time in an audible whisper. When he finished, the arm holding the letter dropped to his side as if weighed down with lead, while confusion filled his face.

"Don't you see what Dudley's saying?" she asked.

"I think so . . ."

Her joy began to dim. "Well?"

"It's—it's hard to believe."

"But not impossible?"

"Let's say I'd like to hear more."

The Pearsons arrived in Washington City in July, well before Jed was scheduled to be seated in the Senate, but not too early to receive his first assignment from his friend, Senator Timothy Shepard, who had been asked to assist Mayor Weightman's Jubilee of Independence Committee, marking the fiftieth anniversary of the signing of the Declaration of Independence. Timothy quickly secured Jed's help.

"First things first," Timothy began. "Lucy has lined up several homes in our neighborhood to show Hannah. One is a very affordable rental. It would be wonderful to have our children grow up together. This project will require many evenings, and living near one another will afford us the convenience of working at home."

"I will help you, but I warn you, I'm not much of a party planner," Jed asserted.

"As well I know from our university days, with you holed up in the library. And all the better since our budget is meager. Every politician these days claims to be a Democratic-Republican—even John Quincy Adams now claims he's one—but deep fractures are dividing the government as they did in the old days. No matter what we do, one camp will say we spent too little, and the other will say we spent too much. The Senate is like the senatorial reenactment of John Randolph and Henry Clay's duel."

"Is that cynicism I hear coming from the mouth of patriotism's most ardent defender?"

"You'll see. This coming presidential contest may leave us all gray, or in the grave."

Jed tugged on a strand of his dark hair. "I will consider myself duly warned."

"Don't laugh. After all you've survived, the presidential race of 1824 may do more to gray your hair than war, near incineration, imprisonment, and even your sister were able to."

Jed's hearty laugh erased the tension from Timothy's face. "Yes, five candidates from one party. It may be brutal, but John Quincy Adams is a gentleman. Surely he can be counted on to run an honorable campaign."

"It's a numbers issue. The Constitution requires a candidate to receive a majority of electoral votes in order to secure the victory. With four candidates, no one may achieve that, forcing the decision into the House of Representatives, which could split the nation once more. I fear we are nearing the end of the blessed era of good feelings we've enjoyed during President Monroe's term in office, making this celebration of our national birth particularly critical."

"Agreed. Where do we begin?"

"Well, President Monroe's staff is handling arrangements for the Marquis de Lafayette's tour of the nation beginning in August," Timothy explained. "His ship is set to dock at Staten Island on August fifteenth to a military salute, and then he'll begin visiting each of our twenty-four states."

"I'd love to be on that tour and see what he thinks of this nation he helped liberate."

"Wouldn't that be something? Imagine how he'll feel when he learns there are people, colleges, and even towns named in his honor."

"As was done to honor President Washington."

Timothy looked thoughtful. "I'm sure it will pain him to return and not have his good friend here. Much of his visit will be spent in Virginia, visiting Mount Vernon and spending time at George Washington's grave. He always intended to return to spend time with his dear friend. Instead, he became a casualty of the French Revolution and ended up imprisoned himself."

"Providing an opportunity for George Washington to serve Lafayette. He was able to provide asylum for Lafayette's son, who was his namesake if I recall."

"That's right. What a blessing, since members of the family were executed by guillotine."

"Beloved here, imprisoned there." Jed shook his head. "Lafayette will certainly feel this nation's gratitude before he leaves our soil."

"Yes, and then we'll launch the official start of the jubilee. Congress commissioned four paintings by John Trumball which will be hung in the Rotunda for the celebration. The capstone of the celebration is his grand mural titled *The Declaration of Independence,* depicting the five writers of the declaration presenting the draft to their colleagues. Here's a sketch."

Jed studied the five images in the center of the sketch. The first three were easily recognizable—Thomas Jefferson of Virginia, John Adams of Massachusetts, Benjamin Franklin of Pennsylvania—but the last two required greater thought. "I'm embarrassed to say I can't remember these two members of the drafting committee, nor some of the other signers."

"Roger Sherman of Connecticut, and Robert Livingston of New York, but I can't name some of the signers anymore. I wonder if future generations will learn their names and know the risk they took when they mutually pledged their lives, their fortunes, and their sacred honor."

Jed grew wistful at the thought. "So few of them are yet alive."

"Charles Carroll is well, but Presidents Jefferson and Adams are in failing health."

"It's remarkable to consider what that generation achieved in fifty years, and yet the cost has been high. Two hundred and fifty years ago the Indians roamed free in virgin forests and welcomed the settlers. Now we are at war with them in many corners."

"We fear them and they don't trust us, often with good cause," Timothy said.

"If only we could share the land and live in peace, but we each have very different visions for America. It's rumored Andrew Jackson will relocate the Indians west if elected president. As much as I love what we're building here, I can't feel good about that."

"It was a primitive new world when the first settlers arrived, as if God hid it in His hand for millennia for a special purpose. I think His hand has ever been and still is over this land."

"And what do you think His purpose is? Even the Founders couldn't agree on religion."

"They differed on the details, but they all believed in Christ. Religion was and is still evolving here since the break with Europe.

Perhaps they purposely kept the language vague in order to accommodate what might yet be."

"Like a visit from God?"

Timothy scowled at Jed. "What?"

Flushing red, Jed wished he could retract the comment. "Don't mind me."

"No, tell me. Who claims to have been visited by God?"

"A young man named Joseph Smith. Hannah is quite taken with him."

"But you doubt him?"

Jed leaned back slightly. "Do you believe God would condescend to come to earth and visit a young man today in response to a prayer?"

Timothy pondered the question a moment. Jed watched his face soften as he thought. "I don't know, but if God wanted to do such a thing, I think this is where He would choose to do it. Religion needs freedom to flourish, Jed, and I believe God helped us establish and preserve ours. Now He's blessed us with a decade of relative prosperity and peace. If He wanted to open the heavens and speak, I think He would do it here, and this might be the time."

CHAPTER 30

Christmas Eve, 1823
Liverpool, England

Daniel tried to find a word to describe the overarching euphoria currently engulfing him. He reached his hand into his satchel and felt again for the five paper bundles there, barely able to bear the lapse of time required to reach the tiny flat he and Ruth called home.

Along the way he saw the gang of young hooligans who terrorized the Mersey River wharf. It dismayed him to see the dark, sad eyes of his former patient—Michael—among the mix. He was too bright, too filled with possibilities that were simply leaching into the filth of the Liverpool streets. Beside him was his brother, a menacing child who slashed his silver blade at anyone who met his gaze. Daniel fingered the eight-inch club he kept stuffed into his right pocket. It wasn't much, but a watchman with the misfortune of drawing the wharf as his nightly patrol had taught Daniel a thing or two about using the weapon defensively. It was all he had.

Daniel tucked his head low as if to ward off a wintry blast, catching a final glimpse of the gang to assure himself that they were not following him. As he did, he made eye contact with Michael, and he thought he saw the young boy subtly tip his felt cap his way. Daniel nodded ever so slightly in return, sorrowing over the lad's wasted promise.

Refusing to allow the moment to dim his happiness, Daniel hurried the three blocks home. He had to chuckle at the curiousness of his and Ruth's abode, decorated with pine boughs, and a small evergreen tree adorned with red bows and candles that shone through their only window, while a menorah filled the place of honor in the center of the table. As he reached for the doorknob, he noticed the chinking he'd done to fill the gaps around the doorway. It needed further repair. He made a mental note to get to it in the morning.

After dusting the snow off his coat, he entered the ground-level flat. The warmth from the coal stove was also the source of the enticing aromas that greeted his first breath. His gaze followed his nose to where Ruth bent over a steaming pot slung over the fire.

"It smells divine," he gushed as he took his wife's shoulders, encouraging her to stand.

"As divine as I could make five carrots, two potatoes and a few slices of salted beef." She groaned from the exertion required to elevate her bulging belly. Daniel led her to a chair, sat down, and then lowered her to his lap, where Ruth curled against him like a cat. She moved slightly, causing the rustle of paper in his satchel. Raising one eyebrow, she asked, "What is in there?"

He could not withhold his smile. "Just a few small things. It's Christmas!"

"But you already brought me gifts for Hanukkah."

"A crooked menorah and candles bartered from a merchant ship, a few apples, potatoes, and a wedge of cheese are hardly what I'd call gifts."

Ruth smiled down on her husband. "That's what *you* saw. I saw cheese latkes, potato pancakes, baked apples. I saw my childhood traditions. I loved my gifts."

Daniel took her hands and placed kisses on each. "And on this special night I want to share *my* traditions with you. And presents are elements of my traditions."

He withdrew the five small, brown-paper-wrapped bundles and set them on the table. Ruth's scowl turned to laughter as she picked up the smallest of the packages. The top was folded down upon itself, and when she released it, several long, white satin ribbons tumbled onto the table. She sucked in an excited breath that released in a sublimely contented "ah."

"I've watched you swoon over the lacy baby clothes with ribbons and bows at Mitchell's store," Daniel explained. "I thought these would dress up the gowns you've already sewn for the baby."

Ruth's delicate fingers slid between each of the exquisite ribbons. As she examined them, wistfulness clouded her pleasure. "These are too exquisite for the simple gowns I've made."

Daniel drew her chin up until her eyes met his. "Where you see simple cotton gowns, I see a beautiful mother's handiwork expressing the love she feels as she awaits her first child."

Her face glowed at the praise, and then she grew pensive again. "These are wonderful, but they are expensive ribbons, Daniel. What did you do to earn this kind of money?"

"Don't worry. It wasn't dangerous. One of the ship captains had a bad burn. He asked me to tend his wounds, and he paid me in cash."

Her smile returned as she placed a kiss on his mouth. "Just so long as you keep your promise to stay away from those ruffians."

Daniel changed the subject as he presented three more packages. "Open these."

Ruth did not hesitate this time, quickly revealing the contents—a package of sugared almonds, a pound of cheese, and a small tin of bath salts. Her laugh grew more ebullient with each surprise, and he saw a return of the joyful girl he knew before the murder of her people.

He gently nudged the last package forward. "I hope you will like this one as well."

Now tentative, she opened the gift—two yards of white satin fabric that left her clearly awed by its pristine beauty. "I've never seen anything more pure and beautiful."

"It's for the christening gown."

Again, worry dimmed her face. "A christening gown . . ."

"We have to hold some service to present this child to God. There are no rabbis available, but there are Anglican churches and ministers aplenty who will name and dedicate our baby."

"No rabbis . . ." She fingered the cloth carefully as her eyes moistened. "I would like us to do *something* to hold to my traditions." She lowered her head and paused, then looked up at Daniel. "If our child is a son, you could perform the brit milah."

"Me? Circumcise a child?"

"You have the skills."

"I'm not a mohel. I—I have no clerical authority."

"You want to dedicate our child to God. Circumcision is a Jewish male's symbol of dedication to God and His covenants."

"It will have no meaning if I perform it."

"It will have a great deal of meaning to me."

He wondered what God would think of such a plan. "All right, all right," he relented. "We'll christen the baby, and if it is a boy, on the eighth day we'll hold a brit milah."

Clock watching became a preoccupation with Daniel Spencer throughout the month of February. Ruth was so near her time that he hurried straight home each evening, running their preparations for the baby's arrival over and over in his mind as he walked.

He passed the offices of the passenger fleets servicing the Mersey River port and glanced, as he did every day, at the names of the ships departing the next day. He longed to purchase passage for his family.

"Is today the day, Daniel?" asked Marco, the ticket agent.

"Perhaps," he answered nervously. "Ruth is due anytime now."

"That's wonderful, but I meant the tickets. You still plan to sail to America, don't you?"

"Oh!" Daniel blushed. "Yes, as soon as I've saved enough for the second."

"Hurry or that baby will grow and you'll need to save for three!"

Daniel laughed as he hurried on. The street slush penetrated his boots, leaving his feet nearly numb. He broke into a run to pound the feeling into them and reach home sooner, but when he turned the last corner near their flat he saw Richard Porter lurking warily outside an alley, his eyes darting around. Daniel stopped and noticed how Porter disappeared into the shadows when anyone came into view. The little band of juvenile delinquents he had assembled was nowhere to be found, but Daniel knew he was concealing something—or someone.

Turning up the collar of his mended coat, Daniel stepped to the far side of the street, keeping his eyes facing downward and his ears so pealed to the potential sounds of feet behind him that he did not see the person walking toward him, until they ran over one another.

Daniel scrambled to remain on his feet, as did the person he assailed. Once steadied, Daniel offered his hand and an apology to his victim, but his voice caught in his throat as his wary stare fell upon the eerily familiar eyes of Michael. The boy seemed just as shocked to see him, and then Daniel caught sight of a satin ribbon trailing from Michael's hand. His blood turned to ice.

Teeth gritted, his breathing rapid and panicked, he grabbed the boy by the scruff of his jacket and lifted him off the ground. "Where did you get that?" he demanded. "Tell me now!"

"She g–g–g–ave it to—"

"Liar! If you've harmed her—if you've so much as touched her, I'll—"

The boy broke loose of Daniel's grasp and raced away into the foggy dusk, while Daniel rushed to his apartment and Ruth. He gave the door a Herculean pull, expecting to find it ajar. Instead he nearly pulled his shoulder from its socket.

"Ruth! Ruth! Are you all right?" he cried out as he pounded on the door. Finally he heard the click of the metal lock and the scrape of wood followed by the appearance of his wife.

"Of course I am. What's the matter? You look as if you've seen a ghost."

He pulled her to him in a desperate embrace, pushed her away to look at her, and then embraced her again. He strained to catch his breath. "Was that hooligan Michael here?"

"Yes." She smiled. "I was on my way to the market for a tart. He sent me home to rest and ran the errand for me. How did you know?"

"I don't want you near him, Ruth! You were the one who said he was dangerous."

"I was wrong. He bought my tart and a rattle for the baby. He said it was to thank you for the time you helped him. He was so fascinated by your books that I gave him a slip of ribbon to use as a bookmark. It wasn't much, yet he seemed moved by that simple act of kindness."

Daniel was unimpressed. "I want you to stay away from him and his family!"

A quiet chill remained in the air throughout the evening. Daniel tried to ignore Ruth's restless silence by reading one of his medical books. He stared at the same page for an hour while stealing glimpses of Ruth's tightly pursed lips and tense eyes. Frustrated, he snapped the book shut. Then a knock sounded on the door. The hairs rose on his arms as Ruth backed into a corner in an unusual display of caution.

They both knew it was too late to be a social call. He cracked the door and found a human lump on his stoop. Under the lump, apparently holding it up, was Michael.

"I had nowhere else to take him. He's badly hurt. Please help him!"

Daniel noticed a red stain spreading along the side of the man's shirt, and he glared at the boy. Michael was slight of build but surprisingly strong and determined, and Daniel figured he was nearly thirteen now. Together the pair laid the patient on the kitchen table.

"I found him in an alley."

Daniel made no attempt to hide his contempt. "You just happened upon him, eh? Perhaps in an alley a block from here? The same one your stepfather was skulking about this evening?" Michael's chin lowered but his eyes remained fixed on the man as Daniel examined him and began cleaning the wound. "He's been beaten, and stabbed . . . with a small-bladed knife. About the size of the one your brother carries, Michael."

"All right! I didn't just find him. I heard he was hurt. Is he going to die?"

Daniel tried to glower at the boy, but like his wife, who was conspicuously absent from the room, he too was succumbing to the boy's innate goodness. "What's his name?"

"I don't know. I just rigged a sling under his arms and dragged him here."

It was all Daniel could do not to smile at the boy's ingenuity. The man groaned and twisted his face in discomfort. "He's coming to. That's encouraging. I think he'll be fine in a few weeks." As Daniel proceeded to dress the man's wound, he added, "By the way, I was hard on you this evening. My wife told me what you did. I owe you an apology."

Another shrug, another fearless reply from the young man. "I didn't do this either, but you've got us pegged right."

"So it was your brother who did this?"

"Hank's a might slow, but he wasn't mean until Porter got a hold of him."

"If the authorities were informed about Porter, they could help you get away from him . . . maybe find you new homes."

"No, they'd separate us!" Michael's response was immediate and firm. "Nobody's splittin' us up! Just patch him up enough so he don't die, and help me get him to St. Andrews."

An hour later, Daniel helped deliver the man to the church. Michael fled away before the vicar answered their knock. Daniel placed three coins in the clergyman's hand. "I don't know who he is, but I've done what I can for him. I hope this will pay for a few days' rest and food."

After settling the man in, Daniel hurried home to find Ruth in hard labor.

"It began before you came home tonight, but I wasn't sure what it was at the time."

Another body-splitting pain hit her, and she doubled over with a scream. Three hours later a robust, healthy baby boy suckled at his mother's breast.

✯ ✯ ✯ ✯ ✯

When a week had passed, the couple dressed their son in the white satin gown and carried him to St. Andrews to be christened. Ruth looked around the church at the paintings and stained glass images of Jesus. She was a Jew in Christendom, a stranger in a foreign land. After the brief service, she wrapped her baby up and held him close to her as the family returned to their apartment. She looked at his perfect face as they walked—her distinctive nose and wide, dark eyes, Daniel's exquisitely shaped face and full lips. This child, part Christian, part Jew, was the only other piece of her heritage she had. She kissed him and felt a fierce bond grow within her.

Later that evening, Daniel laid their bundled son on a white knitted blanket set atop the table. He looked nervously at Ruth as if hoping she would release him from his promise. "Do you remember anything the mohel did or said beforehand?"

Ruth had searched her mind every day since the baby's birth, cursing herself for having been so complacent about her religion. All she had were images of faces now gone, and fragments of songs and prayers offered by them. It pained her to recall the days in Salonika, and in response to that pain her memories had become an unpleasant jumble. She shook her head. "Whatever you say will be fine."

Daniel unwrapped the baby, then opened the Bible to Genesis 17, a chapter of scripture that explained Abraham's receipt of the covenant of circumcision. He read verses one through thirteen aloud. At the end, he simply said, "Our son's name will be David Everett Spencer."

Ruth watched her husband still his nervous hands before attending to the delicate task. David cried out until his tiny body shook. Daniel looked at her, disconsolate, but Ruth closed her eyes and bowed her head. A flood of familiar words and phrases began to flow through her mind with the clarity of light. Instinctively she began to speak the phrases, and with each one her voice grew stronger and more confident. A few minutes passed, and when she opened her eyes she saw Daniel cradling David close as he gazed at her. "You remembered," David said.

She smiled the first full smile she could remember since fleeing Greece. "Yes. I remember many things once more—things I want to share with our son. We'll give him the best of both our worlds, Daniel, and you must begin by writing to your father to tell him about our son."

CHAPTER 31

April 1824
London, England

Arthur Ramsey had not known true peace since his return to England. During the day he scoured the streets of each city and town he passed, hoping against hope to find the McGowan boys. He often walked instead of riding in his carriage, studying every youthful face he passed, uncertain if he would even recognize them if he bumped into them. Ten years had now passed.

He visited orphanages, courthouses, hospitals, schools, and even jails, tossing out the names McGowan and Porter until he finally faced the discouraging fact that they were probably living on the streets around associates more likely to provide information if a reward was offered. And so he hired a private investigator, who spread the word that a cash reward was available for any information regarding the boys, but no actionable information was found.

Six discouraging months passed. At times, Arthur missed his lazy tropical life with his ignorance of Britain's problems, but even then one regret haunted him—Frannie.

London's streets now filled him with despair as he walked where he and Frannie walked during the winter of 1814. The last word Jed had sent of his sister included the news that she and her husband were adopting two orphans. It was a painful revelation. Arthur had rejected Frannie's offer to marry him because he was unable to give her children, and she had argued that they could adopt children together, but he had still declined because he could not be a proper husband to her.

Frannie's happiness was always his primary concern, but he now wished he had been a little less selfless. Perhaps they could have had a good life together despite his handicap. And if their marriage had ended poorly, at least he would have had a taste of love to hold.

There would be no marriage, and no children upon whom to bequeath his fortune, but England had plenty of children in need of someone's concern. Until he could find Hank and Michael, Arthur would cast his wealth upon these other lost and hungry waifs.

Having discovered he still had no burning interest in the shipping business, he had agreed to keep the current management in place. Richard Porter's conspicuous absence made it possible for Arthur to return to more benevolent work, which brought him immense pleasure.

Each week he chose a different shire or village where he would distribute food and clothing to the poor. Sometimes he would hand a tidy sum to a respected member of the local clergy, instructing him to use it to bless the children. On other occasions he would ask the vicar for the names of families in need, and then, like Father Christmas, he would leave baskets of clothing, delightful foods, and a little bag of silver on the doorstep in the middle of the night. Arthur's joy came in the morning, when hidden nearby, he would watch the faces as the treasures were found.

The adventure had become so precious to him that he could no longer pass a toy store or a bakery without buying goodies and then searching for a child on whom to bestow them. His pockets were always laden with candies and coins to hand out. He thought of opening a few schools for the poorest of England's young. Education, he believed, was the best hope of elevating them from the squalor that haunted their lives. He needed advice, and the counsel of someone in the government. Gathering his courage, he decided to pay a call on Lord Whittington.

While Whittington Castle seemed as lovely as ever, there was evidence that much had changed. Where the roads that led to the village were once well worn from the frequent transit of villagers, guests, and goods, they were now covered with grass and weeds, and portions were barely more than paths. The park built at the foot of the walkway that was once filled with village families, now boasted only a few visitors. An older man sat in a new guard house by a latched gate at the edge of the lane. He questioned Arthur's reason for coming. When told Arthur had come on a political errand, he grunted and shuffled over to swing the gate open.

The lawn was still exquisitely manicured, and though the beds boasted spectacular blooms, the gardeners worked as if an overseer stood over them, and none of their magnificent flowers graced any window sills, giving the exterior of the castle a cold, imposing appearance.

No groom arrived to take his horse. Arthur strolled the stone walkway he had once frequented as a welcomed friend, past hedges he had chased Daniel through when the viscount was but ten years old. The memories felt hollow, as if they were images from another life.

Arthur banged the brass knocker. Long moments passed before the scrape of metal signaled the opening of the door. It had barely parted a crack when the familiar, aged face of Ridley appeared. He smiled broadly, and then his smile faded and his head lowered.

"Hello, Ridley. So good to see you well, old friend."

"Very good to see you, Mr. Ramsey. You look very well indeed, sir! I'm so glad to see that the reports of your ill health were exaggerated."

Arthur smiled. "Thank you. As am I, Ridley. Is the earl in? May I speak with him?"

Ridley cast a tense glance over his shoulder into the grand foyer. "I'm afraid, sir, that—that—" His lips drew into a tense, thin line, and then he stepped onto the portico, closing the door behind him. "I've served the earl for over thirty years now, and his father for twenty before that. I confess I love him as a son, so I would never betray a trust, or do anything to cause him pain or embarrassment. But my days on this earth are drawing to a close, Mr. Ramsey, and I fear you may present my last chance to mend the rift between the earl and the viscount."

"I had heard that rift had been mended."

"Mended and then severed clean. There has been but one communication between father and son since Daniel left here to chase the woman he married."

"Married?" It was the first Arthur had heard of this. "Ruth? Did he marry Ruth?"

Ridley's face fell into a somber frown. "A child has now been born, but the earl will not see him or Daniel. I see how Lord Whittington's pride picks at his peace. He will be utterly alone when I am gone. The old staff has all left to seek more amiable employment, and the earl's dour attitude has made him the subject of ridicule amongst the new workers. He lives for his months in Parliament, but when he is home, even the villagers amongst whom he was beloved rarely come."

Arthur had read some of the earl's positions in Parliament. The man was once the voice of compassion, but he now was known for drawing a hard line. Utterly disappointed, Arthur ground his foot into the stone of the porch. "How did you hear of the child? Did Daniel write?"

"A single brief note. He said he will visit, but only if a welcome awaits his wife and son."

"What does the earl require to reconcile with his son? An apology? A pound of flesh?"

Ridley shook his grayed head. "He is aging so quickly. His loneliness feeds upon him like leprosy, but he can't see it. Undoubtedly, he will curse and abuse you if you call on him, but if you have the courage, and care enough for the man who once loved you as a son, you may be the only person who can shake him from his self-destruction."

Arthur agreed to try, but his heart was heavy as he entered the darkened foyer. The drapes were pulled in every room, and the only light shone from the earl's study. Ridley swept his hand in that direction, urging Arthur onward, then dropped back as he moved on alone.

He slowly pressed the door open, but the earl's papers were pulled up before his face, obscuring his eyes. "Who was at the door, Ridley?" he asked in a voice lifeless and unfamiliar.

"It's Arthur, my lord. I've come to call on you."

The papers lowered slowly like the drawing of a curtain on a tragic play. "You . . ." the earl growled. "I thought you were dead."

The earl looked as if someone had shaken a cup of flour over him. Gray streaked his hair, and his skin seemed powdery and frail. "Even if I were I'd be more alive than you," Arthur remarked.

"We are two battle-scarred warriors," said the earl, glowering as he leaned back in his chair. "Perhaps we are each too stubborn to know we are already dead."

"No, I have fought my way loose from the grasp of death many times, and I am now very much alive, but you thrust your own sword in your own belly a little deeper each day."

Shooting to his feet, the earl pointed an accusing finger Arthur's way. "Better that than allow my betrayers to do it."

"How many friends and family members will you label betrayers? You've already banished anyone who crossed you, and anyone who dared dream his own dreams. You've few people left, friend. Accept the offer of family Daniel extends to you before it is too late."

The earl walked to the side table, where a polished wooden box sat. He opened it and removed a hand-rolled cigar, which he dramatically drew under his nose as he inhaled the aroma. "Recognize the brand? It's from the Willows," he cackled. "Jed Pearson called on me on his first trip back to England. Despite the fact that I nearly ruined his defense before the British Admiralty, he wanted to renew civil relations with Britain, and he loved his country enough to abase himself and ask for my help. I respect that." The earl's eyes darkened.

"What I cannot respect is a son who throws everything away—honor, duty, religion, and country—to pursue a selfish agenda."

The earl extended the cigar to Arthur. "Here. Care to renew the memory of that place?" Arthur neither replied nor moved. "I became quite enamored of the brand after receiving Pearson's gift. Daniel knew of my love for these cigars. When he returned from Greece we became very close once more, closer than ever. On his return to Cambridge he stopped to buy me a gift—a box of these cigars. Let me read the note that accompanied it.

Dear Father,

Thank you for being so patient and forgiving, and for allowing me to find my way. Enjoy these. I bought one for myself. I'll save it for finals. Who knows? Perhaps I'll become enamored with them as well. Like father, like son . . .

"'Like father like son,'" Whittington growled. "I honored my father. I longed to continue his work." The earl's eyes closed as he described the events of that day. "That woman called on me that very afternoon, but I sent her away. In a few hours, all our plans and our family's legacy of service to the Crown were gone. He could have had any woman he wanted! He could have chosen from a thousand beauties who would have upheld his country and his religion, but he chose her. Like you, each smell of these now sickens me. And now he has a bastard child."

"He and Ruth are wed. The child is your legitimate heir."

The earl swept the box from the table, shattering it and scattering the cigars across the polished mahogany floor. "I . . . have . . . no . . . heirs!"

Arthur pounded his fist upon the desk and glared back at the earl. "Blood is blood, Everett, and the best of you, and Lady Severina, and even Clarissa, is embedded in your son! Daniel and his son are all that remain of them! And since they cannot defend that boy or his child, that responsibility and honor falls to you. If you lock your heart to Daniel and deny him and his son their rightful legacy, you will have also erased the lifework of those women!"

"Get out!" the earl shouted, causing the windows to rattle.

Arthur cast a final look of disappointment on his former friend as he turned for the door. "As you wish. I will not call on you again."

Ridley's face was twisted in sorrow when he met Arthur at the door. "I heard. Thank you for trying." His voice was filled with resignation as he opened the door for Arthur's exit.

"Do you know where Daniel is living?"

"The letter was posted from Liverpool."

"Very well then. The earl once served as a surrogate father to me when my own failed me. Perhaps Daniel will allow me to return the favor."

The fabled March winds offered no flurry of excitement equal to that produced by Frannie and her children when they burst onto the Willows each spring. James adored his cousins, and Hannah would return to the farm so the little tribe could play together. She noticed the frequency with which James would refer to Sarah and Charles as his brother and sister. When Hannah would correct him, his brow would wrinkle in consternation and he would reply, "But Mama, that's how I love them." The topic came up while Hannah was hulling strawberries one morning with Bitty and Frannie on the porch of the old house.

"He needs a brother or sister," Hannah said as she cut the green cap from a ripe berry.

Bitty remained conspicuously quiet but Frannie jumped in. "What does Jed say?"

"He tries to deflect the topic. I don't know if I can even carry another child. I think I've lost three since James was born."

Bitty's hand pressed over Hannah's, displaying the many wrinkles forming on the tiny woman's brown knuckles.

"What do you think, Bitty? Do I dare hope for another child? Have you ever seen someone lose as many children as I and still deliver a healthy baby?"

Bitty's mouth pressed into a tight line. "The good Lord gave babies to Hannah and Sarah in the Bible, and I've seen women bear babies when they thought they never would." She looked nervously at Frannie. "But you should be talking to Jed about all this, Hannah, not us."

Frannie quickly changed the subject. "I received an interesting offer from Henri. He's actually been invited to take a troupe of singers to Paris for a cultural exchange. They're inviting artists, writers, and scientists. They hope to gather artists from all fields for a sharing of talents and ideas between the nations."

"And you've been asked to go?"

"Yes, and I'd love to, Hannah, but I think the children are too young for such a tedious trip. We're not just going to be in one place the entire time. Henri believes that in order to make the trip profitable we'll need to perform as we travel to and from Paris. That will mean nannies and endless packing and unpacking. I'm not sure they're old enough yet."

"A tour of Europe would be a marvelous experience for children."

"It would, but I don't need to perform to take them there. I planned on taking Sarah to Europe when she was a few years older—maybe when she's twelve. I must confess that I know so little about children and their tolerance for change. What do you think, Bitty?"

She sat back, a thoughtful expression on her face. "I think it's good for children to learn to wait for what they want. Then they're more grateful when it happens."

"That sounds like good advice," Hannah said. "You've been awfully quiet today, Bitty."

Bitty set her knife aside and sighed. "I've got something on my mind, but you got to keep it a secret." The women vowed they would, and Bitty continued. "We just barely married Helen off to Jubal. Now Caleb's asked Jack and Lydia's girl, Miriam, to marry him."

Frannie and Hannah clapped their hands together at the news. "That's wonderful!" Hannah said. "Don't worry over it, Bitty. We'll help you throw them a big wedding with all the trimmings! Won't we, Frannie?"

"Of course we will. Have they picked a date?"

"Not yet, but the timing isn't what worries me. It's something else—something that happened at the market yesterday. A man asked for five of Lydia's hand-rolled cigars. He pocketed two he said weren't worth two bits each, and said he would only pay for the other three even though he kept all five. Miriam challenged him and he got real angry. Caleb was ready to ask the man to leave, but you know Jack—always the peacemaker. He got between the pair of them and started talking to the man in his lazy-speaking way. He gave the man five more cigars for free and got him on the boat without any more trouble."

"And how did Caleb take it?"

Bitty's eyes closed at the memory. "He said he could never feel free here. He went to Abel and asked for the deed to the land out west. He said after he and Miriam marry they're going to homestead that parcel. He wants the rest of us to follow."

The news sobered the two women. Frannie took Bitty's hand. "I'm so sorry."

"I don't know what to say," Hannah said. "Let's hope Caleb changes his mind."

Bitty stood and pressed the bowl close against her. "It's not likely with that young man. The first time he looked at Miriam, he said he was going to marry her. That was ten years ago. He held onto that idea all this time. Once he gets his mind made up, it's not likely he'll change."

She carried the bowl into the house, leaving Hannah and Frannie alone.

"Ten years is a long time," Hannah mused.

"Yes, it is . . ." Frannie drew the words out as if she were traveling backwards in her mind. "If Arthur had honored the terms of our original agreement, we'd be together now."

"I wondered if you still thought of him from time to time."

"Nearly every day, but it doesn't hurt as much as it once did. I am curious, of course— I wonder what he's like, and what he might be doing. And I wonder if he regrets sending me away."

"Why don't you write to him?"

Frannie answered with a quick shake of her head. "Though the hurt has healed some, I've no interest in reopening those old wounds. No, the children and I are doing just fine, and I'll just have to remain content with what I already have."

CHAPTER 32

May 1824
Liverpool, England

The risk of crossing Richard Porter and his wild-eyed son Hank was just too great to entice members of Liverpool's street gangs to provide information on the boys, but today the very man offering the reward was posing the questions, and that opened a wider range of prospects for a cunning opportunist—fifteen-year-old Lawrence "Bled" Bledsoe.

Hiding behind barrels and cargo crates, Bled watched the fortyish man with the visible limp as he made inquiries among the vendors and citizens. His dress and rig were simple and unpretentious, but his gentle manner, groomed hair, unstained hands, and trim nails bespoke a life of comfort, and as he moved along the street posing his questions, he dropped coins into children's hands with the nonchalance of wealth.

"I'm looking for a young man named Daniel Spencer," he repeated to each person he passed. "Perhaps you've seen him—a tall, handsome young man with brown hair, of about twenty-two years? His wife is named Ruth. Do you know them?" His shoulders sagged more and more each time the inquiry failed to produce any information. Then he would ask about the McGowan brothers with an equal lack of success.

Bled heard him ask his question about "Doc" to the fishmonger, who shook his head. "Might you know two young boys by the names of Michael and Hank McGowan, then?" he asked. "They might be associated with a man named Richard Porter."

The merchant didn't bother offering any reply as he hastily gathered his things and moved his cart, leaving the weary man frustrated and alone on the street. Bled sneered at the fool. He was three times Bled's age, yet this naive codger knew nothing about street government. Bled knew no unprotected street vendors would risk having anyone along the docks think they were an informant, and they certainly wouldn't want Richard or Hank Porter to think that.

The man moved on down the street to the shopping district. As the day wore on, his limp had become more noticeable. "You're an easy mark, now aren't ya?" Bled said to himself as he studied the man. "I just need me the right accomplice."

It was nearing dusk, and Arthur was about to quit for the day when he happened into Mitchell's department store. The clerk was quick to answer his inquiry about Daniel Spencer.

"He's not licensed, but folks around here call him 'Doc' because he makes house calls to those too weak and poor to get themselves to the hospital. No one would ever turn him in. In fact, it's rumored that he's the young viscount—the son of the earl of Whittington."

Arthur feigned ignorance on the matter. "Really? The viscount?"

"Yes, I'm certain 'twas he who visited here in the earl's company a few years back. It was the summer before the Spencers moved in. The earl used to come by from time to time and drop a bit of benevolence on the locals, but he hasn't visited here since the viscount was rumored to have disappeared again. We figure the earl doesn't come here because this is where his son came, and since Doc doesn't want to be associated with the title, we play mum about it."

Arthur leaned heavily upon the counter. "Do you know where Doc lives?"

"He and the missus are poor, but we've delivered a few things to them since the baby arrived. It's hard to get a delivery boy to go where they live—dangerous, you know," the clerk muttered as he searched his records. "Yes, here it is." He scrawled the address on a card and handed it to Arthur, who thanked the man as he took the address and left the shop.

The news dispelled Arthur's fatigue. He pulled himself into the carriage and ordered the driver toward the waterfront. As happy as he was to have a lead on Daniel's whereabouts, it distressed him that the beautiful boy he remembered was now reduced to such a life.

The carriage passed streets littered with broken cargo crates and wood-shaving filler, while the air reeked of rotted fish. The smell now churned Arthur's empty stomach. Paper blew from corner to corner where empty crates housed the homeless, but amid the beleaguered scene ran a side street of old but sturdy apartments. The sign read "Howard Street," and Arthur audibly cheered. Like an urban oasis, it breathed light and air into the dingy city. The yards around the buildings were more cared for, and ivy covered the sides and fronts of the old buildings. Arthur read the numbers on the doors until he saw flat 124 on the bottom floor.

"Stop here!" Before the carriage even halted, Arthur had the door open and was exiting.

"How long will you be?" the driver hollered. "This is not a safe area to be in after dark."

Arthur withdrew his billfold and pressed an exorbitant gold sovereign into the man's hand. "Hear me," he said. "If I am here longer than a few minutes, the cause will be so joyous I will gladly triple this when we return to the hotel." With the driver silenced, Arthur stopped to steady his legs and straighten his frame. The persistent ache in his gut began to nag him again but he dismissed it, focusing all his attentions on the freshly painted door bearing the number 124.

He laughed at the nervous shake of his hands, wanting so desperately to see Daniel's happy face appear behind the wood.

Whispering a silent prayer, he knocked, and his petition was granted as Daniel opened the door and burst into a joyous grin.

"Arthur? Saints be praised, it's you! It's really you!"

The two men became a happy tangle of arms that consumed the doorway. Daniel pulled his old friend inside and stepped away. "You look so very well. Every report I had heard—"

"It was very nearly true, but God granted me a reprieve. For these eight years I've wondered why, and now I see. It was to once again set my eyes on the boy I love so dearly."

Daniel's eyes misted as he extended his hand to Ruth. "Arthur, this is Ruth, my wife."

Arthur bowed. "It is an honor to meet the woman who won Daniel's heart." As he came back up he received Ruth's outstretched hand and placed a gentle kiss there. His eyes quickly scanned the cramped but tidy room that served as the kitchen, dining area, and living area. He noticed the skilled needlework adorning the curtains, towels, table runner, and doilies. "You've made Daniel a lovely home, Ruth. I've never seen him happier."

The younger man hugged his friend once more. "I can't tell you how wonderful it is to see you, Arthur. And we have a fine son—David Everett. Bring him, darling, won't you?" he asked Ruth. Moments later, a wriggling, cooing bundle appeared in his mother's arms.

Ruth extended the child toward Arthur. "Would you like to hold him, sir?"

Half enchanted, half frightened by the idea, Arthur stepped back and scolded Ruth. "First we must settle something once and for all. Dear Ruth, you cannot bewitch your husband and then his dear friend, and hold to such formalities. Please consent to be my friend as well, and call me Arthur."

Ruth curtsied in response. "As you wish, Arthur." Her smile stretched broadly across her face as she placed her son in his arms. Daniel led him to a chair where he sat, completely mesmerized over the infant.

"He's marvelous, Daniel. Perfect in every way."

"How did you find us? Did my father tell you where we were?"

Arthur noted the thread of hope in Daniel's voice. "It was Ridley who told me—" *Why give the boy false hope?* "—right after your father tossed me out."

The hope disappeared from Daniel's face, replaced by resolve. "I know it appears we have little of worldly goods, but we are quite content, and we have a good plan. As soon as we've saved enough money, we plan to leave for America."

"So you're going, you're really going. Then give me the honor of financing your way!"

"No, no. Thank you, but we need to do this ourselves. I've always been intrigued with America, but it was those talks we shared about your first trip there that sealed my decision." He placed his arm around Ruth. "Jew's are unwelcome in Britain right now. America has religious freedom, boundless land, and fine medical schools. We have no ties here. Ruth's family was killed in Greece, and I have no family. We'll raise David where he can be free to be whatever or whoever he chooses, and where I can get good work to save for medical school."

Daniel pulled a chair close to Arthur, who was still enthralled with the baby. "I love him so desperately, Arthur. I know my father loved me the same. How can such love become so complicated?"

"I wish I had an answer for you. I've only known this little child a few moments, and yet I already feel such affection for him. If your father would just see him . . ."

"He won't accept Ruth or our son." Daniel threw his hands on Arthur's shoulders. "Why don't you be David's godfather?" Daniel looked to Ruth, who heartily agreed. "Neither Ruth nor I had friends or remaining kin close enough to ask when he was christened. Come stand with us at the church this Sunday. I'll make the arrangements. It would please us so."

"But you're going to America."

"Eventually," Ruth said. "And this will give you reason to visit us when we do."

340

A thrill filled Arthur's heart, warming into contented bliss. "I'd be so honored."

Bled avoided answering Michael's questions as he led him through the dark streets to the Spencers' apartment. "You'll be sorry you bellyached when you see the mark I've picked out."

"What mark?"

"'Is pockets are filled with coins, so I'm bettin 'is billfold is fat as well. Plus, 'e's slow and half crippled. It'll be an easy job."

Michael turned to leave. "You brought the wrong McGowan brother. I don't pick pockets anymore."

"Don't you want to see the fella who's been noseyin' around about you'n Hank? Besides, this ain't a job fer Hank. It requires a gentle touch, and some smarts. Before the fella gets into the carriage, just walk up to 'im with those innocent-lookin' eyes of yours'n ask 'im for a copper. When 'e reaches for the coin, I'll come runnin' down the street and knock 'im down. While you're helpin' 'im up, just lift 'is billfold. Now shh . . . 'e's comin' out."

The boys hid behind a barrel where they could hear and see the man exit Daniel's home. The man shook Doc's hand. "I'll see you bright and early Sunday morning, then."

The voice was familiar to Michael, though he couldn't immediately place it. He cursed the darkness that obscured the man's face, but when the man turned, the lamplight shining through the doorway illuminated his profile enough for Michael to identify him as Mr. Arthur Ramsey, the son of the man who had planned to wed his mother! Images swept across the canvas of Michael's memory—images of Stephen Ramsey, who loved him and treated him as a son, and memories of his mother during the happiest two years of their lives.

Stephen Ramsey's death brought a pall over Michael's mother that Arthur Ramsey had tried to ease. *If only Arthur had not been so weak and sick back then. If only he had not been in Barbados when Mama grew so ill. If only Richard Porter had allowed me to mail Mama's letter . . .*

The boys watched the older man receive a hug from Doc's wife, and after the two men embraced again, Arthur Ramsey turned for his carriage.

"Go! Now!" Bled whispered.

"No! Not this man," Michael replied.

"Are you crazy? Look at 'im! 'E's ripe for the pickin'!"

"Not this man!" Michael growled. "Leave him alone."

"What's a rich codger like 'im to you?"

Michael continued to stare longingly at Arthur Ramsey. "He was good to my mother."

"Good to your mother, eh? I bet Richard Porter would love to know that."

Michael spun on Bled, fire flying from his eyes. "Say nothing about him to Porter!"

CHAPTER 33

Early December 1824
Washington, District of Columbia

Jed's heavy heart warmed at the sight of the candle Hannah had placed in the window to welcome him home. Barely awake enough to lift each foot, he dragged himself up the brick walk to the black-painted door and pulled out his key. Before he could turn it in the lock, Hannah was there, opening the door and taking his hat and scarf.

"Another late night," she said as she helped him remove his coat.

"I'm sorry. I tried not to wake you."

"You didn't. Come in and sit by the fire. I'll fix you a plate."

Too tired to resist her kindness, he smiled and did as she instructed, moving to the overstuffed chair in the family parlor. The butter-colored room was his favorite, bright and cozy and filled with their favorite things brought from the Willows on their last extended trip to the farm—Hannah's piano, James's toy chest, Jed's humidor, a bookshelf filled with their favorite titles. He saw the flannel quilt strewn across Hannah's favorite chair with a book peeking from the corner, and he knew she had been reading until his arrival.

After settling into his chair, he kicked off his shoes and leaned back, then reached for her book to see what had so captivated her attention until nearly midnight. It was her Bible. Several pages of stationery were tucked between the pages. Jed recognized the hand as Beatrice's and assumed the scene had something to do with Joseph Smith.

Things were fine between his wife and him. She doted on him and her affections were sweet and genuine, but he could feel a distance developing between them. It was most noticeable when he caught her alone in thought, when that faraway look overtook her as if she were living a moment foreign to him. There was a new light shining in her eyes as well, and Jed knew it all tied into Joseph.

Jed regretted the irritation that name aroused in him. Never secretive, always inviting, Hannah tried to share each new concept that lit her mind, and there were so many as the tarnish was polished off old ideas, becoming exquisite and new to her. Like all Christians, Jed had been taught about the Crucifixion, but Hannah was astounded by the idea that Jesus was not a name God used when serving as the Savior of men, but instead, He was a separate divine Being, the literal Son of God. Jed had accepted the idea with little of Hannah's passion, as he did after listening to each new concept, asking few questions and offering little rebuttal.

For the most part, like his congressional colleagues, his focus on keeping the nation from splitting apart left little time for pondering God. For Hannah, the opposite was true. She almost seemed frustrated when the minutia of life stole her attention from spiritual things.

And therein lay the chasm opening between them—Hannah was outgrowing him spiritually, and he knew he either needed to work harder to at least understand this part of her, or they would grow so far apart in goals and dreams that they would lose one another.

She came in carrying a tray, looking like an angel. Her long, dark hair cascaded loosely around her flanneled shoulders as if she were eighteen again. Her cheeks were flushed from cooking, and the fireplace light sparkled in her green eyes. Jed took the tray and set it on the side table, then patted his lap for her to sit there. She gladly accepted the invitation and curled against him as he kissed her temple and said, "This moment is the best of my entire day."

Hannah nuzzled closer. "These past two months have been so hard on you. I'm sorry today has also been discouraging."

"Had it been the best of days, this would still be the best moment." He tipped her chin to kiss her, and she found his lips in a sweet touch.

"Are the presidential election results all in now?"

Jed closed his eyes and sighed long and low. "Yes, and the vote is so split no candidate meets the requirement for victory. It's exactly as we feared." He leaned his head back to stare at the ceiling. "The Federalist Party is all but dissolved, and all four candidates attached themselves to the Democratic-Republicans, though their positions on issues and personal rivalries place them oceans apart. Members of Congress point to this disparity in their platforms to argue that the party system has failed and we need a new mechanism for choosing candidates."

"They would throw out the entire constitutional process rather than work to improve it?" Hannah asked.

"Timothy tells me not to worry, that all sides will argue and threaten, but in the end they will work to uphold the constitutional process."

Hannah traced the wrinkles that spread from the corners of Jed's eyes, a measure of the stress he felt. "Is the federal government so different from your experience in the state?"

"The differences between the wants and needs of states within a nation are so much greater than the differing needs within a state. The nation is clearly divided in this election. The northern states favor John Quincy Adams, and his platform of a strong federal government with an equally strong banking system. The western states favor their son, Andrew Jackson, who'd have the entire government run by the will of the electorate if he could. It sounds well and good in spirit, but how many citizens will or have the time to study every issue that comes for a vote? The two lead candidates are polar opposites on the issues, and the harder they pull against one another, the deeper the rift grows in the nation."

"So the election of the next president will fall to the House of Representatives."

"The Founders provided for just such a situation, but it's unprecedented in practice."

"Won't the representatives vote the way their constituents did?"

"Jackson won the popular vote, but he did not claim a clear majority because the vote was split four ways. He also won the most electoral votes, but again without a clear majority. The worrisome thing is that the supporters of John Quincy Adams, who came in second, and Henry Clay, who came in third, have been holding clandestine meetings, and we all think an alliance is being formed to throw Adams the House vote."

"Then the people will say their will wasn't upheld by their representatives."

Jed nodded again as he began rubbing his pounding temples. "Enough of Washington's troubles. Tell me what you've been reading this evening."

Hannah moved to her chair and reached for her Bible, then wrapped her arms around the book and pressed it against her. "I received a letter from Beatrice."

Jed pretended not to know. "Oh? How are the Snowdens?"

"The river is already freezing, so things are quiet. Dudley proved to be a fine farmer—they had a very good harvest. And the mercantile manager reports the store made a tidy profit."

Jed smiled at the good news. "Dudley left so much behind in Palmyra. I'm glad the move has gone well." He hesitated to open the next topic, but knowing how important it was to Hannah, he ventured in. "Was there any further news from Palmyra aside from the mercantile report?"

The question caused a brilliant light to sparkle in her eyes. Tentative at first, she said, "Dudley and Beatrice have been working to repair their relationship with the Smiths, and the Smiths finally shared some details of Joseph's experiences. They told Dudley of another visitation Joseph received from the angel this September."

Jed noticed the way she held her breath as she awaited his response. "Tell me about it."

"On each of these two visits, the angel directed Joseph to a hill near the Smiths' farm where an ancient book was buried—the book

346

mentioned in Isaiah." She tapped the Bible. "It's the record of an obscure Hebrew prophet who was inspired to flee from Jerusalem. He and his family built ships and sailed across the ocean and came to live upon this continent. They became a great people who also knew about the Lord. For hundreds of years they kept a record of their lives and culture as they waited for His birth, and after His death and resurrection, He visited them and taught them His gospel. Imagine it! It's a second record of Christ's teachings, Jed, containing the *fulness* of His word."

"This book . . . is this the one Dudley said was made of golden plates?"

"Yes." Hannah sounded defensive. "But there are lots of mentions in the Bible of records and scribes. It's just that instead of paper or papyrus, this ancient text is inscribed upon thin plates of gold. The angel told Joseph that in time, he would be allowed to obtain the record, and means would be provided for him to translate it."

Jed allowed the ideas to percolate in his weary mind, which to Hannah must have appeared a sign of doubt, for she crossed her arms before her and said, "If God could create a world, He could surely help a man translate a record."

Jed leaned forward and gently took her arms, waiting until the fire left her eyes. "You mustn't expect—"

"You haven't even tried. Not really."

There it is. He leaned toward her and touched his index finger to her lips. "Shh. Let me finish. What I'm trying to say is this—you and I are different. You trust your heart to lead you. I rely on logic and reason. It's not how God wants people to come to Him, but it's how my heart and mind work. When I was a prisoner on that ship, I was able to finally admit I needed Him—really *needed* Him. I had always felt I could eventually work out my own solutions, but not that time. I knew I could do nothing more myself. I surrendered my will to Him wholly, begging for His help, and He heard me, Hannah. I know He heard me, and He answered me in a way He knew a stubborn man like me would accept. So I do believe He can do anything.

"But something happened to me when I came home. Call it pride, or stubbornness—I don't know—but I suddenly saw that submission as weakness, and I retreated from it. Perhaps that's why all this talk of Joseph Smith has made me so uncomfortable. I've always known if I came to believe it was true, it would require something of me . . . something I didn't want to do or give. Isn't that ludicrous? Me trying to hold a standoff with God?"

The more he spoke, the softer Hannah's expression became. She returned to his lap and touched his face. "You're a fine man, Jed. Maybe a bit stubborn at times, but I'm sure God understands that part of you. As you said, He's answered your prayers, and He's still reaching out to you."

"I asked Timothy if he thought God would condescend to personally answer a boy's prayer. He said religion needs freedom to flourish, and that if such a thing were to happen, he believed it would happen here for that reason. I was the last person to leave the Capitol tonight, Hannah. I looked around at the beautiful construction and thought about the fire and how we feared we might lose our sovereignty. We've enjoyed a decade of peace and advancement in this nation, but I fear that sweet season is about to end. This election will divide us once again, and who knows what changes it will bring. But I kept thinking about the years 1814 to 1824. Why did we have that decade of peace?"

Wonder filled her face. "Joseph's vision happened right in the middle of that period!"

"I kept thinking that, too. Perhaps God gave us this time so these concepts could take root."

Silent moments passed, and Jed knew Hannah, too, was considering the implication of that idea.

"Beatrice reminded me of a conversation I had with Emmett Schultz while she and I were in New Hampshire. It concerned a passage of scripture in the third chapter of Acts: 'And he shall send Jesus Christ, which before was preached unto you, Whom the heaven must receive until the times of restitution of all things, which God hath spoken by the mouth of all his holy prophets since the world began.'"

"A restitution of what?"

Hannah's head cocked sideways as she shrugged. "I'm not certain, but I believe it speaks of a restoration of the miracles and authority of God which men thought ended with the Apostles."

"Like God personally answering a boy's prayer, and the ministrations of angels?"

"Yes! What if the heavens really are opening, Jed?" She laid against his chest and sighed. She intertwined her fingers in his. "Something wonderful is about to happen, and more than anything, I want to experience it with you."

"I can't say I believe all of it yet, but I want to learn. You're leaps ahead of me, Hannah. I'll need your patience, but I am willing to see where this takes us."

CHAPTER 34

July 4, 1826
Washington, District of Columbia

Many of their friends closed up shop at Willowsport and headed for Washington for the jubilee, leaving Jed and Hannah's spacious Georgetown home bursting at the seams. But it was no cause of alarm to them. With Bitty at the helm of the kitchen, the time spent indoors proved as joyous as the celebration in the city.

Accounts of other cities' celebrations spoke of a day of feasting, flag waving, and of toasting anything and everything until some revelers would be too inebriated to utter an intelligible word, but in Washington it was a day of reverence for this generation—born the recipients of liberty—who had recently fought to preserve it once more.

Aside from the jubilee, two other topics were bandied about Washington—the conspicuous absence of presidential hopeful and America's hero of the Battle of New Orleans, Senator Andrew Jackson, who resigned his seat in the Senate after the "corrupt bargain" his rival John Quincy Adams struck to win the White House the year before; and the unpopularity of the winner and his British-born wife.

A festive but dignified atmosphere filled the city as crowds swelled in and around the magnificent Capitol that morning. In Lafayette Square, the volunteer military companies saluted the president, leading his escort to the Capitol while the Marine band played. President Adams followed in a carriage, accompanied by a stream of other coaches ferrying members of the cabinet. Military and naval officers followed on horseback. Visitors stood in line to enter the building, which was filled with beautiful artwork, to watch the planned program.

Jed looked out over the Potomac, where ships and boats displayed flags waving merrily in the breeze. He thought how just twelve years earlier British ships had menaced those same waters, threatening to burn Alexandria if she dared fly America's colors. He studied the magnificent lines of the Capitol with her glorious rotunda and dome, and for a moment he saw the charred and smoldering remains of its rocket-burned shell. It took some effort to push the image away, but today was a day to celebrate hope.

He had been born in 1790, fourteen years after the signing of the Declaration of Independence, and seven years after the end of the Revolution. His father and grandfather had fought beside General Washington and Light Horse Harry Lee. Jed felt their spirits with him this day. He never actually knew his grandfather, who died soon after Jed was born, but Jonathan Edward Pearson had been larger than life, as so many men of his day had been— wise Washington, thoughtful Franklin, fiery Jefferson, and Adams, the great orator. They were nearly mythical. The very speaking of their names evoked reverence in Jed, and now only two of the great men were yet alive.

James ran up, holding his tri-corner hat and carrying the wooden musket Jed had made for him. At six years old, the boy was taller and more temperate than most children his age. Jed remembered his parents characterizing him as more pragmatic and thoughtful about things than other children. That was how he saw his handsome boy, and Jed loved him more than life itself.

He ruffled James's hair. "What are you and your cousins up to?"

James pointed to where a group of Indians stood in full dress. "Charles and Sarah are afraid of the Indians, Papa. They won't even leave Aunt Frannie's side."

"Did you explain to Charles and Sarah why they're here? Did you tell them President Adams signed an important treaty with them earlier in the year?"

Hannah strolled over with cookies she had purchased from one of the vendors. She handed one to each of her "men." "We should take our seats soon. The program begins shortly."

Jed slipped his arm around her waist and nodded. "Let's gather Frannie and her children."

After an opening prayer, the Declaration of Independence was read. Each word seemed inspired, and Jed longed to know more of Thomas Jefferson's experiences writing it. A speech and prayer followed, and then a sobering petition was made for people to contribute to a fund for Thomas Jefferson. Many, including Jed, committed money, but it wounded him that the great "Lion of Liberty" was chained by agonizing debt.

The petition to help Mr. Jefferson was particularly poignant in light of the fact that all the remaining signers and former presidents had been invited to attend the jubilee, and though none were able to attend, each sent letters of regret that included each man's thoughts on the significance of the day. Each had been printed in the Washington paper, *The National Intelligencer,* but Jefferson's letter had set the tone of the day for Jed. It was written with the same eloquent tongue that graced his masterful Declaration of Independence:

> *I should, indeed, with peculiar delight, have met and exchanged there congratulations, personally, with the small band, the remnant of that host of worthies who joined with us on that day, in the bold and doubtful election we were to make, for our country, between submission and the sword; and to have enjoyed with them the consolatory fact that our fellow citizens, after half a century of experience and prosperity, continue to approve the choice we made. May it be to the world, what I believe it will be, (to some parts sooner, to others*

later, but finally to all,) the signal of arousing men to burst the chains, under which monkish ignorance and superstition had persuaded them to bind themselves, and to assume the blessings and security of self-government. The form which we have substituted restores the free right to the unbounded exercise of reason and freedom of opinion. All eyes are opened or opening to the rights of man. The general spread of the light of science has already laid open to every view the palpable truth, that the mass of mankind has not been born with saddles on their backs, nor a favored few, booted and spurred, ready to ride them legitimately, by the grace of God. These are grounds of hope for others; for ourselves, let the annual return of this day forever refresh our recollections of these rights, and an undiminished devotion to them.

The words resonated in Jed's heart as they left the Capitol amid the throng. Some attendees planned quiet picnics by the Capitol. The Pearson party headed home and returned that evening for a fireworks display from the White House lawn.

On July sixth, after the last of their company had left, Timothy Shepard appeared at the door, pounding on it with an urgency that chilled Jed. When he opened the door he found his friend grim-faced, his eyes moist as he blurted out, "Thomas Jefferson is dead."

"What?"

"He passed away July fourth at the age of eighty-three," Timothy said as he paced. "I knew he was ill, but he was so looking forward to that anniversary." When he turned and looked at Jed, utter sorrow etched his face. "I cannot imagine this world without him in it."

"Nor can I. Now the only surviving signers are John Adams and Charles Carroll."

"And President Adams says his father is failing as well. The rider from Monticello is rushing to Massachusetts to deliver the news to John Adams as we speak. I pray he arrives in time. I feel like an orphan, Jed—politically fatherless." Timothy walked a few paces away, clearly dumbstruck and reeling. Jed placed his hand on his friend's arm. "Of all the days for him to pass—the fiftieth anniversary of his greatest achievement," Timothy said. "It's almost providential."

That sense of divine intervention seemed more apparent following the news that the fiftieth anniversary of the signing of the Declaration of Independence had not only been the day of Jefferson's passing, but of John Adams's as well. The two great adversaries, who had forged a great friendship in their later years, had died on America's jubilee.

The news caused Jed to become reflective. Numbers began running through his mind—twenty-four states, six presidents, nineteen seated congresses, twelve million American citizens. It was staggering to see what the vision of a few inspired men had brought to pass. Had such rapid development ever occurred before? And not just people and acres, but a unique government, industry, churches and religions, military victories, institutions of learning, inventions, cities and towns, and roads and canals. Jed knew a new invention would likely change the world in a few months. A section of rails was laid, and a steam-powered locomotive like the ones being tested in Britain was being readied. If all went as planned, the Granite Railroad of Quincy, Massachusetts, would soon move not just stone but people over land en masse! Jed was also privy to the fact that Baltimorean George Brown and a group of investors were considering chartering a railroad company between Baltimore and Ohio.

What can't freedom accomplish? he asked himself. *Nothing,* was his reply.

Jed thought again on what Timothy had said about religion needing freedom to flourish. A sense of warmth spread through him at the experiment he was conducting on the matter, exploring how freedom and faith combine. He was grateful he had conquered his fears, agreeing to read the Bible and pray with Hannah and James each night.

Who knew what he would discover?

America had barreled into the year 1826 like an awkward debutante at her coming-out party, but something changed in her after her jubilee. Perhaps it was the passing of Adams and Jefferson, or the victory of reaching fifty years of age, but she was weary of being regarded as a child commercially. Everything lovely was expected to come from Europe, while "American-made" immediately conjured images of homespun and folksy. There was a hunger for America to produce her own artists, her own music, her own elegant goods, and American foundries and factories waited to produce items created from the emerging American vision.

Frannie caught hold of the vision, sponsoring budding American talent. She used an empty storefront to open a gallery, and she encouraged Henri to open a second theater in Baltimore to give new musicians and singers a venue in this budding railroad town.

The railroad began laying tracks in the years following the jubilee, projecting the ability to move people and cargo at previously unthinkable rates. Jed could foresee the changes such mobility would cause as, like dominoes falling, one advancement would further another. He could envision the West opening up and creating a vacuum, drawing liberty-loving, land-seeking people to America to fill the void. But where would the Indians now find refuge?

Such an expanse of population required roads and towns, schools and universities, policing and courts, concerns President John Quincy Adams planned to meet through an expanded government. But populist Andrew Jackson had, in essence, been campaigning since the day the Congress threw the presidency to Adams in 1825, and in early 1827, Jackson was already preparing for a political war.

Jed's democratic convictions blurred. He had always believed in the voice and will of the people, which was strongly in Jackson's corner, but there was something comforting about holding on to the Founders' influence. John Quincy Adams was the last man immersed in their company and weaned on the Revolution. He had been raised by his father while in Europe, and at fourteen he became the secretary for the diplomat assigned to Russia. His reverence for the Constitution was unrivaled, his common sense was stabilizing, and his vision of America was clear. He was a gentle transition between the ideals of the past and the challenges of the present.

And then there was Jackson, a wild hare being championed as the voice of the common man. He was a heralded military leader, but was he qualified to lead a nation? He brought energy, popularity, and renewed passion to the election, but were those qualities enough? Jed just didn't know, but by the fall of 1827, both campaigns were in full battle mode.

Jed regretted the end of a busy but satisfying Willows summer, and the need for the family to return to Washington. Postal service had vastly improved across the entire nation, and it was particularly efficient from city to city. Hannah and her sisters could now exchange letters within a week, which kept the busy women in constant communication.

Neither of Hannah's sisters had seen the new house, nor had the cousins been together in years, so plans were made for all the Stansbury family members to gather at the Willows in early January to celebrate the start of 1828.

Myrna arrived first with a full assortment of advice regarding James's upbringing, all gleaned, of course, from the most "world-renowned" experts on children. Also included in her conversational repertoire were a thousand elongated tales about her life of medical martyrdom and the myriad lives she had personally saved through bandage-rolling and fund-raising. Within six hours Hannah needed a headache remedy from Bitty's medicinal bag.

Twice, Jed issued urgent requests for Hannah to walk with him when a vein running across her temple began to visibly throb. More headache powder and a "medicinal" shot of brandy were required on two days, so the effusive welcome Beatrice received upon her family's arrival came as no surprise to anyone.

"You are my angel of mercy," Hannah whispered to her as the pair embraced.

"Myrna? Is it that bad?"

Hannah simply rolled her eyes as Myrna raced over with her own greeting. "Five children? Good heavens, five? How on earth do you plan on raising such a brood on a farmer's income? Of course it's not for me to say, but—really, Beatrice. How do you survive?"

"Dudley is a partner in the Palmyra Mercantile and in a trading post in Ohio," she corrected.

But Myrna stabbed on. "You're a loyal wife to defend his failed ventures, watching him eek out an existence while you tend a small tribe of his offspring."

Hannah handed Beatrice her very own packet of headache powder.

It became clear on three successive nights that Beatrice and Dudley were trying desperately to find a moment to speak to Jed and Hannah when Myrna was not around. Finding no such opportunity, Beatrice made the ultimate sacrifice.

"Myrna, darling, I so want to hear more about your incredible charity work. Could you spare me a few hours alone? Perhaps we could walk along the river and talk as we go."

Hannah stood behind Myrna, trying desperately to spare her sister from sacrificing herself in this way, but Myrna latched onto the invitation with eagle talons, and the deal was struck. While Myrna fetched the women's cloaks, Hannah pulled Beatrice aside. "Myrna will talk your ear off, and we've only a few hours remaining before you leave for New York."

"Dudley has something urgent to tell you and Jed that must be shared in person," she whispered, "and since we are leaving tomorrow, this is the only way." Beatrice laid her hand on Hannah's shoulder and smiled softly. "We have been foul to joke about our sister. She is a pious widow doing much good, and if she cannot crow about herself to us, who else has she?"

Hannah felt no small shame over her sister's gentle rebuke. "As always, you're right."

Beatrice took her hand and pressed it to her cheek. "No, not always. It was you who righted my course where the Smiths are concerned, and for that I shall always be grateful."

Dudley appeared in the room just before the two women departed for their walk. He and Beatrice shared a quick and knowing glance before she slipped through the door. Dudley turned to Hannah, placing his hand in the center of her back. "Come, I asked Jed to wait for us in the study. I have much to tell you."

The urgency in his voice brought chills to Hannah's arms. As she entered the study she noticed the deep worry lines running across Jed's brow and knew he was equally disarmed by the importance the Snowdens were placing upon this information.

Dudley sat, then stood, then paced, then sat again. "Let me just begin at the beginning. We've shared nothing with you about the Smiths for months because we have heard almost nothing from them. I assumed, since we had heard nothing more, that this September twenty-second passed as the others had—without Joseph securing the record. But it was not so."

Hannah and Jed shot forward in their seats. "Are you saying he has the record in his possession?" Jed asked.

At first Dudley offered no response except a steady gaze that grew increasingly awed and distant as if he were appreciating a far-off scene. A reverent smile slowly stole upon his lips as his eyes closed. He nodded almost imperceptibly and opened his eyes, finally answering, "Yes."

Hannah and Jed glanced at one another, then returned their rapt attention to Dudley. "He has them? In his very possession?" she asked.

On the heels of her question, Jed queried, "Are you saying you've seen them?"

Dudley flapped his hands, gesturing for patience. "I'm getting ahead of myself. In late December, I made a trip to Palmyra to review the mercantile's accounts. I overheard conversations about some 'golden plates,' and I assumed these referred to the record Joseph has been laboring to obtain these past four years. I finally decided to call upon the Smiths at their farm, and they confirmed that Joseph had obtained the record, but he was not there. Not even they could anticipate the opposition that would rise against this work. Circumstances forced Joseph to flee to Pennsylvania to protect the record. But I'm already getting ahead of myself. Joseph married in January of last year. Did you know that, Hannah?"

"He's been married a year? No, I didn't know that."

"His bride, Emma Hale Smith, is a most excellent woman according to Mrs. Smith, and she became his wife and support at a critical time. You already know the disparaging attacks on Joseph's character had begun as soon as reports of his first vision were circulated, but in late winter 1826, his enemies twisted the law to torment him."

Before Jed spoke or moved a muscle, Hannah anticipated his reaction to the disclosure.

"He was arrested?"

Hannah grasped Jed's hand to calm him before his fragile faith dispersed. "Please, Jed, don't judge so quickly. Let Dudley explain."

"Yes, please, Jed," Dudley said. "I have learned all too well that Joseph's course will not be sweet or tidy. Perhaps it is the Lord's will that he, and those who believe him, must do so with naught but faith to support them. Those who require reason or logic will hear his story and seek only gold and gain—or worse—to discredit the divine. And I believe God will allow such to be blinded by their own doubt. So please, I pray you, listen to my whole story before you judge.

"Remember the home Alvin began constructing so his parents could enjoy a comfortable old age? It was stolen from them with only one payment remaining. A trio of men lied to the deed holder, declaring that Mr. Smith had abandoned the farm and that Hyrum was destroying it. He tore up the Smiths' contract and sold the farm to these men instead. Once he discovered the truth, the landowner asked the men to act ethically and morally, but they replied that the Smiths had gold plates and gold Bibles, and they demanded a payment of one thousand dollars within less than two days or they would not budge."

Hannah smacked her hands against her lap. "That's extortion!"

"Clearly their goal was to pressure the Smiths in the hopes that Joseph would produce the gold to end their suffering. In any case, he hadn't yet received the record, and even if he had, the angel forbade the use of the plates for gain. The penalties would be severe.

"The Smiths are now tenants in the home they built, and upon the property they labored to improve. The situation caused Joseph and Hyrum great worry. The primary support for their parents and younger siblings now fell upon them, and they sought work wherever they could.

"A man named Josiah Stowell heard Joseph had a stone with which he could 'see' what could not be seen with the natural eye. At the end of 1825, Mr. Stowell hired Joseph and his father to come to New York and use Joseph's gifts to help him locate an ancient Spanish gold and silver mine. After a few weeks, Joseph ended the venture, but Stowell's nephew filed a charge claiming Joseph's actions violated a state statute against fortune-telling and soothsaying. Joseph was brought before the court to answer the charge of disorderly conduct, but Josiah Stowell came forward to attest to Joseph's character. The case was dismissed, but it will not be the last."

With a nod to Hannah that she knew called for patience, Jed asked Dudley, "Hadn't he been warned of the sacred nature of these things? Why did he not respect the importance of the cause he says he's engaged in? Why did he nose the information around to so many people?"

Dudley shook his head. "Joseph told no one but his family. His father mentioned the plates to one individual—a trusted neighbor named Martin Harris—two years previous. Harris evidently shared the news with someone he likewise but unadvisedly trusted, and soon the word spread far and wide, bringing unforeseen troubles to the Smiths' door long before Joseph even took possession of the plates."

"Tell us about that, Dudley," Hannah said. "How did he obtain the plates?"

"Once people discovered that September twenty-second was the annual date the angel met Joseph at the hill, they scrutinized Joseph's movements so closely that news would spread if he disappeared for even a short while, so the angel told him he must come to the hill at two in the morning. He borrowed a rig and took Emma along as his partner, and finally received the record.

"Since that time, there have been unrelenting attempts to steal the plates. Every step Joseph takes is scrutinized. He has seen his home ransacked, and he has been physically abused and mentally tormented. He has had to move the record many times, striving always to remain a step ahead of thieves and robbers. Finally, realizing there would never be peace enough in Palmyra to allow the translation of the plates to commence, it was decided that they must move elsewhere. In November, Emma's brother moved them to Pennsylvania, where they now reside."

"So we don't yet know what the records say?"

Sympathy filled Dudley's face. "No, Hannah. We'll have to wait a bit longer, I'm afraid."

Jed leaned forward. "Is there any other witness who can at least corroborate his tale, Dudley? Did Joseph allow his parents or his wife to see the record?"

A long, deep breath preceded Dudley's answer. "It is forbidden at this time. But his mother felt the Urim and Thummim—the mechanism or glasses that hold the translation stones—and she was also permitted to feel their breastplate holder through a thin cloth. She was able to describe it down to the very holes where the straps were secured."

Jed sat back, deflated. "But no one else has actually *seen* them."

Dudley glanced at Hannah, his disappointment evident. "No, Jed."

"So . . . no one has seen these plates or these seer stones that have been pulled from a hill by a young man who made his living as a treasure hunter?"

Hannah watched Dudley frown as he appeared to seek words that would satisfy Jed. She likewise prayed that Jed's questions were rooted in a desire to know, rather than a place of doubt, and then a thought came to her. "Remember Markus's stories about his Uncle Ryan? He knew men who found pirate fortunes buried along the coast. And what of all the British strongboxes rowed ashore and buried when ships were sinking during the Revolution? Perhaps it sounds curious to you, but seeking old treasures isn't really that unusual, is it?" She looked from Jed to Dudley and found her brother-in-law's visage peaceful and assured.

"She's right, Jed. We stand on the line between the old days and the new. What was common has become curious, or worse. You balk over the seeing stones, but there are a hundred references in the Bible of wondrous things that came to pass by the use of means we cannot explain. What of Moses and the miracles in Egypt, or Aaron's budding rod, or Jesus and the withering fig tree, or the miracle of the wine? There are ministers in Palmyra who still are hired to pray and then use a divining rod to seek water.

"For thousands of years man believed God was a God of miracles, and that He could and did use divine means to fulfill His work. Here, in 1828, many people still commonly believe this, but science now makes skeptics of us. If a man moves iron filings with a magnet, we call that science, but once upon a time, men would have called that magic—or a miracle. If man can do such things, why do we question whether the Creator can move mountains with His finger? Does knowledge alter the nature of God? And who's to say science isn't but the portion of God's power He reveals to man? Doctors perform miracles every day using bits of revealed knowledge about the body and herbs. Might it be God who reveals that to them?

Dudley went on. "And if you want logic, ask yourself this. Would any reasonable man suffer, or cause the family he loves to suffer, over a false tale? How much easier would it be for Joseph to simply walk away? He lives in another state. He could deny his visions and visitation, move even further west and make a fresh start where no one else has ever heard of him. But he doesn't. He bears the torment and scrutiny and stands by his witness. Why would any man do that, Jed?

"But none of that really matters. No past miracles or logic will be a sufficient foundation for a person to stand on when, as the Bible says, the storms come. Only one foundation will be sure enough—that received through prayer. And I cannot give you that answer. Each person must find that for themselves." Dudley rose and stretched. "And now I must gather the children and begin packing for our return to Colesville tomorrow."

Jed and Hannah rose as well. She went to Dudley and embraced him. "Thank you for sharing this with us."

He placed a kiss on her forehead. "Of course."

Jed stood, offering his hand. "You've given me much to consider."

The two men shook hands. "No matter what you decide about Joseph and his work, it will not change the affection we share," Dudley assured Jed. "Despite what little I know of the actual written record, the thing I am certain of is the feeling I have each time I consider the love God and His Son have for us to have begun this work. Love is at the crux of this, Jed. It's all about love."

Hannah watched as Jed's face flushed, and she saw how the worry lines between his brows faded into softness, but it was his next question that stole her breath away.

"When I'm ready—when I've pondered all you've told me and made peace with it—can you arrange for me to meet Joseph Smith?"

Jed had to steal small moments where he could to study the Bible and ponder religion, praying with Hannah and James intermittently as he frequently rose before the sun and arrived home after they were asleep.

As anticipated, the 1828 political campaign brought increased division to America. Jackson's campaign handlers painted Adams as an out of touch, Europe-loving elitist. Adams's camp battled back against Jackson, charging him to be reckless, inexperienced, and an adulterer. The bitterness drove a massive wedge between political factions, giving birth to a new, two-party political system—the Jacksonian Democrats and the Whigs. They were hotly divided on the division of power in the government, and policies such as the Indian question, banking, taxation, and American development. Jed felt the country polarizing, and he worried where this would lead.

Spring left him longing for the family's planned summer at the Willows, but a letter from Samuel added even greater concerns to his list. Emerson Hildebrand had been a model prisoner, or so the warden said, and he was being considered for an expedited release. That news sent Jed dashing off letters to the warden, to the parole board, and even to the governor of North Carolina, describing the havoc Hildebrand had wreaked upon the Willows and begging them to deny his parole. A reply arrived two weeks later informing Jed of their regrets. His letter had arrived too late. Emerson Hildebrand was already free.

Jed called Jack, Markus, and Abel together to discuss the situation. "What do you think, Abel? I can get a court order and have him picked up if he comes near the farm."

"Do what you can, Jed, but I'm not afraid of Emerson Hildebrand anymore. We're not the same little farm anymore. Over 150 people live here now."

"And a third of those are men who can shoot," Markus added. "These immigrants experienced violence and repression in their old countries. They won't tolerate it here."

Jack agreed. "Markus is right, Jed. The newcomers'll stand with us if the time comes."

"All right then." Jed studied his three friends. As with him, the passing years were beginning to show in the gray streaking their hair, and in the lines around their eyes and brows. He thought how the four of them comprised a most unlikely group. They had built a unique small town from a bold dream, and against great opposition. If need be, they would stand once more and defend their home.

Jed looked at mighty Abel. Though he was still tall, still strong, maturity had left him looking much like his father, Jerome. "How will Caleb take the news about Hildebrand?" Jed asked. "I know he's been threatening to leave for years, and now with the baby coming . . ."

Abel glanced at the ground and scuffed some dirt with his boot. "My son reminds me so much of me when I was his age—ready to fight the world." Abel's laugh was low and thoughtful. "The difference is, he knows he has choices—opportunities I never had back then. We may not have all we want, or all we deserve, but it's progress."

The group nodded, each man seeming to agree with the observation.

"I'll arrange for the restraining order, then," Jed said. "You men can spread the word to the residents."

Jed was headed for the house when Markus rushed to catch up to him. "How's Hannah today?"

"Better." Jed knew the tone of his voice negated his words. "She's melancholy. What woman wouldn't be who lost four babies in as many years? She sees all these new babies being born on the farm— you and Jenny are expecting your sixth, and Caleb and Miriam will soon have a child. Seeing a second generation of children growing up here reminds her that the window is closing for her."

"I'm sure you've told her you're happy with the family you have."

"Of course, a hundred times. If only we hadn't lost Johnny. I still think that's at the root of this panic she feels. She always feels a child is missing, and frankly, I worry about the toll it's taking on her."

CHAPTER 35

July 1828
London, England

A packet of letters arrived from Henri and the Le Jardin singers, who were again touring Europe, tantalizing Frannie with their descriptions of Europe's old-world charm and new innovations. Included was their remaining itinerary, which described a forthcoming stay in London, flooding her with memories of her walks with Arthur along the Thames, and their trips to the opera house and strolls in Hyde Park.

She looked in the mirror and studied her image, noting how much she had changed since her days headlining with Le Jardin. Her auburn hair was now tightly secured in a bun, and though she owned two of the most chic dress shops in the state, her own dress looked as if it had been pulled from Myrna's closet. The wild woman of the Willows was thirty-six years old, a mother of two who had yielded to social pressure, allowing herself to be caged within a detested, tightly laced corset. And though she was not prone to tea parties and sewing circles, neither was she as apt to seek grand adventure as she once had.

Why? She gave the question some thought. After all, Sarah was thirteen now, and Charles was nine. They weren't babies. Both were quite cheerful and adaptable, and they loved to see their mother pretty and perky. So why had she let herself weather like a piece of old driftwood? The answer was simple. She had purposely eschewed the romantic interest of men. One had broken her heart, and two had betrayed her trust. She was not likely to walk that road again.

Still, she told herself, that was no reason to let herself wither like a raisin on the vine, moving from work to home with no diversion other than their trips to the farm. Perhaps the time had come to show the children a glimpse of the dazzling world beyond America's shores.

She immediately sent letters to the rest of the hotels on the Le Jardin's itinerary, advising Henri that she was coming. She and the children left the farm a week later, leaving James so bereft that Jed quickly encouraged Hannah to book passage for herself and their son so they could join the party. He sent along letters of introduction to a few British officials, and they all sailed from Baltimore the first week of August, arriving on Britain's shores twenty-five days later.

Frannie performed three show-stopping numbers written by new American composers. The audience never failed to cry for encores each night, but most delicious to her was the way her children's eyes sparkled when she joined them in her dressing room after the curtain fell.

Charles hugged her tight and offered "I love you"s after every performance, and Sarah all but glowed with pride, saying, "Mama, you're wonderful!"

Even James thrilled at seeing his aunt in this new light, and Hannah was nearly as struck by the whole experience as the children were. Eventually the late nights wore on everyone, and Frannie's nanny encouraged her to ignore their pleas to attend every show and to instead leave them in the suite to return to normal sleep schedules.

Frannie noticed Hannah's fatigue. "You must be as exhausted as the children, taking them out to see sites during the day while I rest, and then attending the shows each night. Isn't that schedule too demanding?"

"I am having the time of my life. I'd forgotten how wonderfully talented you are."

Frannie touched the crow's feet lining the corners of Hannah's eyes. "You look exhausted. Jed will have my head for running you ragged. I want you and the children to remain here when the troupe performs in Brighton next week. I'll only be away for four days, and a more relaxing schedule will do you all some good before we head home."

Hannah moved to a chair by a window overlooking the street. "I'm sure Jed is very relieved to have me entertained by something other than my constant wishing for another child."

"There are other options, Hannah. We both know there are many orphans desperate for love and a good home."

Hannah nodded thoughtfully. "We've discussed adoption, and we're both open to the idea, but I still feel a child of ours is missing from our family."

Frannie stood beside her, laying her head on Hannah's shoulder. "Could it be Johnny you're still missing?"

"I've asked myself that question, but I've even seen this child's face, Frannie, and I feel certain it's a little girl. I was meant to have a daughter." She wiped a tear and laughed sadly. "How ungrateful am I? The Lord blessed me with James to fill my empty arms after we lost Johnny. I should be content and open my heart to a few of the orphans who need to be loved."

"'Ungrateful' is the last word I'd ever ascribe to you. No, generally, you listen to the whisperings of God when the rest of us ignore them. And we all know how fiercely you've prayed to be of one mind with Jed over the Joseph Smith dilemma. Perhaps this 'feeling' is a glimpse of what's to come—a reward because of your faith."

In wonder, Hannah stepped away and studied her sister-in-law. "Thank you, Frannie. Thank you so much. Once again, I've underestimated you. Forgive me."

With a sweep of her hand, Frannie dismissed the apology. "It's no wonder you don't see me as a woman of faith. I haven't done much to provide a religious foundation for the children, but I've recently given the matter some serious thought. Jed and I have had some interesting discussions on the matter."

"You have?"

"I like the changes I see in him. He seems more peaceful, despite everything going on in Washington. He sees it as well."

September 23, 1828
Liverpool, England

Work on the Liverpool and Manchester Railway brought drastic change to the city. The abandoned warehouses many of the streets gangs called home were being razed and replaced with modern construction. The police presence increased as well, and Bled's stomach suffered from the shortfall of income. Richard Porter's temper was short as well, and he beat the little mob of adolescent thieves he harbored because their take hadn't provided sufficiently for his wants. Not that Bled cared. He'd had enough of this place. At nineteen, he was ready to move to London, where the opportunities were better. He simply needed a sufficient stake to set him up.

He had spent the last four years seething at Michael McGowan Porter for his interference the night Bled wanted to rob Arthur Ramsey. Bled was bigger, stronger, and older than Michael, but Michael was decidedly smarter, and at eighteen he already knew enough about the law to defend men in court, as he had done on several occasions. Bled knew Michael could just as easily get a person convicted. No one wanted to cross him. But Michael had one Achilles heel—Hank. And that gave Bled a plan.

There was a different mood uptown because those were Michael's streets. He hadn't lived with Richard Porter and Hank for several years, having moved into the library. He studied during the day and then slept there overnight. It wasn't legal, but no one questioned it. Some local shops lined his pockets with a few quid a month in return for the security his presence provided, while the local baker and butcher saw that he had his fill of good food. It was a comfortable arrangement that allowed him to provide well for Hank while requiring the least possible interaction with Richard Porter, who continued to hold Hank's highest devotion.

Each afternoon around four, the brothers would meet along a patch of grass on Water Street, where they would spend an hour eating together and catching up before both young men headed to work. Michael would begin patrolling the streets of his "area," and Hank would head off to whatever trouble he might find after dark. Sometimes Bled would catch up with Hank, and they would work the harbor in tandem. That's exactly what Bled had planned for tonight.

He had spent three and a half years watching Arthur Ramsey's routine. He arrived every Friday at five to visit the doc and his family, and he'd leave the next afternoon for London. This time Bled would stop Ramsey's carriage on the outskirts of town and roll the bloke.

But something changed. Something was different. Ramsey arrived not in his regular carriage, but in a wagon laden with crates and trunks. He stopped at the doc's cottage as was his routine, and while he was inside, Bled sped off to grab Hank as he came down Water Street.

"I've picked us out a good one, Hank, my boy! We're gonna take us a good haul tonight."

Hank's lazy smile spread. "Richard will be proud of me."

"You'll soon have those boots and that blade you've been eyein'."

Hank put his finger to his lips. "Don't tell Michael. He'll be angry."

"Mum's the word, m'friend." Bled's eyes widened to assure Hank.

He led Hank to Chapel Street, which bordered Lancelot's Hey where the doc's flat was located. The closer they got, the more nervous Hank seemed, until he grabbed Bled by the collar and said, "This is where Doc lives. We can't rob Doc!"

"We're not goin' ta rob the doc. Our mark is 'is friend—Arthur Ramsey."

Hank stopped dead in his tracks and even backed away a few steps. "No. Michael said—"

Bled grabbed Hank by the shoulders and rose on his toes to meet him eye to eye as he delivered the prepared script. "Did Michael tell you Richard Porter hates Arthur Ramsey? 'E'd probably be very happy to hear you roughed the fellow up." He tapped his finger against Hank's chest. "This Ramsey fella was involved with your mother. 'E likely cheated 'er, or worse. You've got a chance to avenge the wrong done to 'er, Hank. And tomorrow, I'll help you."

American Songstress Francis St. Clair!

The headline still tortured Arthur hours after he had read it. With his wagon packed, he had locked the door of his London home with no plans for a return.

His heart was heavy. Daniel and Ruth had finally saved enough for their passage to America, and they and four-and-a-half-year-old David were leaving within a week. The four blissful years Arthur had spent playing surrogate father and grandfather to them was closing, and that made England so unbearably lonely that he had arranged transport back to Barbados.

He purposely had the driver wind past the theater where Frannie and the Le Jardin singers were performing so he could see the poster with her face once more. When they arrived, he stepped from the wagon bed and stood before her larger-than-life image, remembering how it felt to have such a woman on his arm. He touched his mouth absently, savoring the kisses they had shared, wondering if Frannie might be in the theater rehearsing at that very moment. The thought of running into her with her happy little family stung him worse than he could imagine.

He had just turned for the wagon when he heard voices behind him. There were several children and a woman, but the familiarity of the woman's voice shot a combination of fear and want through him. *Fool!* he chided himself as he turned away like a leper.

"Mr. Ramsey?" The incredulity in the voice confirmed his own shock, and he froze. "Wait here, children," she said as she walked to him. "Arthur? Arthur! It's Hannah Pearson."

He glanced at her and looked away. "Forgive me, Mrs. Pearson. I was afraid you were—"

"Frannie?"

He nodded and shook his head in shame as he turned to face Frannie's image once more. "I read that she was performing, and I had to catch a final glimpse of her face. Please don't mention having seen me. I wouldn't want to embarrass her in front of her husband."

Hannah patted his arm and beamed up at him. "Dear, sweet Arthur. Frannie has no husband anymore."

He felt chilled and flushed at the same moment. "What? She's no longer married?"

"No." Hannah laughed as she shook her head rapidly. "She is divorced, and if I may be so bold in speaking, I believe she would welcome a letter from you."

"After all the hurt I've caused her?"

Hannah's brow wrinkled in reaction to the confession. "I'm glad you recognize that she has suffered because of your decision, but I believe she would still welcome your letter."

Arthur patted his trembling lips. "Is she here . . . in the theater right now?"

"No. I'm afraid she's in Brighton for a few days. We sail home next week."

"Then the fates have again aligned against us. I'm headed for the port at Liverpool. Tomorrow I sail for Barbados."

"Perhaps things have aligned just perfectly. I doubt either of you is prepared for an abrupt reunion. She has a family to consider now." She nodded in the direction of the children standing behind her. "I'll not speak of this meeting. I'll leave it to you to contact her. Send it to the Willows. I'll see she gets it, and we'll let her assess her own heart."

With a final clasp of his arm, Hannah gathered the children and herded them down the avenue to the park. Arthur's eyes followed them hungrily. *Which two are Frannie's?* His legs felt weak so he rested, basking in the magnificent shift in his opportunities. Closing his eyes in prayer, he thanked God for his good fortune before climbing in and ordering the driver on.

His euphoria continued all the way to Liverpool and the Spencers' door. Arthur stuffed a pound note into the driver's hand. "Please deliver this wagon load of goods to my ship, the *Ramses,* and then return for me around ten o'clock tomorrow morning."

The Spencers' door opened as the wagon lumbered away. Arthur swept the young couple up in a vigorous embrace that left the trio laughing.

"Ruth has been worried sick that our leaving would cause you distress, but instead, you seem quite excited to be rid of us."

"Not so at all. I'll miss you terribly, but life is filled with opportunities, Daniel—for you, for me—and we must explore each door God opens to us."

They passed their final evening together supping, laughing, and playing with David. The wagon returned the next morning.

"My chariot has arrived," Arthur said as the moment of departure became all too real. He picked up David and hugged Ruth, holding them against him as he pressed his lips to their heads. Handing the child back to his mother, Arthur said, "I wish you three every happiness, Ruth."

Her voice broke as she replied, "You will come to see us in New York, won't you?"

Arthur smiled broadly. "I promise." He patted Daniel's shoulder, and his smile spread even wider. "In fact, I may be spending a considerable amount of time in America in the near future."

"Nothing could please us more, Arthur," Daniel said. "Come, I'll ride with you to the harbor."

The wagon picked its way through the construction until it reached the docks. When they arrived, Daniel sobered. "I can't tell you what a blessing you've been to us, Arthur. We felt we were all alone in the world, and then you came. You've been like a father to me."

Tears wet Arthur's eyes. "It was I who was blessed, and for as long as you care to have me in your life, it will be my honor to be whatever you desire of me—friend or father. But do not give up on your own. If he extends his love, promise me you'll forgive him and accept it."

"I shall, but I shall also remember that it was your hand that always reached out to me."

Daniel helped Arthur step down from the wagon, and then the driver was dismissed. Daniel blinked rapidly as the wagon rolled away. "As soon as we're settled we'll send word to you in Barbados. We will hold you to your promise to visit."

"Nothing could keep me away." Arthur pulled Daniel to him and held him close until the two men noticed two members of the *Ramses'* crew heading down the gangway.

"Your escort is here. I'll take my leave. Goodbye then, Arthur. Be safe, my friend."

Arthur was acutely aware of the ship's crewmen hovering close by. "I'll be with you in a moment, gentlemen," he muttered as his eyes followed Daniel until he disappeared around a slight curve in the road. Even after the young man was past his line of vision, Arthur kept staring down the road until thoughts of Frannie began to brighten his thoughts once more.

"Are you all right, Mr. Ramsey?"

Arthur turned to face the crewmen. "Yes. Thank you."

"We saw those two young thugs running toward the harbor, and we were worried they might have been following you."

Arthur's head snapped back in the direction the two men were pointing. "Thugs?"

"Yes, sir. They seemed to be following your wagon."

Arthur thought back to the day his father had been stabbed along these very docks, and he suddenly feared for Daniel. "Hurry men! Come quickly!"

Hank's eyes were wild and angry as he raced up to Bled. "'E's already gone!"

"Gone? Why didn't you stop 'im? You were the lookout! You're twice his size!"

"It weren't just Ramsey. That wagon driver returned and picked 'im up along wif the doc. And they didn't head down the London Road like you said, but to the docks!"

Bled processed the news and leapt to his feet. "Hurry! One way or another, I will have a prize today."

His heart thundered as he ran toward the docks with Hank on his heels, searching for their prey. He ran down two wrong streets before finding the one where the *Ramses* was moored. The wagon pulled up in the distance, and he pushed his legs harder to reach Ramsey before he boarded, and then Bled saw the bulky crewmen moving toward their passenger, and he knew the opportunity was lost. He and Hank both bent over, heaving, attempting to catch their breath.

"Shh," Bled signaled. "We'll take Doc instead."

Horror crossed Hank's face. "No. I won't hurt Michael's friend!"

Bled spun on him, his merciless eyes bearing down on the younger boy, who cowered despite his greater size. "Yes, you *will* help me. You've blabbered about our big score to half the scoundrels on the waterfront. Porter expects something grand from you, and even if I do the job alone, I'll pin it on you because you're the one who nosed it about."

The muscles of Hank's jaw tensed as if he were actually chewing on the news. When he said nothing more, Bled knew he had won. "Let's get on with it, then."

They moved through the alleys, watching the doc amble home. *He seems distracted—that's good,* thought Bled. As Doc passed by the purser's office, Bled heard the ticket agent call out, "Hello, Mr. Spencer, buying those tickets any time soon?"

Daniel waved as he walked on. "Soon, Marco. We plan to depart on the twenty-second."

The man looked at his sheet. "The twenty-second, you say? Then you'll be on the *Mary Ellen,* the best passenger ship in the fleet. Those tickets are none too cheap, Daniel."

"That's why I've been saving for seven years."

Passage money! Bled could hardly contain his excitement. Grabbing Hank by the arm, he explained, "So this is how we'll play this out."

The pair moved along the alleyways, following Daniel home. Mere yards before he reached his door, Hank stepped from an alley and slipped a blade beneath Daniel's chin, but it was Bled who growled the terms. "Give us that money you've been savin' for your trip."

The Doc froze and said calmly, "We've no quarrel with one another. Don't do this."

Bled enjoyed the fear in Doc's eyes. "Give 'im a taste!" he shouted, but Hank shook his head no. "Do it!" Bled shouted, and wild-eyed Hank drew the blade lightly across Daniel's throat just deep enough to draw blood. Daniel gasped as crimson trickled down his neck. Bled bullied up to him, sneering, "Now you know we mean business. Get us the money!"

Hank punctuated the demand by shoving Daniel forward, causing him to stumble to the ground. Bled compounded the assault with a kick in Daniel's ribs that curled him into a ball in the dirt.

The rapid approach of voices and feet startled Bled, as Arthur arrived with one of the crewmen, and off in the distance, Michael raced with a hoard of street rats likely coming to view the show. Bled's reputation was now on the line, and he was determined not to back down.

"I don't know who you are," Arthur shouted between gasps of air, "but I'm the owner of the *Ramses,* moored at the pier. I beg you, let Mr. Spencer go and take me instead, and my man here will bring you a hundred pounds sterling as a ransom."

Bled eyed Arthur. "A hundred pounds sterling, eh?" He gave Daniel another kick. "How'd you come to know a man what carries around a hundred pounds?" Before Daniel could reply, Bled told Arthur, "All right. Come to me and send your man for the money."

Arthur whispered orders to his anxious crewman, sending him back to the ship while Arthur prepared to surrender himself to Bled.

"No!" Michael yelled as he raced to stand between Arthur and Bled. "Let them go, Bled! Let them all go. You know I'm not going to allow you to leave here with that money."

"Seems to me you're a tad outnumbered, Michael. Hank stands with me."

Arthur's head shot back and forth between the boys. "Michael? Hank? Are you—?"

Michael's gaze dipped to the ground as Arthur Ramsey made the identification. "Yes, Mr. Ramsey. Now you see the sad truth of what's become of the McGowans. Like fathers, like sons."

"No, Michael, no! It's not your father's but your mother's influence I see standing here."

Bled watched Michael's visage change upon hearing those words. His attention shifted to Hank as Michael pled, "Come, Hank, this is not what Mama meant for us. Drop the knife and walk away from this. Come stand with me. Brothers first and always, eh?"

Bled's every nerve poised to react as the scene became clear to him. Ramsey was the anointed rescuer Michael had spoken of as a child—the man he assured Hank would find them and save them from Richard Porter. But he had come too late, after Porter had won Hank's loyalty, and long after the soil of street life had tarnished Michael's innocence. Arthur Ramsey was no threat to Bled's plans, but Michael was, and now Bled watched Hank's face become a palette of confusion as his gaze shifted between Bled and Michael, between Arthur Ramsey and then to the beaten man lying in the dirt. First his eyes softened, then his head dipped, and finally his fingers uncurled, dropping the knife to the ground as Hank stepped away from Bled.

"So, you've made your choice, and I'll have to even the odds!" The words spilled from Bled's lips as he lunged for the knife. He came up, aiming at Hank, but in a shot, Arthur Ramsey leapt between the two young men, and the blade found a different mark—in Arthur's chest.

★ ★ ★ ★ ★

Whistles and shouts sounded as the second crewman arrived, having led the police on a wild search for Arthur, who had charged him at the docks to find help. Bled and Hank both panicked, running helter-skelter like rats as the police chased them down.

Daniel was only vaguely aware of the commotion, awakening as Ruth rolled him to his back to check the cause of the line of blood ringing his throat. Through squinted eyes he saw his terrified son staring at him. He knew that expression, that terror, from his own childhood when Clarissa was murdered, and he would not—could not—let that same fear taint his child's view of the world. Ruth helped him sit up, and with a shake of his head to clear his mind, he reached for his boy. "It's all right, David. Papa's fine. Papa's fine."

The look in David's eyes was not one of relief. He pointed a few yards away to where an officer knelt beside a motionless heap, with Michael weeping by his side.

"Oh, no . . ." Daniel groaned as he crawled to Arthur. "Arthur? Please, no!"

"I didn't do this. I didn't do this," Michael cried.

Ruth helped Daniel assess Arthur's injuries. "Fetch a wagon!" he shouted to the officer. "We need to get him to a surgeon!"

The ripple effect of the incident held the rapt attention of the *London Times'* readers for weeks as stories about criminal youth gangs, the discovery of the missing viscount, and another heroic act by former war-hero Arthur Ramsey graced its pages. The news brought three other visitors to the hospital to join Daniel, Ruth, and David in their vigil—an auburn-haired woman who came in the evenings as Daniel's family left for the day, Arthur's mother from Dublin, and Daniel's father, the earl. And at the end of the first week, Michael also arrived.

Awkwardness permeated the air as the strange group assembled, choking on their past errors, but the past seemed irrelevant as

Arthur hovered between life and death once more. As each day passed, blame eased, fingers ceased pointing, and acceptance slowly came.

During the second week of Arthur's hospitalization, Daniel and Michael were escorted to his room. "He's been asking for you," the attendant said.

Arthur struggled to focus on them, but as soon as he heard their voices a peaceful smile graced his lips. "All my boys are—where is Hank?"

Michael blinked as he answered, "In jail, along with Bled, for the attack on the doc here. He led the police straight back to the hideout, to Porter and the children. The little ones were toted off to the orphans' home, and Hank, Porter, and Bled were hauled before a magistrate to answer a host of charges. I'll defend Hank in court in a few weeks."

"And how are you?" Arthur asked, his brow furrowing over Daniel's bandaged neck.

Daniel touched it gingerly. "I'm fine. It's you we're worried about."

Arthur clasped their hands. "God has blessed me time and again, and now He's answered my greatest prayer. Daniel, I've heard your father came. Are things better with you two?"

"Better. We're still sailing to America, but he invited us back to visit at the castle, and I'm hopeful David will get to know his grandfather after all."

Arthur smiled broadly at the news. Next he looked to Michael. "I hope you can forgive me, Michael. I failed your family terribly."

"It wasn't your fault. Mama wrote you a letter before she died, asking for your help, but Richard Porter destroyed it, leaving himself as the only option for raising us when she was gone."

Arthur's eyes closed in sorrow. "I will do everything I can to make up the loss to you. You were to be my father's son. We are, therefore, brothers, Michael. When I am gone, what is mine will be yours and Hank's."

Michael's hand tightened around Arthur's. "I need my brother, not my brother's fortune."

"Perhaps I can see to that."

The men turned toward the voice. It was an auburn-haired woman.

"No, Frannie, please," Arthur muttered as he turned away. "Don't see me like this."

Straightening her back, she swept past the visitors with an authoritative air, saying, "Could you give us a moment alone, please?"

As soon as Daniel and Michael were gone, her manner softened and she sat on the edge of Arthur's bed. Unable to hide from her, he laid his hand weakly over hers. "So we find ourselves right back where we once were—with me broken and you so beautiful it pains me."

Frannie's eyes were wet. "I read about the attack in the *Times*. Hannah finally told me she bumped into you outside the theater. You should have at least left me a note."

Arthur groaned and laid his free arm across his eyes to hide from her. "What right had I?"

"The right was mine. I deserved some explanation for the past thirteen years."

Of course she was right. He uncovered his eyes and weakly replied, "I planned to spend my entire voyage to Barbados writing to you, explaining everything. You deserve nothing less."

"Then tell me now, Arthur."

"My mind is foggy," he argued. "You deserve better than a ragged synopsis."

"If it's the truth, it will be enough."

He finally dared to study Frannie's appearance. She was dressed like a socialite, in a fitted floral dress that swept straight across her bodice and down into broad, leg-of-mutton sleeves. Her brocade cape was raisin brown, which flattered her green eyes and chestnut hair.

He saw the early appearance of a few gray hairs in the corkscrew curls that framed her face, but to Arthur, they, and the thin lines that marred the previous perfection of her face, elevated her to another plateau of beauty. She was a woman now, and a mother—the product of many experiences faced without him. They had made her strong and wise and successful.

But part of her was fragile. He could see the discomfort in her eyes as she bore his intense study of her. She turned away from him. He wondered how it was that he could so easily disarm her. There was a chasm between them, and Arthur knew he would need to tread carefully.

He squeezed her hand and paused silently for a moment, needing her to feel the sincerity of his next words. "I could barely breathe that morning as your things were loaded on the ship. Frannie, I regretted my decision to send you away the moment your ship left the docks. I still grieve each day the calendar passes that date."

Frannie's face went blank as if she had fallen into a void.

"May 15, 1815," they each said in tandem. Their eyes locked in surprise, then her mouth turned downward, matching her downcast eyes. She quickly withdrew her hand and rose to walk a few steps away. Her back was to Arthur, and her arms hung limply down from squared, defiant shoulders. "I couldn't believe you let me board that ship. All along, I kept telling myself you would stop me and call me back to you, but you did not."

Frannie turned and faced him. Her pained visage was fully unmasked, as if the distance between them gave her the courage to reveal the full weight of her disappointment in him. He bore it, and the coming accusation, though Bled's knife had caused him less pain.

"In desperation I accepted the rigid terms of your agreement, but you withdrew even that from me, leaving me not so much as my promised annual letter. It was heartless, Arthur. You didn't send me away for my good, still hoping for a future together. It was a lie you fabricated to get me on that ship because you were too cowardly to tell me it was over to my face. Admit it now, and finally set me free of you!"

"Do not say that, Frannie!" Arthur sat straight up in a shot, crying out with an involuntary yelp of pain. He saw Frannie flinch at the sound, but she maintained her distance. And though he felt lightheaded, he feared she might leave and take the last chance he had to at least set her heart at ease, so he willed himself to remain lucid long enough to correct her misunderstandings about his devotion.

"Accuse me of anything, but do not lay that charge upon me. I did not fear death the many times it came calling for me. At times I welcomed it, holding fast to my hope in Christ, but I trembled like a wicked man at judgment over the thought of disappointing you. Do you really not know? Even now, can you really not see? The only thing that kept my heart beating all these years was the hope that I had set you on a course for happiness." His words began to slur. *Just a few more seconds,* he prayed silently. *Please, just a few more seconds.* "I sorrow that I did not, but tuck this truth into your heart, Frannie. I loved you then, I've loved you every day since, and if this is the last time I'm blessed to ever behold your face, leave knowing I love you still—"

He felt his body crumple and fall back. When he awoke, Frannie was by his side, her head resting on the pillow by his shoulder. Her cape was off, and though darkness showed through the windows, assuring him it was well past visiting hours, she remained. He smiled inwardly at the ruckus she must have raised to defy the order to leave his side, and with the peace of knowing that the first of many hurdles was past, he moved his head until his cheek touched her, and he fell back into a fitful sleep.

He found her sitting in the hard-back visitors' chair when he awoke. She smiled sheepishly at him and said, "I'm sorry about—"

"Shh . . . no need. I'm sorry you've had to carry all that around for so long. I handled things poorly between us. I've made so many mistakes."

She leaned forward and clasped his hand. "I felt abandoned and unloved. I suppose that's why I accepted Phillip's proposal. Whether or not any of us realized it, you were still influencing my life."

Arthur felt the physical weight of her pain. "I'm so very sorry, Frannie. I both rejoiced and grieved the day word arrived of your marriage. Jed sent a final word a year later, telling me that you and Mr. St. Clair had adopted children, and I realized it could have been us had I not been such a fool. But God is merciful, Frannie, even to old fools. I hope you won't misunderstand it when I say that as much as I regret what might have been between us, I do not regret what I did with my life in the interim. I was not dealt the hand I would have wished for, but I tried to play it as honorably as I could. God helped my life have meaning. I hope you will say the same."

Frannie's gaze drifted until her expression appeared distant. "Neither would I have chosen the path I was given, but I am also grateful for the place it led me. I have two beautiful children, Arthur."

"Yes, you do. Where are they? You are supposed to be sailing back to Maryland now."

"Hannah and the nanny sailed home with them."

"And you? How long are you staying?"

She bit her lip as she pondered the question. "I wasn't certain when I watched my children's ship sail from the harbor, or even when I entered this room yesterday."

Arthur rubbed his hand over hers. "And now?"

"I'll stay until you're recovered, or until you're well enough to travel to Maryland with me. In any case, if I leave England alone, Arthur, it will be the last time you will ever see me."

Frannie rushed about the city buying a fresh set of clothes for Arthur, since all his others were bloodstained or packed aboard the *Ramses*. When she returned to his room, she found him standing cautiously by his bed for the first time, steadying himself with the rail. The top of the pajamas she had purchased for him two days earlier was unbuttoned, revealing the top of his undergarments. His face blossomed into an overly confident cheer when he saw her. "I'm doing well, don't you think?"

Frannie now had doubts about him pressing the physicians into allowing him to leave the hospital so soon. As she set the clothes on the bed, she said, "Perhaps we should give you more time to rest."

"What is there to do on a ship but rest?" Arthur said reassuringly, though nervousness showed in his eyes. He looked at the outfit. "It's a handsome ensemble. Thank you. I—I can manage the trousers, but with my shoulder still stiff, I, uh, I may some help with the shirt."

The intimation that she would need to assist him in dressing sent chills through Frannie, as if she were a young schoolgirl about to have her hand held for the first time. She nodded and moved behind him. It had been thirteen long years since she had been so intimately near to him. She tried to hide the racing of her heart and the prickling of her skin as she placed her hands on his shoulders. She felt his muscles twitch and his body shiver at her touch.

Frannie removed the pajama top first. As she set it on the bed, Arthur fumbled nervously with the buttons of the undergarment shirt. "Darn these fingers," he joked nervously. She understood, as her own hands were shaking, too.

She moved before him and undid three buttons. A small gasp caught in the back of her throat as Arthur's scarred chest peeked through the opening. Memories flooded over her, of his nearly dead body lying in a wagon in a puddle of blood and mud, of Dr. Beanes's efforts to save him, of Arthur's plea for her to get him back to his own troops, so he would not die in America where she would pine away her life grieving over him.

She traced her finger over one of the scars, and Arthur recoiled as he tried to close the shirt. "I am an ugly, broken man."

Frannie opened his shirt wide and placed both her hands upon his chest. "No. I remember, Arthur. I remember it all. You tried to spare me. Everything you did was to spare me. I remember now. And your wounds did not make you bitter. It's as if each one opened a portal to your very heart, allowing love to enter there more fully. No, you are not a broken man. You are better than whole . . ." She pressed a lingering kiss into the hollow of his chest and looked up into the emotional twist of his face. "And now you are finally mine."

Three weeks later, Arthur and Frannie again stood on the docks together. He turned to Daniel, handing him an envelope. "Send word to Frannie as soon as you're settled in America."

"We will. It will be a comfort to have family so near, but what's this?"

Arthur smiled at the "family" reference. "It's tuition for school." When Daniel began to protest, Arthur stood firm, saying, "I know remaining here to check on me has cost you greatly, so take it, and use it to become a fine American physician. And if you're too proud to use it for yourself, save it for David's education—a gift from his Uncle Arthur."

He next turned to Michael. Placing his hands on the young man's shoulders, Arthur looked him in the eye. "Are you certain you won't come to America with us today?"

"Hank needs me, but perhaps we'll come when his sentence is paid."

"Of course." Arthur withdrew two more envelopes from his breast pocket. "Here is a little something for you, Michael. Now go to the university and become a proper trial lawyer." He handed him a key and the other envelope. "I also had my attorney add your name to the deed of the London town home. Take care of it until I return, will you, Brother?"

A smile spread across Michael's face. He extended his hand, but then the two men embraced. "I'll make you proud, Arthur."

"I could not be more proud of you than I already am. And neither could your mother."

With the farewells said, Arthur, Frannie, and his physician boarded the *Ramses*. Arthur knew the four-week journey would be scarcely enough time to recount thirteen absent years, but with a crew bent on meeting the passengers' every desire—and with Sarah and Charles gone ahead with their aunt—each moment would be dedicated to healing his wounded body, and to determining if his and Frannie's fractured emotions could flower into romance once more.

And so it was that with a palette of nothing but sea and sky, they spent the first lazy week talking about the lives they had led since their parting. They laughed and cried, and made peace with their choices, but despite the kiss that symbolized Frannie's acceptance of his ragged body, the daunting fear of physical expression paralyzed Arthur.

Frannie was patient with him, content to walk arm in arm, or to share the simple joy derived from the gentle touch of their hands. But Arthur knew a life together should offer them more than this— that Frannie deserved more than this—but first he must conquer his self-doubts.

It wasn't easy to celebrate milestones like completing three turns around the *Ramses'* deck while passing the vessel's crew of virile sailors, who appeared to be the physical incarnation of Adonis. Arthur had sailed so infrequently that only the captain and senior staff knew him personally. The other men knew him only as the frail but privileged heir of a shipping fortune. He didn't like the resentment they stirred in him. He had spent years battling bouts of envy and self-pity, but he felt those feelings rising in him once again, particularly when he caught the men eyeing Frannie as if she were the evening's entrée.

He wondered if such attention was as flattering to her as it was irritating to him. He knew so little of women, having rushed from divinity school into the military. Frannie was his first and only love, and he realized that as long as he was her choice, he had best honor that gift by acting the part.

They were returning from an afternoon of reading on the deck when Arthur caught two muscular young deckhands tittering and nudging one another as he and Frannie approached. More appalling was the way they hunched their sleeves up over their muscles, as if Frannie would be impressed by such silliness. Arthur did, however, glance her way several times to assess her reaction, which was disconcertingly unclear.

He tightened his hold on her arm and said with forced nonchalance, "I apologize for the spectacle my men are making of themselves."

Frannie raised an eyebrow and smiled at him, and he quickly increased his feigned indifference a notch. Leaning into his shoulder, she whispered, "Any man can ogle and paw at a woman. It requires no character and shows her no deference. But a certain amount of fawning has its place, and a woman does feel flattered when a man cares enough to make a fool of himself over her. As I recall, you were quite good at it yourself when we first met."

The comment took Arthur back to the days after she shot him for trespassing, and to their London winter, and he realized he had lost a part of himself that he needed to reclaim. He turned to face Frannie and took her by the chin. "Dinner will be served soon. Why don't you go on ahead and freshen up? I'll be along presently."

A curious pleasure lit her face as she nodded and departed, glancing back over her shoulder at him as she went.

Arthur gave his vest a tug and left to retrieve a book he had loaned to the captain days earlier. As he returned with the volume, he passed the men and caught a snippet of their conversation.

"Poor woman, stuck with the likes of him. She deserves better."

"Aye. Imagine the women we could 'ave if we 'ad a thousand pounds sterling."

Initially the words stung Arthur, but then Frannie's words warmed him anew. With a jaunty turn, he spun around and said to the men, "I'm slightly crippled, not deaf. And what you said about Mrs. St. Clair is true. She does deserve better than any of us, and yet she has resigned to make me the choice of her heart. And do you know why, gents?"

The two apologetic sailors removed their caps, took a hard swallow, and replied, "No, sir, Mr. Ramsey, sir."

"Then I can't explain it to you, boys. But know this. It requires a lifetime of living to acquire it, so you'd best get at it."

Arthur smiled broadly and patted them each on the chest, then turned and sauntered clumsily away. When he reached Frannie's cabin he knocked on the door, and as she answered he raised his book of poetry and said, "Instead of a before-dinner aperitif, might I interest you in a few of Lord Byron's poems? Perhaps 'She Walks in Beauty Like the Night'?"

A broad smile spread across Frannie's lips. "What has gotten into you?"

"Love," he replied, tossing the book on a side table. He took her in his arms and kissed her, softly at first, then allowing the kiss to linger and deepen. He pulled back and gazed into her own love-filled eyes. "I'm a clumsy romantic, Frannie, but you alone give me the courage to cast aside my inhibitions. I need you, Frannie, and I want you, only you. Will you marry me?"

"Yes," she said, half laughing, half crying. "Absolutely yes."

It was a surreal experience for Arthur to hold Frannie's hand and step on Washington soil, not as a conqueror, but as a guest. Except for the Capitol and White House, both of which exceeded their previous splendor, little of the city seemed familiar to him. He scanned the panorama, trying to recall memories of the blast. The hollow echoes of panic and terror no longer frightened him. The phantom pains of that day, and the years of suffering that followed, seemed no more real than a dream, as if the trauma of the explosion that nearly ended his life had carried the dreadful memories away, allowing fresh new ones to root.

"How does it feel to be back here again?" Frannie asked.

"Curious," he replied as he pulled her to him. "Fine . . . it's going to be fine. I'm more nervous about meeting the children. Shall I call for a buggy to carry us to Jed and Hannah's?"

"I am in charge of your recovery now that we've dismissed the physician. I wish I could prescribe you one day of rest on dry land before subjecting you to the family's inquisition."

He pulled her hand to his lips, stilling his laughter. "Let's hope I pass muster so we can begin a proper courtship and set a date for our wedding."

His comment was answered with a kiss and a raised eyebrow glare. "I've already waited fifteen years for you, Mr. Ramsey. That's courtship enough."

"I agree that that's more than adequate, even for a stuffy Briton, but I don't want to be an intrusion into your family. I want your children to invite me into their lives before we wed. Let's hope it happens quickly, because I, Miss Pearson, am most anxious to be your husband."

CHAPTER 36

May 1829
Georgetown, District of Columbia

The gentle knock on the Pearsons' door that Saturday afternoon should have sounded more like thunder for all the havoc it would begin. The maid announced the arrival of Abel and Caleb, startling Hannah.

"Is everything all right at the farm?" she asked them.

Stress showed on Abel's face as he glanced at his son. "Caleb would like to speak to Jed about a pamphlet he picked up."

"Jed is playing out back with James." She noticed how Abel studied her reaction as he handed the booklet to her. "Oh." She sighed as she recognized the title— "'David Walker's Appeal to the Colored Citizens of the World.' So this is the cause of the stir."

"You've heard of this?" Caleb asked in a voice deep and resonant like his father's.

Caleb had been a bright, inquisitive boy when Hannah first arrived at the Willows, but he was a man now, tall and broad, though not as large as his father. Suspicion replaced the gentleness of his eyes. "Some," she said. "Jed has been fuming about the reaction it's raised in the House and Senate."

Caleb's arms became animated as he summarized the pamphlet. "It says the same thing Jed has always told us—that the Constitution guarantees us the same rights as whites."

"It's a complicated issue, Caleb," Hannah explained. "It takes time to change people's opinions. I wish it weren't so. New York recently emancipated their last slave. It's slow progress, but it's happening."

"Tell that to the slaves in the South, or those in pens in Washington. There are slave blocks a stone's throw from the United States Capitol. The only difference between them and me or my father is a piece of paper you gave us. Freedom and respect aren't gifts. They're rights!"

The words hit Hannah like a verbal slap. "That piece of paper legally emancipated you, but freedom is more than legality. It's also a mindset, and respect is earned, Caleb, not given. You're a free man, and a landowner, and a businessman. Jed gave you an opportunity. You earned people's respect because of what you did with it."

Abel clenched his son's arm, temporarily calming him. "These documents are being distributed all along the waterfront, Hannah. People are riled over them. We just wanted Jed to know."

"We want a lot more than that!" argued Caleb as he turned back to her. "Will Jed be our voice and argue these points in the Senate? David Walker says it's time for colored men and women to stand up and take what's rightfully ours!"

Jed entered with James, who cowered near his father. "Why are you fighting with Mama?" James timidly asked Abel and Caleb.

Directing James toward the door, Jed said, "Take your ball and go upstairs while we talk, all right, Son?" When James was beyond earshot, Jed walked to Hannah, noticing the pamphlet in her hands. "So this is the cause of the discord I heard all the way in the garden."

Hannah handed it to him. "There is tension along the river because of them."

"It was only a matter of time. I've watched it divide the House and Senate. Will we now allow it to divide good friends?"

The question cowed Caleb. "I'm sorry. You're both good people, but when I read these words, and I see how people still see only the color of my skin, I get so angry inside, Jed."

"I know, Caleb. I know. They say God works in mysterious ways. Well, maybe the devil does, too. Good progress was being made in several of the state legislatures. Virginia has been holding serious debates about the possibility of abolition, which caused a panic in South Carolina's representatives, who fear the federal government will then impose abolitionist laws in their state. Those of us in support of Virginia's efforts were working carefully to calm South Carolina so their pro-slavery rhetoric wouldn't erode Virginia's progress, and then this pamphlet was produced, doing just that. The timing couldn't have been worse."

Jed's example only frustrated Caleb further. "Why wait for every state to decide the slavery question? Can't the Congress set all the slaves free?"

"Most states believe this is the business of states. Some Southern states are already threatening to withhold their contributions to the federal government. Some say they'll go so far as to secede if forced to comply with an anti-slavery law. They chant 'Union or Freedom,' because they say we cannot have both emancipation and a *United States of America*."

"Then David Walker's right. Coloreds need to stand up! I plan to get more of these printed, and I'm going to distribute them everywhere."

Hannah looked at Abel for some sign of his opinion, but his face was a blank canvas.

It was Jed who finally answered. "You're a free man, Caleb, free to do what you think is best, but no one can foresee the outcome if you distribute these during such a volatile time. It will agitate pro-slavery zealots, perhaps even incite them to violence or to a call for secession, and that could actually hurt the cause."

After minutes of silence, Abel finally weighed in. "I suppose a man should choose the battles he believes are right, not the ones he fears the least."

Jed and Hannah said nothing more on the subject until after supper, when Abel and Caleb were on their way home. Hannah leaned her head against Jed. "When you warned Caleb those pamphlets could agitate some men into violence, my first thought was of Emerson Hildebrand."

"Mine too."

The opposition fracturing the Congress left Jed delighted to exit Washington by the time the session broke for summer. He longed for the peace of the Willows, where work wearied a man's body instead of his spirit. The anticipated joy over the arrival of Frannie's family eclipsed his governmental frustrations, particularly since Arthur's complete victory in winning Sarah's and Charles's hearts had cleared the way for a late-August wedding.

Frannie's little family arrived in July at the height of the summer heat. The cousins joined the band of some forty children now residing across the acreage of Willowsport. After chores, there were always games and contests, horses to ride, and swimming and fishing. It was an idyllic paradise where children could safely chase fireflies and play until dark.

The men worked hard, and Jed was pleased to see how much Arthur managed to do, despite his somewhat reduced vigor. The wide range of dialects served as a constant reminder of the little community's diversity. One could hear the casual fieldspeak of former slaves, and voices tinged with Irish, Scottish, and Italian intonations. Still, Arthur's cultured British voice and vocabulary set him up for some good-natured ribbing. He tried to assimilate more of the local jargon, which only made his communications more delightful and endearing.

During the busy summer season, the women and older children primarily handled the market. They'd knit and mend, shuck peas and snap beans in between serving the customers who would descend upon them with each boat's arrival, bringing business as well as the latest gossip.

Hannah hung back from the market most days, though it was generally as lively as a party. It seemed in keeping with other curious changes Jed noticed in her. She was more prone to quiet meditation this summer, and less likely to run outside and romp with the children. The clothes she chose were loose and rather dowdy, and she frequently slept in late.

The first few weeks back on the farm had kept Jed so preoccupied with his own activities that he hadn't noticed the changes. He rose early and worked and played to the point of exhaustion, falling soundly asleep at night. He assumed it was the heat that had made Hannah less inclined toward romance, but the twinkle in Frannie's eyes made him consider another cause.

He lingered in bed one morning and snuggled close to Hannah, placing his hand over the unmistakable bulge in her abdomen. She awoke and smiled up at him.

"So you've figured out my secret."

"Why didn't you tell me?"

She shrugged. "I've lost so many. Are you happy about the news?"

He kissed her and hovered near, his nose nuzzling hers. "Very happy. But are you well?"

"A little nervous. I want this baby so badly, Jed. I already know her. I know that sounds strange, but I feel as if we're very familiar with one another."

"And when is this little daughter set to arrive?"

"She will be my Christmas present to you."

Jed left the house an hour later wanting to spread the news to everyone. *A little girl,* he kept telling himself. *A little girl.*

The busy chatter over a particular box delivered that day noticeably silenced when he arrived at the market. Jack and Lydia's son, Moses, brought a pamphlet to Jed. "This is what everyone's talking about. They arrived today. Caleb ordered them all the way from Boston."

Jed began to sweat as he stared at David Walker's abolition pamphlet.

"Caleb already left for Calverton with a whole stack of them, Mr. Jed."

Jed swallowed down his worry and headed to the mill to work. That evening, Caleb's horse trotted down the lane with Caleb stretched across the saddle. Walker's pamphlets stuck out from the back of his trousers like tail feathers. His face was lacerated in a dozen places, and his mouth was so split and swollen he could barely report the pain in his broken hand.

As Jed helped Abel and Jack gently lower him from his horse, he asked, "Who did this to you, Caleb?"

"I didn't see their faces. A whole gang of men dragged me behind the stables."

"Markus, ride to Calverton and get the sheriff here right away."

Caleb raised a bloodied hand to stop him. "He already knows. According to him there's nothing he can do because there were no witnesses."

Bitty and Miriam tended to his immediate wounds, while Markus rode off to bring a doctor back to set Caleb's hand. Jed watched Abel pace outside the cabin, his eyes blazing.

For the first time since he and Abel had become friends, Jed felt awkward with him. He faced a hard reality that night—that no matter how badly he wanted to put himself in Abel's shoes, he'd never be able to. Not really.

"I'm here if there's anything I can do, Abel," he said quietly. And then he left Abel's world.

Tensions ran high along the river for the rest of the summer. Rather than draw additional attention to the farm, Frannie and Arthur opted for a simple, private wedding attended by those already present at the Willows. Their honeymoon was equally simple—a tour of Arthur's new homeland, beginning with days spent in Washington, Alexandria, and Arlington. Two weeks later, the couple returned to the Willows to collect Sarah and Charles before heading home to Baltimore.

Jed gave Frannie a final hug at the docks. "Arthur is the man you were always meant to be with. When something is right, God finds a way." When she smiled at him, Jed asked, "What's so funny?"

"You don't even notice it, do you—the way you attribute everything to God? You sound like Hannah. It's nice."

"If things become difficult here, I may send her and James to you."

"Of course, but don't save them and sacrifice yourself. If you want to protect your family, find a way to end this thing with Hildebrand without getting yourself killed in the process."

CHAPTER 37

December 1829
Georgetown, District of Columbia

Jed had been a prisoner during Johnny's harrowing delivery, and snow had complicated James's arrival. Jed was determined to prepare for any and all eventualities with baby number three, and despite having the best doctor and surgeon in the city on hand, Abigail needed neither, entering the world as peacefully and easily as a dream.

During her pregnancy, Hannah had frequently described the baby she saw in her mind's eye. Just like Johnny, Abigail had Jed's dark, wavy hair, but her eyes were green like Hannah's, and on her shoulder was the same heart-shaped birthmark both Jed and Arthur bore. On the day of Abigail's birth, James checked for each predicted feature and found every one.

"Mama guessed right!" James marveled. Jed knew guessing had nothing to do with it. "Will you tell me about the night I was born?"

The pair curled in a chair together as Jed dramatized the story of the blizzard and Dr. Renfro's snowman-like appearance as he arrived too late to deliver James. The boy's laughter faded into tenderness as Jed then described how he felt when he held James for the first time. Later, he tucked James into bed. He was nearly ten years old, so the days of that ritual would soon come to an end. Jed returned to the master suite and found Hannah staring at Abigail. He couldn't read his wife's glossy eyes. "She's beautiful—just the way you described her," he said.

"I see Johnny when I look at her. I used to be afraid I would lose my memories of him—what he looked like, the sound of his laughter, the way it felt to be a mother for the first time. I'm not afraid of that anymore. I'm never going to forget him. He's ours forever, Jed. I just know it."

The mood in the Congress was the only thing colder than the Washington weather, and though spring eventually brought pleasant warmth to the city, the tempers of the men in Congress fluctuated between icy contempt and white hot anger.

Toward the end of April, Jed came home late one evening, finding Hannah exactly where he expected—in her favorite chair, reading the Bible. "You're late for our study," she quipped. Then, seeing the grim expression on his face, she quickly rose and led him to his favorite chair. "What's wrong?"

He rubbed his weary eyes and leaned his head back. "The topic of anti-slavery legislation was raised today, and a melee nearly broke out right there on the floor of the Congress. I'm afraid it will eventually end in an all-out war." He turned to her, his incredulity on the matter still weighing heavily upon him. "It's as if—as if instead of one Congress, we are two separate camps, each more interested in securing a victory for their side than in securing one for the nation. How can we advance the nation's cause when we walk into the chamber with our opinions set in concrete before a single word is said?"

Hannah hung on every word but said nothing. Jed noticed the concern in her eyes. He took her hands in his. "I'm sorry. I should try harder to leave my frustrations in the Capitol."

"Don't apologize. I just wish I had some wisdom to offer you other than 'Trust God.'"

"'Trust God'. . ." He pulled her palm to his cheek and nestled against it. "Thank you."

"Now there's my handsome husband. For a moment I saw an old man sitting there."

"I feel like an old man. I'll be forty next year—forty! When on earth did that happen?"

"Age is only a number. We have a new baby and a son to keep us on our toes.

Jed pulled Hannah into his lap, sending her into a spurt of giggling. "Is that so, Mrs. Pearson? See how good you are for me? I've been barely home ten minutes and you've completely lightened my mood. Now let me lighten yours. A package arrived for you today—from Colesville."

She sprang to her feet. "From Beatrice?"

"I assume so. It's on the foyer table."

Hannah left and returned in a flash with the rectangular package. She carefully broke the seals on the wrapping, revealing the contents— an exquisitely bound, brown leather book. The aroma enticed her to smell the fine leather. "It's brand new, Jed." She turned it on its edge and read the title aloud. "The Book of Mormon. I've never heard of it." Jed watched as she ran her fingers over the embossed title. "It's a beautiful volume—hand-tooled letters done in gold ink."

She finally opened the cover, revealing the title page. "'An account written by the hand of Mormon, upon plates taken from the plates of Nephi.'"

"Plates?" Hannah froze in wonder. She sucked in a breath with such a start that Jed took immediate notice. "Jed, do you know what this is? It's Joseph Smith's translation! The Book of Mormon is the record Joseph translated from the plates!"

Jed lurched inwardly. The topic of this record had hung over their marriage for six years, and now here it was, in tangible form, to be studied and scrutinized. He could hardly wait to know, once and for all, if Joseph was a prophet or the perpetrator of a great hoax.

He noticed a piece of stationery lying on the floor. "There's a note. It must have fallen out when you unwrapped the book." He handed it to her and Hannah read it aloud.

Dear Jed and Hannah,

This Book of Mormon you hold in your hands is one of the first copies printed from the record Joseph translated from the gold plates. Beatrice and I have read it twice, and have already begun a third reading. I feel like a blind man who has been seeing through a glass darkly, and now my view is clear.

Consider its purpose, which is "to show unto the remnant of the house of Israel what great things the Lord hath done for their fathers; and that they may know the covenants of the Lord, that they are not cast off forever—And also to the convincing of the Jew and Gentile that Jesus is the Christ, the Eternal God, manifesting himself unto all nations."

Oh, how great is the love of God, and how incalculable is the mercy of our Lord, Jesus Christ, that they are reaching to us from heaven. We need only accept it . . .

"Just imagine! God sent an angel to show Joseph where the record was, and now we're among the first to read it!"

Hannah's faith brought Jed low. There she was, holding it reverently, approaching it like holy writ, and there he was, just the opposite, primarily interested in judging the book.

"Shall we begin tonight?" Before he could reply, she sat and opened the book, ready to start. Jed realized attitude affected perception, so he would try to face this with an open mind, an open heart. He owed Hannah that much. "Yes, let's begin."

Before they had left the title page, Jed was intrigued enough to say, "Tell me about Joseph again."

Hannah recounted his lack of formal education and the poor state of the family's finances.

"He had no tutors, attended no schools with vast library collections?" Jed asked.

"They're farmers, though his father was a teacher for a time."

"And you're certain?" When she nodded, he said, "All right, let's read on."

She handed Jed the book and he read the title page aloud, pausing several times to ponder the words. He reached the last line and read, "'And now, if there are faults they are the mistakes of men; wherefore, condemn not the things of God, that ye may be found spotless at the judgment-seat of Christ.'" Jed stopped and stared at the page. *"Condemn not the things of God . . ."*

Hannah laid her hand on his arm. "Are you all right?"

Jed met her gaze with his mouth drawn tightly, as if the state of his mind and heart had just been revealed. He turned the page to The Testimony of Three Witnesses. As he read aloud, his mind repeated some of the astounding phrases:

> ". . . we, through the grace of God the Father, and our Lord Jesus Christ, have seen the plates which contain this record . . . And we also know that they have been translated by the gift and power of God, for his voice hath declared it unto us; And we also testify that we have seen the engravings which are upon the plates; and they have been shown unto us by the power of God, and not of man. And we declare with words of soberness, that an angel of God came down from heaven, and he brought and laid before our eyes, that we beheld and saw the plates, and the engravings thereon; and we know that it is by the grace of God the Father, and our Lord Jesus Christ, that we beheld and bear record that these things are true."

Jed looked up and saw Hannah's glistening eyes upon him. "Imagine what they are saying, Jed—the miraculous witness to which they have pledged their good names and honor." She held his gaze for several long moments until the cry of the baby broke the moment, sending Hannah to attend to her. Jed carried on alone, his mind reeling with his wife's comment.

He thought how the Founding Fathers had likewise pledged their sacred names and honors to the great work of independence, and then he thought about Timothy's comments that religion needs freedom to flourish. Was it all truly as connected as it seemed? The answer, Jed deduced, would be in the reading.

He read until the need to sleep overtook him. After a few hours of rest he awoke and resumed, regretting the need hours later to head to the Capitol. He showed Hannah where he left off, encouraging her to read to that point, and in the late afternoon he hurried home, easily leaving Washington and her woes behind. Once the children were in bed, he and Hannah picked up the book again and read on. And when she could read no more, they were well into the book.

Finally, Jed set the Book of Mormon on the table. "No uneducated person, as Joseph Smith is reported to be, could have written this book. He would have had to have been a biblical scholar to weave together all these obscure bits of Old Testament history. More than that, he would have needed a library at his disposal, on topics from Hebrew customs and culture to Mesoamerica, digested their wisdom, pulled extracts, and knitted them together cohesively in . . . how many days?" He pulled Dudley's letter from the back of the book and scanned the second page. "In sixty-five working days . . . Sixty-five? With only one other person's aid, and that person serving as scribe only? Not as a research assistant or coauthor?"

Hannah smiled and folded her arms on the tabletop, where she then laid her weary head. "Those are logical arguments, Jed. What does your heart tell you?"

"I am, at the very least, intrigued."

As the contentious session of Congress continued on, Jed found himself comparing political colleagues to the leaders in the Book of Mormon. The disagreements in the parties hadn't degraded to war—yet—but Jed knew five individuals whose disputes had been settled by duels, resulting in four deaths. He thought more on the heroes he found in the book—men who placed obedience and sacrifice above power and glory—men like Washington and Madison. *If God's hand has ever been over America, was it not also over her leaders? And did they know?*

That thought illuminated Jed's mind, shedding light on verses he had previously read—verses that described the discovery of a special land and the Gentiles that arrived there by sea. The similarities to America's discovery and her first colonists leapt out at him. He read about the development of a land of promise, and the native inhabitants who suffered at the hands of the Gentiles.

"It's here!" Jed touched the pages reverently. "America is the land of promise!"

Day after day, he rushed home to study with Hannah, marveling over concepts that added to previously learned teachings, as well as completely new and enthralling ideas. He saw references about the Bible and portions of lost doctrine, the mortal mission of Jesus Christ, His visit to this continent after His resurrection, and centuries of peace and faith that followed. Jed read the disturbing reports of a falling away and the downward spiral to the destruction of an entire people. And then he found Moroni's description of a marvelous work that would preserve the records for a future time when what was lost would all be restored. Jed saw references to Joseph and to the plates, and the promises to those who ask for a witness of the truth of the work.

When they finished the book, Hannah asked him again how he felt, and Jed asked for her patience as he began to go through it once more.

On June sixth, he arrived home to find her sitting by the parlor's bay window, staring out into the street, with a letter lying open in her lap. Her expression caused some urgency in him. "What's the matter?" he called out from the doorway. "Is it the children?"

Hannah shook her head, replacing her aloofness with a sheepish smile. "Everything's fine. This letter from Dudley has consumed my attention."

Jed laid his things on the arm of the divan and moved to a chair near hers. "What does it say?"

She handed it to him. "Dudley purchased the copies of the Book of Mormon from the printer, a Mr. Grandin of Palmyra, without the benefit of speaking to Joseph or his family, who were away at the time. After reading the book for the third time, Dudley hurried to Palmyra to tell the Smiths he believed in the book's teachings. It was April fourteenth when he arrived, and Joseph was still living in Harmony, but his family revealed some astonishing news to Dudley."

"Such as . . ."

"On April sixth, Joseph formed a church in Fayette, New York— The Church of Christ."

"Formed a church?" Jed sank into the chair. "But he has no ecclesiastical degree. You've said yourself that he's barely educated at all. And a pastor legally administers over marriages and christenings and such. How can he do that?"

Hannah paused for a moment as if collecting her thoughts. An aura of wonder lit her eyes, but confusion still creased her brow. "He met New York's requirements to begin a church, but there's more. Read what Dudley has written." She pointed to a paragraph on the second page. Nearly an hour passed as Jed read and reread the letter. Hannah left to attend to the children and returned to find him staring out the window as he had earlier found her.

"Is he saying what I think he is saying?" Jed asked.

She smiled and nodded so subtly her head barely moved.

"More visitations?" he scoffed. "From John the Baptist and three of Jesus' Apostles?"

She knelt by Jed's chair and looked into his eyes, as if aware of the struggle his logic was waging with his faith. "It was not a new church, but a restoration of the Lord's own Church that took place that day. Nearly a year prior, all the rights and authorities pertaining to that Church were restored to the earth by those men who held those various authorities—John the Baptist, and the Apostles who led the Lord's Church after His death and resurrection, Peter, James—"

"—and John." Incredulity colored Jed's tone.

"Yes." Hannah touched his elbow as if trying to slow his racing mind. "This restoration had already begun in such a marvelous way, with the visitation of God and His Son in that grove of trees. Should the idea of the Lord's Apostles appearing to Joseph, and to his scribe, Oliver Cowdery, to restore the authority over the Lord's Church, be surprising after that?"

Jed sat back, pressing his hand to his lips. "And these priesthoods?"

"They are the power and authority of God, which He can delegate to men to act in His name on earth, through keys which are the rights and privileges to exercise that power—to govern and reveal things, and to communicate with God."

"And Joseph professes that God has done this—delegated this authority to him?" Jed looked at her curiously. "How is it that you can accept this so readily?"

"I think my gift prepared me. It led me to Emmett, who opened my mind to these ideas long ago. I've always questioned who on the earth God sanctioned with His authority. Kings claim it, but in America we have no king, so from what source do churches here draw their rights? In the Bible, Jesus called and ordained men to the ministry, as Joseph was called and ordained."

"That was millennia ago."

"Emmett and I discussed this many times, as did the Reverend Myers and I. The organization of the Lord's Church changed after the deaths of His Apostles, and why? Because no one retained the authority Jesus had conferred upon them. The chain was broken, and the authority would need to be restored in like manner—by calling and ordaining a new prophet, and by preparing a generation to receive the truth. God and His Son condescended to visit a boy to begin the work, and Jesus' Apostles, who previously held the keys, returned to restore that authority to earth once more. It follows the Lord's pattern. And it needed to happen in a place and time when people were prepared to receive it. I think we are that generation, Jed."

He groaned and stood abruptly, beginning to pace as if he physically needed to walk.

"Please, Jed. Isn't it reasonable that if the book is true the rest must be true as well?"

"But Joseph Smith now claims to be God's prophet? I can accept the Book of Mormon as an inspired document, but all the rest of this?"

"Yes, he's just a man, Jed—a farmer and laborer. There's no shame in that. Others were shepherds, fishermen, tax collectors, until they answered God's call, just as Joseph did."

"I just don't know, Hannah. Dudley plans to be baptized when Joseph visits Colesville in June. I want to be there. I need to meet and speak with Joseph Smith."

CHAPTER 38

June 28, 1830
Colesville, New York

The haste of the Pearsons' departure allowed little time to notify the Snowdens of their plans. They crossed the line into Broome County, New York, late in the afternoon of Saturday, June twenty-eighth, creating no small stir in the village of Colesville.

"Everyone's staring at us, Papa. We're dressed too fancy."

Hannah looked at her blue satin traveling suit and was also aware of the curious stares they were receiving. "We're going to a church meeting, so we're dressed in our Sunday clothes."

"But it's Saturday," James argued.

Jed shot the boy a look that hushed him. "Hannah, the Snowdens' farm should lie on the other side of town, but they may not have received your letter telling them we were coming. What was the name of the family Joseph was coming to visit?"

"The Knights—Joseph Knight, Senior."

"Then I'll also inquire where his farm lies." He searched for a friendly face to whom to make the inquiry. "Hannah, look! Isn't that Reverend Myers passing out handbills over there?"

She squinted to block the setting sun so she could better study the man Jed was pointing to. He was broader than the wisp of a minster who had spent five years attending to the little Willows flock of freedmen. He wore a white shirt, black frock coat, and black trousers.

His one accessory was a black, brimmed hat, which revealed no sign of his signature yellow curls.

The longer Hannah studied him, the more she was inclined to agree with Jed, but the firm set of the man's jaw and the down-turned mouth seemed completely unfamiliar. "He does resemble him, but this man's manner is too gruff to be our Reverend Myers."

"It's been many years since you've last seen him, and you've heard nary a word from him in that time. Perhaps he's changed. Whatever he's passing out is inflaming people."

Their outrage seemed to please the clergyman, while the few people who hung back, or worse—refused his handbills—were subjected to a scrutinizing glare and a brief, fist-pounding sermon.

"I'm sad to say it, but I'm certain that's him," Jed remarked.

Hannah couldn't bring herself to confirm it. Eleven years had passed since the young clergyman had left the Willows seeking answers to his own spiritual questions, answers he had hoped to find at the fiery religious conferences setting upstate New York ablaze.

Leaving the children in the carriage, Jed and Hannah moved into the crowd, catching people's reactions to the document. Joseph Smith's name was vilified from every angry tongue. When Hannah caught a glimpse of the inflammatory document, she saw Joseph's name emblazoned across the printed page. A copy passed into her hands, and she and Jed read the profane accusations written there. He shot her a sideways glance after he read each charge.

Hannah stormed up to the black-suited man and stood directly before him. Gone were the shy eyes and peaceful countenance of the young man she had relied on during Jed's imprisonment. The sweet lips that had once spoken of religious reformation and the Holy Spirit were now twisted into an angry sneer. She barely recognized Reverend Myers at all.

He shoved another handbill at her, but she stood resolute, glaring at him. In a moment recognition began to occur, and for a second she saw her old friend return. He looked down at the handbills as a brief flash of shame washed over him, followed by a return to stony hardness. He shook the handbills at her, exclaiming, "This man is leading people straight to hell!"

"I came seeking this very man. Several years ago, you would have sought him as well."

"You don't know the trouble he's stirring up," Reverend Myers said crossly.

"He teaches that the heavens have parted to restore what has been lost from Christ's Church. Is that not the very hope you left the Willows to seek?"

The reverend's gaze dropped to the ground. "I was misguided."

"Who robbed you of your vision? Did you ask God about Joseph? Did you ever ask that Holy Spirit you once believed in to enlighten your heart? Or did some charismatic preacher shame you into questioning whether God would still answer your questions?"

Hannah spun and began to walk away but felt a hand on her wrist.

The reverend looked into her eyes and said quietly, "He's at the Knight farm, on the south side of the river, near the Colesville Bridge. But hurry—mischief is planned for that place tonight."

Hannah found Jed standing behind her. "What should we do, Jed? We can't risk our children's safety, but Beatrice's family may also be in danger."

Jed laid a discreet but firm hand on the reverend's arm. "You were once our friend, so hear me. Hannah has family visiting at the Knight Farm. Are they in danger from your little mob?"

Reverend Myers shrank back and shook his head rapidly. "No. They just mean to destroy the dam Smith built across the stream to accommodate his baptisms tomorrow. No one will be accosted."

"And Joseph Smith—will he be safe? Swear it to me!" Hannah demanded.

The reverend's expression dissolved into regret. "I cannot stop this now that it's begun, but I'll be there tonight, and I'll make sure no harm is done to anyone."

Despite his pledge, Hannah felt sick as they left the town and headed for Dudley's farm, which lay a few miles ahead. It was dusk when they drew close. Jed planned to see his family safely settled there before heading on to the Knights' farm to warn Dudley, but in the moonlight, Jed saw him unhitching his team from his wagon. Jed slapped the reins and hurried near to warn Dudley of the coming trouble. There was only time for a cursory greeting as the men rushed Hannah and the children into the house and then tended to Jed's team. After quickly saddling Dudley's pair of horses, the men raced to warn Joseph. Even so, they arrived too late. The hoots and hollers of the mischief-makers announced their success at destroying the dam.

Reverend Myers slipped from the group and rode up near Jed. "I suppose I shouldn't be surprised that you didn't trust my promise to prevent a melee. As promised, only the dam was injured tonight, but I'm afraid what began here has not abated the men's anger. It will not be the last effort to stop Joseph Smith." With that, the reverend rode away.

"I'm sorry, Dudley," Jed said. "I suppose your baptism will be delayed now."

Small of build, and weak as he still was, Dudley's response was courageous and resolute. "We'll rebuild the dam a hundred times if that is what we must do."

Jed leaned across his horse. "If this truly is God's work, why would He allow anyone to stand in the way?"

"A delay is not a defeat, Jed. Perhaps it's meant to weed out the weak among us, and maybe it isn't intended for those who believe, but for those who don't."

"You mean men like me?"

Dudley's eyebrow rose. "You believe. You're just too prideful to admit it yet. Watch the crowds tomorrow. The menaces will come to gloat over their work, but you know what else will happen? They'll hear Joseph testify, a thing that never would have happened otherwise."

Dudley's assessment of Jed's heart bit him like a rattler, and it was as correct as his prediction about the next day. Reverend Myers and his mayhem-makers did indeed return that morning. Every nerve in Jed's body tensed for a fight as Dudley pointed to a cluster of people surrounding one man with a mild limp. "That's Joseph."

Love and respect rode unmistakably on Dudley's voice at the mention of Joseph's name. Jed saw the same feelings reflected in Hannah's eyes, which were already fully on the man, assuming that look of peace and expectation that overtook her in quiet moments these days.

Jed scrutinized Joseph, seeing nothing that would, on first inspection, set him apart from other men. Yes, he was tall, with broad shoulders that filled out his suit well, and he had a pleasant-enough face, but he looked more like a banker than a prophet like Moses. Having satisfied the immediate needs of those surrounding him, Joseph turned and scanned the faces of those gathered, and as his gaze passed their group, Jed felt goosebumps rise on his arms at the awe in Joseph's eyes, as if *he* were honored to meet all of *them*.

His welcome pierced Jed personally, as if they were renewing an old, cherished acquaintance, and from the looks on the faces of those gathered, that sense of investment was nearly universal, except for Myers and his followers. Their catty laughter and jeering pulled Jed from the moment, and then Joseph's soft welcome pulled him back, until he felt like a two-man saw, being tugged one way and then drawn the other. He hoped Joseph would deliver a rebuking sermon, but instead, he turned the meeting over to Oliver Cowdery, and Jed's heart sank. He had come with questions he knew only Joseph could lay to rest.

When Oliver concluded, several men bore their testimony. Finally Joseph rose, and Jed felt the hairs rise on his neck as the people drew a collective breath. Joseph scanned the crowd and paused, his countenance exuding a sweet peace, and then he began in a strong, clear voice that occasionally fluttered from emotion. It was not so much a sermon as a statement of his faith.

"The fundamental principles of our religion are the testimony of the Apostles and Prophets, concerning Jesus Christ, that He died, was buried, and rose again the third day, and ascended into heaven. We believe in the gift of the Holy Ghost, the power of faith, the enjoyment of the spiritual gifts according to the will of God, the restoration of the house of Israel, and the final triumph of truth."

As Joseph continued on, bearing witness of these doctrines, Jed cringed. *How many times did Hannah try to satisfy my questions on these very points?*

"The scripture says those who will obey the commandments shall be heirs of God and joint heirs with Jesus Christ. . . . 'The Spirit itself beareth witness with our spirit that we are the children of God, and if children, then heirs of God, and joint heirs with Jesus Christ, if so be that we suffer with him in the flesh that we may be also glorified together.'"

"The Spirit itself beareth witness with our spirit that we are the children of God." Jed ruminated on the import of that sublime phrase for several seconds. He watched as Joseph lowered his head, then smiled and concluded. "Friends, I testify that the Book of Mormon is true, just what it purports to be, and for this testimony I expect to give an account in the day of Judgment."

There. The words satisfied Jed's questions, but as he continued to ponder them they began to warm him like a sweet, steaming cup of cocoa, moving beyond an intellectual satisfaction to an inward understanding. He felt his chest tighten as if his heart had swelled within him, and though his inside was warm, his skin prickled and his heart began to pound.

It was at this very moment that a pastor disrupted the meeting. Jed had previously overheard the man assailing a young woman in the crowd—a female member of his congregation, whom he asked to leave. When she had refused, he departed, but he now returned with a power of attorney and forcibly removed her. The situation appalled Jed, chasing away the sweet reverence he had begun to enjoy, so much so that when the meeting ended and Hannah encouraged him to step forward and speak with Joseph, he quietly declined.

No more was said that night, but Dudley approached Jed early the next morning. "We're going to rebuild the dam. We could use another man."

Jed studied his brother-in-law. "Where is the peace? From what I see, there is precious little for anyone who follows Joseph Smith."

With hands reverently poised, Dudley tapped his chest. "Oh, there's peace, Jed, in here."

Recalling those brief feelings of the previous day, Jed agreed to help rebuild the dam, and when he and Hannah stood on the bank with Dudley's family and the others who awaited their turn for baptism, their expressions of joy and expectation rekindled that moment for him.

He watched Emma Smith smile at her husband as he relinquished her hand to Mr. Cowdery, who led her into the cold, dammed stream and proceeded with the ordinance. As she broke through the water, light radiated from her face. Immediately, she sought Joseph, and the gaze they shared caused Jed's throat to tighten. *There! There is the peace Dudley spoke of.* Jed felt his heart rate increase as his eyes began to burn. Dudley was the next person to enter the water. After he was immersed and then lifted up, he spoke of glory and peace, and Jed hungered to take Hannah and the children and follow. And then the intruders arrived.

The frightened cries of women and children shattered the peace. Jed and Dudley herded their families to the wagons and to safety, keeping an eye on the Smiths, Oliver Cowdery, and the Knights, until they were all safely in Joseph Knight's house. But the mob of nearly fifty men was not content to merely disrupt the service. This time they surrounded the house, as if bent on violence.

"There aren't enough men left to mount a defense," Jed said. "The risk to the women and children is too great."

Dudley scanned the perimeter. "We need the constable here. Let's pray someone already went for him."

The families made haste back to Dudley's farm. Once all was secure, they unhitched the team and had just saddled two fresh mounts, preparing to return to Joseph Knight's farm, when a rider arrived.

"Joseph and Oliver have made their escape to Newel's house, Brother Snowden."

Both men were amazed at the report. "Did the mob leave? The house was surrounded."

The man chuckled nervously. "The mob was unrelenting in their threats and questionings, but the Lord opened a way out, and Brother Joseph and Brother Oliver escaped. The mob now surrounds Brother Newel Knight's house, breathing out threatenings against Joseph. The remaining baptisms will be delayed, but Joseph believes the violence will subside in time for us to gather at Brother Newel's tonight to attend to the confirmation of the newly baptized."

Dudley ran his hand through his thinned hair and look pleadingly at Jed. "Will you stay?"

"Has Colesville forgotten that this is America, where religious freedom is guaranteed?"

Dudley grinned and patted Jed's back. "I'll take that as a yes."

The gathering at Newel Knight's home took place without incident, but just as the meeting was about to begin, the constable knocked on the door with a warrant for Joseph's arrest.

Surprising himself, Jed popped from his seat in Joseph's defense. "On what grounds?"

The constable removed his hat and entered the room. "Officially, the charges are disorderliness and creating a civil uproar with his preaching about the Book of Mormon."

"There is no crime in preaching, sir!" Jed argued.

"Mr. Smith will have his hearing before a judge. But tonight I'm bound by the court to safely deliver Mr. Smith to South Bainbridge in Chenango County, and if he will come along peaceably, I pledge to you that I'll do just that."

Dudley bullied up to the man. "We'll come along and see that you do."

"I'd advise against that, sir. There's a mob waiting for Mr. Smith outside that tree line. I can slip him past, but if they see an escort, it'll turn into a battle, and we don't want that. You come to the courthouse tomorrow, and you'll find that I kept my word."

Jed watched as another opportunity to speak with Joseph slipped away. He turned to Dudley. "I'm not an attorney, but I am versed in the Constitution and willing to help in Mr. Smith's defense."

"I appreciate that, Jed, but you're an outsider here. Lots of folks are still wary of the federal government, and having you on Joseph's defense could further inflame things."

"Mr. James Davidson and Mr. John Reid are men of impeccable characters and well respected in the community," Joseph Knight said. "They're farmers, but they're also well versed in the law. I'll secure them to defend Joseph."

Mr. Knight's appeal to his neighbors proved wise, as the two men appeared in court the next day and successfully diffused the prosecution's ridiculous, almost comedic arguments against Joseph Smith.

The case began with a scrutiny of Joseph's dealings with Josiah Stowell of Harmony, Pennsylvania, the man who had hired Joseph to locate an old Spanish mine. The prosecutors questioned Stowell about a horse he had sold Joseph, attempting to coerce Stowell into saying Smith had stolen it. When Stowell firmly denied the charges, the prosecutors called for Stowell's daughters to be summoned, and when they arrived and took the stand, the prosecutors attempted to assail Joseph's moral character with charges the women refused to corroborate.

More baseless charges and implausible witnesses were produced. Jed noted the toll the proceedings were taking on Emma Smith. "This is a sham," he whispered to Dudley. "Why has the judge allowed it to wear on so long?" The answer soon came. Another constable entered the back of the court, and upon his arrival the judge called for Joseph's acquittal, but the celebration was brief. No sooner had Emma wrapped her arms around her husband's neck than a new warrant was issued, and Joseph was arrested and hauled away to Broome County.

This constable abused and insulted Joseph from the start, without regard for food or water, let alone for his safety. Joseph's friends also made the fifteen-mile journey to the mob-filled tavern that would serve as Joseph's cell for the night. The taunts and jeers of the men echoed into the night, as Joseph was ordered to "Prophesy! Prophesy!" amid laughter and as they spit upon him or insulted him in diverse ways.

In the morning, Joseph was hauled into the Colesville courthouse as another hearing commenced, surrounding a miraculous healing Joseph was purported to have performed on Newel Knight. The questioning reset all Jed's doubts, centering on the casting out of devils and whether Knight had seen the devil—talk too incredulous for Jed to comprehend. And then one of the prosecutors asked a question of Mr. Knight, whose answer caused Jed's mind to reopen.

"Pray, what did the devil look like?" the lawyer asked.

The defense advised Mr. Knight not to answer, to which Mr. Knight turned to the prosecutor and replied, "I believe I need not answer your last question, but I will do it, provided I be allowed to ask you one question first, and you answer me. Do you, Mr. Seymour, understand the things of the Spirit?"

The attorney shook his head and scowled. "No, I do not pretend to understand such things."

"Well then," Knight replied, "it would be of no use to tell you what the devil looked like for it was a spiritual sight, and spiritually discerned; and of course, you would not understand it were I to tell you of it."

Laughter erupted in the courtroom, completely disarming the prosecution, who nevertheless battled on with increasing futility, but Jed heard little of the remaining arguments as his mind centered on the idea of "spiritual understanding." He knew, like this prosecutor, that he too lacked this ability, and he felt certain it was as much a matter of desire as it was a gift.

The defense team leaned heavily upon Joseph's unimpeachable character, giving gratitude to God for the privilege of representing their honorable client. Their voices thundered through their summation with inspired tongues that wielded language and law like honey-dipped swords until the prosecution and their witnesses visibly trembled before them. Again, Joseph was acquitted, but as he turned toward Jed, the sorrow behind his smile caused Jed's eyes to burn.

Joseph's own eyes became glossy as he said, "And thus we are persecuted on account of our religion and faith—in a country, the Constitution of which guarantees to every man the indefeasible right to worship God according to the dictates of his own conscience."

The sting of that hypocrisy, and the pain lining Joseph's face, tore at Jed, and then a scene of incongruous kindness played out. The abusive constable who arrested Joseph extended his hand in apology. "Forgive me for my part in this, Mr. Smith, and let me help you. The mob has been lying in wait with plans to tar and feather you if you were acquitted."

Jed marveled as Joseph provided living evidence of all his defense team had said of him. He grasped his former enemy's shoulders and looked him in the eye, saying, "I do forgive you, sir, and would even call you a friend if you could get me to my wife, who is waiting at her sister's home."

The ease with which Joseph forgave his tormentor entranced Jed. Dudley noticed his incredulity and turned to him. "Now you see the depth of Joseph's character for yourself."

"Joseph's life, and those of his followers and friends, would be sweeter if he would deny his story, but he does not, and why? It can only be because he will not, and cannot, deny what he saw in that grove." Jed rushed to quell Dudley's euphoric reaction. "He is everything you said of him, but I'm still uncomfortable with much of this talk of prophets and angels and such. I still need time to wrestle with my doubts."

"Wait here a few days more. Perhaps things will calm enough for Joseph to teach you."

Jed shook his head. "I cannot. I've business at the farm I need to attend to before my return to the Capitol, but do write to me of Joseph's teachings. I am anxious to learn more."

The next morning, Jed and Hannah packed the carriage and prepared the children to leave for home. As they left the Snowden farm, Hannah grabbed his arm and leaned her cheek against it. "Poor Beatrice. She expected to be baptized a member of The Church of Christ before we left Colesville."

"And what about you? Did you also hope to be baptized before we left?"

Hannah offered him a crooked smile, which he knew was intended to shield him from her disappointment. "A little. There was a moment when I thought you were also feeling the same."

Jed patted her hand. "If this work is truly God's, it will spread far beyond Colesville and New York. It will find us, and we'll see where I am when it does."

Nothing more was said on the subject until they reached Philadelphia on July fourth to rest for a day. As the Pearsons watched the parades and fireworks, Jed thought of Joseph Smith's religious persecution, and of Abel's and Caleb's thirst for total freedom. Many still did not fully enjoy the liberty America celebrated, and that thought energized his desire to return to Washington and raise his voice anew.

CHAPTER 39

July 1, 1830
Willowsport

On July first, a bruised and battered abolitionist from Virginia stepped off a steamboat, asking for Caleb. When the two men met, the abolitionist handed Caleb one of the pamphlets he had passed out a year ago.

"Mr. Miller, I was given this by a slave who said you told him he needed to claim his freedom. I've been looking for you ever since. I stirred up a hornet's nest back in Calverton today, calling for an end to slavery. I'm headed to Washington next and hoped to find a friend here. Travel with me, Caleb. Negroes listen to you."

Markus worried about the price of Caleb's fame, and his worries were soon confirmed. That evening, a portion of the Willows' fencing was knocked down, sending livestock roaming over hundreds of acres. A day later, a boat's mooring lines were cut, setting it adrift. The next day two strangers incited two separate and frivolous altercations with Caleb at the market, prompting the men to close the whole thing down for a week while tempers settled.

On the night of July fourth, Abel and his two younger sons were in the horse barn with Markus, a quarter mile from home, catching snippets of sleep during shifts as they tended to Windmere's troubled foaling.

Two riders slipped over the rise that marked the dividing line between the Willows and White Oak, checking their rudimentary hand-sketched map before picking their way toward Abel and Bitty's cabin, where a thin trail of wood smoke escaped from the chimney.

"Block the chimney," one man ordered the other. "We'll smoke him out."

Like a repeating nightmare, thick, suffocating smoke began pouring out of the fireplace, swiftly filling every corner until no sweet air remained.

"Prissy, douse the fire!" Bitty shouted to her daughter as she grabbed a pot and began breaking the window glass. Momentary relief rushed over her as the smoke escaped through the windows in thick, dark plumes. The dogs started barking, and Bitty tuned to the voices of the assailants, who were cursing the dogs for awakening the other residents. She saw the glow of lamplight in previously darkened windows and knew it was only a matter of time before her neighbors began checking on the cause of the alarm.

She pulled her crying daughter to her. "It'll be all right. They'll leave now."

Two men burst through the door with hoods over their heads, shouting, "Where's Abel?"

Far in the back bedroom, the two women huddled together in a corner as tiny Bitty did her best to shield her seventeen-year-old daughter, who was nearly twice the size of her mother. The stockier assailant pushed the barrel of the gun against the girl's head as he growled at Bitty. "Tell me where Abel is, or I'll shoot this girl!"

Bitty saw the brown skin of the man's hand and thought she'd try to reason with him. Quietly, she rose to her feet and approached the man. "Abel's gone, sir. All my menfolk are gone tonight. You got no cause to rile a couple of defenseless women, do you?"

She tried to smile as her eyes begged the man for mercy. A string of expletives shot from the white man's mouth, while the Negro man reacted to Bitty's petition by punching the gunstock against her head with such force it sent her flying back into the corner.

The white man pointed to Priscilla. "Tie this one up," he ordered his accomplice.

As his partner proceeded to bind the weeping girl, the white man issued instructions to Priscilla. "You tell your father he and that upstart son of his brought this upon themselves. Tell him we came for him, but we took his woman instead."

The Negro glanced out the broken window. "I see lanterns comin'. We gotta go!"

"Grab the old woman." And then they were gone.

Markus's twelve-year-old son, Sean, cracked his parents' door open to find his mother standing by the window, peering into the dark. "Mama, where's Papa? The dogs are barking."

"I know, Sean. Papa is in the foaling barn, remember?" She reached a hand to her red-haired son, who came readily to her. She kissed his head. "Come, let's have a look."

From the veranda she could see bobbing lanterns racing through the dark, signaling something was wrong. Bitty and Abel's youngest son, twenty-year-old Grandy, raced by as if on a critical errand. Jenny called to him, and he stopped to reply.

"I've got to saddle some horses, Miss Jenny. I went back to the cabin to get some of Mama's tonic, and I found Prissy all tied up. The men who did it kidnapped Bitty Mama!"

Before the last syllable left his lips he was off like a shot, racing toward the meadows. Jack came by next. Clearly shaken, he was breathing so hard he could scarcely support his weight. Jenny could see the worry in his eyes.

"Jack," she called to him. "Is it true? Someone's taken Bitty?"

He doubled over and nodded his head with worry. "They took Bitty to lure Abel out, and we don't know when Jed'll be back. I'm afraid something terrible's going to happen tonight."

Every able-bodied male in Willowsport spread out on horseback and foot, trying to follow tracks in the dark, while others searched the surrounding area with dogs, hoping they'd catch a scent of Bitty's trail. Markus discovered some interesting wagon tracks near the property line, indicating a third assailant might have been waiting there. A group of seventeen white and Negro men followed the tracks all the way to Calverton, where Abel forced them to stay behind while he went into the town alone, willing to give himself up in return for Bitty's safety.

An hour turned to two, then three, but as daybreak began appearing across the horizon, it became apparent Bitty's captors weren't coming to make the trade, and the men waiting at the edge of town wandered in. Locals became nervous at the sight of so many agitated Negroes, and the sheriff suggested they search elsewhere while he nosed about the town for Bitty.

It took the bulk of the seventeen men to remove Abel from the village limits. At a loss over what to do next, he told the men, "Double on back and search the brush along the roads."

"What are you plannin' ta do?" Markus asked.

"What would you do if it was your wife they took?" challenged Abel.

Markus knew exactly what he would do. "Probably something stupid that might get me killed."

"If you find Bitty, tell her I love her and that everything will be all right."

Markus grabbed Abel's arm. "Don't do this! We'll find her."

With his free hand, Abel cold-cocked the Irishman, knocking him out flat. Abel's face twisted in sorrow. "I'm sorry, Markus, but this is something I have to do."

Jenny left the children in the nanny's care to find Jack, the lone Willows sentry. He escorted her to the cabin to comfort Priscilla, and while there, they both noticed the muddy boot prints left by the kidnappers. "It hasn't rained enough to cause this much mud anyplace but—"

A light went on in Jack's worried eyes. "The swamp."

"That's what I think, too." Jenny picked a piece of debris off the floor. "What plant would you say this is from? Lobelia?"

Jack studied the crushed piece of plant. "That'd be my guess. It confirms that the riders could have come in from the swamp, but the wagon came across Stringham's fields."

"Our men followed the wagon tracks, but the attackers brought the wagon to carry big Abel out. They wouldn't need it to carry someone as tiny as Bitty. They were also in a hurry. Maybe after they took her they left on horseback, the way they came in."

"It's worth a try. Let's pray they didn't leave her in the swamp for the animals to get."

"I'll take Priscilla back to my house, then I'm coming with you. If Bitty is there, she'll need nursing while you drive."

Twenty minutes later they were heading for the swamp in a wagon loaded with blankets, a bottle of brandy, and Bitty's bag of medicinal herbs. The swamp was a lasting reminder of the damage left by the water spout that put out the fires set by mercenaries in 1814. Over the years it had become home to a stunning array of wildlife that preyed upon one another. Thick with cattails, it seemed an eerie, dead place at night, but tonight, when they wished for silence to listen for Bitty, the swamp was teeming with cries and calls of every kind.

They unharnessed the horses and rode bareback, calling for Bitty and then waiting for a response. After repeating the exercise in various locations, they finally heard a noise in response to their calls—a series of splashes that eventually led them to the tiny woman. She was bound and gagged, and she had a nasty head gash that had clotted over. Her normally vibrant eyes were dim. She was soaked to the bone, lying atop a bed of downed cattails, except for her left hand, which rested in the water.

Jack loaded his sister into the wagon and rushed to re-hitch the horses while Jenny removed Bitty's wet clothes and wrapped her in the blankets. They raced straight to the main house and put her to bed, and then Jack fired off three quick rounds to notify the searchers. Everyone came home but Abel.

Abel spent three days scouring the roads and trails, searching for the wide wagon tracks. He began spending time at the docks, furtively watching wagons come and go, until he finally felt certain he had identified the wagon. He waited patiently until late evening, when the two drivers arrived and climbed in, obscured by the darkness. Abel controlled his fury, knowing there was much more at stake than personal retribution. He thought about waiting until Jed arrived home, but the mighty man pushed caution aside and headed off alone to follow the wagon.

As the wagon stopped, Abel hid among the ragged brush. Then he drew closer and caught a clear view of the man holding the reins. He was a powerful Negro whose bearing and features were familiar to Abel. Then a sick recognition came. *Leon.* He had been one of the militiamen at Fort McHenry, a man who openly hated "uppity niggers" like Abel and Caleb, because they could read and write, and acted "white." The realization that Bitty had been attacked by one of their own turned Abel's stomach. But now he had a new concern. Where had the other man gone? He had just turned to search the brush when a heavy thud crashed down upon his skull.

He had no idea how much time had passed, but somewhere in the murky space between unconsciousness and clarity, he heard three voices. Two were familiar. One belonged to the Negro driver, while the other compassionless voice was that of Emerson Hildebrand. Before Abel could register what was happening, the other two men had bound his feet.

424

"Don't bother hauling him into the wagon." Hildebrand walked over to where Abel lay in a semiconscious lump. "Tie the rope to the back and drag him behind."

With a click of Hildebrand's tongue, the horses took off, pounding Abel's head into the rocky ground until unconsciousness retook him again. He awoke like one raw wound, with bloody burns from his head to his feet. He heard the lazy slap of water against the shore below, triggering pure panic as he realized he had been dumped on a narrow rock outcropping thirty feet above the Patuxent River. His shallow, rapid breaths matched the cadence of his thundering heart, which nearly drowned out the sound of his captors' taunts from the ridge above.

"Seven years in prison changes a man—gives him time to think. I was going to forget all about you, Abel, and start fresh, but you and your boy weren't content with what you had. No, you went around passing out those pamphlets, changing the balance of things. You shouldn't have done that. You had it better than Leon here, but he made peace with his station, and for a few dollars and a bottle of rye, he's as anxious as I to put you in your place once and for all. And I've planned something special for your end. You think you're my equal? You're nothing. You were never anything special. I want you to die realizing what a frightened, crying beggar you are. And you, Leon? The only thing worse than an uppity nigger is a traitor."

Able heard the crack of a pistol, and a thud, and then a dark hand dangled lifelessly over the edge. He heard his two remaining tormenters' laughter fade as they dragged Leon away.

For what seemed hours, proud Abel stood, pressed against the earthen and rock wall, trying to control his panic. *Someone will find me. Someone will find me . . .* Then the rain began.

He made many attempts to get a foothold or handhold to climb the wet wall, but each one slid his body closer to the edge. Though he clawed at the mud-slick ledge, he was unable to dig in, and slowly his shins, and then his knees and thighs slid over, toppling him. A sharp pain bit his skull as it scraped the rock wall, and that was followed by a surreal, momentary sensation of floating, which ended as he plunged into the black water below. Disorientation and hysteria overtook him. He gasped for air while underwater, quickly filling his lungs and sealing his fate.

Fog and an eerie cold front haunted the river as Jed and Hannah returned to the devastating news that Abel's body had washed up two miles south of the Willows dock the day before. The mournful sounds of Bitty's cries pierced the Willows' men's hearts. Jed was convinced it was murder and that Emerson Hildebrand was behind it, but the man had covered his tracks well. No witness could be found willing to testify that he had even been in Maryland, let alone along the Patuxent.

Caleb came to Jed and asked, "Did I cause this by distributing those pamphlets?"

Jed didn't know what to say. "Wicked people will always find an excuse for the harm they cause. Take care of your mother now. We'll get justice for your father. I promise you that."

"It's not right. It's just not right, Jed," Caleb howled before turning to attend to his mother.

Jed rubbed his fingers over his eyes. "Poor Bitty. How will she bear it, Markus? I can't accept that I'll never see Abel again. I never even had a chance to say goodbye."

"No one did, Jed . . . except me, I guess. That's what's makin' this so hard on 'is family. I'm sure 'e knew how Caleb would react ta 'is goin' off alone, so 'e just walked away from our search party without makin' a stir. It's how 'e wanted it."

"Did he or Bitty say anything that would give us a lead?"

Markus shrugged as he stared absently into the trees. "Two small things. Bitty said one of the men who attacked her was a large Negro, and we know they had a wagon with very wide wheels. Abel's plan was to follow those tracks. When 'e was late returnin' to the farm, Jack and I tried ta pick up the trail, but it just disappeared in Calverton."

"Then I'll head back to Calverton and see if I can pick up that trail again," Jed said. "Either Abel found Hildebrand, or Hildebrand found Abel."

"We don't have a shred of proof Hildebrand did this, but it sure bears 'is mark—pullin' stunts for days ta lure 'is targets out, and then bushwhackin' 'em. Abel knew what the stakes were when 'e left. He was desperate to protect 'is family from that devil. I guess 'e just forgot that Hildebrand didn't just target 'is family. He went after all the Willows."

Jed leaned against a tree. "And yet he has support, including members of Congress."

"Don't tell Caleb that. He's not thinkin' straight as it is. We need ta rein 'im in."

"Send him out with Jack to scout those wagon tracks. That will keep him busy until we have some answers. Once we do, he has the right to look this devil in the eye."

It pained Jed to open the door to Bitty's cabin. Every square inch reflected Abel's pride at being a free man, from the two upholstered chairs that sat by the fireplace, and the hand-rubbed bookcases, to the frames he had fashioned after the fire, to hold their freedom papers and Bitty's needlework. It was the comfortable home of a landowner, and it seemed utterly hollow without him in it.

Jed knelt beside Bitty's chair. Her arms clutched a pile of Abel's shirts, into which she kept burying her face. Jed took hold of her hands and kissed each one. "He loved you so much, Bitty."

"Wood chips and lavender . . . I'm going to miss those smells." Tears slowly filled her eyes. "How will I sleep without his snoring? That sound always made me feel safe because I knew my man was near. I loved the way we started the day. He'd wolf down a stack of buckwheat cakes and tell me he was a lucky man to have a good cook for a wife. It makes a day near perfect when it starts out with someone telling you they feel lucky because you're theirs." Her face slowly warmed from sorrow to peace. "He said it every day—that I made his life sweet. Even now, I'm comforted to know I made his life better."

When Jed left Bitty's home he headed to his own, and there, watching for him by the window, was Hannah. She met him on the porch, slipping into his embrace without a word and pressing nearly into him, as if she were soaking him up. She knew. And Jed knew it.

"When are you leaving?" Her question was uttered into his shoulder as he held her.

"Tomorrow. We need to make this home, this world safe for James and Abigail."

"They need you."

Jed pulled back, forcing her to meet his eyes. "You understand all this, don't you?" He felt her shiver in his arms, and he tightened his embrace. "I thank God every day for you, Hannah. Every happy moment I've spent has been about you, and if you look back on our life and forget everything else, remember this—I loved my life because you were in it."

They headed to James's room. Jed's hands shook slightly as he tucked the quilt more tightly under his boy's chin. Back in the bedroom, Jed tucked his finger into Abigail's tiny fist for a moment, and then he and Hannah went downstairs. He built a fire to abate the unseasonable chill. The pair curled up in his favorite chair, holding one another.

"You are my life, Jed Pearson. You remember that."

Her concern and love so overwhelmed him that the pair never made it upstairs to bed. Instead, they spent that night together, loving one another by the fire's amber glow, but before dawn's first light broke across the horizon, he slipped from her arms and into the dark.

By dawn Jed reached Calverton, where a restless unease was prevalent. Whispers about the outsiders—the abolitionists—followed his every step. There had been a shift in people's attitudes toward

Jed following Caleb's distribution of the pamphlets, but it was pervasive this day. He moved from the main street to the waterfront, visiting the watermen's haunts, asking questions about the wagon. An oysterer explained that a local hauling company owned a wide-wheeled wagon. It was a rental, hired out multiple times a day. Jed refused to accept another dead end.

"A large Negro man of about thirty years might have hired that wagon recently. He's not quite as big as Abel, but big enough to make a person notice him. Have you seen such a fellow?"

The oysterer's eyes narrowed in thought. "Now that you mention it, a fellow came into town yesterday, haulin' a dead slave in the back of that wide-wheeled wagon—said the runaway tried to kill him so he had to shoot him dead."

Jed pulled out the Hildebrand family portrait. "Do you see that slave owner here?"

Without a moment's hesitation, the man pointed to Emerson Hildebrand's face. "That's him."

Jed now had proof that Hildebrand was not only behind Abel's murder, but that he had killed off his own Negro accomplice. The victory was sweet, but small and brief as Jed now noticed the attention being paid him by the patrons, and by one man in particular who left the tavern soon after he did, and who seemed to be following him around Calverton.

Feeling it wise to get off the docks, Jed nevertheless felt a lone rider made an easy target, so he quietly boarded his horse and booked passage on a steamboat headed north. He wondered if he'd ever get past the sense of suspicion and danger he saw lurking in every unknown face, in every situation. His nerves were on alert, his muscles tight, his mind anxious. He moved to the railing near the bow, finding comfort in the familiar shoreline, feeling home so close at hand.

As the captain gave the orders for the crew to prepare the lines, a man approached Jed from behind. "Senator Pearson!" he greeted as if he were an old friend.

The man disarmed Jed with his smile and extended his right hand, which Jed courteously received as he struggled to identify him. An unsettling moment of silence passed between the two as the other passengers jostled about, preparing to disembark.

The man's grip tightened, and his smile broadened to a sneer. As the first horn blast erupted, Jed saw the man's face brace in preparation as he shifted his stance and thrust forward. A beam of moonlight revealed the glint of a blade a breath before Jed felt pressure against his side, followed by the crack of the glass on the Hildebrand family portrait in his pocket. The steel glanced left and into Jed's flesh. His groan was smothered in the blare of the horn. He shoved his left hand into the man's face, drawing him and his blade back, but in the narrow confines of the bow there was only one escape—backwards into the water. And with a mighty swing, Jed threw himself and his assailant into the churning Patuxent.

CHAPTER 40

July 14, 1830
Baltimore, Maryland

Frannie paused before taking Arthur's extended hand and descending from the stagecoach. "I feel as if we should do something magnificent to mark this moment."

Arthur indulged her whim with a smile. "Mrs. Ramsey, this trip to Philadelphia to finalize the adoption of our children has already been the most marvelous trip of my life."

"I know, but we're returning home for the first time as the Ramsey *family.*"

"I do love the sound of that. So what would you suggest?"

Fannie clapped her hands together. "Let's not unpack. Let's head straight to the Willows. Surely Hannah and Jed are back from their trip to Beatrice's now. I want us all to be together."

Fifteen-year-old Sarah and eleven-year-old Charles heartily agreed, and as exhausted as he was, Arthur kissed his wife's palm and called for a carriage to ferry them from the station to home. The driver lowered his eyes as he held the door, saying, "I'm so sorry for your loss, ma'am."

Having no idea what he meant by the comment, Frannie brushed it away, but as the carriage rolled past the Washington Monument, she noticed the flag at half mast, the way heads bowed solemnly, and how the men removed their hats at her passing.

"Something's wrong—something's terribly wrong, Arthur!" She hung out the window trying to get the driver's attention until her husband pulled her back in. "Look at how people are reacting to me, as if I'm in mourning!"

Arthur called for the driver to stop and then got out. Soon, he returned to the carriage grim-faced and carrying a copy of the day's paper bearing the headline "Senator Pearson Believed Dead."

Without hesitation they rode on, arriving at the Willows in the dead of night. The ruckus caused by their arrival brought to the door a tired maid and a haggard-looking Hannah dressed in her nightgown, clutching Jed's silk wrapper around her.

Frannie gathered up her traveling skirt and raced up the steps with Arthur close behind. "I wouldn't believe it until I heard it from your lips, but it's true, isn't it? Oh, no! Not Jed!"

She pulled Hannah to her as Arthur scooped them both into his arms, leading them inside, while the driver and the maid attended to the children and the luggage.

"Wait in the parlor while I make arrangements for you for the night," Hannah said, "and then I'll come and explain." Moments later, she returned and pulled a chair up close, forming a cloistered circle. "We suffered for three days thinking Jed was dead, but he was found alive, Frannie, though we must continue to act as if he is dead until we know by whom and why he was attacked."

Frannie buried her face in Arthur's shoulder. "Thank God."

As Frannie struggled to compose herself, Hannah placed a hand on her sister-in-law's arm. "I'm sorry you found out this way. I was in a fog until word reached me that he had been found alive. I wanted to spare you that shock, so I sent a courier to your home."

"We came straight here from the stagecoach station," Arthur said.

"Then you don't know the rest—dear Abel is dead. Bitty was kidnapped, and Jack and Jenny found her while Abel was searching for her kidnappers. He was found floating downriver a few days later. We moved Bitty and Prissy here now. They're fine physically, but still very shaken."

When Frannie lifted her face it was set as hard as flint. "Was it Hildebrand?"

Hannah shrugged. "We think he was behind Bitty's kidnapping and Abel's murder, but Jed's attacker was a man named Felcher, and we have yet to establish a tie between them."

"It's there—it has to be."

"Perhaps, but Jed has many enemies now, as do others with an anti-slavery position."

Frannie stood abruptly. "I want to go up and see him."

"How I wish he were here." Hannah's mournful eyes teared up. "James won't accept that his father is alive until he sees him, and we can't risk that until we know whether his attacker acted alone. The sheriff was unable to find one witness, and Mr. Felcher claims Jed tripped and pulled him overboard."

"That's ridiculous!"

"If he's not here, then where is he?" asked Arthur.

"At White Oak. Frederick found him. Once word of the accident got out, Frederick combed the shoreline. He remembered the overhangs all along the riverfront, and how Jack taught you three to hide there when you were children. Sure enough, he found Jed curled up in some exposed roots where he hid from his assailant, who he later found out was nearly drowned, lying downriver."

"Who else knows?" Frannie asked.

"Five besides us. When the sheriff arrested Mr. Felcher, we told him nothing about Jed. I told Markus, Jack, and Bitty, and I called for Samuel Renfro to tend to Jed's wound. Timothy had to know in order to handle whatever issues would arise with the Senate."

"How long can you keep this up? Jed must be beside himself over there."

Hannah leaned forward again. "I think this whole experience has greatly affected him. He asked me to send a copy of the Book of Mormon to him to read while he recuperates. *Imagine that,* I thought to myself. I shouldn't have been so surprised. Affliction can break us, but it can also strengthen and teach. He's written me wonderful letters these past three days. I think the book has given him some much needed clarity."

"I'd like to read that book," Arthur said. "Frannie told me a little about it, and about Mr. Smith. It's a very curious publication surrounded by even more curious rumors."

Hannah pulled a copy from the bookshelf where three other copies sat. Handing it to Arthur, she said, "We brought extras back to share. Jed says he saw life like a disjointed series of events and duties, all swirling about one another. Reading the Book of Mormon has helped him see how they are all related and part of a great plan God has for us, for this land, for everyone."

"And Jed believes all this now?" Frannie asked.

Hannah rubbed the cover of another copy. "You should ask him that."

Frederick Stringham peeked in from the doorway of Jed's room. "How are you feeling?"

Jed laid his Book of Mormon against his chest. "Grateful, humble, and foolish to begin with. I've misjudged you, Frederick. I owe you an apology. You saved my life, yet a week ago I'd not have counted you much of a friend."

Frederick lowered his head as he entered the room, dressed in his riding attire. "I strained our friendship over the years, so I'm grateful for the chance to make amends. These just arrived." He handed Jed a thick stack of correspondence from home.

Jed's eyes filled with tears as he leafed through the letters. Then he leaned back and stared out the window toward his home. "I thank you and Penelope more than I can express, Frederick. I owe you two my life, but I need to get home."

"Not today, I'm afraid. The wound in your side did considerable damage. You need to allow it to heal. Dr. Renfro told me to shoot you in the foot if you left that bed within a week."

Jed could not bring himself to smile at the joke. As the moment grew awkward, Frederick pointed to the Book of Mormon. "I glanced at it while you were asleep. I figured any book that can keep Jed Pearson in bed is worth a look. What is it?"

Jed didn't know how to reply. How could he answer when he was just beginning to understand the true purpose and power of the book? Somehow, for all his reading, he had previously missed the book's purpose—to lead people to Christ, and to testify of Him and His love. How had he missed it?

The subtle glint of the knife had cut through all of Jed's noble preoccupations, illuminating what really mattered. Images of Hannah and the children flashed before his eyes, along with other beloved faces he'd leave behind if he died. In that instant, his love for his family eclipsed all else. He knew Dudley had been right. The book, Joseph's work—it was all about love, and Christ was the way.

Jed wondered why it had taken another near-death experience to pierce his pride and humble him enough to admit he needed God's Son's miraculous mercy. All his life, he had glossed over the biblical witnesses of Jesus and His ministry, failing to intimately feel the personal price Christ paid to redeem *him* and those he loved. It shamed Jed that Christ's miraculous love, woven through pages and pages of the Book of Mormon, had been read but not personalized the first few times. Now Jed felt it. Now he was beginning to understand the necessity of Christ's atonement. Jesus was, in very deed, the Son of God the Eternal Father, and the Savior of the World. He offered Himself as a sacrifice for all the rest of God's children, and why? For the same reason Jed risked his life to save his own family. For love.

He questioned why the account of Christ's agony in Gethsemane, His crucifixion, and His death had not cracked the shell around his heart. Why did he not weep the first time he read the Book of Mormon's account of Christ's resurrection and appearance to the believers after the destruction of the land? Jed had marveled over its accounts of leadership and military strategy, while missing the promises of protection over the lands of those who followed Christ, and the devastation that followed when people followed their own wisdom. But no more. Jed now understood what Markus had tried to tell him years ago—that pride had placed him at odds with God. For all the good Jed had tried to do, he thought he could do it alone, and now he realized he had lied to himself all along. God had been there, at the helm, always.

Previously, Jed had received but a glimpse of America's purpose, but now he saw the divinity of her principles woven within the pages, cementing his conviction to protect the Constitution, while also dedicating himself to be a witness of Christ. And now he must begin by bearing testimony of the book. And if the book was true, and if Joseph had been the instrument of its translation, then he was what he claimed to be, and he saw what he claimed to have seen!

Jed's throat was tight as he extended the Book of Mormon to Frederick. "It was written for *our* day, Frederick—as a second witness of Jesus Christ. He rescued a portion of the house of Israel by leading them across the sea to this continent. They also prophesied that the Son of God would come to earth and establish His kingdom here. America and her liberties are critical to God's plan, Frederick. It's in here. He knows us. The challenges and possibilities of our day are described within these pages."

Frederick did not appear as stunned by the disclosure as Jed expected. He took the book and opened it. "Government, slaves, and Mormons. You, Jed Pearson, are the champion of thankless causes."

"No, Frederick, hear me out. Each is a cause of liberty. Keep it. Read it."

Frederick weighed the book in his hands before returning it. "Perhaps in time. I've already introduced a great deal of change into my life. I must admit, when I saw you lying there, nearly dead, I saw the future. This slavery battle is coming to a head, and I knew I could either be a merciless master and live in fear of an uprising on my own land, or I could take a good look at myself and make some much-needed changes. I didn't like what I saw, Jed.

"One day, I held my hand out to my wife to help her into the wagon, and she was shocked by that simple act of kindness. Shocked! I realized I've been ruling over my family as tyrannically as I've been ruling over my slaves. I don't want to be that person anymore. I want Humphrey to be a better man than his father or grandfather, and I want his life to be untarnished by the burdens that beset us. So after counseling with Penny, I'm slowly freeing my own slaves."

A warm smile spread across Jed's face as he studied his friend for several moments. "You'll find that freeing them frees you as well."

"I'll be unpopular amongst our neighbors, though not nearly as unpopular as you, of course." The two men laughed, and then Frederick sobered. "You've many enemies, but slavery set off this attack. The locals hold you responsible for the actions of the freedmen."

"Has the man who tried to kill me said that?"

"Mr. Felcher hasn't confessed to anything, but he and plenty of others have expressed these sentiments. The locals are frightened by the arrival of abolitionists and pamphlets encouraging slave insurrection. Besides that, no one saw Felcher attack you, so no crime can be proven, and he will soon be set free. Yet if you let people know you're alive—"

"Someone else may come looking for me, or my family."

"So how shall we play this? You need to decide soon or he'll be released."

"I've been giving this some thought." Jed looked at the Book of Mormon in his hand. "I think I understand Hildebrand now, and I know his Achilles heel. It's pride, a topic I know a bit about as well. I need to recuperate at home where I can put my family's mind at ease. But I could use your help in flushing Hildebrand out."

Frederick extended his hand. "Just like the old days."

The Stringhams hid Jed in the back of their wagon and drove to the Willows, presumably to call on the grieving family. When night had fully set in, Markus and Jack helped Jed into the house through the back entrance, where an anxious Hannah, James, and Abigail waited.

The strain of the past four days was told in the circles surrounding Hannah's eyes, and in the set of her determined, trembling mouth. James hovered beside his papa, holding firmly to his pocket, while without a word, Hannah moved beneath Jed's arm. He kissed her head, saying, "I'm sorry."

She shook her head, dismissing his apology. "We're together. That's all I care about."

"I'm going to fix this, Hannah. I've got a plan."

The relief at being home obscured Jed's pain for a time, but it soon began to show. Bitty rushed to tend to him. Downstairs, Timothy arrived, and everyone was brought upstairs as an impromptu meeting commenced on how to deal with Emerson Hildebrand.

"I had Frederick send for Timothy to address any legal concerns in the plan I'm proposing," Jed explained. "To begin with, I plan to come forward and testify against Mr. Felcher."

Hannah nodded her approval. "But we still don't know if others want to kill you."

Jed smiled sadly as he took Hannah's hand. "I'm sure they do, but we'll address them by squaring off with Mr. Hildebrand. I hope seeing me alive will frighten Felcher into testifying to any role the Mr. Hildebrand may have played. If not, I intend to challenge Hildebrand to a duel."

Hannah and Bitty gasped aloud. "No! That's barbaric!" Hannah said.

But Timothy actually seemed to ponder the idea. "We haven't had a senator involved in a duel since Senator Randolph challenged Secretary Clay four years ago. And President Jackson still carries a ball in his chest from his duel with Charles Dickinson."

"I hope it won't come to shots being fired," Jed said, "but it will draw Hildebrand out."

"You can barely stand. How can you duel, and how will you find him?" Frannie asked.

"First, I need to issue an explanation about my attempted murder and why I remained hidden after Frederick rescued me. After that, I plan to take out an advertisement detailing Hildebrand's cowardly attacks on this farm and her people and run it weekly in every paper from here to Alabama, demanding that he confess his crimes to the court or face me on the field of honor for a duel on September first. I'll be better by then, and I have no doubt he'll show."

Hannah jumped from her seat, working her hands as she walked about the room. "You wrote to me about the evidence you have linking Hildebrand to Abel's murder and the kidnapping of Bitty. Just have the sheriff arrest him when he arrives."

He reached a hand to her, but she was reluctant to be mollified. "Hannah, I will have the sheriff here, I promise." A sly glint lit Jed's eye. "I have more damning evidence than that. The other day I realized Hildebrand didn't think things out very clearly when he went after Abel. He forgot that Abel was his insurance."

Jack's mouth fell open as Jed's meaning became clear. "That's right! We never prosecuted Hildebrand for attacking the schoolhouse in 1814 because we had to protect Abel."

"I'd forgotten, too!" Frannie said, noting Arthur's confusion. "Arthur, you couldn't know because you and Jed were on a ship headed for Britain when it happened. Abel served at Fort McHenry with Hildebrand and a Private Skully. They all received commendations, but Hildebrand couldn't accept a Negro being honored that way, so, soon after the Battle of Baltimore, Hildebrand staged an attack on the Willows. Abel thought everyone was in peril. In his attempt to rescue everyone, he shot and killed Hildebrand's accomplice— Private Skully."

Arthur looked at Jed and said, "I remember the day the letter arrived from Hannah. Jed wept when he heard the news that he'd nearly lost her and the baby, but we had no idea it was because there had been an attack on the farm."

Latent anger flushed Jed's face. He reached a hand to Hannah, who moved to his side as Jack picked up the story.

"It was a blessing that Dr. Foster was riding along with Abel that day, but he arrived seconds after Skully was shot. Knowing the courts would hang Abel for shooting a white man, he made a deal to save Abel. Dr. Foster took responsibility for Skully's death, and Hildebrand walked away without being charged for attempted murder."

"'Twas a dark day for all of us," Markus added. "Then fourteen years ago, Foster was found hangin' in 'is barn, in a feigned suicide. We all knew Hildebrand did it."

A satisfied glint filled Jack's eyes as he said, "But now that he's killed poor Abel, there's nothin' protectin' Hildebrand from the law anymore."

With Timothy's legal advice and Hannah's literary help, the announcement of Jed's rescue was prepared for the papers. He needed it to arouse readers' sympathies by conveying the severity of the threats to his family that compelled him to keep his survival a secret. When he was satisfied with its content, he handed the article to Timothy.

"Take my story to the sheriff first. I'll be waiting right here for him to depose me. Then, please explain all this to our colleagues in the Congress after you deliver it to the newspaper office in Washington. Explain how the vitriol over slavery is tearing our nation apart. Tell them I implore them to commit a portion of the coming session to a constructive debate on this issue."

Timothy folded the paper and tucked it into his coat pocket. "I'll do my very best, friend. I know you'll have dueling seconds aplenty for when Hildebrand arrives. Markus, Jack, and Arthur will stand by you, though I still think Frannie would be your most intimidating partner."

Jed laughed and then winced from the pain it caused in his side. "I'm blessed with good friends. Jack says all the men in Willowsport will stand with me."

"Willowsport . . . Do you realize you created an entire town, Jed? With a school, a church, a mill and market, docks and roads throughout? You've accomplished a great deal in your forty years. It's a life you can be proud of."

After Timothy left, Jed turned his attentions to the advertisement for the duel:

> *Having suffered years of torment and abuse at the hand of a man who has inflicted terror upon my person, my wife, my children, and my friends, I, Jed Pearson, do hereby summon Mr. Emerson Hildebrand to answer for the following crimes:*
>
> *The attempted murder of fourteen women and children in a schoolhouse, which was barricaded and then set on fire.*
>
> *The attempted murder of my unborn son, whose premature birth was brought on by said attack.*
>
> *The murder, by hanging, of Dr. Randolph Foster.*
>
> *The kidnapping of my son, Jonathan Pearson IV, from his bed.*
>
> *The destruction, by deliberately set fire, of one house belonging to the Miller family.*
>
> *The kidnapping of my dear friend and surrogate mother, Mrs. Bitty Miller.*
>
> *The murder of her husband, Mr. Abel Miller, a veteran of the Battle of Baltimore.*

As a co-conspirator, the attempted murder of my person by the hand of one Reginald Felcher.

The slaughter of one fine mare and two excellent steers, and numerous acts of mischief that have unsettled us and stolen our peace.

For these many crimes I will be satisfied only with a confession to the proper authorities that results in the appropriate penalties of law being paid, and an end to all harassment by any and all cohorts.

Failing this, I challenge Mr. Emerson Hildebrand to a duel on neutral ground, at White Oak Plantation, September 1, 1830, at nine o'clock in the morning.

Signed,
Jonathan Edward Pearson III

The list of Hildebrand's crimes staggered Jed, and as he laid his pen aside, he felt his hands shake at the thought of the havoc one man could wreak. He sent for Frederick, who arrived quickly.

"Thank you for your help, Frederick. How right it feels to enjoy your association again."

His friend smiled shyly. "Many things are better now. Penny is happier than I've ever seen her, and my son and I are on the best of terms. I thank you for your forgiveness."

Jed picked up the document and handed it to Frederick. "I'm happy for you, and I appreciate your help. What ill will passed between us is nothing compared to what this man has brought upon my house. When you reach the office of the *Baltimore Patriot,* ask them to print it right away, and to also set it in a full-page broadside in the largest type." Jed handed him a letter as well. "Here's my release to distribute the broadside along the Atlantic. Included are billing instructions."

"I'll take care of it, Jed."

"Thank you, Frederick." Jed leaned back and sighed with fatigue. "And now we wait."

The wait was brief.

It began with the barking of the dogs. Jed didn't know if it was a hound on the trail of prey, but it set his nerves on edge. Even the beating of his heart and his breath became an annoyance as he listened to every chirp and howl. He looked at Hannah, lying still beside him. He could trace the course of gray streaking through the long, dark tendrils spilling across her pillow, and for a moment the peaceful expression on her face calmed his heart.

He lay carefully down, protecting his wounded side, as the dogs' barking faded. *They're giving chase,* he told himself, but when the sound began to grow louder and more urgent, he again sat up, head craned, ears tuned.

The thunder of horse hoofs pounded along the river road. Again, Jed relaxed, relieved to know the cause of the dogs' irritation, but then suddenly the sound turned up the Willows lane, and before he could get to an awkward stand he knew the danger had already arrived.

Craaacckkk!!! The vibrato of a gunshot into the trees reverberated through an open window, raining wood chips and leaves onto the floor. A horse whinnied wildly and bolted away. James ran in and slammed the door behind him, fear twisting his face, while Abigail's wails sent Hannah flying to her cradle. With one arm around her baby and the other around her boy, she crouched in a corner as Jed reached in his nightstand and pulled out his pistol.

Arthur pounded on the bedroom door. "Jed, is everyone all right?"

"Arthur, take my family to the south end of the house with yours. And tell Frannie to stay out of this!"

Craaacckkk!!! Craaacckkk!!! Two more shots fired in rapid succession. More wood, more leaves, more terror.

443

"Jed Pearson! What have you done to me?" came the drunken cry from the ground below. Jed moved to the wall beside the window, searching for the source of the attack. Illuminated in the moonlight stood Emerson Hildebrand, a rifle in one hand, a bottle of liquor in the other. A pistol was tucked into his belt, where an ammunition pouch hung. His shirt was ripped open, his face and hands bloodied and bruised, and he alternated pulling down a draw on the bottle and reloading.

"You want to duel with me? Come down, Pearson! Come down!"

Craaacckkk!!!

Cedar chips from the roof splintered in a spherical pattern like wooden fireworks. Jed urged Hannah to leave the room and follow Arthur.

"Wait for help, Jed! Please wait!" she cried.

He knew they each needed to act while Hildebrand reloaded, but Hannah only buried more deeply into the corner with the children.

Jed groaned and returned his attention to the window, hollering down, "I called for an honorable duel, Hildebrand. Is this your answer? Terrorizing women and children in their sleep?"

"You've emblazoned cowardice upon my name! Come down here and finish the job. Do not leave me a hollow man."

Come down here and finish the job . . . Jed noted misery, not anger in the man's voice. Hildebrand was calling Jed out when he knew he had a good shot where he stood, but why?

"Were my charges not true? Did you not commit every act listed on that sheet?"

Maniacal laughter was interrupted by another draw on the bottle. "You gave me too much credit. You must have others who hate you as much as I."

An icy chill raced down Jed's back. "Which charge do you deny?"

"No. You want to talk to me? Come down."

Hannah's eyes begged him to stay, but Jed's conscience tore at him. Had he been wrong?

"James, lock the door when I leave and don't open it for anyone unless Mama says it all right. Do you understand?"

444

His son followed him to the door and pointed to a red stain appearing on his nightshirt. "You're bleeding, Papa," he cried.

Ignoring the seeping wound, Jed laid his hand at the back of his son's head and smiled. "It will be all right." He drew James to him as he offered Hannah a reassuring smile. In an even voice he said, "There's another pistol in the dresser. You'd better get it out."

He left the room, delaying his descent down the stairs until he heard the click of the lock behind him. Arthur stood in the hall, a pistol in his hand. "Frannie's agreed to stay with the children, but I'm coming with you."

There was no time to argue as the pair made their way to the front door. "I'll go out on the porch and talk to him," Jed said. "You keep your eye on his guns."

Jed opened the door and found the devil he had spent years seeking, standing a few yards away from his very doorway, his arms spread, his guns aimed at the ground. Jed stepped into the open doorway and stared down at the man who had caused so much pain for so many people Jed loved. He knew a single shot would end the reign of terror and give him the satisfaction of revenge. Part of him wanted it, hungering for the sweet peace it would bring.

"I will not give you that confession," Hildebrand said. "I know you want me dead, but kill me outright, not like this. Seven years in a tiny cell gives a man too much time to think. I thought about so many things. Did you know I have a child, Pearson? A sixteen-year-old mulatto boy." He brought the bottle to his split and bloodied lips again and drank. "How could I hate my son when I once loved his mother so? But she didn't love me back." His eyes grew menacing. "How dare she refuse me? She was a slave! How dare she?"

Jed noticed the approach of lanterns and knew he had minutes, maybe less, to subdue Hildebrand before other lives would be in jeopardy. "What did all that hatred get you?"

"What indeed! You've marked me. People look at me as if I'm a dog to be kicked and beaten." His arms swung wildly. "I could have killed your boy years ago, but I didn't. I showed mercy. I kept warning you, and warning you," he whimpered, "and now it's too late."

"What are you talking about?"

Hildebrand's gaze drifted to the ground as he rambled on in a drunken slur. "I told myself I'd die before I went back to prison again, so for two years I lived quietly, kept to myself, avoided confrontation. My family even welcomed the prodigal son home again, but I didn't fit there. It had already started." He finished the bottle and flung it away angrily. "Abolitionists were stirring things up. Your niggers were passing out handbills, cozying up to them. I only meant to put a scare in Abel, to shut his family up, but then I saw it in his eyes."

"What?"

Hildebrand huffed. "He really believed he was my equal, just like Belle."

"We were all created equal," Jed spat back. "It was the nation's weakness that kept the Founders from abolishing slavery. It's that same weakness that causes us to turn on one another."

Hildebrand gestured wildly with the gun. "You think you have all the answers. So did I. Now an old sin becomes my undoing. Foster knew as long as he or Abel lived, I'd be immune from my past. I didn't know Foster killed himself. I'd never have killed Abel if I had."

Jed took a step toward Hildebrand. "You didn't kill Foster?"

"Ha ha!" he cackled. "Didn't know that, eh? I suppose Foster couldn't live with the lie, so he planned his death to set me up." Hildebrand pointed at Jed's bloody side. "And I had nothing to do with Felcher coming after you, either."

"Liar!"

Hildebrand chortled wildly. "It was much easier when you believed the devil had only one face, wasn't it? But now you know you have others to fear—men who don't like these changes you're so determined to bring about. They will fight them with every resource they have."

A cold sweat broke along Jed's back. "What are they planning, and when?"

"I don't know when it will come, but it will come, and it will be worse than any fight the British gave us. We won't be fighting a foreign enemy. It will be neighbor against neighbor, father against son, tearing this country apart. This isn't what I wanted, and I don't want to be here for it. That's why we're finishing this tonight. You've told the world what a coward I was in life. I'll not die as a woman-killing dastard in some prison. We'll hold this duel—tonight."

Waving his gun, Hildebrand urged Jed onto the lawn. Jed longed to pull the trigger and end the torment. It would be so easy—so justified. He had done it a thousand times in his dreams, but that was before. He was different now. "I won't fight you tonight. Not like this."

"Do not deny me!" Hildebrand raised his gun and fired, clipping Jed in the arm. From across the lawn a rifle blast sounded. Hildebrand registered surprise, then shock as the ball slammed into him, dropping him to the ground. Arthur and Jed rushed over as Caleb arrived, his smoking rifle attesting to the origin of the shot.

When Jed reached Hildebrand, he was surprised to see a smile on the dying man's lips. He gestured to Jed to draw close, then with his dying breath, he said, "I am the lucky one, Pearson. The day is not far off when you and your children will see that." And then he was gone.

✵ ✵ ✵ ✵ ✵

The news of Jed's disappearance reached the Colesville papers just as things were beginning to settle down at the Willows. Beatrice, Dudley, and their family raced to Maryland to comfort Hannah and James, and found Jed recovering but very much alive.

"So it's finally over," Dudley said as the two men sat on the front porch enjoying glasses of lemonade.

Jed set his glass aside. "I'm afraid it's just beginning. Factions are determined to take this division over slavery to the brink of civil war."

"Joseph has prophesied about such a war. The Saints and the slaves are in much the same situation. People dislike change, which is why having a friend in the Senate will help us."

"Me? I doubt I will be invited to return. My positions are in disfavor."

"On slavery?"

"And on the Mormons." Jed smiled at Dudley. "I know it's true, Dudley—all of it. I know Joseph is God's prophet today, and I know the Book of Mormon is God's word."

Dudley wrapped Jed up in a warm embrace. "I thought I felt a change in you. You've finally surrendered your will to God."

"I suppose we'll need to travel back to Colesville or wherever Joseph is, to be baptized."

"You once told Hannah that if the Church were true, it would spread until it found you. It has this day. I've been confirmed since you left. Joseph spoke with me at length and ordained me to perform the ordinance of baptism for others. Let's hurry and tell Hannah!"

The Pearsons lined up along the Patuxent shoreline, and one by one Dudley took them by the hand and led them into the water. Jed went first, hanging on every word of the ordinance. Dudley immersed him, and as Jed rose from the water, he looked across the river at the Snowden family, and Beatrice's happy tears. He saw Frannie's and Arthur's intense curiosity as they gazed in wonder at him. *Do I look different?* He knew he was changed, at once overwhelmingly full of love, or the Spirit of God, or perhaps both. Yet simultaneously he felt light, as if he could float away. And then he knew the sense overcoming him. He grabbed Dudley's shoulders and cried aloud, "I'm clean! I'm clean!"

He sought Hannah, and when their eyes locked she handed the baby to Beatrice and waded into the water, her arms reaching for Jed. He wept into her hair as they embraced, and then he guided her hand to Dudley, who performed the ordinance for her. As Jed watched her rise from the water she seemed transformed into a being of light,

IN GOD IS OUR TRUST

more bright and beautiful than when they were young and he first realized he loved her.

Together, they stood on the shore as James was immersed, and when his face broke the water's surface he turned to smile at them, and for a moment they felt Johnny there, too.

Dudley followed James to the shore and placed a hand on Jed's and Hannah's shoulders. "You're thinking about Johnny, aren't you?"

Hannah's lip quivered. "Has Joseph said anything yet about the circumstances of the unbaptized dead?"

Though Dudley shook his head, there was hope shining in his face. "Nothing doctrinal yet, but I know it weighs heavily upon him, and there is much in the Book of Mormon to give us hope. My hope lies in King Benjamin's address, the third chapter of Mosiah, near the end. The angel tells Benjamin about a day when all the world shall have knowledge of the Savior Jesus Christ, and then he said this, 'And behold, when that time cometh, none shall be found blameless before God, except it be little children.' Surely God is telling us they are welcome in His kingdom."

Jed felt a familiar shiver, not from the cold, but rather from this new feeling he was becoming accustomed to as the Spirit touched his heart with greater frequency.

When they were dried and dressed, they enjoyed a sumptuous dinner, the first decent meal in weeks since the sad pall of mourning fell over the farm. Bitty seemed to be nearly herself again, but Caleb announced he was packing up his family and moving west to lay claim to Abel's deed of land.

"Are you going too, Bitty?" Jed asked.

She shook her head as she matter-of-factly ladled more food onto her plate. "This is where my people are buried. This is my home."

Caleb looked to Jed for support. "Tell her what Hildebrand said, Jed. Tell her things are going to get worse here."

"Jed done already told us everything, Caleb," his stepmother said. "You've got to make your way, and a way for your family. My way has already been laid, and it leads back here."

After supper, the men headed outside to complete the evening chores. Arthur and Dudley fell in beside Jed, and Dudley raised a new topic. "We still need to confirm you members of the Church and bestow the gift of the Holy Ghost upon all of you. Can you travel back to Colesville with us so the elders can attend to this?"

"The Holy Ghost," Arthur mused. "I have many questions about this from my reading."

Jed stopped walking. "Are you reading the Book of Mormon, Arthur?"

"Frannie and I are reading it with the children. Does that surprise you?"

Jed smiled and shook his head in wonder. "I assumed your clerical training would predispose you against the book. And Frannie has never voiced an interest in religion."

"If Joseph and this book prove to be what he claims, this is far more than a religion, Jed. It's—it's the opening of heaven and the foundation for Christ's return! Why are there so many religions and interpretations of God's law? Because man has been attempting to interpret it on his own, but if God is indeed speaking through a prophet again, we will clearly know God's will.

"Frannie has been anxious to find a church for our family, and from the moment Hannah handed us a copy of the book, I marveled at how many of the questions that plagued me through divinity school have been answered by Joseph's first vision—questions such as the nature of God, and who holds the authority to act and speak for Him on earth. I was also amazed at the emphasis the Book of Mormon places on Old Testament prophecies from Isaiah. Suddenly, I could see new meaning in these verses, relevant to our day."

Arthur's excitement continued to bubble over as he hurried on. "I feared how Daniel, a Christian, and Ruth, a Jew, would ever find common religious ground, but the Book of Mormon shows how the house of Israel and the promises made to Abraham remain crucial to modern Christians. I think the teachings in this book will help Ruth accept Christ as the Messiah, and bring her great comfort."

He turned back to Dudley. "We'd like to come along to Colesville and meet Mr. Smith. I also have two brothers in England. I'd like to ask Joseph about them—if they will have the opportunity to read the book and be baptized if they accept it."

"Don't hesitate to send them a copy, Arthur," Dudley said, placing his hand on the man's shoulder. "Let them begin to learn. In time, your brothers will hear the gospel preached in their own land. Joseph assures us this work will roll forth across the entire earth."

"Imagine that," Jed said. "I was afraid of it for so long, and here you were, hungering for it. Sadly, I still see that same fear in Bitty's eyes, and in Markus's each time Jenny speaks to Hannah about the book."

Dudley laid a hand on Jed's back. "Give them time. They'll take their cues from you, Jed. We are each called to the work, and now you'll become a teacher of the gospel."

"Hardly," he quipped. "I'll be leaning on you for a long time."

"Not so long, I'm afraid. I've been waiting for the right time to tell you this, but we'll be moving soon. The persecution has become so intense that Joseph has been asking the Lord for direction on where he should go. I don't think it will be long before Joseph relocates the body of the Church."

Jed frowned. "Would you actually leave your new farm to follow him?"

"Revelation is pouring down from heaven. Oliver says these are days never to be forgotten, and I don't want to miss a moment of it. God is building His kingdom on earth—a place called Zion, so yes, if Joseph moves, we'll follow the Church. Come with us when we do, Jed. You said yourself you will likely not be re-selected to the Senate."

Jed's gaze swept along the Patuxent River and across the land. It was easy to recall the terror of enemy ships moving along the river during the War of 1812. It was already being called a "nothing war" by some, but Jed knew better. Some ravaged cities had been rebuilt, some never would. Their rubble stood as a reminder of how fragile liberty is. It had brought a passel of new leaders to the political forefront, and turned a loose confederation of states into a united nation. It was the first test of America's Constitution and of the presidency, and they had each held. *What if they had not?* Jed wondered. *Would Joseph's efforts and this peculiar church have had a chance? More importantly, what if they fail in the future?* He shuddered.

"No, I'll be staying here. Whether I'm still a senator or merely a citizen, this is my watch." He pointed to the village of Willowsport. "Liberty will always need defenders. Their voices are still unheard. The Saints and others will need the Constitution's protection as well so they can worship unmolested. It may make the difference in getting this Zion built."

Dudley grew pensive. "Liberty is a godly principle, but you're right. Protecting it will be an ongoing struggle. Freedom is tied to faith. The Book of Mormon promises that God will protect this land only so long as it is a land of righteousness."

"And faith requires liberty to flourish."

Dudley smiled. "God and country. The Founders understood that."

"I wonder how much the Founders actually did know," Jed said. "The Declaration of Independence and Constitution acknowledge the hand of God in the nation's founding, yet religion is mentioned only in broad language."

"Perhaps because they knew a marvelous work was yet to commence."

Jed watched the sunset color the Patuxent orange as he thought about that. "A marvelous work—yes, yes, it is."

Sources

Burstein, Andrew. *America's Jubilee: How in 1826 a Generation Remembered Fifty Years of Independence*. New York: Alfred A. Knopf, 2001.

Bushman, Richard L., and Jed Woodworth. *Joseph Smith: Rough Stone Rolling*. New York: Alfred A. Knopf, 2005.

Forman, Martha Ogle, and W. Emerson Wilson. *Plantation Life at Rose Hill: the Diaries of Martha Ogle Forman, 1814–1845*. Wilmington, DE: Historical Society of Delaware, 1976.

History of the Orphan Asylum, in Philadelphia: with an Account of the Fire, in Which Twenty-three Orphans Were Burned. Philadelphia: American Sunday School Union, 1832.

Holzapfel, Richard Neitzel, and T. Jeffery Cottle. *Old Mormon Palmyra and New England: Historic Photographs and Guide*. Santa Ana, CA: Fieldbrook Production, 1991.

Orton, Chad M., and William W. Slaughter. *Joseph Smith's America: His Life and Times*. Salt Lake City, UT: Deseret Book, 2005.

Smith, Joseph. *History of The Church of Jesus Christ of Latter-day Saints*. Vol. 1. Salt Lake City, Utah: Deseret Book, 1991.

Smith, Lucy Mack. *The History of Joseph Smith by His Mother*. Rev. George Albert Smith and Elias Smith. American Fork, UT: Covenant Communications, 2004.

Laurie (L.C.) Lewis was born and raised in rural Maryland, surrounded by history-rich Philadelphia, Washington, and Baltimore. She and her husband Tom reside in Carroll County, Maryland, where they raised their four children.

In God Is Our Trust is Laurie's seventh published novel. Her other novels include *Unspoken* (2004), *Awakening Avery* (2010, as Laurie Lewis), and the previous four volumes in the FREE MEN and DREAMERS historical fiction series: *Dark Sky at Dawn* (2007), *Twilight's Last Gleaming* (2008), *Dawn's Early Light* (2009), and *Oh, Say Can You See?* (2010).

Dark Sky at Dawn and *Twilight's Last Gleaming* were finalists in the 2008 USA Best Books competition. *Oh, Say Can You See?* was a 2010 Whitney Award finalist.

Laurie is a popular historical speaker and workshop presenter, and a freelance contributor to Deseret Media Companies. She is a member of the LDStorymakers authors' group as well as ANWA, a writing group for Latter-day Saint women.

Laurie combines all her loves—LDS and American history, travel, family, and interesting locations—to produce family and historical dramas. She loves hearing from her readers and may be contacted through her website, laurielclewis.com, on Twitter as laurielclewis, or on her blog, laurielclewis.blogspot.com.